P9-EKT-960

The LEARN® Program *for* Weight Management

10th Edition

LIFESTYLE

EXERCISE

ATTITUDES

RELATIONSHIPS

NUTRITION

KELLY D. BROWNELL, PH.D.

YALE UNIVERSITY

AMERICAN HEALTH Publishing Company

Copyright © 2004 American Health Publishing Company
Printed in the United States of America

All rights reserved. No part of this book may be reproduced or transmitted in any form or by any means, electronic or mechanical, including photocopying, recording, or any information storage and retrieval system, without permission in writing from the publisher.

Written requests for permission to make copies of any part of this publication should be addressed to:
Permissions Department
American Health Publishing Company
P.O. Box 610430, Department 10
Dallas, Texas 75261–0430
Facsimile: 817–545–2211

Library of Congress
ISBN   1–878513–41–9

Address Orders to:

The LifeStyle Company®
P.O. Box 610430, Department 70
Dallas, Texas 75261–0430
World Wide Web address:
E-mail address:

In Dallas: (817) 545–4500
Toll Free: 1–888–LEARN–41
Facsimile: (817) 545–2211
www.TheLifeStyleCompany.com
LEARN@TheLifeStyleCompany.com

ACKNOWLEDGMENTS

I am grateful to several trusted colleagues and friends for providing comments and suggestions for this manual. Their help was invaluable. They are:

Dr. Steven N. Blair, President and CEO, The Cooper Institute, Dallas, Texas.

Dr. John P. Foreyt, Professor of Medicine and Director, Nutrition Research Clinic, Baylor College of Medicine, Houston, Texas.

Dr. G. Alan Marlatt, Professor of Psychology, University of Washington, Seattle, Washington.

Dr. James Rosen, Professor Emeritus, Department of Psychology, University of Vermont, Burlington, Vermont.

Dr. Sachiko T. St. Jeor, Professor and Director, Nutrition Education and Research Program, Department of Family and Community Medicine, University of Nevada School of Medicine, Reno, Nevada.

Dr. Thomas A. Wadden, Professor, Department of Psychiatry, Director, Weight and Eating Disorders Program, University of Pennsylvania School of Medicine, Philadelphia, Pennsylvania.

Permission to reprint cartoons was granted by, Creators Syndicate, Inc., King Features Syndicate, North America Syndicate, Tribune Media Services, United Feature Syndicate, Inc., United Media, Universal Press Syndicate, Washington Post Writers Group, Bob Thaves, and Randy Glasbergen.

Finally, I thank my students, colleagues, and especially my clients for providing the challenges and stimulation that encouraged me to undertake this writing.

LEARN®, The LEARN WalkMaster®, The LEARN LifeStyle Program Series®, and The LifeStyle Company® are registered trademarks of American Health Publishing Company, Dallas, Texas.

Table of Contents

Introduction and Orientation

I hope you are excited about the program you are beginning. It wraps into a single package the best that science has to offer on weight management with experience I have had working with many, many people. I have developed this program to be comfortable and friendly, and most important, to work for you now and in the future. At times, you will celebrate the progress you make, and at other times, you may struggle to make changes. I'll be here with you along the entire way.

You may wonder whether you can make lasting changes when you may have tried before. I think you can—you are motivated now; working together we can make a real difference. Most of all, you are beginning a new approach.

My Welcome and Your Future

I am confident you can succeed at managing your weight. By opening this manual, you have taken the first step down a new path—a path that leads to weight loss to be sure, but a path that gets you to your destination in a new way. Let's look at why this path is so important.

 LIFESTYLE PROFILES

Christina and Kate both lose 30 pounds but do so in different ways. Christina uses a fad, herbal product she saw advertised on television and cuts out her favorite foods as if they were poison. She is convinced that the herbal product is responsible for her weight loss.

Kate, on the other hand, makes reasonable changes in her diet. She limits problem foods but does not eliminate them from her diet. Kate makes sensible increases in her physical activity and does her best to make activity fun and enjoyable. She changes old patterns of thinking and develops a peaceful, new relationship with food and exercise.

Christina and Kate both arrive at the same initial destination—30 pounds lost. But, here the comparison ends. Christina falls for a quick-fix scam, while Kate develops a long-term plan. Christina invested in a bottle of pills, hoping for a miracle, while Kate invested time and ef-

fort in her future. One is doomed to pursue the next miracle diet, the other is proud of her accomplishments. One has a good chance at lasting success, and the other has a snowball's chance. As you can see from this example, the path is everything.

Today, we start down a new path together. This path can lead to more self-assurance, a healthier relationship with food and exercise, more positive thoughts, and improved body image—not to mention the many positive physical changes you will experience. You will impress yourself.

Watch for the Tape/CD Symbol

Tape/CD 1
Section 2

When you see this symbol alongside text in this manual, it means that the topic I am discussing is covered on *The LEARN Program Cassettes/ CDs*. I have recorded a series of four audiotapes and CDs to accompany this program. The audiotapes and CDs are not a repeat of the program. They are additional and supplemental material to clarify the program and to lend support to you at critical times. The tapes or CDs can provide additional motivation, inspiration, and education.

People use the tapes/CDs in three ways. First, as you read a section in the manual with a tape/CD symbol next to it, you may want to listen to that section on the tape or CD for supporting material. I will refer you to the particular tape/CD section where you can find the material I am discussing in the manual. Second, some people just listen straight through the tapes or CDs. This

gives them an up-front overview of key topics. They later refer back to the tapes/CDs as needed. Third, you can use the tapes and CDs at times of crisis. If you hit a plateau, struggle with cravings, or want to eat in response to difficult moods, the tapes and CDs can help. When you find it difficult to get out and walk, the tapes and CDs can help get you going. Examples of the topics covered in the tapes and CDs include the power of constructive thinking, ways to reward yourself, stress and eating, getting support when you need it, hitting a plateau, compulsive eating, keeping motivated, and much more.

People listen to the tapes and CDs in the car, when walking or doing some other form of exercise, when busy around the house, and in many other ways. The tapes and CDs provide me with another way to speak with you.

If you have not ordered the cassette tapes or the CDs and would like to, see Appendix H—Supplemental Resources and Ordering Information in the back of this manual that begins on page 257. Alternatively, you can order online by visiting the Internet at www.TheLifeStyleCompany. com.

About The LEARN Program

Different people benefit from different approaches to weight loss. Some prefer a structured diet, and others hate the lack of choice; some enjoy being physically active, and others get tired just thinking about exercise; some like support from family and friends, and others are more private. The

key is finding the approach that works best for you.

**Tape/CD 1
Section 4**

Your chances of finding the best approach increase with flexibility. Being flexible means having choices and tailoring your approach to fit your life. The LEARN Program will help you maximize your flexibility. The principles of LEARN can help you make long-term changes, no matter what type of nutrition and exercise plan you use.

The LEARN Program is the most thoroughly tested lifestyle-change program for weight management available. I wrote the first version about 25 years ago and have revised, updated, and improved it every year or two since then. The objective of the program is to help people develop the confidence and learn the skills necessary to lose weight and keep it off in today's challenging environment.

In my work at Brown University, the University of Pennsylvania, and now at Yale, I have used The LEARN Program with thousands of individuals. They have helped me make it better. My hope in creating both this new edition and the stabilization program that follows is that you can change your lifestyle once and for all.

I named this program LEARN for two reasons. The first is that learning implies an educational process in which the learner masters crucial information that he or she can apply to everyday life. Second, the word "LEARN" is an acronym created from the first letter of the five essential components of the program: **L**ifestyle, **E**xercise, **A**ttitudes, **R**elationships, and **N**utrition.

The name LEARN is now being used with other programs for lifestyle change such as stress management, exercise, and so forth. When I talk about "The LEARN Program," I'm talking about this program. Refer to Appendix H—Supplemental Resources and Ordering Information for a list of other programs in the LEARN LifeStyle Program Series®.

The LEARN Program Format

Each lesson begins with a brief introduction that provides you with a preview of the lesson. Do your best to complete each week's assignments as completely as possible. Plan to read one lesson each week. Be sure to read all the way through the assigned lesson at the *beginning* of the week. This will allow you plenty of time to focus on the activities of each lesson.

The lessons conclude with a My Weekly Goals section and a Knowledge Review. The Knowledge Review is for *you* to decide whether you have mastered the important information in the lesson. The section on weekly goals asks you to experiment with different approaches discussed in the lesson. This will help you learn what works best for you and help highlight the progress you are making.

As you go through The LEARN Program, you will become a student of your habits. You will learn when, how, and why your habits occur and how to change them. You will practice new skills and techniques so they become part of your everyday lifestyle—now and in the future. This is what separates the LEARN approach from other programs—the focus is on permanent results.

I should mention two other features of the program. First, you will not be assigned to eat certain foods. I will not ask you to banish any foods from your diet. You will not be asked to rid your life of apple pie or faint with envy when your friends dip into the Häagen-Dazs. Likewise, you will not be running to the fruit stand for papaya and mangoes so you can abide by a senseless series of magic foods. The LEARN Program is structured around your lifestyle, not vice versa.

The second feature of The LEARN Program is that you can individualize the program to your unique circumstances. The focus is on learning new habits, whatever they may be for you, and making them a permanent part of your new life. You can weave the principles and techniques of LEARN into the fabric of your life and individual lifestyle.

The NEW LEARN Program

I have structured this edition of The LEARN Program to have the Introduction and Orientation you are reading now, followed by 12 weekly lessons. Each of the 12 lessons contains one week's worth of material. Hence, the program lasts for 12 weeks.

The LEARN Program Schedule

The LEARN Program for Weight Management—10th Edition
A 12-Week Weight Loss Program

♦ Introduction and Orientation
♦ Lessons 1–12 (one lesson each week)

The LEARN Weight Stabilization and Maintenance Guide

♦ Introduction and Orientation
♦ Lessons 1–4 (one lesson each week)
♦ Lessons 5–10 (one lesson every two weeks)
♦ Lessons 11–16 (one lesson every four weeks)
♦ Commencement Lesson

The Introduction and Orientation introduces The LEARN Program, addresses your readiness to change, and talks about how you can get lifestyle change working for you. This is a quick read—you may be able to pour through this introductory material in a single reading. Lesson One begins the nuts and bolts of the program.

The Schedule of LEARN Lessons

Each lesson in The LEARN Program is written as a weekly lesson, hence 12 lessons, 12 weeks. The idea is for you to read one lesson each week and to work on the material in that lesson before proceeding to the next. I will introduce you to dozens of ideas for changing your lifestyle. You will discover the ones that work best for you.

After the initial 12 weeks, you will be ready to progress to *The LEARN Weight Stabilization and Maintenance Guide*. This guide begins with weekly lessons and gradually increases the time interval between each lesson, with the last lessons being monthly lessons. The focus in this guide is on making permanent (stable) changes you can enjoy and live with. The term "maintenance" is used to refer to sustaining the lifestyle changes necessary to manage and "stabilize" your weight for good. My commitment is to work with you as long as it takes. If you go through both manuals, we'll be together for about a year. So, let's work together to make the best team possible!

Tracking Your Progress

As you go through The LEARN Program, your role will be an active one. I will ask you to keep records, complete some forms, and try assignments each week. This is an important part of the program because being proactive in the lifestyle change process allows you to understand yourself better, know why you eat, realize how physically active you are, and make more rapid progress. Having worked with thousands of people over the years, I can tell you emphatically that those who do the work do far better than those who do not.

Along the way, you will see icons that highlight key aspects of the program:

 LIFESTYLE PROFILES offer personal examples of individuals who have experienced the topic being discussed.

 EXERCISE ESSENTIALS highlight important information and tips for becoming and staying physically active. Physical activity is one of the most important components of weight management success. I will talk about it often.

 ATTITUDE ALERT will help warn you against potentially hazardous internal attitude traps that can derail your progress.

 RELATIONSHIP RESOURCES offer ideas and suggestions for building and maintaining interpersonal relationships. For many people, social support plays a key role in their weight management program.

 NUTRITION NOTES will help you learn important information and skills necessary to achieve and maintain a healthy and balanced diet.

 DID YOU KNOW? offers interesting facts about many weight management issues.

 MY WEEKLY GOALS will include specific goals for you to work towards that are based on the material in that lesson.

 KNOWLEDGE REVIEW is a section at the end of each lesson designed to help you determine if you have mastered important concepts.

Making this the Right Time

Before we begin this program, let us consider whether the time is right. With some simple guidelines, you can decide whether to move ahead now or to wait for a better time.

Losing weight is much easier than keeping it off. Some people have lost and regained as much as 1,000 pounds, in what nutrition expert Jean Mayer labeled "the rhythm method of girth control." Losing and regaining weight is discouraging, so beginning a program when motivation is high is best.

The first step is to ask whether you are prepared for the commitment of a weight loss program. Despite claims from diet books, most people cannot lose 15 pounds without trying. They do not get addicted to exercise by buying flashy running shoes and warm-up suits. Moreover, most people do not suddenly yearn for broccoli and tofu when they are used to eating bacon, pork chops, and hot fudge.

Right now you are probably saying, tell me something new! You know that weight management requires effort. Yet, many people start programs when they are only mildly motivated. They may be pressured by family members, distressed by clothes that don't fit, or wish to look better for a special event, such as a wedding or reunion. Sometimes these reasons for losing weight provide sufficient motivation, but not always.

Losing weight requires time and effort. The LEARN Program can help, but the key results will come from your own efforts. Because your own efforts are central to your success, it is important to ask yourself if you are ready.

Weight loss readiness may seem unimportant to you at this time, because after all, you are reading this manual and may be enrolled in a class. Still, readiness is important to consider.

Readiness refers to your motivation and commitment, not just now, but over the weeks and months to come. Starting a program when you are truly ready can put you in the best position to succeed over the long run. In addition, if your readiness is low in certain areas, there may be things you can do to boost it.

I have developed the Weight Loss Readiness Test. This test has 23 questions that are divided into six categories:

❶ Goals and Attitudes

❷ Hunger and Eating Cues

❸ Control Over Eating

❹ Binge Eating and Purging

❺ Emotional Eating

❻ Exercise Patterns and Attitudes

The purpose of the test is to help you determine whether you are ready for the steps ahead. I suggest you take the whole test by logging onto the following website and looking under the heading of "Self-Assessments":

www.TheLifeStyleCompany.com

This test is available at this website and will be scored automatically as you take it. If you do not have access to the Internet, I am giving three of the key questions here. Score yourself from 1–10 on each question, with 10 being the highest score and 1 being the lowest. Use this as a general guide to how motivated and committed you feel. If your score is low (5 or less on a given question), you may think about trying strategies to increase your readiness.

Three Key Questions

_____1. Compared to previous attempts, how motivated are you to lose weight at this time?

_____2. How certain are you that you will stay committed to a weight loss program for the time it will take to reach your goal?

_____3. Consider all outside factors at this time in your life (the stress you're feeling at work, your family obligations, etc.). To what extent can you tolerate the time and effort required to stick to a program?

If, after answering these questions, you have concerns about your readiness, you have several ways to proceed. One is to find the barriers that are keeping you from moving ahead and then do something to clear your path. For instance, if stress is a major factor, perhaps there is a way to reduce the stress or to learn new ways of coping (perhaps by learning stress management skills). If difficult relationships are in the way, counseling may help. If you feel the barriers cannot be overcome, waiting for a later time when motivation is higher may be in order.

Weighing the Benefits and Sacrifices

In addition to readiness, you should consider the benefits and sacrifices of starting a weight loss program. For instance, the benefits of losing weight may include improved health, a better figure, increased self-confidence, a more active social life, increased energy, wearing attractive clothing, and much more. The sacrifices could include issues like hunger, irritability, explaining your new lifestyle to others, problems eating out, and so forth. Also,

consider the time you will need to devote to your program to be successful. Each week, you will need to set aside time to read the week's lesson, complete the lesson's assignments, keep records, and plan for upcoming events. The more time you invest in your weight loss efforts, the better your chances of success.

LIFESTYLE PROFILES

The illustrations on the right provide examples from two individuals contemplating a weight loss program. Bob wants to lose 40 pounds, and his wife is pressuring him to lose weight. Becky has 27 pounds to lose. She is tired of being heavy. Becky is applying for jobs after taking courses at night, and she wants to look as good as possible.

Bob and Becky weighed the benefits of losing weight and the sacrifices of beginning a program and came to different conclusions. The positive side of the ledger was stronger for Becky, so she pressed ahead and achieved her goal. Bob was different. He decided against starting a program because it held so many disadvantages for him. He later found himself more motivated and lost his excess weight.

We can learn two morals from Bob's story. First, deciding not to begin a program is sometimes wise. A person who attempts to lose weight and fails can feel bitter and guilty. The decision to wait until later is not a failure—it may prevent a failure.

A second side to Bob's story is also possible, however. A person who decides the time is not right may be looking for a convenient excuse. Such people may deny or avoid the realities of their weight problem or may question their ability to succeed. I recommend that such people take a two-week trial of eating less and exercising more as a test of how they will do later. Difficulty may be a sign that starting a program should be set aside and undertaken later. If they do well, their attitude may

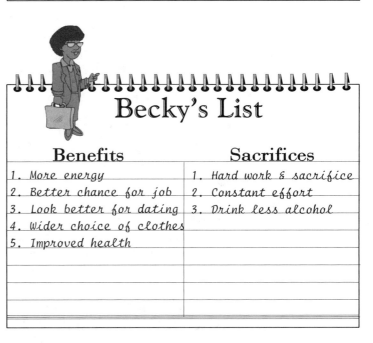

continue to improve as they lose weight. Consider this two-week trial if you are uncertain about starting a program now.

List as many of the benefits and sacrifices you can think of in the figure titled "My List" on page 8. Be sure to consider the importance of each cost and each benefit to your health, your lifestyle, and your overall quality of life—now and in the future. This exercise may help you to see if the balance

My List

Benefits	Sacrifices

of benefits and sacrifices leans in the direction of starting a program. If the list of sacrifices outweighs the benefits, you may want to reconsider whether the best time to begin a program is now.

A Word about Changing

Individuals come in many packages with many personalities. Some like to make changes on their own and do not want other people involved. Others like the help and support they might get from family and friends. I call the first group solo changers and the other group social changers. You may know already how you would like to proceed with your weight management efforts. If so, terrific! If you're unsure, read ahead in Lesson Four, on page 57. There, I discuss solo and social changing along with some guidelines for selecting a program partner.

Being a Good Group Member

Many people who use this program do so on their own. Others are part of a group program. If you are part of a group there are several important matters to consider.

Being in a group can be a wonderful experience, with support, encouragement, and good ideas flowing from one member of the group to another. This is why groups can be so valuable. To make the group a positive experience, each member must realize that working in a cooperative way and with a team spirit will allow the group to reach its potential. Each member in the group has the opportunity and the responsibility to follow certain guidelines. Some effort will be required, but the payoff will make it worthwhile.

I have included detailed guidelines for being a good group member in Appendix D, beginning on page 227. If you are participating in a group program, I urge you to read these over, and take the advice seriously. Being a contributing and constructive member of the group will support the other group members, who in turn will support you. This can go a long way toward motivating you when times are tough and giving you fresh ideas.

Your Quality of Life

Tape/CD 1
Section 7

People begin weight loss programs because of the benefits they hope will occur with weighing less. Looking better, feeling better, having more energy, and having more self-confidence are examples of what we call "quality-of-life" issues. These and other factors affect how you feel every day.

As you progress through this program, you will have a natural tendency to focus on the scale. This can be a problem when the scale shows no change, even though you may be making important changes. Keeping your eye on these changes will be useful. This helps you appreciate the positive effects of your hard work and shows just how many areas of your life can improve by eating better and being more physically active. Focusing on areas other than the scale also gives you more than one means of evaluating your progress.

Please complete the Quality of Life Review provided on the right to get a feeling about various aspects of your current, daily quality of life. I will ask you to complete this assessment several times later in the program to see if the scores change. Be sure to record your score in the appropriate place in Appendix B on page 213.

Helpful Resources

Additional materials have been developed to supplement The LEARN Program that may be helpful to you (see page 257 or log onto the website www.TheLifeStyle Company.com). Here is a snapshot of some of the resources.

The LEARN Program Cassettes/CDs are a motivational and informational supplement to *The LEARN Program for Weight Management*. The tapes/CDs do not repeat the program, but provide additional material to clarify and reinforce key principles. The information is designed to help motivate and inspire you as you encounter challenging situations.

In addition to *The LEARN Program Cassettes/CDs* mentioned earlier, *The LEARN Program Monitoring Forms* were developed at the request of many people who had completed The LEARN Program. Although I provide you with one daily monitoring form that you may copy from the relevant lessons, many individuals find it more convenient to have a pocket-sized form that contains a week's supply of food and physical activity monitoring.

The LEARN WalkMaster® is a helpful way for you to monitor your physical activity. This handy little device keeps track of

---

Quality of Life Review

Please use the following scale to rate how satisfied you feel *now* about different aspects of your daily life. Choose any number from this list (1 to 9), and indicate your choice on the questions below.

1 = Extremely Dissatisfied
2 = Very Dissatisfied
3 = Moderately Dissatisfied
4 = Somewhat Dissatisfied
5 = Neutral
6 = Somewhat Satisfied
7 = Moderately Satisfied
8 = Very Satisfied
9 = Extremely Satisfied

1. _____ Mood (feelings of sadness, worry, happiness, etc.)
2. _____ Self-esteem
3. _____ Confidence, self-assurance, and comfort in social situations
4. _____ Energy and feeling healthy
5. _____ Health problems (diabetes, high blood pressure, etc.)
6. _____ General appearance
7. _____ Social life
8. _____ Leisure and recreational activities
9. _____ Physical mobility and physical activity
10. _____ Eating habits
11. _____ Body image
12. _____ Overall Quality of Life[1]

[1] Record your Overall Quality of Life score in the space provided in Appendix B, page 213.

---

your steps, how far you walk, and how many calories you use. I will discuss this more in Lesson One, but for now, please know how helpful a step counter may be.

Finally, *The LEARN Weight Stabilization and Maintenance Guide* is the follow-up companion to this manual. It is a continuation of The LEARN Program with more information on making permanent changes you can live with forever.

Information on other materials can be obtained by calling or writing to the address shown below.

LEARN—The LifeStyle Company®
P.O. Box 610430, Department 70
Dallas, Texas 75261–0430
Telephone: 1–817–545–4500
Toll Free: 1–888–LEARN–41
Fax: 1–817–545–2211

E-mail:
LEARN@TheLifeStyleCompany.com
Internet:
www.TheLifeStyleCompany.com

Providing Feedback

I am a great believer in feedback, and I'd very much like yours. If you can suggest changes to improve the program, please let me know. Additions, deletions, alterations—I am open to them all. I can say with sincerity that this manual, now in its 10th edition, has improved dramatically over the years with input from people using it. If you enjoy the manual and it helps you, please let me know. Good news is always gratifying to hear. Also, your words may inspire other people. So, if you contact me, let me know if I can use what you say (without citing names) in future versions of this manual or on the website listed.

To send feedback to me, you may write a letter to my attention and mail it to American Health Publishing Company, P.O. Box 610430, Department 10, Dallas, Texas 75261–0430. You may also fax feedback to me at 1–817–545–2211. If you have access to the Internet, you may e-mail your feedback to me at: LEARN@TheLifeStyleCompany.com. I read every word.

I often meet people who use this manual and see books with pages that are ragged and bent at the edges, notes written in the margins, and many sentences underlined or highlighted. I am delighted to see this level of connection with this program. Use this book for all it's worth. I'd love to see you connect to the program in this way.

Congratulations and Good Luck

Congratulations on your decision to take control of your weight and health. You can be proud of making an important decision. I wish you every success and look forward to working with you. So, without any further delay, let's move on!

Lesson One

Today you begin Lesson One of The LEARN Program. This program contains the best of what science and clinical practice have to offer on weight management. In writing this manual, my intention is for us to form a partnership. Together we can make it work for you.

When you lose weight on this program, only one person deserves credit—you. I would be happy to claim credit, but I deserve it no more than the Rand McNally Company does when you use its atlas to drive from one city to the next. The atlas provides the possible routes and may even suggest the best one to follow. Yet, you choose the route, and you determine whether you reach your destination. Most important, you do the driving. Reminding yourself of the credit you deserve as you make changes is important.

Remember the Tape/CD Symbol

When you see the tape/CD symbol, it indicates that the topic is covered in detail in *The LEARN Program Cassettes/CDs*. The set has four cassette tapes or CDs with me speaking to you about topics such as motivation, commitment, dealing with plateaus, compulsive eating, dealing with food cravings, rewarding yourself, crisis intervention, body image, and stress and eating. The tapes/CDs are designed to be educational, inspirational, friendly, and supportive. They help me share with you my experiences gained over many years.

The LEARN Approach

As you know, the word "LEARN" represents the five components of this program: **L**ifestyle, **E**xercise, **A**ttitudes, **R**elationships, and **N**utrition. The lessons in this program contain information in each area. In some weeks, the information in one area is particularly important, so it will receive the greatest emphasis.

Appendix A on page 209 has a Master List of LEARN Techniques that you will be learning as you go through the program. I have referenced each technique by page number to show you where I discuss the technique. Refer to this appendix often when you find yourself having difficulty with a particular lifestyle-change technique.

Because we are partners, your role will be an active one. You will have forms to use and much time to experiment with new approaches to eating, becoming more physically active, and changing other lifestyle behaviors. This process is both exciting and challenging.

Your role in The LEARN Program will be an active one. You will be experimenting with many different approaches to developing important weight management skills.

Tape/CD 1
Section 4

Herein lies a key issue. Changing habits is not something that happens while a person is *on* a diet and then stops later when the diet ends. This implies a temporary solution, a quick patch job that only requires effort over the short term.

We are seeking a permanent solution. Instead of a quick, temporary fix, we want *permanent* lifestyle change. This involves establishing new habits and working hard to make them part of day-to-day life. Most people who struggle with weight have a chronic problem, and chronic problems require attention over the long term.

The LEARN Program is not a diet; it is a system for lifestyle change. This is more than just a matter of words—it is a fundamental difference in philosophy that affects nearly every aspect of the LEARN approach. This approach is what sets LEARN apart from other programs.

Reflect for a moment on the difference between going on a diet and changing your lifestyle. The lifestyle approach is the hallmark of The LEARN Program, emphasizing gradual, sustainable, and permanent changes in eating, exercising, thinking, feeling, and acting. As you go through the program, you will learn important skills that will help you develop the confidence to succeed.

The LEARN Program can be used in a variety of settings. In some cases, this manual will be used in conjunction with classes or with some degree of professional assistance. The LEARN Program also is used as a companion or guide in many other weight management programs. I developed this program for you to use as a self-help program or in a group setting. Remember that group sessions do not replace the manual. Group sessions simply cannot cover the details of a program like a manual can. The manual permits you to examine the information at your pace and at a convenient time. Be sure to read the manual each week, and use it as a reference after the program ends.

Diet vs. Lifestyle Change

The word *diet* conjures up images of deprivation and suffering, but most of all, it is something that you go on or off. Whether someone is "on a diet" or "off a diet" is part of our modern culture and language.

Building Skills and Confidence

Tape/CD 1
Section 1

A highly respected psychologist at Stanford University, Albert Bandura, developed a concept known as self-efficacy; it has two parts. The first states that an individual's chance of accomplishing a goal depends on having the skills to make the change. The second part is whether the individual has the confidence that the changes can occur. This idea applies beautifully to weight management.

As I said earlier, The LEARN Program is a skill-building program. I will suggest many approaches to developing skills. You will take each for a test drive and find the ones that work best for you. The skills will deal with what you eat, how you stay physically active, and perhaps most important, the thoughts, feelings, and attitudes you have about these and many other important issues. Thinking helpful thoughts and looking at the world in a constructive way are skills that you can cultivate.

Confidence is the second part of the picture. If you are confident that you can handle high-risk situations, bounce back when you falter, and keep your motivation high, you'll have the strength to hang in there when things get tough. You will approach situations with a new sense of control. I will be speaking often about confidence.

ATTITUDE ALERT

Sometimes the discussions of confidence will sound like a pep talk, but pep talks can be helpful. One of the most important things you can do is to have your own internal pep talks. What you say to yourself when you succeed can have an important impact on your future. Moreover, what you tell yourself when you slip will be central to your success. I will talk often about the discussions you have with yourself.

Starting with Your Goals and Expectations

Tape/CD 1
Section 5

This program can help you achieve a "healthier" weight. The LEARN Program produces average weight losses of 12–25 pounds over a 12-week period. Studies from our research group and from scientists at other centers around the world have documented these numbers. This translates into a one- to two-pound weight

The skills you will learn deal with what you eat, whether you are active, and perhaps most important, your thoughts, feelings, and attitudes.

loss per week. What does this mean for you?

Averages can be deceiving. For example, if one person loses 50 pounds and another loses none, their average weight loss is 25 pounds. Whether the program is a success depends on which person you consider. Some people lose more than the average, and some lose less; but in general, the program aims for a steady weight loss that you can maintain. By the way, you are more likely to achieve the best results by reading and completing each lesson faithfully and by achieving your personal goals each week. A recent study showed that the more weekly goals people accomplished during the program, the greater their weight losses.

If you have 30 pounds or less to lose, this program provides a good opportunity for you to reach your goal weight. If you have more to lose, you can estimate the 12- to 25-pound loss for the initial 12-week program and then can continue to lose by going through *The LEARN Weight Stabilization*

Even modest weight loss can provide you with important health benefits and an improved quality of life.

and Maintenance Guide that follows this program. If you stop losing before reaching your goal, a good strategy is to stabilize your weight for a period of time until you feel comfortable maintaining your new weight. Then you can start the program again with additional weight loss as a goal.

Long-Term Results

The best news about The LEARN Program is the long-term results. Compared with the very high relapse rates from most programs, the maintenance of weight loss for this program is quite good. Again, some people lose even more after the initial 12 weeks while some regain.

These numbers have more meaning when compared with the results of other approaches. Dr. Albert Stunkard, from the University of Pennsylvania, estimated many years ago that fewer than 5 percent of people on weight loss programs lose more than 40 pounds and keep it off. The figures are better now, but by every estimate, maintaining weight loss remains a challenging problem. Many people (as many as 66 percent) who enter the popular commercial and self-help programs will drop out within six weeks. Techniques like hypnosis, herbal programs, and the best-selling diet books are usually of little use. The key to successful weight management, of course, is weight stabilization and the maintenance of lifestyle changes that led to weight loss in the first place.

We will be working on maintenance of weight loss from the very beginning of this program. When I speak of maintenance in this sense, I am talking about *maintaining* new lifestyle changes. I want to help you develop a mind-set of permanent lifestyle change. You will be changing fundamental behaviors and attitudes that affect your eating and activity. We will work together so you can make changes that become part of the way you live. Perhaps more than any other program, The LEARN Program blends methods to maintain weight loss with ways to lose weight initially. Together, we can make it work for you.

Many programs and books promise quick and easy results, some as much as 10 pounds in a few days. Such diets are drastic measures that may endanger your health. These quick weight losses are more water than fat, because the body rids itself of water when intake of salt and carbohydrate decreases. The water returns when a person abandons the rigid diet. Losing weight slowly allows your body to adjust to a new weight and will help you look and feel better as you reduce.

Slow and gradual weight loss is not as flashy as a fad diet, but may ultimately be more effective. In the Introduction and Orientation, I shared the story of Christina and Kate. This is an excellent example of why the path to success is so crucial. Losing more than three to four pounds of body fat per week is physically impossible, even by fasting. So, a weight loss of 1–2 pounds per week is quite good. Slow and steady are the key words. This represents the most reasonable approach to weight management.

Setting Realistic Goals

You will be most satisfied with your results if you set clear and realistic goals that you have a good chance of attaining. During this program, I will speak often about realistic goals, appropriate expectations, and "reasonable weight."

Take a minute now and think about what a 10 percent weight loss would be for you. This is a good starting goal. Whether or not you lose more, the 10 percent loss will be an important achievement. Clinical studies have shown that weight loss in this amount improves important factors related to health, such as blood pressure and lipid levels. In the space below, write down what a 10 percent weight loss would be for you (divide your current weight by 10). We will refer back to this number later in the program.

**A 10 percent weight loss
for me will be _____ pounds.**

Bare Bones Nutrition

*Tape/CD 1
Section 10*

I will speak a lot about eating a healthy and balanced diet throughout this program. However, you do not need to read one page further before beginning a new approach to weight management. You can start by eating sensible meals regularly throughout the day, including breakfast. Try cutting your portion sizes down and increasing your intake of fruits and vegetables.

As you'll learn, you can eat more than you think and still lose weight. Nevertheless, you have to be careful about what you choose. For instance, if you have a 3-oz portion (about the size of a deck of playing cards) of meat (like chicken) with seasonings, a salad (with two cups of lettuce, some cucumber and tomato, and two tablespoons of light salad dressing), one-half cup each of three vegetables, and some fruit, you will have a healthy and quite filling meal, with surprisingly few calories (about 500–600).

Calorie Guides

You will need a calorie guide to record the number of calories in the foods you eat. For some foods, you can probably look at the food label on the package and find the calories. Other foods, like fruits and vegetables, do not come in packages, so the calorie count is not readily available. In addition, you may eat out and have foods

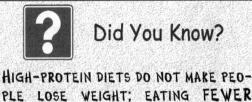

Did You Know?

HIGH-PROTEIN DIETS DO NOT MAKE PEOPLE LOSE WEIGHT; EATING FEWER CALORIES IS THE REASON WEIGHT LOSS OCCURS.

served to you by friends or family and will need to know how to estimate calories.

I have included a calorie guide in Appendix G for you to use. The guide contains commonly eaten foods along with some exotic foods you might want to try. This guide also includes Food Guide Pyramid serving sizes, calories per serving, and the nutrients that have calories for each food (grams of fat, protein, and carbohydrate).

I have also included a fast-food guide in Appendix F. This guide does not include all fast-food restaurants, but does include the more familiar ones.

Another option is to go to a bookstore and look in the section on diet and nutrition. Easier yet, ask someone who works there to help you find a book with the calorie and nutrition values of foods. The different guides may vary a bit in the calories and nutrition listed for given foods, but these differences tend to be insignificant.

NUTRITION NOTES

Accurately estimating your daily calorie intake will require you to do some arithmetic. For instance, a calorie guide may list a pat of margarine as having 36 calories. If you have two pats on a roll, the contribution from margarine will be 72 (36 x 2) calories. If you have only one-half of the pat, you will record 18 (36÷2) calories.

Your judgment is important when estimating calories because a calorie guide provides only estimates and may not apply exactly to the food you are eating. For example, a guide may show that a roast beef sandwich has 347 calories. This refers to a

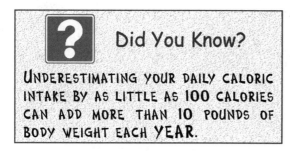

Did You Know?

UNDERESTIMATING YOUR DAILY CALORIC INTAKE BY AS LITTLE AS 100 CALORIES CAN ADD MORE THAN 10 POUNDS OF BODY WEIGHT EACH YEAR.

regular sandwich with about 2 oz of meat and does not include mustard, mayonnaise, or cheese. If your deli sandwich has two inches (rather than 2 oz) of roast beef, the calories could be three or four times what the guide lists.

The challenge is to estimate the portion sizes and composition of the foods you eat. This is not easy when eating out, but make your best guess. At home, using a food scale and measuring cups and spoons can simplify the job.

Many people feel they do not need a food scale, especially the veterans of weight loss programs who have been keeping calorie records for years. Some colleagues and I did a study on this. We had individuals estimate the quantities and calories in common foods and beverages, such as milk, green beans, meat, and soda. Some estimated high and some low, but the average error was 60 percent! Food scales are readily available and inexpensive. For information on ordering a food scale, look in the Supplemental Resources section of this manual on page 257.

Finding the hidden calories in foods is also important. Examples include butter on vegetables, whipped cream on desserts, dressings on salad, and sugar used as a sweetener. Be painfully honest because these are sources of extra calories and extra pounds. One extra pat of margarine per day, which has only 36 calories, can add up to four pounds of weight gained in one year!

As you progress through the program, you will be able to estimate food portions, food composition, and calories more easily and more accurately. The Monitoring Form, which I talk about later in this lesson, will become easier to keep as you go through the program.

Bare Bones of Physical Activity

Tape/CD 1
Section 9

You will read a lot about being physically active in the lessons that follow. Physical activity is really, really important. In fact, physical activity is one of the best predictors of long-term weight management success. The best news of all is that you don't have to knock yourself out to become physically active. Even in modest amounts, exercise can be good for your health, weight loss, self-image, mood, and your overall quality of life.

One issue I will discuss several times is just how much exercise you should do. Contrary to old notions that you have to exercise a certain number of minutes at one time and get your heart rate into a target zone, short bouts (a 5-minute walk) of exercise accumulated during the day can improve your overall level of health and fitness. The task is to increase your movement and activity beyond what you do now. Work your way into a pattern of regular,

Copyright © 1990 by Thaves. Distributed from www.thecomics.com.

healthy physical activity. Remember, *anything you do to increase your physical activity can be helpful and "counts" as exercise!*

You can start being more physically active right away by doing two things. The first is to use every chance you get to be a bit more active. Try walking places, using stairs when possible—just making an effort to move around will help. Every time you are active is a reminder that you are making progress. The second thing you can do is to walk regularly—even in small amounts. Begin with short walks that are comfortable for you, then work your way up. Doing a series of short walks is as good as taking one long walk. You can use a watch to time the number of minutes that you walk each day. You also can use a step counter to count the number of steps you take each day. Throughout the program, I will discuss the advantages of using a step counter.

A Very Helpful Device

As we go through The LEARN Program together, I will speak many times about increasing your physical activity; but, I do not talk about heavy exertion or spending hours every day on the stair machine, the treadmill, or sweating in a warmup suit. On the contrary, small increases in activity can *really* help you lose weight and keep it off. This happens for biological reasons but also because you feel better about yourself. Experiencing these benefits right away is helpful; so, make a commitment to begin increasing your physical activity right away.

Consider purchasing a handy and helpful device called a pedometer (step counter). The more advanced versions of the pedometers not only track how far you walk but other important factors as well, such as calories burned. These devices measure motion and calculate the number of steps you take. People usually keep a log of how many steps they take each day or the total distance they walk.

The LEARN WalkMaster® is one of these devices—one that my colleagues and

I use ourselves. It gives you credit whether you are running the Boston Marathon or are meandering through the house. The WalkMaster can detect increases in your activity even when you don't notice. This feedback can be highly rewarding and can be a constant reminder that any increase in your activity can be helpful. The WalkMaster measures the number of steps you take, the total distance you move, and the calories you burn. Information on ordering a WalkMaster is on page 257.

The LEARN WalkMaster counts all of your daily activity and provides important feedback about your activity level.

An Impressive Study

Let me mention a study conducted by Drs. Ross Andersen, Thomas Wadden, and colleagues at the University of Pennsylvania. This study compared people on two quite different approaches to weight management. Both groups received The LEARN Program. The researchers gave one group a traditional approach to exercise—step aerobics at a fitness facility, three times a week, requiring about 60 minutes each time.

The other group was encouraged instead to increase "lifestyle activity." Individuals in this group were asked to increase their activity by 30 minutes most days of the week by adding short bouts of activity throughout the day. Examples included walking rather than driving short distances, taking a walk during lunch, walking during television commercials, and so forth. People in this group used a device like the WalkMaster.

At a one-year follow-up after the initial program ended, both groups had lost the same amount of weight, and both groups showed the same changes in important medical factors, such as blood pressure. This shows that reasonable, attainable amounts of activity can be valuable, even if it is not strenuous.

Record Keeping

**Tape/CD 1
Section 8**

The first and perhaps most important lifestyle behavior you will learn is record keeping. You will be keeping records of your eating, exercise, and weight. You'll have more records than an accountant! Some people resist keeping records, so let me tell you what the research shows. Studies have shown that individuals who keep records do better than those who do not; hence, record keeping is one predictor of success. If you are one who resists keeping records, chances are that you may need this the most. Moreover, you may be surprised by how much you benefit from keeping good records. My advice to you is give it a try.

Purpose and Importance

This lesson introduces two records. The first is the Monitoring Form, which is a daily record of the food you eat and your physical activity. The second is the Weight Change Record, which is a weekly graph of your weight change. Both will help you in-

crease the awareness of your eating and and physical activity and how they affect your weight. Here is why records help:

➡ *Awareness* is a key step in changing habits. You may already know a great deal about your habits and your weight patterns, particularly if you have kept records for an earlier program. You will be surprised by how much more there is to learn.

➡ *You learn about calories.* Calories are lurking where you least suspect. One cup of fruit yogurt can have more calories than an ice cream cone. Ten innocent potato chips contain 110 calories, more than five cups of plain popcorn. Becoming a calorie expert insures you won't be derailed by calorie surprises.

➡ *You become aware of what you eat.* You might be thinking, "Of course, I know what I eat." However, one does not always recall the exact number of Doritos consumed at happy hour or the ounces of milk poured into the bowl of Cheerios. These are easily forgotten calories, sometimes because we want to forget them!

➡ *You learn how to bank calories.* Your body is like a bank account in which you make calorie deposits and withdrawals. If you eat less, you have some calories to bank for a special occasion. If you have a party to attend on the weekend, you can cut back during the week. With this knowledge, you can afford to indulge a bit more. Calorie re-

cords give you the information to make informed food choices.

➡ *You increase control over eating.* Knowing exactly where you stand with the day's calorie count is important. This helps you to judge whether you can afford to eat certain foods. Choices are much easier with this information.

➡ *Your eating patterns become clear.* You may discover that most of your eating takes place between dinner and bedtime. Some people eat when they have certain feelings (anger, anxiety, etc.), and others find they eat when doing something else, like watching TV. Knowing your patterns is a big help in changing habits.

➡ *You learn not to despair.* You may experience one or more weeks during this program when you fail to lose weight, or even worse, gain weight! Many reasons exist for this. I will discuss them later. Such a discouraging bout with the scale can make life difficult. Reviewing your change in weight over many weeks can prevent this despair. A slight gain is easier to tolerate when your records remind you that you have been losing weight in a steady manner.

The Monitoring Form

The Monitoring Form allows you to record amounts and calories of the foods you eat. Recording everything you eat and estimating calories may be hard to do initially, and when it becomes easy, you may find it repetitive. Conquering this resistance and keeping the records is important. Research has shown this to be one of the most, if not the most, important part of lifestyle change.

A blank Monitoring Form for this lesson is provided on page 24, along with a sample that has a typical person's eating records filled in on page 23. I will provide blank monitoring forms for each lesson in The LEARN Program. You may make photocopies of the blank forms for your own use.

Record keeping is an essential ingredient of The LEARN Program.

Many people find it helpful to have pre-printed forms. *The LEARN Program Monitoring Forms* (listed on page 258 in the back of this manual) can be ordered by calling toll-free 1–888–LEARN–41 or on the Internet at www.TheLifeStyleComany. Com. Each of these forms contains a week's worth of monitoring and can easily be carried in a pocket or purse.

Be sure to record everything you eat and be on the lookout for hidden calories.

Here are the instructions for completing your Monitoring Form in this lesson.

➡ *Record everything, forget nothing.* Every morsel of food goes in the Monitoring Form. If you eat pretzels, count how many. Enter every ounce of food and beverage. Don't forget to count the foods you taste when you are cooking.

➡ *Record the food, the amount, the calories.* Record the type of food you eat, how it is prepared (baked, fried, etc.), how much, and the number of calories.

➡ *Record immediately after eating.* Do not wait until you are ready for bed, until the next morning, or even later! You will have trouble remembering how much you ate. When you finish eating, bring out the Monitoring Form and make your entries. If you are with others and are embarrassed, excuse yourself and find a private place, like a phone booth. Clark Kent did it!

➡️ *Carry your Monitoring Form always.* Food lurks everywhere, so keep your Monitoring Form with you (except when swimming or in the shower) so you won't be caught off guard. Some people use a pocket notebook or small notepad during the day and then transfer the information to their Monitoring Form later.

The Weight Change Record

*Tape/CD 1
Section 8*

You can track your progress by using the Weight Change Record. Once each week, record the date and your weight change from the previous week. I have provided a sample on page 21.

Keeping the Weight Change Record has several advantages. First, it is a reminder of how you fare with the program. Second, it shows the relationship between your eating and your weight. The record can help you estimate how many calories you need to lose weight. You can do this by taking the average daily calorie values from several weeks of your Monitoring Form and comparing the values with your weight changes from your Weight Change Record. Third, the graph puts your weight change in perspective. If you gain a pound during your eighth week, you can take heart from the steady loss in earlier weeks.

You will notice that the Weight Change Record is a graph of weight change, not of weight per se. This is done so people can

place the graph in a public spot, like on the refrigerator door, if they wish. Your weight does not have to appear on the graph, just your progress. Many people like to have the graph posted in a place where they see it frequently, so it can act as a source of encouragement.

On the sample graph provided on page 21, you will see that weight loss does not occur in a straight line. The realistic line on the graph shows some weeks where weight stays stable and even weeks when weight increases.

A terrific help in setting reasonable goals is to think ahead to how much weight you are likely to lose by landmark dates. Let's use the sample graph on page 21 as an example. A person's anniversary might be at week 4 of the program, a daughter's birthday at week 7, and family reunion celebration at week 11. A good weight loss goal is one to two pounds a week. So, this individual might lose about 8 pounds by the anniversary, 14 pounds by the daughter's birthday, and 22 pounds by the family reunion. When the person reaches these dates, he or she can see if the expected goal was reached. People usually expect too much!

I have provided a blank My Weight Change Record in Appendix B on page 216 for you to use. Take a few minutes to pencil in some landmark dates on this graph for the next 12 weeks. Use holidays, birthdays, or other special dates as target dates. When those dates roll around, compare your weight loss with the graph. A weight loss

that seems disappointing may look good when compared with a reasonable standard.

Setting Goals

Tape/CD 2
Section 2

Each lesson of The LEARN Program will end with a section on setting weekly personal goals. This section includes specific issues for your attention, based on the material in the lesson. In some ways, this is an assignment to practice the new activities you read about in the lesson. This also will offer you a chance to reflect on what you want to accomplish before moving on to the next lesson. Sometimes the goals will be broad, like being more aware of temptations to eat, but others will be more specific. An example is being physically active for a certain number of minutes each day.

Goal setting is important. It gives you something to strive for, a standard against which to measure your progress. As you establish your weekly personal goals, remember several things. The first is to set reasonable goals. The tendency for many people is to set goals too high. This makes good progress seem trivial. I will discuss this issue of setting realistic goals in greater detail as the program moves along.

Tape/CD 3
Section 8

The second thing to remember is to reward yourself, even with a few kind words. Too often people dismiss important changes they make and focus instead on how far they have to go. People are notoriously reluctant to reward themselves, perhaps because it seems like bragging. Yet, you can be your biggest fan—you know how much time and effort you have invested in making important changes. Most people would not dream of praising themselves for something they would routinely praise a friend for doing. Refrain from using food as a reward. Later in the program I will give you some exam-

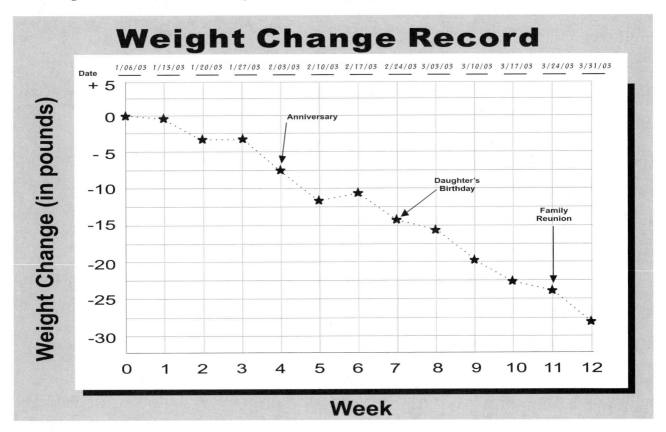

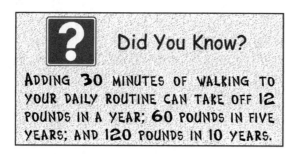

Did You Know?

ADDING 30 MINUTES OF WALKING TO YOUR DAILY ROUTINE CAN TAKE OFF 12 POUNDS IN A YEAR; 60 POUNDS IN FIVE YEARS; AND 120 POUNDS IN 10 YEARS.

ples of how to reward yourself. For now, just be aware of the notion of rewarding yourself for doing a good job—it's okay to pat yourself on the back. Getting in the habit of praising yourself is a good habit indeed!

 MY WEEKLY GOALS

The primary goal this week is not to start a diet but to learn about your eating and weight habits. The Monitoring Form and the Weight Change Record are an important first step in this learning process. I will discuss specific calorie levels in Lesson Four. Set a personal goal this week to make copies of the blank Monitoring Form provided on page 24 of this lesson. If you have ordered the pocket-sized forms listed on page 258, that's terrific; you won't need to make copies. Complete your Monitoring Form each day of the week, and begin to chart your weight change on the My Weight Change Record on page 216.

Setting personal goals to complete these forms is critical for three reasons. First, it is a good test of your motivation, so think of ways to fire yourself up. Second, the information will teach you about your habits. Third, the information will be valuable to a group leader or professional who may be working with you.

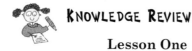 **KNOWLEDGE REVIEW**

Lesson One

(For each question below, circle T for true or F for false.)

T F 1. The LEARN Program is a lifestyle change approach to weight management, not a diet.

T F 2. You can expect to lose five pounds per week on The LEARN Program.

T F 3. Setting goals that you will have little chance of achieving is a good way to keep you motivated and working hard.

T F 4. Record keeping may be the most important aspect of a weight management program.

T F 5. Keeping track of the calories you eat is not all that important for weight loss.

T F 6. People who exercise at a gym lose more weight than people who do lifestyle physical activity.

T F 7. Very few people can accurately estimate the quantity and calories of foods.

T F 8. Using a tool like a step counter is not very helpful for weight management.

T F 9. The purpose of the Weight Change Record is for you to track your actual weight each week during the program.

(Answers in Appendix C, page 219)

Monitoring Form—Lesson One (Sample)   *Today's Date:* Jan 6, 2003

Time	Description	Place	Calories
6:30 am	**Breakfast**	Kitchen	
	Orange juice, 6 fl oz		77
	Cheerios, 1 cup		110
	Skim milk, 8 fl oz		79
	Toast, white bread, 1 slice		90
	Total calories from breakfast		356
12:45 pm	**Lunch**	Restaurant	
	Apple, 1 medium		59
	Vegetable, vegetarian soup, 2 cups		157
	Chicken salad sandwich/wheat bread, 2oz, 2T fat-free mayo		305
	Whole wheat crackers, 5		89
	Diet Pepsi, 12 fl oz		0
	Total calories from lunch		610
7:00 pm	**Dinner**	Dining room	
	Sirloin steak, lean, broiled, 3.5 oz		200
	Green beans, steamed, 1 cup		44
	Cauliflower, steamed, 2 cups		100
	Bread, whole wheat, 1 slice		69
	Apple pie, 1 slice (1/6 of 8" pie)		277
	Water, 16 fl oz		0
	Total calories from dinner		690
10:00 pm	**Snacks**	Kitchen	
	Yogurt, raspberry, fat free, 8 oz		147
	Total calories from snacks		147
Total calories eaten today			1,803
Number of steps walked today			2,542

Time	Description	Place	Calories
	Monitoring Form—Lesson One *Today's Date:* _____		
	Breakfast		
	Total calories from breakfast		
	Lunch		
	Total calories from lunch		
	Dinner		
	Total calories from dinner		
	Snacks		
	Total calories from snacks		
	Total calories eaten today		
	Number of steps walked today		

Lesson Two

Welcome back after your first lesson! I hope you did well and are on your way to permanent weight loss. Many people think of weight management as "going on a diet." Banish this thought from your mind, and think instead of making good food choices and being more physically active in enjoyable ways. This new way of thinking leaves the door open to be at peace with food, to enjoy being active, and to be happier and healthier. You can do this; you CAN lose weight and keep it off.

Reasons for Overweight

*Tape/CD 1
Section 11*

Why people are overweight is still somewhat of a mystery, although scientists from many countries have been working on the problem for years. Exciting discoveries occur frequently, yet we still have a long road to travel before we can unravel the complex causes of weight problems. Meanwhile, examining the popular reasons people use to explain overweight is helpful.

I cover this information here because the reasons people use to explain weight problems create attitudes that can help or hinder efforts to lose weight. A person who feels genetics has determined his or her weight may be discouraged from attempting to lose weight. The information that follows may counter some misconceptions.

➡ *Glands.* An underactive thyroid used to be a popular reason to explain weight problems. The truth is that most overweight people have no gland problems. If they do, the problems are not serious enough to account for much of their excess weight. If you suspect gland problems, don't hesitate to see your doctor. But, remember that fewer than 5 percent of overweight persons have these difficulties.

➡ *Metabolism.* I will talk about the subject of metabolism later in our discussion of exercise. Metabolic rate, which is the energy (calories) our bodies use for living, varies widely among individuals. This influences the way people gain or lose weight. Some women will lose weight rapidly on 1,600 calories per day while others, in rare cases, may lose slowly on only 800 calories per day. A thrifty metabolism that conserves energy and promotes weight gain curses these people. Determining your exact

metabolic needs is more costly than it is worth, because you approach weight loss in the same way regardless of your metabolism. If you have a thrifty metabolism, exercise is especially important.

➡ *Genetics.* Overweight runs in families. A child with no overweight parents has less than a 10 percent chance of being overweight. If one parent is overweight, the chances increase to 40 percent. With two overweight parents, the odds are 70 percent. This, of course, could reflect the tendency of families to pass along their eating and exercise habits to children.

Fatness can be bred. Farmers have been breeding animals to have a certain body fat for decades. But, what do we know about humans?

The past 20 years have brought an explosion of research on the genetics of body-weight regulation. Among the ways to study genetics is to examine identical twins. Studies have compared body weights of twins who were reared together to weights in twins reared apart. If genes were important, we would expect the weights within twin pairs to be similar, whether or not they were reared together. If the twins reared apart were more dissimilar than twins reared together, the environment

People become overweight for a variety of complex reasons. Yet, when all is said and done, the fact remains that people gain weight because they eat more calories than their bodies use.

would seem to exert an important influence. The studies show that the similarity in body weights within twin pairs is nearly the same whether twins are reared apart or reared together. This suggests that genes are important.

This does not mean, however, that genetics completely controls a person's body weight. How we eat and exercise will determine whether our genetic predisposition to be heavy or thin is expressed. One virtue of this research is that it relieves some of the blame people place on themselves for being overweight. One danger is that people may overstate the importance of genetics. They may come to feel they are destined to be heavy and that they can do nothing about it.

➡ *Fat cells.* The body accumulates and stores fat in fat cells, also called adipose tissue. Some people have too many fat cells (called *hyperplastic* obesity) while others have the normal number but their fat cells are too large (called *hypertrophic* obesity). Still others have both types. People who were overweight in childhood or are very heavy as adults tend to have an excessive number of fat cells as well as enlarged cells. Early researchers in this area speculated that people with too many fat cells would have difficulty losing weight, but this has not been shown conclusively.

➡ *Family upbringing.* Some families foster overeating for emotional or even cultural reasons. As a result, some people may eat for psychological reasons related to their family upbringing. A program aimed at behavior change is the right approach for these people. Behavior change helps to separate emotions from eating and helps to identify other sources of gratification.

➡ *Psychological factors.* Many overweight people have trouble controlling their eating in response to stress, depression, loneliness, anger, and other emotions. Does this mean that being

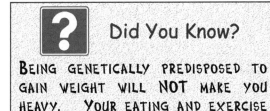

Did You Know?

BEING GENETICALLY PREDISPOSED TO GAIN WEIGHT WILL **NOT** MAKE YOU HEAVY. YOUR EATING AND EXERCISE HABITS PLAY A MORE IMPORTANT ROLE.

overweight is a symptom of deep psychological distress? If so, the remedy would be to root out the underlying psychological problems in hopes that the symptom of overeating would disappear. This theory rings true intuitively for many people but does not have much support among experts. Many normal-weight persons have psychological problems but cope without overeating. In people who undergo intensive psychotherapy, weight problems generally remain after their psychological difficulties have been resolved. If you feel that psychological problems are at the root of your weight problem, deal with either the weight (through this program) or the psychological problems (with therapy). Do not labor under the notion that you must remedy the psychological problems before you can lose weight.

When all is said and done, and all the reasons for overweight are debated, the fact remains that people gain weight because they consume more calories than their bodies use. Becoming overweight is usually a gradual process and may result from small errors in what we eat for a given level of physical activity. One business executive gained five pounds each year for 20 years. The five pounds each year were not too obvious, but he sure noticed the 100 pounds he accumulated over the 20-year period. This could have occurred from nothing more than two to three drinks per week. The solution to such a problem is a gradual change in eating and exercise habits so that long-term weight loss can occur.

Eating a Sensible Meal

Making meals count is important. By this, I mean you want your meals to be satisfying, good tasting, pleasing to the eye, nutritious, and have a texture that is pleasing to your palate. Otherwise, you will feel deprived when there is no need to, and you will keep your body from getting the nutrients it needs to stay healthy. You do not have to eat a sparse and boring "diet meal." Your meals can be filling, nutritious, varied, delicious, and still be low in calories, sugar, and fat. You may have to do some advanced planning and make good food choices, but this is not difficult to do. A little practice can go a long way to preparing and eating excellent meals.

Eating Great Meals

You will hear me talk a lot about eating "sensible" meals. I am a firm believer that you should enjoy every bit of food you eat. The objective is for you to eat delicious, filling, and nutritious meals—not a plate with one stalk of asparagus and a beet. Keeping your calories low, accomplishing your dietary goals, and being satisfied is quite possible—if you make good choices.

Some people like to feel full when they eat. If this sounds like you, a well-planned meal will probably do the job. For example, you might eat a green salad, baked chicken breast, baked potato garnished with butter buds and dried chives, grilled or steamed squash and carrots, and fresh strawberries and melon for dessert. Eating a sensible meal can mean eating a fun meal, a delicious meal, and a meal that makes you feel virtuous.

Adding variety to your meals can increase your eating pleasure. You can substitute soup for the salad or replace vegetables and fruits from time to time. You may have turkey, fish, and chicken, and still eat delicious, low-calorie meals. So, when you hear "sensible" meal, think of good food, plenty to eat, and a boost for your body.

Reviewing Your Monitoring Form

Tape/CD 2
Section 8

Your Monitoring Form contains information about the foods you eat and other important issues—your eating patterns. The better you understand these patterns, the easier it will be to establish new ones. After a week of recording, you should have a better idea of how many meals you typically eat each day and the types of food you enjoy. You should also be more aware of when you are most hungry and where you are most likely to eat, both at home and away from home. Your job now is to become a detective who analyzes your eating habits and tries to correct the troublesome ones. Sometimes this requires only small changes such as taking a piece of fruit or a small bag of pretzels to work to prepare yourself for the three o'clock munchies. In other instances, you may have to take more time to plan your meals. Let's now search to see what some of your eating patterns might be.

Searching for Patterns

One purpose of the Monitoring Form is to examine your eating patterns. Much eating is automatic and occurs with little thought or appreciation. We miss much of the pleasure in food and eat more than we need. Think of munching from a large bag of potato chips. Would you remember how many you ate? Would you taste each bite of

Carefully reviewing your Monitoring Forms will help you discover your unique eating patterns.

each chip? Would you have just the right amount to satisfy yourself?

LIFESTYLE PROFILES

A good example of automatic eating comes from a client of mine named Ginny. She loved ice cream and would have a bowl every night. With instruction, she began counting her bites and noting the pleasure in each one. She averaged 16 bites. She found that the first four bites were delicious, and then there were about 10 bites where she paid little attention to what she was eating (automatic eating). The final few bites were good because she was nearly finished. With her increased awareness, Ginny decided that the middle 10 bites were needless calories.

Examine your Monitoring Forms for the past week and look for patterns. The patterns you find will be the foundation for later parts of the program. I will give you guidelines for tailoring techniques to your specific eating and exercise patterns. On page 30 is the My Eating Patterns Worksheet to help you identify your unique eating patterns. The last column in the worksheet is for you to list the eating patterns you'd like to change. As you review your Monitoring Forms for the last week and complete this worksheet, pay careful attention to the following topics as you search for *your* eating patterns.

➡ *Time.* Look for times of the day when you are likely to eat. A typical pattern shows little eating at breakfast and lunch, but much eating and snacking at dinner and afterwards. Do you crave a snack just before bed? Do you always have something to eat in the mid-afternoon? Are your meals irregular? Do you skip meals?

➡ *Amount.* Look over the quantities and calories of the food you eat. One key is to enjoy the food you eat so that you do not waste calories. Are there foods that you could eat less of or avoid completely? Do you eat specific amounts

DIET COUNSELOR

I KEPT A LOG OF EVERYTHING I ATE THIS WEEK, BUT NOW I'VE GOT WRITER'S CRAMP.

THAVES

each time without thinking about how much you need and want?

➡ **Foods.** Pay close attention to the foods you eat. Can you find patterns in the foods you choose? Which foods contribute most to your calories? Can you think of substitutes for high-calorie foods?

➡ **Places.** Are there certain places where you eat? Do you frequently eat in places other than your kitchen or dining room? Some likely candidates are the den, the office, and the car.

An Expanded Monitoring Form

This week you will find several categories added to a new Expanded Monitoring Form. These categories are Feelings and Activity. In addition to the food and calories, you will be recording how you are feeling and what you are doing while you eat. These are important factors in the eating habits of many overweight people.

Use the Expanded Monitoring Form as you did the Monitoring Form for Lesson One. In the next lesson, I will discuss the interpretations of the new form. A blank Monitoring Form is provided in this lesson on page 36. I have also included a sample from one of my clients on page 35 to show you how the form might be completed. Be sure to make enough copies of the blank Monitoring Form to use between now and the next lesson. Good luck with the new form!

Rating Your Diet

Nutrition is one key to successful weight management. What you eat affects how you feel, whether you are healthy, and how you look. Much information on nutrition awaits you in this program. To start the process, let's evaluate your diet.

 NUTRITION NOTES

I have provided in Appendix E on page 231, the "Rate Your Diet Quiz" for Lesson Two. This quiz was developed by the Center for Science in the Public Interest and published in the *Nutrition Action Healthletter*. Take a few minutes to complete the quiz and to score your answers. You have probably changed your diet since beginning this program. Complete the quiz as you would have before starting the program, so you will see how you would score ordinarily.

Better diets will receive higher scores on this quiz. You will see which choices for each question contribute to or subtract from the total score. Taking the quiz can be educational because it may help provide new ideas for healthy food choices. Later in the program, I will ask you to take the quiz again to see how your eating habits have changed.

Exercise

I want you to have a clear understanding of what exercise is and what it *can* and *cannot* do for you. This is an important concept, so read carefully! The more realistic your expectations and the more positive

My Eating Patterns Worksheet

	Description	My Eating Patterns	Eating Patterns to Change
TIME			
AMOUNT			
FOODS			
PLACES			
OTHER			

your outlook, the more likely you are to enjoy physical activity, both now and in the future.

 EXERCISE ESSENTIALS

As I view it, *exercise* involves any activity in which you move your body and expend calories. This is why you will see me refer to *exercise* more often in this program as *physical activity*. Moving your arms in circles is a type of physical activity, as is rolling down a car window (if you can still find a car without electric windows). Similarly, walking up the stairs in your home or apartment counts as exercise and so does working out on a stair machine at a health club.

Any duration of physical activity counts, whether it is 15 seconds, 15 minutes, or 15 hours. You burn calories when you get up to change the TV channel, take a walk during your lunch break, or ride all day in the Tour de France. Over the course of a day, brief bouts of activity can add up to a lot of exercise. Just ask anyone who has waited tables. You do not have to exercise for a certain amount of time to improve your well-being—any type and amount of activity *counts* as exercise.

Benefits of Physical Activity

The principal benefits of regular physical activity are improved physical and emotional well-being. Exercise improves blood pressure, cholesterol, blood sugar, and

overall health. This was shown in a recent study in which overweight individuals who were physically active and fit had a lower risk of heart disease and premature death than people who were thin but inactive and unfit. It is possible to be *fat* but *fit*.

Perhaps the best reason to exercise is that it makes you feel good about yourself. Even a quick two-minute walk can help clear your mind and give you a boost. Over time, longer bouts of activity can make you feel more self-confident and more attuned to your body. Many of my clients tell me that simple activities such as stretching, dancing, and walking help them rediscover their bodies and enjoy movement for the sake of movement. In the next lesson, I discuss some more specific benefits of physical activity as they apply to weight management.

Physical Activity and Weight Loss

You have probably noticed that I have not emphasized the weight-reducing benefits of physical activity. I do this intentionally. Most people know that exercise burns calories, however, it takes a lot of exercise to lose one pound of fat. For most people, losing one pound of fat would require walking 25 to 30 miles or spending five to six hours a week in an intensive aerobics class. This is a lot of physical activity.

Second, judging the benefits of exercise based on weight loss is bound to disappoint you some weeks. Your bathroom scale probably cannot reliably detect a weight loss of a half-pound or less. Sooner or later you will get on the scale and hear yourself say something like, "This isn't fair. I exer-

cised five days this week and didn't lose anything! What's the point?"

The way to keep from falling into this trap is to separate activity from weight loss. Increase your physical activity for the sake of the pleasure and improved health it brings. These payoffs alone are better than any pill or magic potion you can take. In addition, there are a host of long-term rewards.

People who exercise regularly are far more likely to maintain their weight loss than those who are not physically active. Exercise can facilitate long-term weight management by improving mood, food choices, and self-control—in addition to burning calories. Most of my clients who are working to stabilize their weight tell me that they exercise because they love it. Keeping off lost weight is only one of many benefits.

I hope you keep these points in mind as you increase your physical activity over the next few weeks. You may want to tag this page in some way so you can refer back to this discussion about exercise. In Lesson Three, I will help you determine if increasing your exercise is safe for you. Then, I'll help you begin a walking program.

Why Losing Weight Is Difficult

Let's face it—losing weight is hard work, and maintaining weight loss can be even more challenging. Most overweight people really want to lose weight, but often find it difficult. Many factors can contribute to this difficulty. I will discuss several

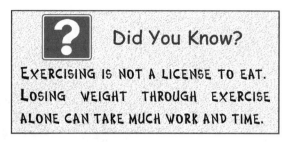

Did You Know?

EXERCISING IS NOT A LICENSE TO EAT. LOSING WEIGHT THROUGH EXERCISE ALONE CAN TAKE MUCH WORK AND TIME.

here. Appreciating the complexities of weight management is important so that you don't get demoralized when you encounter tough times.

Eating is a complex activity. When you face tempting food, say a piece of cake after dinner, many factors collide that determine whether you will indulge. Physiology is at work because seeing the cake might stimulate hunger. Your family upbringing can enter the picture because you may have learned that foods, especially desserts, are associated with love. Culture plays a part, particularly if you are dining with someone else and you feel obliged to eat everything, including dessert. Psychology may take part if you are feeling depressed or lonely and want food for gratification. We cannot pinpoint a single reason for eating the cake.

Being physically active also can be difficult. When you're out of shape, don't like to be seen exercising, and find the experience unpleasant, it is hard to mobilize. Being inactive is easier and is reinforced by our environment. People used to get paid to exercise—it was called a *job*. Today, few jobs require physical exertion; so, it becomes harder and harder to get out there and move.

To keep your attitude on the right track, remind yourself that getting the actual eating and exercise habits under control is the best course to weight loss and long-term weight loss maintenance. Instead of feeling guilty about what you eat, resentful about what you cannot eat, or beating yourself up for being inactive, you can learn about food and calories; you can learn how to become more physically active; and, you can learn to enjoy yourself along the way!

What Losing Weight Can Mean in Your Life

Tape/CD 2
Section 1

Living with extra weight can be extremely difficult. The good news is that you can do something to help manage your weight. You deserve to feel better and be healthier. You deserve to succeed.

Success at weight loss can be wonderful. I can think of many benefits, such as having more energy, improving your health, looking better, and feeling better about yourself. Think of the boost in self-esteem that comes from overcoming a very difficult problem. Think of how wonderful it feels to receive compliments on your progress and for others to be genuinely happy for you. This is all part of well-being—being well as a person. Let's work together to be well.

Using the LEARN WalkMaster

You may remember that in Lesson One, I mentioned the LEARN WalkMaster. This handy device counts your steps, the distance you move, and the calories you burn. It serves a simple, yet very important purpose—to keep you motivated and to give you positive feedback about increases in your physical activity.

Because it detects small changes in your activity, the WalkMaster provides a nice way for you to see the progress you are making. It shows that even small changes do count and add up over time. The WalkMaster can help you increase your overall physical activity because it counts *everything* you do as exercise, even simple things that you may not have considered to be exercise in the past. Research shows how helpful this "lifestyle" approach to exercise can be, so consider using a pedometer like the LEARN WalkMaster. In the next lesson I will give you more specific guidelines on using the WalkMaster. For now, simply record the number of steps you take each day on your Monitoring Forms.

Mastering the Scale

Tape/CD 2
Section 9

Using the scale wisely can be a great help, but it also can be troublesome. Weighing too often is generally the problem, yet avoiding the scale when one slips is also common. Developing a plan for optimal use of the scale would be simple if one strategy worked for everyone, but such is not the case. Some people benefit from more frequent weighing such as once a day; others benefit from weighing once a month or less. Once a week is about average.

I will describe the advantages and disadvantages of weighing yourself, then you can experiment and learn what works best for you. The primary disadvantage is that ups and downs unrelated to your behavior can generate strong feelings, and these feelings in turn can derail a program. You must decide what works best for you.

I encouraged you at the outset of the program to weigh yourself weekly and to record your weight change on the My Weight Change Record on page 216. Many people wonder how frequently they should weigh themselves. One popular self-help group, Overeaters Anonymous, does not have its members weigh themselves at all. The theory is that more frequent weighing gives "too much power to the scale." Other programs recommend that participants weigh regularly to get feedback on their progress. Some people weigh themselves many times each day. The average for people who enter weight loss programs is about once per day.

The scale represents various things to different people; it can be either friend or foe. Feedback from the scale can be a kind incentive for some individuals. It reminds them of the progress they have made and spurs their efforts. Others despair when the scale shows no change, and they look with horror at how much weight they have to lose to reach their goal. Please remember that the scale can be a powerful influence in your weight loss efforts—both positive and negative; so think seriously about how often you and the scale should communicate.

This is where your judgment must prevail. Weigh yourself as often as you see fit. I recommend no less than once each week and no more than once each day. If you are a frequent weigher, you may get discouraged by weight gains beyond your control. Fluid shifts alone can lead to gains or losses of several pounds. However, if you feel the scale can be a motivating factor, try weighing more often.

One problem with paying too much attention to the scale is that it can lead to undeserved euphoria or disappointment. An example would be a person who does not do well on his or her eating plan. The scale may show a weight loss anyway, perhaps due to water loss from a menstrual cycle. This person may think he or she can stray from the plan and still lose weight. The opposite side of the coin is the person who does well on the program and gains weight anyway. Again, this can happen for several

reasons, including fluid shifts. The danger lies in the person assuming that his or her efforts are fruitless.

The scale should be a general guide about progress, not a day-to-day index of whether your program is working. This is why the Monitoring Forms at the end of each lesson ask you to record your calorie intake, your behavior changes, and your exercise. If these change appropriately, you *will* lose weight. Paying attention to all the lifestyle changes you are making will make you less vulnerable to the vagaries of the scale.

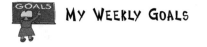 ## MY WEEKLY GOALS

You have several program goals for this week. First, make copies of the new Expanded Monitoring Form on page 36 and complete it each day. Record the types and amounts of food you eat, times, feelings, and activities associated with eating. You can order blank week-at-a-time Monitoring Forms as mentioned in the Supplemental Resources section on page 258. Second, make your meals count and work on making them enjoyable, delicious, and nutritious. Review your Monitoring Form from Lesson One and search carefully for patterns. Using the Rate Your Diet Quiz—Lesson Two beginning on page 231, rate your diet. Be sure to rate your diet as it was before you started this program.

Finally, think about your attitudes toward physical activity as you prepare to increase your activity this week. Can you view exercise in a more positive light after reading this lesson? If you do not have a pedometer, consider getting one like the LEARN WalkMaster. Increased physical activity brings many rewards, one of which is long-term weight management. Remember, even small increases can help. Don't forget to record your weight change for week two on the My Weight Change Record on page 216. Good luck achieving your personal goals for this week!

 ## KNOWLEDGE REVIEW

Lesson Two

T F 1. Discovering the psychological roots of your weight problem is the most important factor in weight reduction.

T F 2. All overweight people have an excessive number of fat cells.

T F 3. There is no such thing as a slow or underactive metabolism.

T F 4. Being on a weight management program means that you can't enjoy good meals.

T F 5. Automatic eating is common in overweight people and distracts them from the taste of food.

T F 6. It is possible to change dietary habits to lose weight and still eat meals that are satisfying, good tasting, and nutritious.

T F 7. The Monitoring Form helps uncover patterns in your eating habits.

T F 8. Exercise doesn't really help with weight loss unless it is done at a high-intensity rate for at least 20 minutes at a time.

T F 9. You should weigh yourself every morning.

(Answers in Appendix C, page 219)

Expanded Monitoring Form—Lesson Two (*Sample*) Today's Date: Jan 13, 2003

Description	Time	Feelings	Activity	Calories
Breakfast				
Coffee, 6 oz	7:30 am	Tired	Reading paper	0
Poached egg, 1 medium				66
Bagel, ½ 3"				78
Orange juice, 8 fl oz				110
Total calories from breakfast				254
Lunch				
Roast beef sand, 3 oz, wheat, 2T mayo	12:30 pm	Hurried	Working, desk	328
Raspberry yogurt, fat free, 8 oz				147
Water, 8 oz				0
Total calories from lunch				475
Dinner				
Chicken breast, grilled, 3½ oz	7:30 pm	Relaxed	Watching TV	164
Green beans, steamed, 1 cup				44
Carrots, cooked, 1 cup				70
Wheat bread, 1 slice, dry				65
Skim milk, 16 oz				172
Total calories from dinner				515
Snacks				
Celery, 4 12" stalks	10:00 am	Busy	Working/desk	41
Apple, 1 med	3:00 pm	Hurried	Working/desk	80
Total calories from snacks				121
Total calories eaten today				1,365
Number of steps walked today				2,850

Expanded Monitoring Form—Lesson Two				*Today's Date:*____
Description	Time	Feelings	Activity	Calories
Breakfast				
Total calories from breakfast				
Lunch				
Total calories from lunch				
Dinner				
Total calories from dinner				
Snacks				
Total calories from snacks				
Total calories eaten today				
Number of steps walked today				

Lesson Three

Congratulations! You have now been using The LEARN Program for two weeks and have probably lost some weight. I hope you are pleased with your progress, both with your weight and your lifestyle changes. The small changes you make now will pay big dividends over the long run.

You may be wondering whether you can make the lifestyle changes a permanent part of your life, especially if you have tried before. Sure you can; you are motivated, and you now have the help of a state-of-the-art program. I hope you are enjoying working together as a team. Many more exciting things are yet to come!

Reviewing Your Expanded Monitoring Form

Now that you have experience with the Expanded Monitoring Form, let's discuss what the information means. We are looking for several things. The first involves eating patterns that tell us whether your eating follows a reliable course from day-to-day. The second are triggers—the circumstances that provoke overeating. Let's see if you can find some patterns and high-risk situations.

The Search for Patterns

The Expanded Monitoring Form included spaces for the time of eating, feelings, foods, and other activities. Did you find any patterns? Below are some of the typical patterns:

➡ **Time.** Did your eating cluster around certain times of the day? Your eating times may vary depending on the day of the week. Some people keep a strict schedule on weekdays and then have less control on weekends. If you find times when control is difficult, think about scheduling alternative activities, like exercise.

➡ **Feelings.** Did you eat when you were bored, depressed, anxious, angry, or lonely? Other feelings may also be involved, like resentment, hostility, jealousy, or even joy. Seeing a pattern is a sure sign that you may want to develop more adaptive ways to cope with difficult feelings.

➡ **Activity.** What do you do while eating? Watching television is the main culprit, but reading a newspaper, listening to a radio, or surfing the Internet also can signal problems: Doing two things at once insures that neither gets full attention. Eating already

My Eating Patterns Worksheet

	Description	My Eating Patterns	Eating Patterns to Change
TIME			
FEELINGS			
ACTIVITY			
FOODS			
OTHER			

gets less attention than it deserves. Later in the program, I will discuss how eating can be separated from other activities.

➡ *Foods.* What types of foods do you eat? Do you crave carbohydrates at certain times? Do you eat foods because they are available, or do you seek out the foods you love? Are some foods very difficult to eat in moderation?

I have provided you with a worksheet above titled "My Eating Patterns Worksheet." You may find this worksheet helpful in uncovering your unique eating pat-

terns. Take time now to complete this review before moving on.

Now that you have reviewed your Expanded Monitoring Forms from last week, let's focus on triggers that may cause you to begin eating.

High-Risk Situations—Triggers for Eating

What are your eating triggers? Talking to your mother-in-law may do it, being bored at home or having your spouse eat ice cream in front of you may be eating triggers for you. It could be a trying day at work, a fight with someone, or worries about money. Most people have well-defined eating triggers. What are yours?

This is where the notion of high-risk situations becomes so important. Throughout this program, you will learn methods for avoiding or coping with situations that spell trouble. Identifying these situations, or triggers, is the first step. The knowledge you gain from studying your behavior provides valuable information for later stages of the program. You can learn to predict the situations that increase your risk of overeating and plot your strategy accordingly.

Triggers are typically a mixture of the factors included in your Expanded Monitoring Forms. Given the right time, feelings, and other circumstances, eating can be hard to resist. You may encounter positive pressure, like offers of food from friends, or negative pressure, such as feeling upset. Once the trigger loosens your restraint, stopping can be difficult.

List your four main triggers in the "My Eating Triggers" worksheet on the right. Remember these; I will make many suggestions later about how to counter your particular eating triggers.

On the Move

Tape/CD 3
Section 3

Much has been said about the glories of exercise. Some joggers boast of a runner's high, and others believe that sweating and panting are the paths to heaven. Some people react to this hysteria by giving up on exercise completely. However, the LEARN concept of physical activity is not the typical exercise-prescription program of high-intensity exercise. Instead, this program promotes enjoyable activities. I gave you a brief overview of physical activity in Lesson Two on page 29. The objective of The LEARN Program is to make physical activity fun and to increase the number of activities you consider "exercise." The first

My Eating Triggers

Trigger 1:
_____

Trigger 2:
_____

Trigger 3:
_____

Trigger 4:
_____

Identifying your eating triggers is the first step toward developing alternative coping strategies.

example is walking. Other activities will follow later in the program.

The Role of Physical Activity

Tape/CD 1
Section 9

I have talked a lot about the benefits of carefully examining your eating patterns, as well as different methods of eating a balanced diet. I will speak about this often throughout the program. Keeping calories low is one good way to help your body create an energy deficit. However, there is much, much more you can do. Now it is time to talk about the other side of the weight loss equation—increasing the number of calories you expend by increasing your physical activity. Are you ready?

 **EXERCISE ESSENTIALS**

I cannot overstate the importance of increasing physical activity. Theoretically, you can eat less, exercise more, or do both to alter your energy balance and your weight. I feel strongly that doing both is the best approach. This comes from experience with hundreds of clients and from research showing that people who exercise regularly are more likely to achieve long-term success than those who are not physically active. Let's see why this is so.

The Importance of Being Active

Don't get nervous! Increasing your physical activity does not have to involve calisthenics, weight lifting, or marathon running. I'm not going to ask you to join an expensive gym. Many people avoid exercise because it hurts, it takes time, they are embarrassed, and they are not skilled at athletic activities. Solutions exist to these problems. I will discuss these in upcoming lessons. For now, I want you to be aware of the importance and benefits of being active. Before I talk about the many benefits of exercise, I want to share a new view of exercise.

A New View of Exercise

Most of us labor under the old idea that exercise has to be taxing to be beneficial. "No pain, no gain," right? This sermon was preached for years and years. Much to the delight of people struggling with their weight, the view of exercise has changed entirely in the last several years. What we know now, and what prestigious groups like the American College of Sports Medicine and the Centers for Disease Control and Prevention have emphasized, is that *moderate-intensity* physical activity can be very beneficial for health and weight management. For most sedentary adults, moderate-intensity physical activity means moderate to brisk walking at a pace of 15–20 minutes per mile or lifestyle activities such as raking leaves.

This new view of "exercise" turns everything upside down. It means that small increases in physical activity *count* as exercise. Even with modest increases in your physical activity level, you may improve your health considerably. This also means that we can set aside the biggest barrier to exercise—the thought that long bouts of high-intensity exercise are necessary to get any health benefits. I hope you don't tire of me saying that any amount of exercise is beneficial, because I raise this issue often throughout the program.

Staying Motivated to Be Active

You may remember that in Lesson One I talked about using the LEARN Walk-Master, a device that counts steps, distance, and calories. This device has a simple yet very important purpose—to keep you motivated and to give you positive feedback about increases in your physical activity.

Because it detects small changes in your activity, a step counter provides a nice way to see if you are increasing your activity. It shows that even small changes do count as exercise, and that doing things you may not have considered helpful before, like walking a little extra distance, can really help increase your overall physical activity. Research shows how helpful this "lifestyle" approach to exercise can be. This is why I strongly recommend you use a step counter.

The Benefits of Exercise

In the last lesson, I promised to talk more about the specific benefits of exercise as they apply to weight management. Physical activity is central to weight management for seven reasons. Most people know only the first—that it burns calories. Let's explore the others as well.

➡ *Burns calories.* Exercise does burn calories, but the other benefits might be more important. Be careful to avoid feeling that a modest amount of exercise entitles you to more calories at the table. In reality, you will probably eat more calories than the exercise burns.

➡ *Counteracts the ills of overweight.* Exercise can help improve the physical and psychological problems often associated with being overweight. Regular physical activity can lower blood pressure and cholesterol and improve the metabolism of carbohydrates. In addition, regular physical activity improves mood, self-esteem, confidence, and well-being.

➡ *May help control appetite.* Some studies with animals and humans suggest that exercise may help control appetite. It certainly does not stimulate appetite when people exercise in moderate amounts. If you exercise and feel increased hunger, your mind may be at work rather than your body.

➡ *Preserves the body's muscle.* Your body loses both muscle and fat when you lose weight. The objective is to maximize fat loss and preserve lean body tissue (muscle). Combining exercise with diet does this more effectively than diet alone.

➡ *Helps to increase metabolic rate.* When you eat less and lose weight, your metabolism slows down. This is bad news because your body then uses less energy (calories) for basic functioning at a time when you want to burn more calories. Exercise may help to speed up

❓ Did You Know?

YOU DON'T HAVE TO EXPERIENCE PAIN OR SWEAT LIKE A WATER HOSE TO GET IMPORTANT HEALTH AND WEIGHT MANAGEMENT BENEFITS FROM EXERCISE.

your metabolism, although the degree and duration of this increase are subject to debate. At the very least, exercising while restricting caloric intake may help offset this drop in your metabolic rate.

➡ *Improves confidence and psychological factors.* Exercise makes people feel good. Each time you are active is a symbol that you are making positive changes. This improves confidence and gives you a boost that can carry over to your eating plan. In addition, many people exercise to relieve stress. This is a much better strategy than eating to lower stress, and it burns rather than adds calories!

➡ *Correlates with long-term success.* Exercise is one of the best predictors of who will lose weight and keep it off. If people are followed a year or more after a weight loss program, those who are exercising tend to be the ones who keep the weight off. Those who exercise during weight loss do better than those who just restrict their caloric intake.

Is Exercise Safe for You?

Today I hope you can begin a walking program. If you are doing more vigorous activity, keep it up if you feel comfortable and have medical clearance. If you are not exercising regularly, the walking program may be just for you. Before you begin, you must ask if exercise is safe for you.

Moderate activity, including the walking discussed here, is safe for most people. Some people with physical problems, however, should not begin an exercise program

The Physical Activity Readiness Questionnaire (PAR-Q)

Many health benefits are associated with regular physical activity, and the completion of the PAR-Q is a sensible first-step to take if you are planning to increase the amount of physical activity in your life. Start by answering the seven questions below. If you are between the ages of 15 and 69, the PAR-Q will tell you if you should check with your doctor before you start. If you are over 69 years of age and you are not used to being very active, check with your doctor.

Common sense is your best guide in answering these few questions. Please read the questions carefully and answer each one honestly. Check YES or NO for each question as it applies to you.

YES NO

☐ ☐   1. Has your doctor ever said that you have a heart condition and that you should only do physical activity recommended by a doctor?

☐ ☐   2. Do you feel pain in your chest when you do physical activity?

☐ ☐   3. In the past month, have you had chest pain when you were not doing physical activity?

☐ ☐   4. Do you lose your balance because of dizziness or do you ever lose consciousness?

☐ ☐   5. Do you have a bone or joint problem (for example, back, knee or hip) that could be made worse by a change in your physical activity?

☐ ☐   6. Is your doctor currently prescribing drugs (for example, water pills) for your blood pressure or heart condition?

☐ ☐   7. Do you know of *any other reason* why you should not do physical activity?

If you answered YES to one or more questions:

Talk with your doctor by phone or in person BEFORE you start becoming much more physically active or BEFORE you have a fitness appraisal. Tell your doctor about the PAR-Q and which questions you answered YES.

➲ You may be able to do any activity you want—as long as you start slowly and build up gradually. Or, you may need to restrict your activities to those which are safe for you. Talk with your doctor about the kinds of activities you wish to participate in and follow his/her advice.

If you answered NO to all questions:

If you answered NO honestly to *all* PAR-Q questions, you can be reasonably sure that you can:

➲ Start becoming much more physically active—begin slowly and build up gradually. This is the safest and easiest way to go.

➲ Take part in a fitness appraisal—this is an excellent way to determine your basic fitness so that you can plan the best way for you to live actively. It is also highly recommended that you have your blood pressure evaluated. If your reading is over 144/94, talk with your doctor before you start becoming much more physically active.

Delay becoming much more active:

➲ If you are not feeling well because of a temporary illness such as a cold or a fever—wait until you feel better; or

➲ If you are or may be pregnant—talk to your doctor before you start becoming more active.

Please Note: If your health changes so that you then answer YES to any of the above questions, tell your fitness or health professional. Ask whether you should change your physical activity plan.

without getting medical clearance. This should extend beyond a simple checkup. You should tell your physician that you want an examination to know whether regular exercise is advisable and safe for you.

The Physical Activity Readiness Questionnaire (PAR-Q) on page 42, provides a simple assessment you can complete to see if increasing your physical activity is safe. Read and answer each question carefully. If you answer "yes" to any question, see your physician before doing any exercise. This is serious and goes beyond the usual warning to "see your doctor" found in most diet books. If you are uncertain about what the terms mean or how to answer any question, play it safe, and consult your physician. The questionnaire here has been adapted from the Canadian version.

Starting Your Walking Program

This week you will begin your walking program. I cannot emphasize enough the importance of monitoring your physical activity. If you are using a step counter, put it on the first thing in the morning. At the end of each day, just before you go to bed, review your daily activity. Record the number of steps you walked during the day on your Monitoring Form in the space provided. Be sure to reset the step counter after you have recorded your steps.

Your goal this week is to walk at least 4,000 steps each day. If you already walk more than this, keep up the good work. Maintain the level that you have been walking. Your goal will be to increase the number of steps by at least 200 steps per day each week, beginning next week. I have included a Walking Goals chart on page 44 to help guide your walking program. Remember, if you are currently walking more than 4,000 steps each day, use your current number as your starting point, and add at least 200 steps per day each week. If you can increase your number of steps more than the 200 I suggest, that's fine. However, make sure that your

increases are reasonable and that you can achieve them.

For optimal health, some experts recommend an ultimate goal of 10,000 steps per day. This would be a great achievement, but for now, focus on near-term changes. Let's look at why walking can be so helpful.

Walking has many advantages. Below are a few:

➡ *It can be done by almost anyone.* Compared with many activities like swimming, basketball, or horseback riding that require special equipment or facilities, walking is an activity available to most people.

➡ *It is convenient.* You don't have to go to the gym to walk. You can walk just about anywhere—in your neighborhood, at the mall, around the office, in a parking garage, or while standing in place in your living room.

Walking is a terrific way to increase your physical activity. Six 5-minute bouts of walking provide the same weight loss benefits as one 30-minute bout.

Regular physical activity is a crucial component of your weight management program. So, do your best to increase your physical activity.

Walking Goals

Week	Steps per Day
3	4,000
4	4,200
5	4,400
6	4,600
7	4,800
8	5,000
9	5,200
10	5,400
11	5,600
12	5,800

➡ *It can be done at any pace.* You don't have to strain with exertion when you walk. Even slow walking can be helpful.

➡ *It is enjoyable.* Think of all you can do and see while walking. You can enjoy the sights, listen to a portable tape/CD player, or talk with friends.

➡ *It is inexpensive.* You do not need a health club membership or expensive equipment. Proper clothing and a good pair of walking shoes will do the job.

➡ *It can be a social event.* You may like company while you walk. It is a delightful time to be with someone you enjoy.

This may surprise you, but walking burns almost the same number of calories as running the same distance. How far you go is more important than how fast you go in terms of burning calories. In Lesson Four, I discuss some of the barriers to being active and provide you with some ideas to overcome some of the more common barriers.

Clothes, Shoes, and Weather

Before you begin, consider clothes, shoes, and weather. Wear clothes that make you feel comfortable. Expensive running suits have nothing special about them. Walking will help just as much if you adorn yourself with an old sweatshirt and jeans.

Shoes are important and are well worth the money for a good pair. Go to a sporting goods store, and try on several brands. Pick one that feels good. Good shoes provide support for your feet, keep you from tiring, and reduce the chance of orthopedic injury.

Weather can be tricky. Exercising indoors when the weather is too hot or too cold is wise. If the temperature is above 90 degrees or is below zero, exercising inside is best. This still leaves most days of the year available for outdoor walking. Most dedicated walkers manage to do their walking in nearly any weather.

Wear layers of clothing in cold weather. When it gets quite cold, you might wear a

cotton T-shirt, several sweatshirts, and a windbreaker. The cotton will absorb the perspiration. Some materials are designed specifically to absorb moisture from your body and keep you dry. You may feel cold for the first few minutes, but you will warm up rapidly. If you get too hot, you can remove a layer. Wear a hat because much of the body's heat loss occurs through the head (especially if you are a hot head!). Mittens will keep your hands warmer than gloves.

Being careful in hot weather also is important to prevent heat-related injuries. Walking in the morning or evening may help avoid the hottest parts of the day. Wear as few clothes as possible, and never wear rubber suits or other clothes designed to make you sweat. Trapping the body's heat in hot weather can be dangerous. Be sure to drink plenty of water. It is fine to drink water before, during, and after exercising.

Mall Walking

Shopping malls are a good place to walk no matter what the weather is like outside. In many parts of the country, mall walkers go to malls early in the morning and walk alone or in groups. This is a terrific idea that allows you to walk no matter what the weather outside is doing.

The walkers who go with friends often make new friends and find the social contacts helpful in adhering to a regular exercise schedule. Also, walking by the stores each morning leaves you poised for action the minute your favorite store posts a new "SALE" sign!

The Mysterious Calorie

In Lesson Four on page 64, I discuss your option of counting calories or using food exchanges. No matter which option you choose, you need to know more about calories.

The word "calorie" is on the lips of millions of Americans. Food products boast about being "low calorie" and diet soft

drinks sell because they have "no calories." Just what is this thing we call a calorie?

A Calorie Is

Tape/CD 2
Section 5

The calorie is a measure of energy available to the body. This is much like a gallon is a measure of volume, the inch a measure of length, and the pound a measure of weight. When you eat something, the number of calories it contains is the number of energy units it provides to the body. The calorie is also a measure of energy your body uses, so it is a measure of both intake and expenditure. This is why I talk about the number of calories burned during exercise.

How do we measure the calories in foods? This is done by burning food in a special instrument called a bomb calorimeter. The food is first dried to remove water and then is placed in a special container that rests in water. When the food burns, heat is transferred to the water. The amount the burning food heats the water is the measure of calories. One calorie is the energy needed to raise the temperature of one gram of water one degree centigrade.

Shopping malls are excellent places to walk, especially when the weather is bad and there are new sales signs to see.

"How many calories are you?"

Foods contain proteins, carbohydrates (sugars and starches), and fats, each of which provide calories. The water, vitamins, and minerals in food provide no calories.

Most foods are measured in kilocalories, which is 1,000 times the energy in a single calorie. In common usage, as in diet books and calorie guides, the word calorie actually refers to kilocalorie.

This may sound technical, but you do need to know the calorie values of foods. A piece of apple pie has 400 calories, and a fresh apple has 100. The pie gives you four times the energy (calories) as the apple. This would be fine if you were starving, but when your basic energy requirements are met, the body stores the excess as fat. The pie contributes four times as many calories to your fat stockpile.

Energy Balance

The notion of energy balance is quite simple. Our bodies use and store energy (calories) much like an automobile uses and stores energy. If you put 20 gallons of gasoline in your car's tank and use only 5 gallons during the day, the remaining 15 gallons are stored. The same thing happens when you eat more calories in a day than your body uses. If you eat 2,200 calo-

ries in a day and your body uses only 1,800 calories, the remaining 400 calories will be stored as *excess* calories. Similarly, if you eat 1,800 calories in a day and your body uses 2,200, you will be creating a calorie *deficit*. Your body will retrieve the needed 400 calories from storage to fuel your body's functions. This is how you lose weight, by creating a calorie deficit.

Estimating Your Daily Energy Expenditure

Modern science and technology have provided us with many helpful tools for estimating our body's daily energy expenditure. Some people find the arithmetic somewhat cumbersome and complicated. A simple way to estimate your body's daily "resting" energy needs is to multiply your weight (in pounds) by 11. Remember, this is only your resting energy needs. You would need to add your energy expenditure from physical activity to this number to estimate your body's total "daily" energy needs. A more accurate way to estimate your body's "daily" energy needs is to log onto the following website, click on "Daily Calorie Needs" and simply answer a few questions:

www.TheLifeStyleCompany.com

If you have access to the Internet, I highly recommend that you do this now and about once each month as you lose weight. This can help you set a target intake calorie level later in the program. For example, if your body's daily calorie needs, at your present weight and activity level, are 2,400 calories, you know that you need to eat less than this to lose weight. A 500 calo-

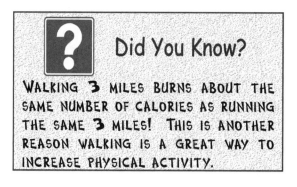

Did You Know?

WALKING 3 MILES BURNS ABOUT THE SAME NUMBER OF CALORIES AS RUNNING THE SAME 3 MILES! THIS IS ANOTHER REASON WALKING IS A GREAT WAY TO INCREASE PHYSICAL ACTIVITY.

rie-a-day deficit will produce about a one pound per week weight loss. A 1,000 calorie-a-day deficit produces a weight loss of about two pounds per week.

Not All People Are Created Equal

People differ greatly in how their bodies use calories. We all know people who eat like crazy and gain very little. These fortunate folks do well in a society where food is abundant and thin is in. In a famine, however, they would be the first to go. Their bodies are not efficient at converting ingested calories to energy stores (fat).

The unfortunate ones among us are those who are food efficient. Their bodies make good use of calories, so they are prone to gain weight. This is adaptive if food is scarce, but promotes weight gain when food is abundant. To lose weight, these individuals must cut their intake to low levels. This is one reason that some people have a more difficult time losing weight than others.

 ### LIFESTYLE PROFILES

Let's consider two individuals who fight different battles. Sheri and Bonnie both weigh 180 pounds. Sheri eats 2,500 calories each day to maintain that weight and will lose about one pound each week by cutting to 2,000 calories. Bonnie, on the other hand, maintains the 180 pounds on only 1,800 calories each day, and must reduce to 1,300 calories to lose the one pound each week. It would not be surprising if Bonnie had a more difficult time losing weight than Sheri. Because of these individual differences, prescribing the same calorie goal to these two different people would not be fruitful.

What Makes a Pound?

We often hear that 3,500 calories equals a pound (it takes 3,500 extra calories to gain one pound). If we decrease intake by 3,500, one less pound will grace our bodies. The typical arithmetic is as follows. If you eat 500 fewer calories each day than your ordinary intake, you will create a 3,500 calorie deficit in a week and will lose one pound. These numbers are helpful to show how we can translate calories into pounds, but again, the numbers are rough averages. People are highly variable in the number of calories necessary to lose a pound, so these numbers may or may not apply to you. The key question is, therefore, "How do you choose a calorie goal for yourself?" Think about this question over the next week. In Lesson Four, I'll help you set a calorie target for yourself.

Following a Balanced Diet

Tape/CD 1
Section 10

Recording what you eat and the times, places, and activities associated with eating, will make you more conscious of your food choices. Some people can use this information to design a healthy meal plan, but many like to learn more about the components of a nutritious, well-balanced diet. There is no end to advice on nutrition. When I visit bookstores or listen to the radio, I am amazed at the half-baked schemes concocted by "experts." One day it is apricot pits for cancer or papaya juice for arthritis. The next day it's mega doses of vitamins for stress and prune pulp for bad breath.

It is inviting to believe in popular diet plans because they provide hope for difficult problems. But, think back over the years. We have all witnessed the Scarsdale Diet, the Rotation Diet, the Beverly Hills Diet, the Carbohydrate Addicts Diet, the Zone Diet, and many, many others. Each promised breakthroughs, grand solutions, and results that seemed guaranteed. Do you know anyone who lost weight and kept it off on one of those diets? Where are the diets now? How much would you bet that the next miracle diet book will be different than the rest—that it will deliver on what it promises and offer a final solution?

When it comes to nutrition, there is no magic, just common sense and rational eating. The key word to remember is balance. This means eating a variety of foods from the different food groups. This may sound like what you learned in the sixth grade, but the message is just as important today.

NUTRITION NOTES

Your body needs a balance of nutrients. It does not function well with too little or too much of any nutrient. If your body needs a certain amount of vitamin E each day, you will be worse off with one-half that amount or with 100 times more. This is similar to making your favorite cake. Each ingredient is important. One ingredient may give the cake a very good taste, but too much will ruin it.

Some people ask why nutrition is so important. The answer is simple. What you eat helps determine how healthy you are, which in turn influences how you cope with life—both physically and psychologically. You could lose weight by eating nothing but grapefruit, but your body would suffer greatly from deficiencies in the nutrients grapefruit does not provide. How much you eat (calories) is only part of the answer. You must also consider how well you eat.

You will notice that I say not a word about forbidden foods. Prohibition can be difficult for people losing weight. If you like cheesecake, but feel it is illegal, you may eventually eat it and feel guilty. This may weaken your restraint even more. If you have the expectation that the first bite will send you into a frenzy and you will then eat all the cheesecake in sight, you are setting yourself up to fall apart when you might otherwise have a little and be satisfied. It

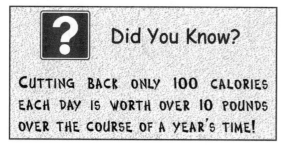

Did You Know?

CUTTING BACK ONLY 100 CALORIES EACH DAY IS WORTH OVER 10 POUNDS OVER THE COURSE OF A YEAR'S TIME!

is fine to eat cheesecake, as long as it occurs within the guidelines for sensible nutrition and fits within your calorie goal.

Dietary Guidelines for Americans

Every five years the U.S. Department of Agriculture (USDA) and the Department of Health and Human Services (HHS) jointly issue a *Dietary Guidelines for Americans* report. Based upon the most current scientific and medical knowledge, this report is intended to provide nutritional and dietary information and guidelines for the general public. These guidelines are designed to help all Americans develop a healthy eating plan. The following represent the 2000 Dietary Guidelines for Americans:

AIM FOR FITNESS . . .

➡ *Aim for a healthy weight.* Many studies show that maintaining a healthy weight can reduce your chances of having high blood pressure, heart disease, certain cancers, a stroke, and the most common kind of diabetes.

➡ *Be physically active each day.* Being physically active is needed for good health. Aim to accumulate at least 30–60 minutes of moderate physical activity most days of the week, preferably daily.

BUILD A HEALTHY BASE . . .

➡ *Let the Pyramid guide your food choices.* Different foods contain different nutrients and other healthful substances. No single food can supply all the nutrients in the amounts you need. To make sure you get all the nutrients and other substances you need for health, build a healthy base by using the Food Guide Pyramid.

➡ *Choose a variety of grains daily, especially whole grains.* Foods made from grains (like wheat, rice, and oats) help form the foundation of a nutritious diet. They provide vitamins, minerals, carbohydrates (starch and dietary fiber), and other substances that are important for good health.

➡ *Choose a variety of fruits and vegetables daily.* Fruits and vegetables are key parts of your daily diet. Eating plenty of fruits and vegetables of different kinds, as part of the healthful eating patterns described by these guidelines, may help protect you against many chronic diseases.

➡ *Keep food safe to eat.* Foods that are safe from harmful bacteria, viruses, parasites, and chemical contaminants are vital for healthful eating. Safe means that the food poses little risk of food-borne illness.

CHOOSE SENSIBLY . . .

➡ *Choose a diet that is low in saturated fat and cholesterol and moderate in total fat.* Fats supply energy and essential fatty acids, and they help absorb the fat-soluble vitamins A, D, E, and K and carotenoids. You need some fat in the food you eat, but choose sensibly. Some kinds of fat, especially saturated fats, increase the risk for coronary heart disease by raising the blood cholesterol. In contrast, unsaturated fats (found mainly in vegetable oils) do not increase blood cholesterol.

➡ *Choose beverages and foods to moderate your intake of sugars.* Sugars are carbohydrates and a source of energy. Dietary carbohydrates also include the complex carbohydrates starch and dietary fiber. During digestion all carbohydrates except fiber break down into sugars. Sugars and starches occur naturally in many foods that also supply other nutrients.

➡ *Choose and prepare foods with less salt.* A diet that is low in sodium can help reduce your risk of high blood pressure.

➡ *If you drink alcoholic beverages, do so in moderation.* Alcoholic beverages add calories, but provide little nutrition. Alcohol also can contribute to

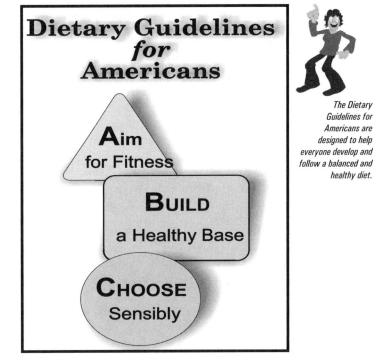

The Dietary Guidelines for Americans are designed to help everyone develop and follow a balanced and healthy diet.

many other health problems and may lead to addiction.

You can see from these dietary guidelines that the key message is moderation. As we progress through the program these guidelines will become more and more familiar to you. Review each of the guidelines again, and check to see how many you are now following. At this point in the program I want you to be familiar with the guidelines so that you can be thinking of how they apply to you and your eating habits.

The Food Guide Pyramid

The Food Guide Pyramid is a graphic illustration of Dietary Guidelines for Americans. The Pyramid divides foods into five separate groups as shown below. The Pyramid also includes a category for fats, oils, and sweets. Each group in the Pyramid includes suggested daily servings that are listed beside the groups. Small circles are used throughout the pyramid to identify food groups that contain high-fat foods, and triangles identify foods that have added sugars.

At the top of the Pyramid is the section containing foods that you should eat sparingly. It should not be surprising that this smallest section consists of fats, oils, and sweets. As the food groups progress toward the bottom of the Pyramid, they become a larger part of your diet. For instance, the bread and cereal group is the largest section. Foods from this group should make up the largest portion of your daily diet.

Many things we eat are a mixture of foods from the five groups. Pizza, for example, has bread (dough), vegetables (tomatoes, peppers, etc.), cheese, and meat in some cases. A chicken pot pie has pastry, vegetables, meat, etc. You will become an expert at identifying the components of combination dishes.

In this lesson, I want you to become familiar with the five food groups in the Pyramid. This graphic will become more familiar to you as you continue through the program. In the lessons that follow, I will describe each tier of the pyramid in more detail. At this point in the program, do not be concerned with the number of servings you should be eating from the various food groups or how much food it takes to make one serving. I will discuss this and other information about each of the five food groups in later lessons. For now, be aware of the five different food groups and try to include each group in your diet. In your Monitoring Form this week, try your best to identify foods from all five food groups.

The Food Guide Pyramid is a useful way to see that you get balanced nutrition, but it is possible to follow the guide and still take in too many calories to lose weight. Eating the recommended number of servings will generally help the average person maintain his or her weight, but since you want to reduce, the number of servings may have to be reduced. As you find the level of calories you need to lose weight, you will be able to adjust the number of servings from the Pyramid.

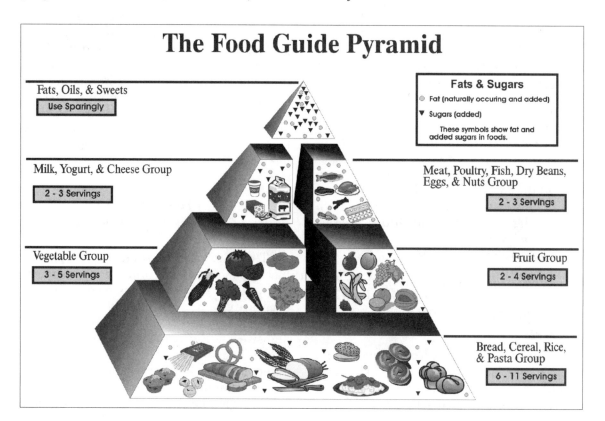

The Food Guide Pyramid

Fats, Oils, & Sweets
Use Sparingly

Fats & Sugars
- Fat (naturally occuring and added)
▼ Sugars (added)

These symbols show fat and added sugars in foods.

Milk, Yogurt, & Cheese Group
2 - 3 Servings

Meat, Poultry, Fish, Dry Beans, Eggs, & Nuts Group
2 - 3 Servings

Vegetable Group
3 - 5 Servings

Fruit Group
2 - 4 Servings

Bread, Cereal, Rice, & Pasta Group
6 - 11 Servings

In thinking about good nutrition while losing weight, both the Food Guide Pyramid and a means of counting calories are important. Within the number of calories you budget for yourself each day, try to choose the right balance of servings across the food groups in the Pyramid.

Introducing a New Monitoring Form

This lesson ushers in a new Monitoring Form. An example of a completed form appears at the end of this lesson on page 53. The new form has three sections. The section on the top is to record food intake, time, and calories, and food-group servings. Although the sample form illustrates food-group servings, don't worry about completing these right now. There are no longer separate sections for breakfast, lunch, dinner, and snacks. List foods in the order you eat them. This will be the Monitoring Form you will be using for the remainder of the program—that's how important it is.

The middle section of the new form is for you to keep a record of your physical activity. Spaces are included for the types of activity you do and the number of minutes you do each one. This section also is part of the form from now on. List every activity here, like using stairs, working in the yard, walking, and playing sports. The idea here is to estimate the caloric expenditure associated with each activity. On page 95, I have provided you with a list of typical activities and the calorie values for 10 minutes of each activity. If you are using a step counter, your job will be much easier. You can simply record the calories burned during the day from your steps. Be sure to also include those activities that are not measured by the WalkMaster, such as swimming, water aerobics, and cycling.

The last section of the new form is for recording your goals for the week that I discuss in each lesson. For this week, the personal goals include:

❶ Meet or exceed walking goal of _____ steps each day

❷ Record food intake on the Monitoring Form

❸ Eat servings from the five food groups

❹ Record daily physical activity on the Monitoring Form

❺ Review Monitoring Forms for patterns

❻ Eat less than _____ calories each day

You simply mark down whether you achieved your goals "Most of the Time," "Some of the Time," or "Rarely." You will have different goals for each lesson.

Some of the techniques you will be trying may be listed under the Most of the Time, Some of the Time, or Rarely part of the Monitoring Form, even though the goals may not fit neatly in these categories. For example, in Lesson Seven you will be encouraged to shop from a list to avoid impulse buying. However, most people do not shop for food each day, so it is difficult to note each day on the Monitoring Form whether you shopped as you planned. In

cases like this, put N/A (for not applicable) if Most of the Time, Sometimes, or Rarely do not apply.

 ## My Weekly Goals

The main goal for this week is to begin your walking program. Walk as many days as possible by using the guidelines included in this lesson. Be sure to take it easy if you have not been exercising regularly. Do your best to complete the Monitoring Forms each day. Remember what you learned from reviewing your previous week's Monitoring Forms. See if you can develop even more insight into situations that place you at high risk for overeating. A blank Monitoring Form for this lesson is on page 54 for you to use. Make a copy for each day of the week. Finally, record your weight change for *week three* on My Weight Change Record on page 216.

Knowledge Review

Lesson Three

T F 1. You can identify your triggers and high-risk situations for over-eating by keeping a Monitoring Form and examining it carefully.

T F 2. Exercise isn't of much use for weight loss because it burns relatively few calories.

T F 3. Exercise must be strenuous and must be done at a certain intensity and for a certain amount of time to be of any help in losing weight.

T F 4. Physical activity can help prevent the loss of muscle tissue during weight loss.

T F 5. Walking one mile burns almost as many calories as running the mile.

T F 6. A step counter can be motivational by showing you the small changes in your level of physical activity.

T F 7. Expensive exercise suits are worth the money because the special materials help the body.

T F 8. A calorie is the measure of the amount of fat in food.

T F 9. If you eat an equal number of servings from the five food groups of the Food Guide Pyramid, you will have a balanced diet.

(Answers in Appendix C, page 220)

Monitoring Form—Lesson Three *(Sample)* *Today's Date:* Jan. 20, 2003

Time	Food and Amount	Calories	Milk & Dairy	Meats & Protein	Vegetables	Fruits	Bread
7:30 am	Apple juice, 6 fl oz	84				✓	
	Special K cereal, 1 oz	115					✓
	Skim milk, 1 cup (8 fl oz)	86	✓				
10:00 am	Banana, 1 med	110				✓	
12:30 pm	Turkey sandwich, 3 oz, wheat, 2 tbs low-fat mayo	286		✓	✓		✓✓
	V8 vegetable juice, low sodium, 12 fl oz	90			✓✓		
	Water, 8 fl oz	0					
	Soda crackers, low sodium, 10	130					✓
	Carrots, raw, ½ cup	35			✓		
	Celery, raw, ½ cup	33			✓		
	Water, 8 fl oz	0					
7:30 pm	Salmon, Atlantic, baked, 4 oz	206		✓✓			
	Tossed green salad, 2 tbs fat-free ranch dressing	71			✓✓		
	White rice, ckd, ½ cup	121					✓
	Mashed potatoes, ½ cup, w/ butter buds	100			✓		
	Strawberries, fresh, 1 cup	46				✓✓	
	Skim milk, 1 cup (8 fl oz)	86	✓				
9:30 pm	Apple, raw, 1 med	80				✓	
Total Daily Caloric Intake & Food Guide Pyramid Servings		**1,679**	**2**	**3**	**8**	**5**	**5**

Daily Activity Record (Caloric Expenditure)

Time	Activity	Calories	Minutes	No. of Steps
All day	Walking per WalkMaster	175		4,625
6:30 pm	Bicycling with kids	180	30	

Personal Goals this Week	Most of the Time	Some of the Time	Rarely
1. Meet or exceed walking goal of __4,000__ steps each day	✓		
2. Record food intake on the Monitoring Form	✓		
3. Eat servings from the five food groups	✓		
4. Record daily physical activity on the Monitoring Form	✓		
5. Review Monitoring Forms for patterns	✓		
6. Eat less than __1,700__ calories each day	✓		

Monitoring Form—Lesson Three

Today's Date:_____

Time	Food and Amount	Calories	Milk & Dairy	Meats & Protein	Vegetables	Fruits	Bread
Total Daily Caloric Intake & Food Guide Pyramid Servings							

Daily Activity Record (Caloric Expenditure)				
Time	Activity	Calories	Minutes	No. of Steps

Personal Goals this Week	Most of the Time	Some of the Time	Rarely
1. Meet or exceed walking goal of _____ steps each day			
2. Record food intake on the Monitoring Form			
3. Eat servings from the five food groups			
4. Record daily physical activity on the Monitoring Form			
5. Review Monitoring Forms for patterns			
6. Eat less than _____ calories each day			

Lesson Four

We are ready to move on to new and exciting things. The emphasis in this lesson is to focus on a new way of thinking about weight loss (attitudes). I will ask you to consider enlisting a program partner and to think about how others can help you stay committed. Our attention will then turn to physical activity, and I will discuss some of the common barriers to being more active (exercise). Finally, in the nutrition arena, I will discuss two different eating plans.

Progress Is More than Weight

People use programs like LEARN because they want to lose weight, but there is much more at stake. Better health, living longer, being more vital and energetic, sleeping better, and having more confidence are just a few of the other reasons to change eating and physical activity habits. How much your weight changes is only one index of the success you have.

People often become too focused on the scale. This single-minded way of evaluating your progress can lead to disappointment when the scale moves less than you'd like and deprives you of opportunities to feel good about other changes. This is why I ask you to complete quality of life assessments throughout this program—to draw your attention to the total picture of how much your overall life is changing.

The changes you make in diet and physical activity can improve your life in many ways, regardless of the impact they have on your weight. Your body will celebrate these changes, so it is important that your mind does the same. Pay attention to the changes you make, reward yourself for them, and make sure you consider changes in energy, sleep, vitality, and how you feel about yourself when you stop to size up your progress. There is much to be proud of.

A Revolution in Thinking about Weight Loss

Most of us have worried for years about "ideal weight." Height-weight tables are everywhere, and in many programs, a goal weight is given to program participants based on the ideals from these tables. The message is that you must lose to a magic level to benefit from weight loss. Far from being "ideal," these weight tables are a source of enormous frustration, given their unrealistic view that "one size fits all."

More recently, tables using Body Mass Index (BMI) have replaced the old height-weight tables. BMI is better but still leads people to think of ideal weight.

A great deal of scientific evidence now converges on an important conclusion —that even a modest weight loss can have important health benefits. High blood pressure, diabetes, elevated cholesterol, sleep disturbances, and a variety of other medical problems can improve with a modest 5–10 percent loss in body weight. Most experts now agree that losing this amount is a reasonable and achievable weight loss goal. This changes everything.

The new weight loss goals are designed to help people achieve a *healthier* weight and to push aside the notion of *ideal* weight. Most people can achieve a healthier weight at which they will feel better, have more energy, and reduce their risk of health complications. Let's spend a few moments talking about your vision of reasonable weight changes.

Say good-bye to the notion of an 'ideal' weight. Instead, visualize yourself at a healthier and happier weight.

Your Vision of Reasonable Weight Changes

People begin weight loss programs with differing ideas about how much weight they will lose and how fast the weight will come off. A common story might be of Sally, with 50 pounds to lose.

 ## LIFESTYLE PROFILES

Sally may begin a program in March in anticipation of the upcoming swimsuit season. She may not consider how much weight might *reasonably* be lost in the few months ahead. Instead, she focuses on how she will look when she walks on the beach.

Suppose Sally loses 20 pounds in three months. This is terrific progress, yet when she steps on the beach, Sally may feel like a failure knowing that she is still 30 pounds heavier than she wants to be. This feeling could translate into self-doubt, anger, hurt, resignation, and the feeling that losing weight was not worth trying in the first place.

 ## ATTITUDE ALERT

You can avoid this attitude trap of unreasonable weight loss expectations and allow yourself to have the good feelings you deserve when you do well. First, having a clear idea of how much weight you might lose is important. I'll give you a suggestion for accomplishing this.

On page 217 in Appendix B, I have provided another blank weight graph called "My Reasonable Weight Loss." Assume you will lose 20 pounds by week 12. This is slightly more than 1½ pounds per week. Draw a line from the zero mark (no pounds lost) at the beginning of the program (week 0) to the 20-pound weight loss mark at week 12. Next, at the bottom of the graph where I have numbered the weeks, put in the dates for each of the weeks so you have a specific date recorded for each week of the program. For instance, if you began the program on February 1st, week 1 would be

February 1, week 4 would be February 22, week 7 would be March 15, and so forth. Next, make a special mark on the weeks in which some important date occurs (your birthday, your parent's or child's birthday, July 4th, Thanksgiving, Halloween, Valentine's Day, etc.). These landmark dates should be similar to the ones on your "My Weight Change Record" on page 216.

When a specific week rolls around, like when your birthday arrives, you can look at your graph and review your progress. This gives you a reasonable standard against which to assess how you are doing. A person beginning a program on February 1st could pull out this graph on St. Patrick's Day in March, see that a reasonable weight loss would have been about five to 9 pounds, and then feel great about a 12-pound loss.

Completing this exercise is important. Referring to your "My Reasonable Weight Loss" chart may make the difference between feeling good about your progress (as you should) or bad (as is possible) later in the program. Feeling bad about your weight management efforts is a state we want to avoid!

Solo and Social Changing

In the Introduction and Orientation, I brought up the notion of being a solo or social changer. Individuals come in many packages with many personalities. Some like to make changes on their own and do not want other people involved. Others like the aid and support they might get from family and friends. I call the first group *solo* changers and the other group *social* changers.

Solo changers like to travel the weight loss path alone. They often do not tell others when they start a program, and they don't enjoy questions about their weight or their eating. Social changers, on the other hand, like company. They talk with others about their program and are pleased when others notice their progress. They may join

a program with a friend or enlist someone in the family to exercise with them.

Being a social changer is fine. Being a solo changer is fine as well. What is important is to determine what best fits you, and structure your program accordingly. I discuss much material in this manual about enlisting the aid and support of family and friends. This is likely to be helpful to the social person but not the solo type. Solo changers can be upset when others attempt to assist them, even when another person offers assistance for the right reasons.

Think about whether you are a social or solo changer. If you are more social, the "Relationships" part of The LEARN Program may be very helpful, beginning with the information on partners in the next section. If you are unsure as to whether you are more of a solo or social changer, let me suggest that you enlist the support of a partner for at least a portion of your program. A walking partner is a terrific place to gain social support.

Consider the support from others as a resource to be cultivated. If you are a social changer, decide exactly when and how you would like others to be involved. Support from others is a resource only if *you* find it helpful. Many other social resources are also at your disposal.

Why Social Support Can Be So Important

Tape/CD 3
Section 4

Many scientists have studied the impact of social networks on health and well-being. In early days, researchers evaluated whether people had friends and interacted frequently with family members. They then studied whether these events were related to health. The problem with this approach is that a person may have many social contacts, but the contacts may not be positive (say in the case of a distressed marriage). More recently, experts have agreed that the *quality* of a person's relationships is the key. People who

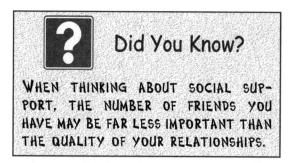

Did You Know?

WHEN THINKING ABOUT SOCIAL SUPPORT, THE NUMBER OF FRIENDS YOU HAVE MAY BE FAR LESS IMPORTANT THAN THE QUALITY OF YOUR RELATIONSHIPS.

have relationships they can count on for emotional support (e.g., love, caring, concern, etc.) and tangible support (e.g., baby-sitting, financial assistance, and other practical issues), live longer and are healthier and happier than those who do not have these relationships.

If support can be so helpful, you have to ask yourself two questions:

❶ Why is it so helpful?

❷ What can I do to get more support or to take advantage of the support I have?

As for the first issue, support may be helpful for many reasons. Just feeling cared for may help by inspiring you to lead a healthier lifestyle, to do things that make you happier, and perhaps even influence things like your immune system. Whatever the reason, it is clear from many studies that *quality* social support can be beneficial.

The question then becomes how to get the support that will benefit you. Before talking about this, let me reiterate that social support is something that benefits some people more than others. Some people are perfectly content doing things on their own, and they do not want or need others involved in their business. This is perfectly fine as I discussed earlier in this introduction. For those who feel they would benefit from additional social support, even if it occurs at a modest level from only one person, there is much to discuss.

Would a Partner Help?

Program partnerships can be very powerful. They occur when a person enlists the aid of another. Sometimes the partner is also on a program, but excellent partnerships can work well when the partner is not doing the program with you. How can you tell if a partnership is for you?

First, there are different types of partnerships. The most logical one is with a spouse. A husband or wife can be a real aid, but not in all cases. Many of my clients have formed successful partnerships with coworkers, good friends, neighbors, or relatives.

You may already have a partner in mind. In Lesson Five on page 74, you can complete the Support Partner Quiz to determine whether this person would be a good choice. Feel free to jump ahead right now and complete the quiz if the notion of a partnership sounds helpful for you.

A program partnership is much like a friendship; it is based on give and take. Not all the support flows from the partner to you. You must reciprocate. There will be good times and bad. As with any relationship, some energy is required to keep the partnership intact.

Do you think you would profit from a partnership? While you think about this question, let me explain what scientific studies have shown. About 20 studies on partnership programs have been completed, including several that I have conducted with colleagues. In some studies, working with a partner greatly increased weight loss. In others, there was no advantage to the partnership approach. I interpret these inconsistent findings to show that losing weight with a partner is helpful for some, but not for all.

RELATIONSHIP RESOURCES

Several examples may illustrate how others can help or hurt. Marjorie enlisted the aid of her husband in her program. He was supportive and showed his concern by walking with her and by not eating treats when she was around. This encouragement helped Marjorie.

Sharon's case was different. Her husband made fun of her and was bitter about her weight loss problem. He ate in front of her and nearly always made discouraging comments. It would have been difficult for Sharon to engage her husband in a helpful partnership. Only you know whether this approach will work for you.

Think about having a weight loss partner. Remember, this person does not have to be overweight. It is important that you feel comfortable with this person and that he or she is able to encourage and motivate you. Next, think about your own style and personality. Do you like to do things with others or alone? Do you confide in others or do you keep things to yourself? Could you discuss weight management troubles with another person or would you rather not share them? Finally, what is your *gut* feeling? Do you think the partnership approach would work for you?

You will have time to ponder these important matters, because guidelines for starting a partnership will appear in the next lesson. Think about your own style and decide if a partnership would help you. Sort through your friendships and form a pool of possible partners.

Optimizing Your Success

You have already completed three weeks of The LEARN Program. I hope you are progressing with flying colors. Let's review a few points that will help ensure continued progress. This topic fits nicely with the discussion about program partners.

Friends and Family

Talking with family members and close friends about your program can be very helpful. When you do, take a few minutes to explain the program, and answer any questions. As you continue to make lifestyle changes, friends and family members may become even more interested in your program. Share the information in this manual with them, and encourage them to

Some people like to make changes on their own, and other like the aid and support from family and friends. You are in the best position to decide what works best for you.

get a copy of the manual or to share yours if they are interested in making changes of their own.

You may also want to tell friends and family members how they can support you. As I discuss in later lessons, little things such as inviting you to go on a walk or not offering you snack foods can make a big difference. Express your appreciation when loved ones support you.

Ultimately, you know your family and friends best. If you think that talking about your program will cause problems, trust your judgment. Such discussions are a help in most cases, but as with all things I talk about, you know best what is helpful for you. Take a moment now to list your additional resources and support on the worksheet on page 60.

Determining Your Target Calorie Level

In Lesson Three on page 45, I discussed the calorie and asked you to think about what a reasonable calorie level is for you.

My Additional Resources

We now come to the point in the program when it is time to identify your target calorie level. As you explore your body's calorie requirements and become more proficient in estimating your body's daily energy needs, you will soon learn (if you do not know already) whether you are more like Sheri or Bonnie, the two people mentioned on page 47 in Lesson Three.

The guidelines are simple. You want to find the calorie level at which you can lose one to two pounds each week. This means that you need to eat about 500–1,000 fewer calories than your body uses each day. Faster weight loss can be a clue that you are making drastic changes that may be difficult to maintain. Several methods are available for estimating your body's daily calorie requirements.

If you have access to the Internet, you can log onto The LifeStyle Company's website at www.TheLifeStyleCompany. com and go to "Self- Assessments." From there, go to the "Daily Calorie Needs." You will need to answer a few simple questions, then the calculator will give you an estimate of your daily calorie needs to maintain your current weight.

Your body's daily calorie needs include resting energy expenditure plus the calories used from being physically active during the day. Your body uses about 11 calories for every pound of body weight while at rest during a day (24 hours). Hence, your body weight (in pounds) multiplied by 11 will give you a good estimate of your daily resting calorie needs. If a person weighs 150 pounds the calculation would be: 150 lbs. x 11 = 1,650 calories per day while at rest. While up and about during the day in "light" activity, your body will use an additional .23 calories *per* pound of body weight *per* hour. Remember, this is in addition to the calorie needs during rest. Let's assume our 150 pound person is up for 16 hours during the day. The calorie needs for this 16 hours of light activity are: 150 lbs. x .23 x 16 hours = 552 calories. The total calorie needs for this 150 pound person from rest and light activities would be: 1,650 + 552 = 2,202. Keep in mind this does not include any activity above light activity during the day. If this 150 pound person did no additional physical activity above the "light" level, this would be a good estimate of his/her current daily calorie needs to *maintain* current weight.

After you have estimated your daily calorie needs to *maintain* your current weight, subtract 500–1,000 calories to create a daily calorie deficit. This will give you a daily target calorie level to lose 1–2 pounds per week.

If you are still uncertain about the calorie level, consider using 1,200 calories per day for women and 1,500 for men. These are commonly used figures that represent calorie levels at which many people will lose weight. As you know, this is just an av-

erage, which means that some people will need fewer calories and some can afford more.

Over the next few lessons, you will have time to experiment with this beginning calorie level and to arrive at your target number. This number is important. I will ask you to enter your daily calorie target onto your Monitoring Forms for each week in future lessons. You will note your daily calorie target number on each daily Monitoring form. You will then have a record of whether you attained the goal each day of the program. The space for the precise calorie level in the Monitoring Form is left blank, so you can write in your personal number.

Dropping your calorie level below 1,000 calories per day is not advisable. By eating fewer than 1,000 calories, you may be losing weight at the expense of good nutrition. A physician should supervise diets of less than 1,000 calories per day.

Diets with few calories (800 calories per day or lower) are called very-low-calorie diets (VLCDs). Again, these diets should be used only under medical supervision, preferably in a program where a registered dietitian is available to provide expert nutritional input. The body goes through complicated changes when these diets are undertaken. If a person is not screened and monitored adequately, a potential for danger exists if the food or supplement to be eaten does not contain the right mix of nutrients.

If your Monitoring Forms reflect a 500–1,000 per day caloric deficit, and you go a few weeks without noticing a weight loss, there are several ways to proceed. Before I share this with you, I want to emphasize that your Monitoring Form is an *estimate* of the calories you eat. Several studies have shown that individuals in weight management programs tend to *underestimate* their caloric intake and *overestimate* their energy expenditure—even when they are being as honest as they can. These studies have shown caloric intake to be underestimated by as much as 50 percent and energy expenditure to be overestimated by as much as 50 percent.

The take-home message from these studies is that the more accurately you estimate your caloric intake, the more closely reflected these estimates will be on the bathroom scale. Carefully reading food labels, measuring the food and beverages you consume each day, and writing down every thing that you eat and drink can go a long way to increasing the accuracy of your food intake. Record your target calorie level in the space below.

**My target calorie level is
_____ calories per day**

Barriers to Being Active

A number of barriers stand in the way of many people being physically active. Extra weight can make exercise physically difficult. People who have been overweight all their lives may have little experience with vigorous exercise, and the experiences they do have may be unpleasant. They may have been teased or chosen last for sports teams. Finally, some people are afraid of what others will think when a heavy person jogs by or cruises past on a bicycle.

Put aside these feelings right now! You have absolutely no reason to be ashamed or embarrassed. Your weight loss and health are more important than being shy or embarrassed. Losing weight is a long process as it is and will be even longer if you wait to trim down before starting to exercise. Don't worry about what others think. In fact, most reasonable people give heavy individuals credit for being active and making positive changes. I'll share an example with you from one of my clients.

 ### LIFESTYLE PROFILES

Ellen was walking one evening at the local high school track when the track team sprinted by her. She turned to the coach and said "Gee, I must look pretty ridiculous out here, walking so slowly, with all the kids racing past me." Without missing a beat, the coach replied, "No Mam, the people who look ridiculous are the ones who are at home sitting on the couch!"

The 5–10 Minute Prescription

In the last lesson you began your walking program. The Walking Goals chart on page 44 provided you with an initial walking goal of 4,000 steps each day. Beginning gradually and working your way up is important. Starting with less than you can tolerate is not dangerous, but starting with more can be painful and discouraging. If you are using a step counter, tracking your physical activity is simple. If not, the next

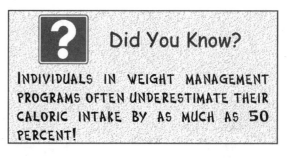

Did You Know?

INDIVIDUALS IN WEIGHT MANAGEMENT PROGRAMS OFTEN UNDERESTIMATE THEIR CALORIC INTAKE BY AS MUCH AS 50 PERCENT!

best thing is to count the minutes that you walk each day.

 ### EXERCISE ESSENTIALS

Consider beginning by adding 5–10 minutes of walking to your day. If you are not used to walking, begin with a few minutes each day. If you are walking each day already, keep up the good work and try adding 5–10 minutes to your current routine. Your goal will be to increase your walking time by 5–10 minutes per day each week until you are walking about an hour each day. This may seem like a lot, but keep in mind that you can *accumulate* this time *incrementally*—5 minutes here, 10 minutes there—it all adds up! If you have difficulty walking 15 minutes all in one bout, try three 5-minute walks. When you can do this with ease, increase by 5 minutes each day to the point you feel some exertion. If the 15-minute walk is too difficult, subtract time until you feel comfortable. Remember, the *ultimate* goal is to walk 30 minutes to one hour each day. Try to increase your walking to this level gradually, so as not to make it difficult or unpleasant.

You know best when your schedule can adapt to your walking. Below are a few suggestions:

❶ Get up 30 minutes early to walk

❷ Walk at lunch

❸ Walk during work breaks

❹ Walk after work

❺ Walk after dinner

❻ Walk before bedtime

❼ Walk during TV commercials and between programs

❽ Walk around during your child's soccer game

Do your level best to walk every day. Making it part of your routine is important, like brushing your teeth, making your bed, or taking a shower. This is the only way you will integrate walking into your lifestyle. However, don't despair if you miss a day now and then. The long-term picture is more important than if you occasionally miss a day. I will discuss your attitudes about exercise later in the program.

Experiment with walking different places, at different times, and with different people (or try it alone). Find the way you like it best. In Lesson Five, I will present specific ideas about making walking fun and even more enjoyable.

Using a Step Counter

I have talked much about using a step counter to measure your daily physical activity. This is because physical activity is such an important component of weight management, and using a step counter is a simple way to track your daily activity. A step counter has a simple but very important purpose—to keep you motivated and to give you positive feedback about increases in physical activity.

Because it can detect small changes in your activity, a step counter is a nice way to see if you're getting more activity. It also shows that every step counts as physical activity and that small, gradual increases in daily activity can make big differences in just a few weeks.

One way to use a step counter is to set incremental step goals throughout the day. For instance, you can set a mid-morning goal, a noon goal, an afternoon goal, an after work goal, and so on. If your noon goal is to have 2,500 steps and you have only 2,000 steps, then you may want to go for a walk during your lunch hour. If your goal has been reached by noon, then you can reward yourself by socializing with coworkers or reading your novel.

A Walking Partnership

This is a good time to continue the "R" (Relationships) part of the LEARN approach and couple it with the "E" (Exercise) component. Since we are focusing on walking, we can discuss its social aspects. Some people like to walk with others, while some like to go solo. You are the best judge of what is right for you. Even if you decide not to involve others in your weight loss program, you may find that a walking partnership can be very rewarding.

Walking with another person can be a powerful way to make it more enjoyable. The company is a nice distraction because you can talk about politics, speculate about the stock market, bet on ball games, or best of all, plot your strategy to win the lottery! A partner also can help by establishing a regular time for walking. You may be tempted to stay home on some days, but knowing that a partner is waiting may be

Walking and other forms of exercising with another person can be a powerful way to make physical activity more fun and enjoyable.

just the stimulus you need to get out and going.

As I said earlier in this lesson, having a partner is not for everyone. Walking can be a delightful time to enjoy yourself, to reflect, and to think about important matters. Don't feel pressured to have a partner, because going it alone may be best for you. Think about the advantages of walking with a partner or walking alone. You might try it both ways to see which you like.

The Principle of Shaping

In Lesson Three you read about the Food Guide Pyramid and its recommendations for the number of servings to eat from each food group. In this lesson you set a target calorie level to lose one to two pounds per week. You may be wondering how you will be able to decrease your calorie intake while increasing your intake of fruits and vegetables. Making all of these changes can seem overwhelming! Rest assured, however, that I am not asking you to meet your calorie goal perfectly and eat the recommended number of servings of each food group right away. Instead, I will be encouraging you to *shape* your behavior throughout this program.

Shaping refers to making gradual, step-by-step changes in your behavior. Making gradual changes is often easier and

"I'd like to contact my willpower. It died last night at Angelo's Pizza Palace!"

less daunting than making drastic changes all at once. When you succeed at making small changes, you gain confidence in your ability to change. Let's look at some examples of how this works.

If your weakness is donuts and you begin every day with three of your favorite kind, dropping them completely may be difficult. You could start by cutting down to two donuts, then one, and finally to none. You might follow a similar strategy to reach your target calorie level. If you have been eating 2,500 calories per day, limiting your intake to 1,200 calories may be difficult. You may want to start by aiming for 2,000 calories per day, then 1,800, 1,400, and then 1,200.

You have already been applying this principle to your physical activity goals. I have encouraged you to start with manageable levels of physical activity and then gradually add 5–10 minutes (or 200 steps) of physical activity until you reach your ultimate goal of 30–60 minutes (or 10,000 steps) of physical activity per day. If you jumped right in and set a goal to do 60 minutes of activity every day, when you haven't been very active recently, you might injure yourself or feel discouraged when you fail to reach your goal. Remember, you are starting a physical activity program that will become a lifelong habit, so you have plenty of time to reach your ultimate goal!

Selecting an Eating Plan

Several food plans are available for eating nutritiously. I talked about the importance of following a balanced diet in Lesson Three, on page 47. One common plan is to count calories while eating a specified number of servings in the five food groups in the Food Guide Pyramid. I introduced the Food Guide Pyramid in Lesson Three. This approach is one many individuals are familiar with because counting calories is the way most people learn to judge how they are doing with a weight loss plan. For this reason, I use this approach in The LEARN Program.

An alternative eating plan is the Exchange Plan developed by the American Dietetic Association (ADA) and the American Diabetes Association. The Exchange Plan places foods into six categories: starch/bread, meat and meat substitutes, vegetables, fruit, milk, and fat. The Exchange Plan lists foods and amounts in each category so that all foods have approximately the same carbohydrate, protein, fat, and calories. A food in a given category, therefore, can be exchanged with any other food in the same category. Copies of the exchange list guide are available for $2.50 each plus $5.00 shipping and handling. If you would like to receive a complete guide for the Exchange Plan, you can call 1–800–877–1600 ext. 5000 or write to:

The American Dietetic Association
P.O. Box 97215
Chicago, IL 60678-7215

Both the calorie counting and the Exchange Plan methods represent sound nutrition. If you are in a program run by a health professional, he or she may have a preference, so I discuss both plans here. If not, choose the plan you feel most comfortable with, and follow it throughout the program.

My Weekly Goals

The main goal for this week is for you to continue your walking program and to increase your level of physical activity. Walk as many days as possible by using the guidelines provided in this lesson. Be sure to take it easy if you have not been exercising regularly. Complete your "My Reasonable Weight Loss" chart on page 217 in Appendix B. Determine your target calorie level and record it in the space provided on your Monitoring Form.

Continue using the new Monitoring Form introduced in the last lesson. A blank form is provided for you on page 66 of this lesson. Don't worry, as you become more familiar with this form, it will become much easier for you to use. The Monitoring Forms will help you identify patterns and triggers. Remember what you learned the previous week and see if you can develop even more insight into situations which place you at high risk for overeating. Finally, record your weight change on the My Weight Change Record on page 216 of this manual.

KNOWLEDGE REVIEW

Lesson Four

1. T F Everyone should walk with a partner because the company increases pleasure.

2. T F Many overweight people are reluctant to exercise because they are embarrassed.

3. T F A modest weight loss of 5–10 percent of initial body weight can produce important health benefits.

4. T F To lose weight more rapidly, you should eat fewer than 1,000 calories per day.

5. T F Increasing your physical activity by 30 minutes per day right away is a good way to help you lose weight faster.

6. T F A step counter is difficult to use and is not very helpful in motivating individuals to be more active.

7. T F To lose one pound per week, you need to create a calorie deficit of 500 calories per day.

8. T F Shaping refers to encouraging others to help you lose weight.

(Answers in Appendix C, page 220)

Monitoring Form—Lesson Four

*Today's Date:*_____

Time	Food and Amount	Calories	Milk & Dairy	Meats & Protein	Vegetables	Fruits	Bread
Total Daily Caloric Intake & Food Guide Pyramid Servings							

	Daily Activity Record (Caloric Expenditure)				
Time	Activity	Calories	Minutes	No. of Steps	

Personal Goals this Week	Most of the Time	Some of the Time	Rarely
1. Meet or exceed walking goal of _____ steps each day			
2. Record food intake on the Monitoring Form			
3. Eat servings from the five food groups			
4. Record daily physical activity on the Monitoring Form			
5. Set realistic diet, exercise, and weight loss goals			
6. Eat less than _____ calories each day			

Lesson Five

Y ou have now been using The LEARN Program for one month. I hope you are pleased with your progress. We'll begin this lesson by taking a few moments to review and appreciate the accomplishments you have made during the past month. You may be surprised to see all that you have achieved. Our attention then turns to the ABC's of behavior change. I'll then talk more about physical activity then dive into nutrition in more detail.

One-Month Review

Over the last month, you may have noticed changes in your health. You may feel more alert and energetic or may be sleeping better. People frequently report such changes soon after they begin a healthier diet and become more physically active. If you are planning to see your doctor, ask about any changes she or he notices.

Your Health

Tape/CD 1
Section 12

Your doctor can assess many changes in your physical health. For example, if your blood pressure, cholesterol, or blood sugar were high before you started this program, they may show some improvement. Your overall health should continue to improve over the next few months as you progress through the program. What a wonderful accomplishment—to improve your health and well-being!

Your Quality of Life

Another way of assessing the changes you have made in the first month is to complete the Quality of Life Review on page 68. Rate how satisfied you are with each of the 12 areas listed, including your mood, eating habits, and body image. Complete these items based on how you feel today.

Now compare your responses to those before you began the program. Use the Quality of Life Review Comparisons form on page 214 in Appendix B to help you make this comparison. In column (b) of the form record your scores from the Introduction and Orientation on page 9. In column (c), record your scores from the Quality of Life Review on page 68. Column (d) reflects the positive (+) or negative (-) change in your responses. The positive (+) numbers reflect increased satisfaction with life in the related category. The negative (-) numbers represent de-

Copyright © 1990 by Thaves. Distributed from www.thecomics.com.

Quality of Life Review

Please use the following scale to rate how satisfied you feel now about different aspects of your daily life. Choose any number from this list (1 to 9), and indicate your choice on the questions below.

1 = Extremely Dissatisfied

2 = Very Dissatisfied

3 = Moderately Dissatisfied

4 = Somewhat Dissatisfied

5 = Neutral

6 = Somewhat Satisfied

7 = Moderately Satisfied

8 = Very Satisfied

9 = Extremely Satisfied

1. _____ Mood (feelings of sadness, worry, happiness, etc.)

2. _____ Self-esteem

3. _____ Confidence, self-assurance, and comfort in social situations

4. _____ Energy and feeling healthy

5. _____ Health problems (diabetes, high blood pressure, etc.)

6. _____ General appearance

7. _____ Social life

8. _____ Leisure and recreational activities

9. _____ Physical mobility and physical activity

10. _____ Eating habits

11. _____ Body image

12. _____ Overall Quality of Life[1]

[1] Record your Overall Quality of Life score in the space provided in Appendix B, page 213.

your diet and becoming more physically active.

I suspect that your satisfaction has increased in at least one area, if not several. Many people report increased satisfaction the first month with their mood, energy level, general appearance, eating habits, and physical mobility and activity. What is remarkable is that these changes occur relatively quickly and with only a modest weight loss. This is an excellent return on your weight management investment!

Satisfaction may come more slowly in other areas, such as with your social life or leisure and recreational activities. If you have specific desires in these areas, such as meeting new people or taking up tennis or golf, make a plan for how you can start achieving these goals. Do not make the mistake of thinking you have to be at some magical goal weight in order to socialize more or take up a new hobby.

 ### LIFESTYLE PROFILES

Eric used to enjoy riding his bicycle, but he was afraid that he wouldn't be able to ride at his heavier weight. He thought the seat would be too small and uncomfortable, and he wouldn't be able to climb the hills in his neighborhood because he was out of shape. With the encouragement of his weight loss group, Eric found a more comfortable gel seat for his bicycle. He used a training stand which allowed him to ride his bicycle inside his house to improve his fitness before tackling the road and the hills. Soon, Eric started riding outside again. To his surprise he discovered that he enjoyed riding as much as he used to! He didn't wait until he reached his goal weight to resume a pleasurable activity.

Weight Loss

Improvements in quality of life and physical health are the real measures of success in a program like this, but it's hard not to focus on weight loss. We all like to get things done quickly, and people like losing weight fast. If you're satisfied with

creased satisfaction with life. If you have negative (-) numbers in any of the categories that have been covered in the first four lessons, now is a good time to go back and review this material. Positive (+) numbers in the categories that have been covered in the first four lessons mean that you have done well and are ready to move on. If you have negative (-) numbers in any of the categories that have been covered, try not to be discouraged. It may take you a little longer to see improvements. Continue working on your progress, fine. Sometimes, people lose weight slowly and get discouraged. Let's talk numbers and put your weight loss in perspective.

During the first month in behavioral weight loss programs, women typically lose 4–6 pounds, and men experience a 6–8 pound loss. Don't worry if you've lost more or less; people vary in weight loss just like cars differ in gas mileage. If your weight loss is in this range, you may be disappointed for not having lost more. Sometimes people who lose weight slowly have great success at keeping it off. In addition, weight loss of this magnitude is typical and is cause for celebration, not disappointment. You may notice changes in how your clothes fit before the scale changes all that much. Feeling positive about what you have accomplished is important. This provides motivation and energy to forge ahead.

You may have had the opposite experience the first month and lost far more weight than you had expected. Women who have lost more than 8 pounds and men more than 12 pounds should be cautious that they are not engaging in a drastic diet. Women should make sure that they eat at least 1,000 calories each day and men 1,200 calories per day. Increasing your calorie intake may be necessary if your weight loss does not slow in the next few weeks. Rapid weight loss can increase the risk of developing gallstones and other health complications. If you have any questions at all about this, be sure to see your physician.

Calorie Intake

A smaller than anticipated weight loss can also result from not decreasing your calorie intake sufficiently. As I discussed in Lesson Three, if you eat 500 fewer calories a day than your body burns, you will lose a pound a week. If, instead, you eat only 250 fewer calories a day, you will lose only about one-half a pound a week. If you lost less than four pounds the first month, plan to pay extra attention to your portion sizes and your Monitoring Form. Try to incorporate these tips:

Don't wait until you reach your 'goal' weight before engaging in pleasurable activities.

➡ Record your foods and beverages immediately after consuming them. This will ensure that you remember to record everything.

➡ Measure portion sizes *carefully* to ensure that you are eating the amounts that you think you are. You may want to purchase a food scale if you don't already have one. Most people underestimate their daily calorie intake, so be careful.

➡ When reading food labels, be sure to determine how many servings the item contains. For example, a 20-oz soda contains 2½ servings (one serving equals 8 oz). Each serving has 100 calories or a total of 250 calories for the 20-oz bottle. That is a big difference from thinking that the bottle contains one serving and only 100 calories. I'll talk more about reading food labels in Lesson Eight.

➡ Keep a running total of your calories throughout the day. This way, you will

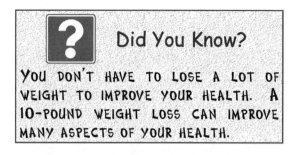

Did You Know?

YOU DON'T HAVE TO LOSE A LOT OF WEIGHT TO IMPROVE YOUR HEALTH. A 10-POUND WEIGHT LOSS CAN IMPROVE MANY ASPECTS OF YOUR HEALTH.

know if you have enough calories left for a second serving at dinner or for a bedtime snack.

➡ Set a calorie goal for the week, not just each day. This way, if you exceed your goal on Thursday, you can eat a bit less on Friday, Saturday, and Sunday—and still meet your goal for the week. The closer you come to your calorie goal each week, the better your weight loss will be.

The ABC's of Behavior

As you progress through The LEARN Program, you will learn ways to change your behavior. I will use the ABC approach to help you change behaviors. The letters stand for Antecedents, Behavior, and Consequences.

Antecedents

Antecedents are the events, situations, thoughts, and feelings that occur *before*

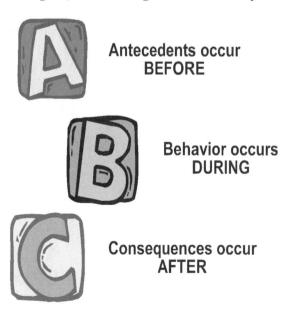

Antecedents occur BEFORE

Behavior occurs DURING

Consequences occur AFTER

behaviors such as eating or being inactive. These usually occur together in a series of steps called the Behavior Chain, which I will discuss in Lesson Twelve.

Behavior

Behavior refers to the particular conduct itself and to the related events, situations, thoughts, and feelings. The relevant factors for eating include the speed of eating, rate of chewing, taste of food, and the events that take place *during* eating. Factors that affect physical activity include intensity (pace) of the activity, the type of activity chosen, how long the activity lasts (duration), and how you feel while doing the activity.

Consequences

Consequences are the events, situations, thoughts, feelings, and attitudes that follow the behavior. What happens *after* the behavior can determine whether the same behavior will occur again. Coming home tired (antecedent) and watching television until bedtime (behavior) one evening when you had planned to go for a nice long walk may trigger feelings of being a failure, which in turn could lead to an "it's no use" attitude, resulting in giving up completely (consequences).

 LIFESTYLE PROFILES

You can see each aspect of the ABC approach in the case of Steve. He was home on the weekend watching a football game. The game excited Steve because he bet $20 with his neighbor. He went to the kitchen to get his favorite TV snack, cheese curls. Steve ate the cheese curls rapidly and did not taste each one. Steve ate until he was very full, and then he felt guilty about eating so much.

The antecedents were being at home, watching the football game, being excited, and having the cheese curls available. The behavior was eating rapidly until very full. Steve did not taste all the cheese curls. The consequences were an unpleasant, full feel-

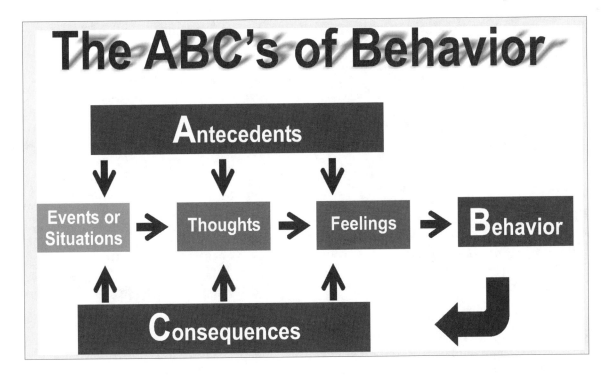

The ABC's of Behavior

Antecedents

Events or Situations → **Thoughts** → **Feelings** → **Behavior**

Consequences

ing in his stomach followed by much guilt about overeating.

This analysis gives us many ideas about reducing Steve's chances for overeating. Steve could alter the antecedents by doing something other than watching the game. This activity is a high-risk situation for Steve. He could also alter the antecedents by not having the cheese curls in the house. The behavior could be changed by eating slowly and savoring every bite or by eating a measured amount in the kitchen during a commercial. The consequences could change if he had different attitudes and coping strategies that would prevent the self-doubt and guilty feelings he experienced, which in turn could stimulate even more eating. For example, Steve might say to himself, "I ate more than I planned, but that doesn't mean I'm a failure. I'll eat a smaller dinner then go for a 30-minute walk. I'll get back on track!"

We will use the ABC approach in upcoming lessons. You can prepare yourself by thinking about the antecedents, behaviors, and consequences related to your eating and exercising. One way to do this is to review your Monitoring Forms from the past weeks and raise your level of awareness a notch or two. You have been thinking about events that trigger eating (the antecedents), but think of the eating itself and the consequences. If you think ahead to situations that may be risky for you, you can predict in advance what the A, B, and C parts are likely to be. This puts you in a good position to cope with even the greatest challenges.

Let's now look at the example of Sandy. Sandy generally goes for a walk when she gets home from work on Wednesday evenings. One day she runs an errand after work (antecedent) and arrives home an hour later than usual (antecedent). After getting home, Sandy feels tired and skips her walk (behavior). The next evening, she decides to skip her planned walk because she feels as though she "blew it" the day before (consequences).

What can Sandy do? She can change the sequence of events in several ways. She could change the antecedent by running the errand at lunch instead of after work. Sandy could change her behavior by walking at the mall after she completes her errand. Finally, she could change the consequences by telling herself that missing one day of planned activity is not the "end of the world." Sandy could schedule three five-minute walks the following day while at work.

Perfecting Your Walking Program

Tape/CD 2
Section 10

How are you doing with your walking program? Do you feel good about this positive activity? It may still be too early to know how you will like walking, but if your initial reactions are positive, then you are on the right track.

Maximizing the Pleasure of Walking

Walking can be a lot of fun if you work on making it enjoyable. Remember, regular physical activity is a key to being successful in weight management. So, the more fun you have, the more you will walk and the more successful you will be. Here

are some ways to make walking more enjoyable:

➡ **Pay attention.** There are many interesting things to see wherever you walk. Look at the style of the houses or buildings you pass or what your neighbors plant in their yards. What sort of cars go by ? What type of people do you see? This is a good way to take advantage of what has always been available.

➡ **Bring entertainment.** Some walkers like to carry portable radios, MP3 and cassette/CD players. Listening to the news, music, or the LEARN tapes/CDs is a terrific way to make walking more enjoyable. Another idea is to listen to a Book on Tape, and to only allow yourself to listen to the book while you are walking. Choose a mystery, and you'll be eager to take your next walk! Decide whether you want to enjoy the outside world or drown it out. You may be surprised by how many wonderful things there are to enjoy when you are outside being active.

➡ **Don't overdo it.** A sure way to undermine an exercise program is to do too much too soon. You will be sore, frustrated, and discouraged. Be careful not to become a "Weekend Warrior."

➡ **Take a gradual approach.** *Gradual* is a key word in this program. Start exercising at the level you need. Work your way up from there, but do it sensibly. Beware of the tendency to increase your exercise too fast, even though you may be enjoying yourself. This is the principle of *shaping* that I discussed in Lesson Four.

➡ **Walk with a partner.** Walking with someone you enjoy is a terrific way to increase the pleasure of walking. This is also a good strategy to enhance motivation. Simply knowing that someone else is counting on you can motivate you to be active when you may otherwise want to sit on the sofa.

Physical activity is key to weight management success. The more fun you have while being active, the more likely you are to stay active.

Did You Know?

ONE RECENT STUDY SHOWED REGULAR AEROBIC PHYSICAL ACTIVITY TO BE AS EFFECTIVE AS ANTI-DEPRESSANT MEDICATIONS IN TREATING DEPRESSION.

Increase Your Walking

In Lesson Three, I provided you with a Walking Goals chart if you are using a pedometer and counting steps. If you are not using a pedometer, I recommended in Lesson Four that you add 5–10 minutes of walking to your day each week until you reach a daily walking goal of between 30–60 minutes. If you have not been active, begin more gradually. Try adding three 2–5 minute walks to your daily routine throughout the day. When you can do this comfortably, increase the time. Again, your judgment must prevail. Do no more than you can handle, but try to make it a routine part of your day.

I recommend that you continue to add 5–10 minutes of walking each day per week until you reach your goal of 30–60 minutes of walking each day. As you add time, stop when you feel muscle fatigue or when you are uncomfortable. For example, you may feel fine when increasing from 15 to 20 minutes, but may feel fatigue or discomfort when going to 25 minutes.

If this happens, back up to the 20-minute comfort level, and stay there until you are ready to move ahead. Some people will stay at one level for many weeks before moving ahead while others can progress more rapidly. Tailoring these guidelines to your needs is important.

Choosing a Support Person

Tape/CD 3
Section 4

If you think that you would benefit from the support of another person, you have a number of choices for doing so. The most extensive involvement is to have a weight management partnership. In this case, you and another person would both be losing weight and working with each other. This can work wonderfully in some cases, but again, it is not for everyone.

You can get less intensive but equally important support from others, including a spouse, parent, child, friend, coworker, or anyone who encourages you. The person could be involved in a big way, say by asking you each day about your goals and accomplishments, or in a smaller way, by just being there when you ask for help. Of course, whom you choose and what you ask them to do is best decided by you.

One reason social support can be so powerful is that it comes in many forms. Emotional support is one such form. It involves the caring, understanding, acceptance, kindness, and other positive human feelings that flow from one person to another. This type of support can be power-

Support Partner Quiz

____1. It is easy to talk to my partner about weight.

   True—5   False—1

____2. My partner has always been thin and does not understand my weight problem.

   True—1   False—3

____3. My partner offers me food when he or she knows I am trying to lose weight.

   True—1   False—5

____4. My partner never says critical things about my weight.

   True—3   False—1

____5. My partner is always there when I need a friend.

   True—4   False—1

____6. When I lose weight and look better, my partner will be jealous.

   True—1   False—3

____7. My partner will be genuinely interested in helping me with my weight.

   True—6   False—1

____8. I could talk to my partner even if I was doing poorly.

   True—5   False—1

If you scored between 30 and 34, you may have found a terrific partner. A score in this range indicates that you and this person are comfortable with one another and can work together.

If you scored between 25 and 29, your friend is potentially a good partner, but there are a few areas of concern. Try asking the partner to take the quiz and predict how you answered the questions. This may help you make a decision.

If you scored between 17 and 24, there are potential areas of conflict, and a program partnership with this person could encounter stormy going. Think of another partner.

If you scored between 8 and 16, definitely look to someone else as a partner. A program partnership in this case would be a high-risk undertaking.

fully reinforcing and feels good to both give and receive.

Other forms of support also can be helpful. For instance, practical support is the aid another person might provide to help with life's duties. A person who gives you a ride when you need it, helps with money if you are in a crunch, offers to watch the children, or does other practical things is offering this type of support. Another type of support comes when someone provides helpful information, feedback, guidance, and so on.

Different people respond to different types of support. Giving careful thought to what others might do to help you and what you can do for them in return can be helpful. Let's look at how to decide whether a given individual would be a good support person.

A Quiz for Choosing a Support Partner

I promised in Lesson Four to give you a quiz for evaluating whether a person would make a good partner. Such a partner could go through the program with you or support your efforts even if they are not trying to lose weight. Your job was to think of possible partners, and then to use the quiz to make a final decision. The Support Partner Quiz is on the left.

To take this quiz, think of the person you would have as a partner, and answer the questions honestly. First, answer each question either true or false. Beside each of your answers is a number. Write this number in the space provided immediately before each question number. Add the numbers of your responses, and then use the scoring guide at the bottom of the quiz.

These guidelines should help in choosing a partner. Once you have done so, discuss the possibility with the person you have in mind. Below, I will make some specific suggestions on how to proceed.

Let me stress again that you need not have a partner. The decision is yours. If you do decide on the partnership approach, these questions could help in selecting a supportive partner. If you are uncertain about proceeding with a partner, even after taking the quiz, experiment with it. Use what you learn about partnerships to see if you profit from the aid of another person. If not, consider yourself a solo changer and move ahead.

Communicating with Your Partner

The Support Partner Quiz can help you decide whether certain individuals may be good support partners. Now you are ready to discuss your program with this person and start the ball rolling. There is a lot you can do to get the most out of this effort.

In later lessons, I discuss methods for dealing with family and friends. Your interactions with family and friends may be different than your interactions with a partner who has agreed to play an active role in supporting you. With the family, there are many ways that support can be provided and sabotage can be prevented. If you feel your family is a problem or can be a useful resource now, it may be helpful to read page 119 in Lesson Eight. In the meantime, let's discuss partnerships.

Here are specific ideas for starting a program partnership. Communicating is the first and most important step. If you and your partner can communicate effectively, you are on the way to a successful partnership. Here are some ideas for making this happen.

It is essential that you and your partner talk together. Sit down and have a friendly talk with the person you have chosen as a partner. Discuss the topics below in an open and honest way.

➡ *Are you both ready for a partnership?* Is your partner ready to listen to requests for help and make the required effort? Is he or she ready to help you during good times and difficult situations? Are you ready to help your part-

ner in return? Some degree of commitment is necessary from both of you.

Communicating is the first and most important step in forming a good partnership.

➡ *Tell your partner how to help.* A common and crucial mistake is to expect your partner to read your mind. If your spouse is your partner, you may think he or she should know what you want and need. Most people are not good mind readers, so leave nothing to chance. Tell your partner specifically what he or she can do. Do you want to be praised when you do well or scolded when you do poorly? Should the person avoid eating in your presence? Can your partner help by exercising with you?

➡ *Make specific requests.* The more specific your requests, the easier it will be for your partner to comply. If your request is vague and general, like "Be nice," your partner is at a disadvantage. A more specific request is better, such as "Please tell me you love me when I lose weight." Instead of saying, "Don't eat in front of me," say, "It helps me when you eat your evening bowl of ice cream in the other room." Replace a general statement, like "Exercise with me," with "Please take a half-hour walk with me each morning."

→ *State your requests positively.* It is better to ask for something positive than to criticize something negative. Clever changes of words can help. If your partner nags, you can say, "It really helps me when you say nice things." If your partner offers you food, you can say, "I appreciate the times when you don't offer me food. It is easier to control my eating then." Human nature responds well to the chance to do something positive, so try this approach with your partner.

→ *Reward your partner.* For your partner to help you, you must help your partner. One-way relationships don't last long. If you are going through this program together, you can work out weight-related ways of helping. If your partner is not on a program, be forward, and ask what you can do in return. Remember, being a partner can be challenging, so you need to acknowledge your partner's help.

Use these techniques to start the ball rolling with your partner. Upcoming lessons will give you more ideas for working with your partner. Laying this groundwork first is important.

The Mighty Calorie

We eat at least a half-million calories each year. You might wonder, therefore, what difference a few calories can make. They can make a *big* difference. Even the smallest number of calories adds up over the course of a week, a month, or a year.

As I mentioned earlier, 3,500 calories translate into a pound of body weight. If you consume 7,000 calories more than your body uses, you will gain two pounds. These are rough estimates, and people vary greatly in the precise number of calories needed to gain or lose weight. What is clear is that calories do count. Let's examine the effects of adding an innocent 10 calories per day to your total.

If you add 10 calories per day to what you ordinarily eat, you will gain an extra pound in a year. Added over a decade or two, this is 10–20 pounds; and all from 10 crummy calories per day! If the difference each day were 100 calories, this would be 10 pounds per year and 100 pounds for 10 years! Let's look at the 10-calorie difference for the moment. The chart on page 77 shows you how little you have to eat to get just 10 extra calories.

Think how easy it is to have an extra teaspoon of ketchup, one bite of an orange, or less than 1 oz of Pepsi. This highlights the need for carefully estimating the calories that you write down on your Monitoring Form and for having a vigilant attitude about foods. You also can take a positive outlook on this calorie equation. Cutting out 10 calories each day will save you a pound each year. You certainly won't miss the 10 calories, but you can easily do without the additional pound of weight.

Small Changes in Your Diet

You may be feeling a bit overwhelmed by all the information you have read over the last two weeks about different methods of following a balanced diet. You learned about the Food Guide Pyramid, and in this lesson, you will learn more about the number of servings you should eat from each of the five food groups. Don't be alarmed if your present meal plan won't win an award (or even honorable mention) from the nutrition experts.

Changing your eating habits takes time. For example, if you eat no fruit most days, start by adding just one serving a day, and make it an easy one. You can probably add a banana to your morning cereal, take an apple with you to work, or have a 6–oz glass of orange juice for an afternoon snack. Each week, try to make one small change you can live with. These small changes will yield big results over the long term.

Taking Control of Your Eating

The Monitoring Forms have helped you discover patterns in your eating, and this section will give you some concrete suggestions on how to disrupt those patterns. These are classic strategies that countless people have used to succeed at weight management. Let's see if they might work for you.

Many people have situations, times, or activities that stimulate eating. These events become *coupled* with eating so that just the event alone can make you feel hungry. Here are a few examples. You may read the paper every day at breakfast. You may watch television every evening and have a snack. You may always eat when you sit in a certain chair. If eating is coupled repeatedly with these events, the events can make you feel like eating. If you sit in your chair, watch TV, or read the morning paper, you will feel like eating, irrespective of physical hunger.

Separating eating from other activities is important. This removes the ability of these activities to stimulate eating, freeing you to respond to actual hunger. Several skills and techniques can help make this happen. I discuss four such techniques here.

Do Nothing Else While Eating

This means reading the paper at another time, eating before or after you watch TV, waiting to read the book, etc. Eating should be a pure experience. Don't contaminate it with extraneous activities. If this seems awkward, it is a sure sign that you are hooked on the association of eating with other activities. The more this technique bothers you, the more you may need it.

You may be one of those individuals who does other things while eating. You may eat while working on a hobby, talking on the phone, writing letters, watching TV, reading a magazine, and so forth. This has two disadvantages. I mentioned the first earlier; eating can become coupled with

Look where you can get just 10 calories!

1/26 of a hamburger	1/30 of Danish pastry	1 SMALL french fry
1/10 Tablespoon of Butter	1/10 Tablespoon of Peanut Butter	1 teaspoon ketchup
1/8 teaspoon mayonnaise	1 oz of soft drink	1 bite of orange

other activities. Second, the activity distracts you from eating, so you get all the calories but only part of the pleasure.

Ten little innocent calories can add up to many unwanted pounds over a long time.

Calories Should Be Tasted, Not Wasted

Many a monitoring form shows people who eat half a bag of popcorn, 45 Fritos, 22 pretzels, or three-quarters of a pound of mixed nuts. Many of the calories are wasted, not tasted. Pay careful attention to how *every* bite tastes. Eating less can increase your enjoyment of what you do eat.

Follow an Eating Schedule

You may have uncovered *time* patterns from your Monitoring Forms. If you eat many times each day, and if you always feel like eating at those times, an eating schedule will help. This does not necessarily mean three meals a day at conventional times. It does mean finding a schedule that is convenient for you.

Judy's Sample Eating Schedule

Time	Meal
7:00 am – 7:20 am	Breakfast
10:30 am – 10:45 am	Morning snack
12:30 pm – 1:15 pm	Lunch
3:00 pm – 3:30 pm	Afternoon snack
6:30 pm – 7:00 pm	Dinner
9:00 pm – 9:20 pm	Evening snack

Plan a schedule for your eating. If you eat breakfast at 7:00 a.m., write it down. If you have a mid-evening snack, add it (if necessary). Keep the number of times you eat under control. This may involve eating three conventional meals, but remember to choose a plan you can tolerate.

"It says, 'One pill before breakfast controls your appetite all day.'"

Following a schedule will help you eat less and think more. You might have a snack planned at 9:00 p.m. If you feel like eating at 8:15, you can wait out the urge, and then see if you are still hungry at 9:00. You may get by with no snack at all! The illustration to the left is an example of an eating schedule made by Judy, one of my clients.

The worksheet on page 79 titled "My Eating Schedule" contains blanks for you to plan your eating schedule. List the times and meals you can live with, and do your best to stick with the schedule. There will, of course, be times when you violate your schedule, but do your best. When you feel like eating at times other than your schedule permits, think carefully about whether you are hungry or are responding to associations of eating and other factors.

Eat in One Place

Some people eat *anywhere*. They eat standing up, sitting down, at the kitchen counter, in an easy chair, lying in bed, or driving the car. They eat in the den, living room, bedroom, basement, and bathroom. One of my former clients even tied Oreo cookies in a bag and hung them with a rope out the window into the shrubs to hide her eating. This isn't exactly what I have in mind when I say to keep problem foods out of the house.

Here is a hypothetical example I use with my clients. Let's say that for the next 10 years you came to my clinic every day to eat a delicious meal while seated in a yellow chair. At the same time, you would have a chair in your home where no eating would occur. After the 10 years and 3,650 meals, your response to the two chairs would be quite different. You would be tempted to eat in the yellow chair even when you weren't hungry. This would not happen in the chair at home.

Select one place in your home where you will eat. Do *all* your eating there, but do *nothing else*. Do not use the place to play chess, pay the bills, or plot a way to beat the stock market.

Do Not Clean Your Plate

It is time to turn the tables on your plate. Until now, you may have been a slave to the rule issued by every mother, "Clean your plate!" It is nice to avoid wasting food, but think for a minute of the folly in cleaning your plate.

When you eat everything on the plate, you are at the mercy of the person doing the serving, even if you serve yourself. Unless the person has mystical powers and knows your body's energy requirements, you will be served too much or too little. Given our cultural tendency to overdo it, you will usually be served more than enough. If you clean your plate, you are responding to the *sight* of food, and eating stops only when no more food is in sight. When you serve yourself, remember that you do so *before* you have eaten, so you might be inclined to serve large amounts.

You can exert control by breaking the habit of cleaning your plate. Try to leave some food on your plate each time you eat. Leave only small portions if you like (two peas or one bite of mashed potatoes), but leave a small amount of everything. You can ask for second servings, but only if you are really hungry. This puts *you* in control of what you eat, not the chef.

Goal Setting

Tape/CD 2
Section 4

I have talked about setting reasonable goals in earlier lessons and will bring up this topic often in the lessons that follow. One common attitude problem is having unrealistic goals. Some individuals do not recognize they are setting unattainable goals, but they do so nonetheless. Examples of this are starting a program in May for swimsuit season when you have 50 pounds to lose. Having fantasies of being thin and having life improve immediately is another example. These things may happen, but not right away.

My Eating Schedule	
Time	**Meal**

Think about your goals for the program. Think of specific answers to these four questions:

➡ How much weight do you expect to lose each week?

➡ How soon do you expect to be thin?

➡ Will your life be different when you lose weight?

➡ Do you expect losing weight to be easy and quick?

These are just examples of some tricky areas. You are a sensible person and can formulate reasonable goals. Do you think your hidden or unconscious goals are unrealistic? If so, remind yourself time and time again that setting unrealistic goals is a setup for trouble.

In the space on page 80, list your four major goals for this program and decide whether they are realistic. The goals may be specific weight loss accomplishments (to

My Goals for this Program

GOAL #1:

GOAL #2:

GOAL #3:

GOAL #4:

lose one pound each week, or to lose 25 pounds total) or other changes (clothes will fit better, look better for daughter's wedding).

Servings from the Five Food Groups

I introduced you to the five food groups of the Food Guide Pyramid in Lesson Three. As we continue through the program, the Pyramid will become a familiar friend. We can now be more specific about the number of servings to have every day from each food group. Selecting the correct number of servings from each food group is important to insure the right mix of nutrients and total calories. The graphic illustration on page 81 lists the recommended average number of servings per day for adults.

The number of servings you choose from each food group will depend upon your target calorie level. Below, I have included a Menu Planning Guide to be used with the Pyramid. Use these tools as a guide to structure your diet. Do your best to eat the recommended number of servings every day (based upon your target calorie level) and record them the best you can in the columns on your Monitoring Forms. You may want to refer back to the example on page 53 in Lesson Three. I will focus on each of the food groups in upcoming lessons and provide you with common food lists from each group.

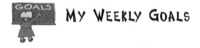 MY WEEKLY GOALS

You have several goals this week—some old, some new. Work on maintaining your target calorie level. Make copies of the Monitoring Form and complete it each day, recording the types and amounts of food you eat. Your Monitoring Form lists the following goals for the upcoming week that include:

Food Group	1200 calories (number of servings)	1400 calories (number of servings)	1500 calories (number of servings)	1800 calories (number of servings)	2000 calories (number of servings)
The Food Guide Pyramid Menu Planning Guide					
Milk, Yogurt, & Cheese Group	2 (nonfat)	2–3[1] (nonfat)	2–3[1] (nonfat)	2–3[1] (nonfat)	2–3[1] (nonfat)
Meat, Poultry, Fish, Dry Beans, Eggs, & Nuts Group[2]	5 oz lean meat (or equivalent)	5 oz med-fat meat (or equivalent)	5 oz med-fat meat (or equivalent)	7 oz med-fat meat (or equivalent)	7 oz med-fat meat (or equivalent)
Vegetable Group	4	4	5	6	6
Fruit Group	3	3	3	4	4
Bread, Cereal, Rice, & Pasta Group	6	6	7	8	9
Total Fat Calories (grams)[3]	360 (40)	420 (46)	450 (50)	540 (60)	600 (66)

[1] Women who are pregnant or breast feeding, teenagers, and young adults to age 24 need 3 servings.
[2] Meat group amounts are in total ounces.
[3] Based upon a maximum of 30 percent of total daily calories from fat.

➡ Meet or exceed your walking goal

➡ Do nothing else while eating

➡ Eat on a planned schedule

➡ Eat in one place

➡ Leave some food on your plate

Finally, think about your attitudes toward physical activity, as you prepare to increase your activity this week. Can you visualize walking being more fun and enjoyable? Increased physical activity brings many rewards, one of which is long-term weight management. And, even small increases can help. Remember to record your weight change on the My Weight Change Record on page 216. Good luck on your fifth week!

KNOWLEDGE REVIEW

Lesson Five

1. T F Weight loss is the best measure of success in The LEARN Program.

2. T F During the first month in behavioral weight loss programs women typically lose 8–10 pounds and men lose 10–12 pounds.

3. T F The ABC approach stands for Alternatives, Behaviors, and Consciousness.

4. T F You should increase your walking by 20 minutes per day until you reach the goal of 60 minutes of walking each day.

5. T F You should find a program partner to be successful at weight management.

6. T F You should tell your program partner in specific terms how he or she can help.

7. T F Eating 10 extra calories per day will add one pound of weight over a year.

8. T F Eating on a schedule is not advisable because it is too regimented.

9. T F Cleaning your plate is harmful because the server decides how much you will eat.

(Answers in Appendix C, page 221)

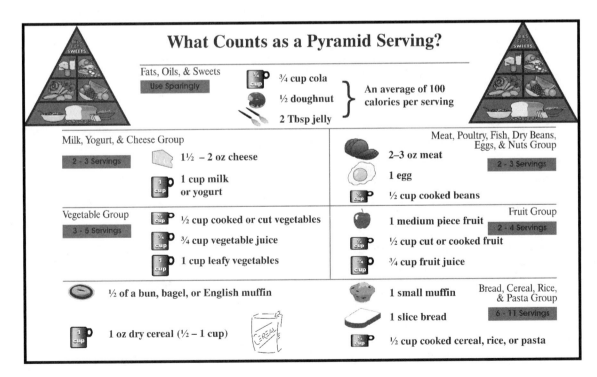

What Counts as a Pyramid Serving?

Fats, Oils, & Sweets
Use Sparingly

¾ cup cola
½ doughnut
2 Tbsp jelly
} An average of 100 calories per serving

Milk, Yogurt, & Cheese Group
2 - 3 Servings

1½ – 2 oz cheese
1 cup milk or yogurt

Meat, Poultry, Fish, Dry Beans, Eggs, & Nuts Group
2 - 3 Servings

2–3 oz meat
1 egg
½ cup cooked beans

Vegetable Group
3 - 5 Servings

½ cup cooked or cut vegetables
¾ cup vegetable juice
1 cup leafy vegetables

Fruit Group
2 - 4 Servings

1 medium piece fruit
½ cup cut or cooked fruit
¾ cup fruit juice

½ of a bun, bagel, or English muffin
1 oz dry cereal (½ – 1 cup)

1 small muffin
1 slice bread
½ cup cooked cereal, rice, or pasta

Bread, Cereal, Rice, & Pasta Group
6 - 11 Servings

Monitoring Form—Lesson Five

*Today's Date:*_____

Time	Food and Amount	Calories	Milk & Dairy	Meats & Protein	Vegetables	Fruits	Bread
Total Daily Caloric Intake & Food Guide Pyramid Servings							

Daily Activity Record (Caloric Expenditure)

Time	Activity	Calories	Minutes	No. of Steps

Personal Goals this Week	Most of the Time	Some of the Time	Rarely
1. Meet or exceed walking goal of _____ steps each day			
2. Do nothing else while eating			
3. Eat on a planned schedule			
4. Eat in one place			
5. Leave some food on your plate			
6. Eat less than _____ calories each day			

Lesson Six

You have now had a thorough introduction to the five components of The LEARN Program. In this lesson, we continue our journey by focusing on your speed of eating. We'll revisit the Food Guide Pyramid, and I'll show you how to estimate food portions. We continue our discussion about lifestyle activity, and I will give you a chart showing the number of calories you burn for various activities. I will also introduce you to an alternative way to better estimate your body's total daily energy expenditure. Finally, we'll work on the "Attitudes" component of LEARN by addressing the topic of negative self-talk. So, if you're ready, let's move on.

Slowing Your Eating Rate

Could you qualify for the Olympic speed-eating trials? Many people, both heavy and thin, eat so fast that their taste buds see only a blur as the food speeds by. This minimizes the enjoyment of food. More importantly, eating rapidly can fool your body's defense against eating too much.

Your body has an internal satiety (fullness) mechanism. When you have eaten enough to satisfy your body's energy needs, the mechanism sends out signals saying "Enough is enough!" Most experts believe this takes about 20 minutes, although it is a very complex process involving the stomach, hormones in the small intestine, brain chemicals, and other factors. If you eat rapidly, you will consume more food than your body needs before the mechanism kicks in. You will outpace your body's internal controls.

Slowing down your eating can be like halting a runaway freight train. You have had many meals in your life, so you have practiced the habit of fast eating thousands of times. Be patient and practice the following techniques to slow your eating until you replace old patterns with new ones.

Techniques to Slow Your Eating

The following two techniques can help you to slow your eating. Both can help put the brakes on eating and can increase your enjoyment of food.

➡ **Put your fork down between bites.** When you take a bite of food, put your fork down, chew the food completely,

THE GIANT BAGEL AND THE DRAWSTRING WAIST.

THE JUMBO FRIES AND THE ELASTIC WAISTBAND.

THE SUPERSIZED SODA AND THE RELAXED-FIT PANTS.

TODAY'S FOOD AND CLOTHING TRENDS COMBINE FOR A POWERFUL NEW LOOK:

GOODBYE, FASHION PLATE. HELLO, FASHION PLATTER.

swallow, and then pick up the fork for another bite. Do the same with a spoon. If you are eating finger foods like a sandwich, put the food down between bites.

➡ **Pause during the meal.** Take a break during your meal. Start with a brief pause of perhaps 30 seconds. Gradually increase the time to one, then two, and finally three minutes. This pause gives you time to reflect on what you have eaten, so you can make a conscious decision to proceed with more. This may also help you eat less. One study with animals found that interrupting the meal led to fewer total calories, even though the animals could eat all they wanted after the break.

More on the Food Guide Pyramid

I introduced the Food Guide Pyramid in Lesson Three and discussed the number of servings and serving sizes for each of the tiers in the Pyramid in the last lesson. Accurately estimating portion sizes and the calorie content of the food you eat can be

important to your success. The more accurate you are in recording the calories you eat, the better you will be at providing your body with just the right amount of fuel. Once you master the technique of estimating, you will need to measure portion sizes less often. It is a good idea, however, to keep these skills polished. So, you may want to measure portion sizes a few days every month.

A Food Portion Quiz

On page 85 is a Food Portion Quiz for you to take. Take this quiz now to get an idea of how accurately you may be estimating your food portions. Dr. Judith Ashley and Frances Poe, both registered dietitians from the University of Nevada School of Medicine, developed this quiz. If you answer "no" to any of the 10 questions, then you may need to improve the accuracy of your estimating abilities. The sections that follow will help you enhance these important skills.

Accurately measuring portion sizes of the foods you eat is important for estimating the total number of calories you eat each day. If you are using the exchange plan, measuring is equally important. Some foods are measured by weight in ounces or grams. Food scales are the most common method of weighing food. Scales are inexpensive and you can purchase them at most department or food stores. Cereal, meat, cheese, and dried crunchy snacks are examples of foods that are measured by weight. Other foods and drinks are measured by volume in cups, tablespoons, and teaspoons. Milk, cooking oil, cooked vegetables, cut-up fruit, fruit juices, rice, and dried beans are examples. Still, other foods are measured by size. Size can vary anywhere from a measured size in inches to a more subjective food size like a "medium" apple. Finally, foods can be measured by item count, such as one slice of bread, one egg, or five crackers. Understanding the basics of measuring foods and beverages is important for controlling calories.

A Visual Guide

As illustrated by the table in Lesson Five on page 80, the Food Guide Pyramid suggests a certain number of daily servings from each of the five food groups, depending upon the number of calories you want to include in your daily diet. The graphic illustration on page 81 highlights what makes up a single serving from each of the five food groups in the Pyramid. Many people confuse *serving* sizes with *portion* sizes. A serving is the exact measurement to equal one serving. An example would be one cup (1 cup) of milk. A portion, on the other hand, is what you actually serve yourself. For instance, a glass of milk that contains one and a half cups of milk would be a portion, and this portion would contain one and one half servings. As you can see, accurately measuring your food portion sizes is a key to controlling the number of calories you eat each day.

The chart on page 86 is a helpful Visual Portion Guide. Study this guide carefully to help you more accurately estimate the portion sizes of the foods you eat. You may even want to make a copy of this handy guide to carry with you. Share this information with your family and friends. Many people find this visual guide helpful in estimating portion sizes.

The Importance of the Five Food Groups

The Food Guide Pyramid arranges food groups by the key nutrients that they provide. For example, food choices from the Meat, Poultry, Fish, Dry Beans, Eggs, and Nuts Group are high in protein, B vitamins, iron, and zinc. The Milk, Yogurt, and Cheese Group includes foods high in protein and provides other key nutrients like calcium and vitamin D. The Vegetable and Fruit Groups along with the Bread, Cereal, Rice, and Pasta Group are excellent sources of dietary fiber along with other important vitamins and minerals. Choosing the right number of servings from the different food groups each day helps you achieve a balanced diet.

Food Portion Quiz

1. Yes No Do you own a food scale?

2. Yes No Do you have measuring cups and spoons where you serve food?

3. Yes No Do you keep a ruler handy in the kitchen?

4. Yes No Do you know how many ounces the glass you usually use at home holds?

5. Yes No Do you know how much the cup you use at work holds?

6. Yes No Do you know how many ounces are in the hamburgers, chicken, or fish you usually eat?

7. Yes No Do you count the number of strawberries, cherries, nuts, or french fries on your plate?

8. Yes No Do you know how many calories are in an ounce of your favorite cheese?

9. Yes No Do you read food labels to find out how much is in a serving?

10. Yes No Do you compare the calories per serving in possible food alternatives of your favorite foods?

Source: Ashley JM, Poe RE. Too much of a good thing: Keeping an eye on nutrition. *The Weight Control Digest* 1998; 8:742. Reproduced with permission.

Reviewing Your Target Calorie Level

Back in Lesson Four, you began experimenting with calorie intake to identify the level at which you will lose weight at the recommended rate of one to two pounds per week. Look back now to Lesson Four on page 61 to see what calorie level you selected as your best guess.

Now that you are several lessons wiser and have had more experience with your body's response to making changes, it is time to select a more official Target Calorie Level. Enter this number in the space provided below. In the Monitoring Forms you are using, you will continue to record whether you meet your calorie goal each day. The forms have a space for you to complete the following item: "Less than _____ calories." The blank spaces are where you

Visual Portion Guide

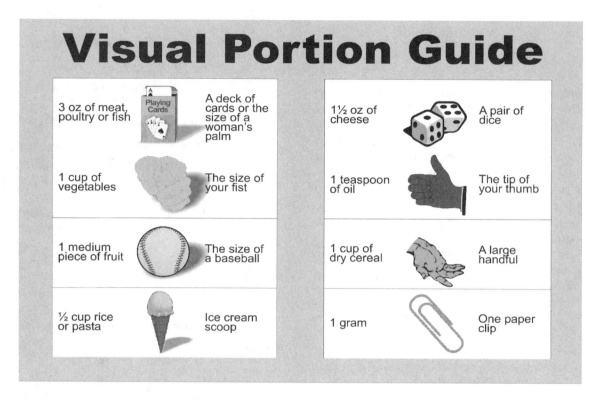

3 oz of meat, poultry or fish		A deck of cards or the size of a woman's palm
1 cup of vegetables		The size of your fist
1 medium piece of fruit		The size of a baseball
½ cup rice or pasta		Ice cream scoop
1½ oz of cheese		A pair of dice
1 teaspoon of oil		The tip of your thumb
1 cup of dry cereal		A large handful
1 gram		One paper clip

fill in your Target Calorie Level. Remember, this is to be the calorie level at which you will lose one to two pounds each week. To do this, you need to create a daily caloric *deficit* of 500–1,000 calories per day. The number can be modified as you progress through the program. Remember to keep your calorie level above 1,000 (women) or 1,200 (men).

My New Target Calorie Level is Less than_____Calories Each Day

The Role of Fat in Your Diet

Fat is what it's all about, right? You want to eat less fat and reduce body fat. How are dietary fat and body fat different? What role should dietary fat play in your diet? You may think that fat is just what we see on meats and that it goes right to our store of body fat. The picture is more complex and very interesting.

The Importance of Fat

Dietary fat plays an important role in everyone's diet. It has received much attention due to its association with heart disease and cancer. Yet, dietary fat in the right amounts is essential for good health. Dietary fat provides essential fatty acids that carry the fat soluble vitamins (A, D, E, and K) throughout the body and a semi-essential fatty acid that helps prevent growth deficiencies and builds cell-wall membranes. Dietary fat also provides flavoring in many of the foods we eat.

Body fat protects vital organs and prevents excessive heat loss. It also is a valuable source of energy, particularly for endurance activities; carbohydrate is the quick energy source. Too much body fat, however, can lead to serious health problems.

Our bodies can manufacture many of the essential fatty acids we need from the carbohydrate or protein we eat; however, there are some fatty acids that our bodies cannot manufacture. These fatty acids must be included in the foods we eat. Dietary fat is a combination of fatty acids and glycerol. All fats in foods are mixtures of three different types of fatty acids: saturated, monounsaturated, and polyunsaturated. You can visually identify *saturated* fats because they are usually *solid* at room temperature. Saturated fat comes primarily from animal sources, such as meat and dairy products, although some vegetable fats, like coconut, palm, and palm kernel oils, also contain saturated fat. As a rule, saturated fats are harder and more stable. Butter, stick margarine, lard, shortening, and the fat in meats and cheeses are good examples.

Monounsaturated fats are found mainly in olive, peanut, and canola oils. These fats are generally easy to identify because they are liquid at room temperature. Polyunsaturated fats can be either liquid or soft at room temperature and are found mainly in safflower, sunflower, corn, soybean, and cottonseed oils and some fish.

The distinction between saturated and unsaturated fat is important for health reasons. Again, the saturated fats are easy to distinguish because they are usually solid at room temperature and come primarily from animal sources (butter, lard, meat). High consumption of these fats has been associated with heart disease and is likely related to an increased risk for colon and breast cancers.

On the other hand, monounsaturated and polyunsaturated fats are usually liquid or soft at room temperature and come from vegetable sources (vegetable oils, margarine). These are generally healthier than the saturated fats. This is why so many people have switched from butter to margarine, reduced their intake of high-fat meats like beef and pork, and cook more with vegetable oils. The best unsaturated oils are corn, soy, sunflower, and safflower (the

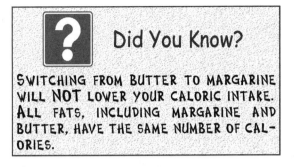

Did You Know?

SWITCHING FROM BUTTER TO MARGARINE WILL **NOT** LOWER YOUR CALORIC INTAKE. ALL FATS, INCLUDING MARGARINE AND BUTTER, HAVE THE SAME NUMBER OF CALORIES.

most highly unsaturated oil). A noteworthy point is that *all fats contain the same number of calories.*

Trans fats have received recent media attention because of their apparent link to an increased risk for heart disease. These fats occur naturally in low amounts in certain meats and dairy products. Trans fats also are produced synthetically from unsaturated fats by food manufactures through a process known as hydrogenation. When oil is partially hydrogenated, trans fats are formed. This process converts liquid, unsaturated vegetable oils into more solid, spreadable fat with increased shelf life. Food manufacturers use partially hydrogenated oils because they help produce high quality food products that stay fresh longer and have a more desirable texture. For example, hydrogenated vegetable oil is used to make some margarine products that are lower in saturated fat than butter and that can be used immediately from the refrigerator. Foods that contain these oils must list "partially hydrogenated vegetable oil" in the ingredient statement of the food label. Examples include cakes, cookies, crackers, pies, margarine, some breads, fried foods, salad dressings, and some snack foods.

Many dietary health experts now suggest that individuals limit their intake of trans fats. Trans fat consumption has been shown to elevate LDL cholesterol which increases the risk for coronary heart disease. Because of the link between trans fats and heart disease, the Food and Drug Administration (FDA) has proposed that the amount of trans fat be added to the amount of saturated fat per serving on the Nutrition Facts panel of food labels. A foot note would state how much trans fat is included in the product.

How Much Fat Should I Eat?

Three basic facts are important to remember about dietary fat. The first is that fat provides a lot of energy, which is bad news for a person trying to lose weight. Fat contains twice the calories (9 calories per gram vs. 4 calories per gram) of either protein or carbohydrate. This means that if you choose foods that are high in fat you will need to eat smaller portions to meet your calorie goals than if you choose low-fat foods. You will get more calories from the fat on a single steak th an from an equal amount of pure sugar.

Second, the amount of fat you eat is associated with an increased risk for several serious diseases. The average American consumes close to 40 percent of total calories from fat. This is 10 percent above the recommended limits of no more than 30 percent of total calories from fat. Saturated fat should be limited to less than 10 percent of calories or about one-third of total fat intake. Reducing your fat intake to these recommended levels should help with both weight loss and general health.

Third, I mentioned earlier that fat calories are more easily converted to body fat than are calories from other sources, such as protein and carbohydrate. Therefore, keeping fat intake under control can go a long way toward helping you reduce your weight.

To calculate the amount of fat you should eat each day, begin with your total daily calorie goal. Multiply this number by

---

My Daily Fat Intake (Example)

Total daily target **calorie** intake		1,500
Target max **percentage** of total calories	x	30%
Daily target **calories** from fat	=	450
Calories in one gram of fat	÷	9
Daily target **grams** of **total fat**	=	50
Daily target **calories** from **saturated fat** (10% of total calories)		150
Daily target **grams** of **saturated fat** (⅓ of total fat grams)		16

My Daily Fat Intake Calculation

Total daily target **calorie** intake		___
Target max **percentage** of total calories	x	30%
Daily target **calories** from fat	=	___
Calories in one gram of fat	÷	9
Daily target **grams** of **total fat**	=	___
Daily target **calories** from **saturated fat** (10% of total calories)		___
Daily target **grams** of **saturated fat** (⅓ of total fat grams)		___

---

30 percent to determine your daily calories from fat. Because each gram of fat contains 9 calories, divide your daily calories from fat by nine to determine your daily grams of fat. See the example in My Daily Fat Intake above. Use the blank chart above to calculate your daily fat-gram goals. You may want to record fat grams and/or fat calories on your monitoring form next to the "calories" column. This can help keep your daily fat intake to the recommended level.

Sources of Fat

We generally don't realize how much fat we eat. This is because about 60 percent of dietary fat cannot be seen. We often refer to this as hidden fat because it is contained in other food products, such as meat, cheese, nuts, breads, etc. In determining the amount of fat in your diet, it is important to account for both *visible* and *hidden* fat.

The table on page 90 provides you with a list of common foods from each of the five food groups of the Food Guide Pyramid. This table includes the number of food-group servings of each food and the calories from fat for each food listed. Take a minute to look at this table carefully. The amount of fat in some of your favorite foods may surprise you. Let's take a close look.

You can get one serving from the Milk Group by drinking one cup of skim milk that contains 86 calories, of which 4 calories are from fat. If you choose ice cream from the Milk Group, you would have to eat 1½ cups to get *one* Milk-Group serving. The ice cream would add 398 calories to your diet, of which 196 calories would be from fat. In other words, one cup of skim milk and 1½ cups of ice cream are each both equal to one serving from the Milk Group. You can see from this example that carefully selecting foods from within each food group is important for controlling calories.

Let me make one more important point here about serving sizes. In Lesson Eight, I discuss how to read a food label. Until then, **beware** that the *servings* listed on food labels **are not** Food Guide Pyramid servings—they are *portions* based upon the "amount of the food people typically eat." If you are confused by this, you're not alone. Use the table on page 90 along with a calorie guide to help you reduce your dietary fat, control calories, and eat a balanced diet.

Dietary Fat Adds Up

The fat in some foods adds up quickly. As I mentioned earlier, fat contains more than twice the calories of protein or carbohydrate. One gram of fat has 9 calories, whereas 1 gram of carbohydrate or protein has only 4 calories. One teaspoon (one pat) of butter or margarine has 4 grams of fat; that's 36 calories of fat for every teaspoon. It is important to watch out for those extras that contain high amounts of fat. For example, a bologna-and-cheese sandwich made with two slices (2 oz) of bologna, two slices (2 oz) of cheese, and 2 teaspoons of mayonnaise, includes about 36 grams of fat—that's 324 calories just from fat. A similar sandwich, however, made with lean beef, lettuce, tomato, and low-fat mayonnaise, and served with a cup of nonfat milk instead of cheese, has only about 6 grams of fat, or 54 calories from fat.

Reducing the Fat in Your Diet

Many techniques are available to help you lower your daily intake of dietary fat. The first step is to determine a target intake of fat as you did in the calculation on page 88. You can count fat *calories* or fat *grams*, whichever method works best for you. Next, you should become aware of the fat content of the foods you eat. In addition to reading food labels, many good books are available that can help. Here are some ad-

© 1997 Randy Glasbergen.
www.glasbergen.com

GLASBERGEN

"Our new synthetic fat substitute is made entirely from wool. With our product, dieters will shrink when they get wet!"

Fat from the Food Group Choices

Description	Cal	Fat Cal	FG[1]	FS[2]
Fats, Oils, and Sweets				
Butter (100% milk fat), 1 tsp	36	36	n/a	0.3
Chocolate bar, milk, 1.5 oz	145	78	n/a	4.4
Coca Cola, classic, 12 fl oz	146	0	n/a	10.1
Coca Cola, diet, 12 fl oz	2	0	n/a	n/a
Fruit drink, low cal, 6 fl oz	32	0	n/a	2.1
Gelatin dessert mix, ½ cup	80	0	n/a	4.7
Jam, preserves, 1 tsp	19	0	n/a	1.1
Margarine, corn, stick, 1 tsp	36	36	n/a	0.3
Mayonnaise, 1 tbs	100	99	n/a	0.9
Salad dressing, ranch, 1 tbs	75	72	n/a	0.6
Salad dressing, ranch, fat free, 1 tbs	24	2	n/a	0
Sherbet, orange, ½ cup	102	13	n/a	4.8
Sorbet, citrus fruit, ½ cup	92	0	n/a	5.8
Sour cream, 1 tbs	30	27	n/a	0.2
Sour cream, nonfat, 1 tbs	10	0	n/a	0
Milk, Yogurt, and Cheese Group				
Cheese, American, 2 oz	186	126	1	0
Cheese, cheddar, low-fat, 1½ oz	74	27	1	0
Cheese, cottage, 2 cups	464	183	1	0
Cheese, cream, 1 oz	99	89	0.7	0
Cheese, mozzarella, 1½ oz	120	83	1	0
Ice cream, vanilla, 1½ cups	398	198	1	9.3
Ice milk, vanilla, 1½ cup	203	54	1	2.5
Milk, chocolate, 1 cup	208	76	1	0
Milk, skim, 1 cup	86	4	1	0
Milk, whole, 1 cup	150	73	1	0
Milk, 2%, 1 cup	121	42	1	0
Milk, 1%, 1 cup	102	23	1	0
Yogurt, vanilla, frozen, 1 cup	203	23	1	7.1
Yogurt, fruit, low-fat, 1 cup	250	24	1	8.8
Yogurt, vanilla, low-fat, 1 cup	209	28	1	8.5
Yogurt, vanilla, nonfat, 1 cup	223	4	1	7.8
Meat, Poultry, Fish, Dry Beans, Eggs, and Nuts Group				
Beans, black, ckd, 1.2 cups	272	10	1	0
Beef, bologna, 2½ oz	221	182	1	7.2
Beef, ground, baked, 21% fat, 2.6 oz	212	139	1	0.7
Beef, ground, broiled, 16% fat, 2.6 oz	189	108	1	0.4
Cod, fillet, bkd/broiled, 2.6 oz	77	6	1	0
Chicken, dark w/ skin, fried, 2.6 oz	210	112	1	0.8
Chicken, dark w/o skin, fried, 2.6 oz	176	77	1	0.3
Chicken, white w/ skin, roasted, 2.6 oz	145	52	1	0
Chicken, white w/o skin, roasted, 2.6 oz	122	24	1	0
Egg, fried veg oil, 1 med	121	95	0.4	0
Salmon, filet, bkd, 2.6 oz	134	54	1	0.5
Peanut butter, creamy, 5 tbs	474	367	1	2.8
Peanuts, dry roasted, 4½ oz	746	570	1	4.5
Pork, lean tenderloin, broiled, 2.6 oz	138	42	1	0

Description	Cal	Fat Cal	FG[1]	FS[2]
Vegetable Group				
Beans, green, ckd, ½ cup	22	2	1	0
Broccoli, steamed, ½ cup	22	2	1	0
Carrot, raw, .6 cup	37	1	1	0
Cauliflower, raw, ½ cup	13	2	1	0
Celery, raw, ½ cup	33	2	1	0
French fries, 15 each (2.6 oz)	236	112	1	0.9
Lettuce, Romaine, chopped, 1 cup	8	1	1	0
Peas, green, bld, ½ cup	67	2	1	0
Potato, baked, ½ cup	57	1	1	0
Potatoes, mashed w/ milk & margarine, ½ cup	111	40	1	0.3
Tomato, raw, ½ cup	19	3	1	0
Fruit Group				
Apple, raw, 1 med	80	0	1	0
Apple juice, 6 fl oz	87	2	1	0
Avocado, raw, ¼ med	81	69	1	0.6
Banana, 1 med	109	5	1	0
Cantaloupe, fresh, ½ cup	31	2	1.1	0
Kiwi fruit, fresh, .8 cup	86	6	1	0
Orange juice, fresh, 6 fl oz	84	3	1	0
Pineapple, fresh, ½ cup	38	3	1	0
Strawberries, fresh, ½ cup	23	3	1	0
Bread, Cereal, Rice, and Pasta Group				
Biscuit, plain mix, dry, .8 oz	121	39	1	0
Bread, wheat, 1 slice	65	9	0.9	0
Cake, Angel food mix, 1.8 oz	129	1	1	0.6
Cake, white w/ white icing, 2½ oz	266	86	0.9	9.2
Cookies, oatmeal, 1 oz	139	53	1	2.6
Corn flakes cereal, 1 oz	105	0	1	0
Crackers, saltine, 10 each	130	32	1	0
Croissant, 2 oz	198	96	1	1.9
Danish, apple, 2 oz	184	73	1	3.3
Doughnut, 6", 2 oz	229	116	1	4.2
Pancake, plain, 4", 1 each	83	26	1	0
Pasta, noodle shells, ½ cup	81	3	0.8	0
Pie, apple, 9", 1 piece, 5.5 oz	411	174	1.2	1.1
Rice, long grain white, ½ cup	103	2	1.1	0

[1] This column represents the number of servings from the respective food groups of the Food Guide Pyramid.

[2] This column represents the number of servings from fats, oils, and sweets of the Food Guide Pyramid.

Note: Be sure to read product labels carefully as nutrient values and serving sizes may vary by food manufacturer.

ditional tips that will help you lower the amount of fat in your diet.

Milk, Yogurt, and Cheese Group

Use skim or low-fat milk instead of whole milk for drinking as well as cooking. Also, use nonfat or low-fat fruit yogurt instead of whole-milk yogurt. Frozen yogurt or ice milk is a nice substitute for ice cream. You can get one serving from ice cream that has a whopping 398 calories or from 1½ oz of low-fat cheddar cheese that has only 74 calories. This is a difference of 324 calories!

Meat, Poultry, Fish, Dry Beans, Eggs, and Nuts Group

Eat modest portions of meat, poultry, and fish. About three cooked ounces is the recommended portion size. Choose lean cuts of meat that include the name "loin" (e.g., sirloin, tenderloin, loin chops, pork loin, etc.), round steak, extra lean ground beef, and center cut ham. Ground turkey breast can be a good low-fat alternative to ground beef, but be sure to read the label carefully because some ground turkey can be loaded with fat. Limit your use of processed meats that tend to be high in fat. When in doubt, read the food label. If the fat content is not listed on the food product, be extra cautious. If cholesterol is a problem, limit your use of organ meats (liver, kidneys, brains, etc.) and limit the number of egg yolks to three or less per week. Legumes (dried beans and peas) are good alternative sources of protein and have little or no fat. Use them in mixed dishes instead of meat, or combine them with a small por-

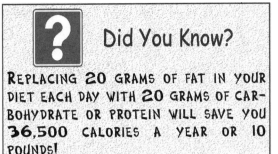

Did You Know?

REPLACING 20 GRAMS OF FAT IN YOUR DIET EACH DAY WITH 20 GRAMS OF CARBOHYDRATE OR PROTEIN WILL SAVE YOU 36,500 CALORIES A YEAR OR 10 POUNDS!

tion of meat or poultry. Be careful in your food choices, however, and don't forget to look at total calories. Look again at the table on page 90. You can get *one* Meat-Group serving by choosing a 2.6 oz fillet of cod (77 total calories and 6 calories from fat) or 1.2 cups of cooked black beans (272 total calories and 10 calories from fat).

Vegetable and Fruit Groups

Fruits and vegetables provide a good supply of fiber, vitamins, and minerals—all with low fat and no cholesterol. Use them generously at mealtime and for snacks. For both cooked and fresh vegetables (including salads), try seasonings and substitute flavorings, such as herbs, spices, butter buds, or a splash of lemon or balsamic vinegar instead of using butter or salad dressings. Remember, there are 4 grams of fat in each teaspoon of butter, margarine, or mayonnaise. Cutting out the salad dressing can save up to 72 calories of fat for each tablespoon.

Bread, Cereal, Rice, and Pasta Group

Use rice, pasta, and other grain products as the mainstay of a low-fat eating

plan. Small portions of meat, fish, and poultry go a long way when combined with grain products. Eating whole-grain products will help you maximize your intake of fiber and other important nutrients. Choose a slice of whole-wheat bread (1 gram of fat) rather than a croissant (11 grams of fat). Be extra cautious about looking for the hidden fats in baked goods.

Cooking Tips to Reduce Fat

Trim away all visible fat from meat before cooking. Remove skin and fat from chicken and turkey before cooking. Use nonstick pans and sprays for cooking. In sauces, salads, and soups, substitute low-fat or nonfat plain yogurt for sour cream or mayonnaise. Broil or bake meats instead of frying.

Fat in Snacks and Desserts

Eat plenty of fresh fruits and vegetables every day. Most supermarkets have small trays of prepared fruits and vegetables that are ready to eat. Pop your popcorn in a microwave or air popper. To add flavor, spray the popcorn lightly with hot vegetable oil or vegetable spray and add seasoning salts. Sorbet, flavored ice, and frozen fruit bars are a nice snack. Danish pastries, doughnuts, cookies, and frosted cakes are high in fat and should be eaten sparingly. In addition, potato chips and other crunchy snacks are often high in dietary fat. Be sure to read the food label for the fat and calorie content of these foods.

*Remember to count **ALL** of your physical activity as exercise—even the fun stuff.*

A Word of Caution about Fat

Because of all the media attention given to dietary fat over the past decade, food manufacturers have rushed to the market with low-fat and fat-free products. This is both a blessing and a curse.

Foods that are low in fat are generally lower in calories than their high-fat counterparts. However, there are exceptions. For example, one Archway "fat-free" oatmeal-raisin cookie has 106 calories and the regular oatmeal-raisin cookie contains 110 calories. Manufacturers sometimes replace the fat with sugars so people will still like the products.

Remember, it's not *fat* that makes a person gain weight, it's the total number of *calories* consumed. Eating a diet that is relatively low in dietary fat, yet still loaded with calories, is much easier today than just a few short years ago. This is why counting total calories is important for weight management. Try not to fall into the trap of thinking that you can eat all you want of foods that are low in fat and not gain weight.

Making Physical Activity Count

The time has come to distinguish between *lifestyle* and *programmed* physical activity. Lifestyle physical activity is simple and can be done in your day-to-day routine. An example would be using stairs rather than an elevator when you go to work. Programmed activity is a traditional exercise regimen of running, biking, aerobics, racquetball, and so forth. I will discuss programmed activities beginning with Lesson Eight. For now, let us focus on lifestyle activities.

Lifestyle Physical Activity

*Tape/CD 3
Section 9*

You can imagine the virtues of lifestyle activity; it is easy, takes little time, does not hurt, does not require special clothes or equipment, and can become habit with little effort. Regular physical activity makes you feel better, both psychologically and physically.

The idea here is to sneak in activity wherever and whenever possible throughout your day. The suggestions that follow may help you get started with another part of the assignment for this lesson—*increasing your lifestyle activity*.

Use the Stairs

Stairs can be a good friend because they are so readily available. Climbing stairs burns more calories per minute than a casual stroll. If you work on the fifth floor of a building, take the elevator to the fourth floor, and walk the remaining flight. As your fitness improves, get off on lower floors. One of my favorite examples is a client who lived in a two-story house with bathrooms on each floor. She decided to use the bathroom on the floor where she wasn't located, which gave her several extra trips per day up and down the stairs.

Park Further Away

When you drive to the mall, don't circle around like a vulture in search of a spot by the door. Park where only the people with new cars pull in—away from the crowd.

Increase Walking

If you take the bus downtown, get off one or two stops early, and walk the extra distance. If someone gives you a ride to the store, have him or her drop you off a few blocks away. At home, take things up the stairs in several trips instead of letting them accumulate for one trip.

Count All Activity as Exercise

Count everything you do as exercise. If you are using a step counter, then your job is much easier. When you do housework, turn on a timer, and keep moving. Use the vacuum an extra day each week. Time yourself as you wash the car, rake the leaves, or mow the lawn. You will be surprised how fast the minutes go by, and you will accomplish another task as well.

The beauty of these small bouts of activity is that each one provides an opportunity for you to feel virtuous—to be reinforced for doing something positive. And, this is not just a trick—you really *are* doing something positive. Anything you do to increase your lifestyle activity is beneficial and makes you feel better. You deserve a pat on the back whenever you make an effort to do something good, and you're the closest one around to do it. My hope is that you will count yourself among the ranks of people who consider themselves exercisers. This can build on itself to the point where you are feeling much better about your body and your physical condition. It doesn't take much to notice improvement.

These are just a few examples of the general *principle* of increasing lifestyle activity. Think of more methods to fit your

own routine. The section that follows, on the calorie values of exercise, may give you more ideas. Be sure to record all of your lifestyle physical activities on your Monitoring Form. You deserve credit for doing these activities, so they should show up in your records.

Tracking Your Progress

When you are making positive changes, *feeling* like you are making progress and *reinforcing* your accomplishments is important. Having a way of assessing how you are doing is quite helpful. The activity section on the monitoring forms of each lesson is an excellent place to begin, but some people like to do more.

Some people like to keep a graph or a log of when they are active. Either could include the number of minutes you are active, how fast you do some activity (like walking a certain distance), or how far the activity takes you (distance). Another helpful index of progress can be to use a pedometer. These are available in sporting goods stores and have been refined in the last several years to be much more accurate than earlier models. I discussed such a device in earlier lessons when I talked about the LEARN WalkMaster. If you don't have one of these you may want to call 1–888–LEARN–41 to order one or log on to the Internet at www.TheLifeStyleCompany. com. Some devices measure how far you walk and others give the number of steps you take. The ones with the number of steps are nice because you can see evidence of even small increases in activity.

I have worked with individuals who set up reward systems for themselves by making a contract. The contract states that certain non-food-related rewards (e.g., a movie, a new CD, clothing, etc.) are earned for attaining a certain level of activity. These are fine, but whether or not you have a reward system, it is important to track your activity so you have a sense of how much you are improving. This helps you feel virtuous when you deserve it.

The Calorie Values of Physical Activity

How many calories do you burn when you wash the dishes? Is it more than when you rake leaves? Is it easier to burn calories by swimming, jogging, or cycling? The physical activity table on page 95 will help you answer these questions.

The physical activity calorie table highlights several important points. First, any activity uses energy (calories), so any increase in activity can help. For a 175 pound person, sitting uses approximately 20 calories per 10 minutes, while standing uses 25, and walking briskly uses 65. Even something as simple as standing rather than sitting can use a few extra calories. Second, heavier people burn more calories than lighter people while doing the same activity, because more energy is required to move the extra weight. Third, several routine activities like using stairs and walking are useful methods of burning calories.

You must consider several facts when viewing these calorie figures. One is that calorie expenditures vary enormously for many activities depending on their intensity. Two people shoveling snow may differ greatly in how quickly they shovel, how

MET Values and Calories Expended in 10 Minutes of Physical Activity

Activity	METs	175	200	250
Personal Necessities				
Dressing or washing	2	26	30	38
Sitting (Talking)	1.5	20	23	28
Sitting (Watching TV)	1	13	15	19
Sleeping	.9	12	14	17
Standing (Talking)	1.8	24	27	34
Locomotion				
Cycling at <10 mph	4	53	60	76
Cycling at 13 mph	8	106	121	151
Running at 5 mph	8	106	121	151
Running at 7 mph	11.5	152	174	217
Walking downstairs	3	40	45	57
Walking upstairs	5	66	76	95
Walking at 2 mph	2.5	33	38	47
Walking at 3 mph	3.3	44	50	62
Walking at 4 mph	5	66	76	95
Home Activities				
Child Care	3	40	45	57
Cooking/food preparation	2	26	30	38
Dusting	2.5	33	38	47
Gardening	4	53	60	76
Making Beds	2	26	30	38
Mowing grass (manual)	6	79	91	113
Mowing grass (power)	5.5	73	83	104
Painting	4.5	60	68	85
Raking leaves	4	53	60	76
Scrubbing floors	3.8	50	57	72
Shoveling snow	6	79	91	113
Vacuuming	3.5	46	53	66
Washing car	3	40	45	57
Washing dishes	2.5	33	38	47
Occupational Activities				
Carpentry	3.5	46	53	66
Construction	5.5	73	83	104
Electrical work/plumbing	3.5	46	53	66
Farming	5.5	73	83	104
Light office work, sitting	1.5	20	23	28
Store clerk, filing, standing	2.3	30	35	43
Typing, electric, computer	1.5	20	23	28
Writing, desk work, sitting	1.8	24	27	34

Activity	METs	175	200	250
Recreation				
Badminton	4.5	60	68	85
Ballroom dancing (slow)	3	40	45	57
Ballroom dancing (fast)	4.5	60	68	85
Baseball	5	66	76	95
Basketball (shooting hoops)	4.5	60	68	85
Bowling (nonstop)	3	40	45	57
Canoeing	3.5	46	53	66
Dancing (aerobic)	6.5	86	98	123
Football, touch	8	106	121	151
Golf, using power cart	3.5	46	53	66
Golf, walking/pulling clubs	4.3	57	65	81
Hiking	6	79	91	113
Horseback riding	4	53	60	76
Ice skating	5.5	73	83	104
Jogging	7	93	106	132
Racquetball	7	93	106	132
Rollerblading	12	159	181	227
Roller skating	7	93	106	132
Rope jumping (slow)	8	106	121	151
Rowing	7	93	106	132
SCUBA diving	7	93	106	132
Skiing (cross country)	8	106	121	151
Skiing (downhill)	5	66	76	95
Skiing (water)	6	79	91	113
Softball	5	66	76	95
Squash	12	159	181	227
Swimming laps, slow	7	93	106	132
Table tennis/ping pong	4	53	60	76
Tennis (singles)	8	106	121	151
Tennis (doubles)	5	66	76	95
Volleyball	3	40	45	57
Water aerobics	4	53	60	76
Weight lifting	3	40	45	57

Note: The MET values were taken from the Compendium of Physical Activities: Ainsworth, B.E., Haskell, W.L., Whitt, M.C. et al. (2000). Compendium of Physical Activities: An update of activity codes and MET intensities. *Medicine and Science in Sports and Exercise*, 32(Suppl): S498-S516.

MET values above include resting energy expenditure. To calculate total daily energy expenditure using *incremental* MET values, subtract 1 MET from the MET values in this table. For example, the incremental MET value for walking at 4 mph is 4. Calorie values in this table were calculated from the MET values.

much snow they move with each scoop, and how much they move around while shoveling. Similar differences can occur with skiing, tennis, yard work, and so forth. Therefore, the figures in the table are only averages.

The second fact is that the table shows the calories burned for 10 minutes of continuous activity. If you do an activity for five minutes, divide the value in the table by two. If you are active for 30 minutes, multiply the value by three.

Incremental MET Values

Light-Intensity Activities (.5–2 Incremental METs)

This category is where you will spend most of your time. It includes sitting, working at the desk, and standing.

Moderate-Intensity Activities (2–4 Incremental METs)

This category includes those activities above light activities where you can *talk and sing* comfortably. For example, walking 3 mph (20 minutes per mile) requires 2 incremental METs, and walking 4 mph (15 minutes per mile) requires 3 incremental METs. Most adults can comfortably walk at a pace of 3–4 mph. This pace is typically described as a brisk pace. It is not race walking or a casual stroll; it is the pace that you might move if you were in a bit of a hurry to make an appointment. Even sedentary and unfit individuals can walk at this speed for several minutes without undue fatigue. Other examples include:

- **Callisthenic exercise**
- **Carpentry work in workshop**
- **Golf (not riding in a cart)**
- **Horseback riding**
- **House painting**
- **Mowing lawn (not riding)**
- **Raking leaves**
- **Sailing**
- **Scuba diving**
- **Snorkeling**
- **Softball**
- **Sweeping floor**
- **Table tennis**
- **Vacuuming carpet**
- **Volleyball**
- **Walking 3–4 mph**
- **Weeding the garden**
- **Weight lifting**

Hard-Intensity Activities (4–6 Incremental METs)

Hard activities are more strenuous. When you engage in hard-intensity activities you can *talk* but *NOT sing*. Doubles tennis is a good example. Classifying sport activities can be a bit tricky, so you need to use good judgment. For example, tournament doubles tennis may belong in the very hard category whereas recreational doubles would fit in this category. Then again, it is possible to play doubles tennis and scarcely move around at all. So, for sports and other programmed activities, such as household, occupational, and recreational activities that can be performed at different paces, you have to use some judgment when assigning incremental MET values. I like using the *talk/sing* test. If you can talk but not sing comfortably, the activity is a hard activity. Other examples include:

- **Aerobic dance**
- **Basketball**
- **Construction work**
- **Digging in the garden**
- **Doubles tennis**
- **Downhill skiing**
- **Fishing in a stream**
- **Hiking**
- **Hunting**
- **Skating, ice or roller**
- **Show shoveling**
- **Square, folk, or fast dancing**
- **Stair climbing (moderate pace)**
- **Swimming (slow pace)**
- **Walking at 4.5–5.5 mph**
- **Water skiing**

Very-Hard-Intensity Activities (7+ Incremental METs)

Activities in this category are quite strenuous for most people. They include those activities where you cannot *sing or talk* comfortably. Sedentary and unfit individuals cannot sustain very hard activities for more than a few minutes without becoming fatigued. Running at any pace qualifies for this category. Vigorous sports involving a lot of running such as soccer or basketball are typically very hard activities. Examples include:

- **Backpacking (hilly country or rough trails with a heavy pack)**
- **Basketball, soccer, singles tennis, or racquetball (competitive)**
- **Cross-country skiing**
- **Mountain climbing**
- **Rope jumping**
- **Running**
- **Stair climbing (fast pace)**
- **Swimming (fast pace)**
- **Vary hard physical labor**

The word *continuous* is important to understanding the table. The table shows that a 250-pound person burns 57 calories for 10 minutes of bowling. This is 10 minutes of nonstop bowling and does not include time to keep score, chat with friends, polish the ball, or visit the snack bar. The 10 minutes for skiing would not include time waiting in the lift line, marveling at the scenery, or watching others fall down! So, to calculate the calories you burn for a given activity, calculate the time you are truly active, and then use the table on page 95 as a guide.

Physical Activity and METs

Another way of estimating the total number of calories your body uses in a day is to know the number of hours you spend in activities at various MET levels. MET is an abbreviation for Metabolic Equivalent or the energy (measured in calories) you expend while resting quietly. METs are expressed as multiples of this resting rate. For example, 3 METs would mean that you are burning calories at 3 times your resting rate. The table on page 95 includes MET values for selected physical activities.

For every hour that you are resting quietly, your body uses about 1 MET. The caloric expenditure for a person's 1-MET value is equal to the person's weight in kilograms. To calculate your body weight in kilograms simply divide your body weight by 2.2. So, your body weight divided by 2.2 is equal to your body's 1-MET value. If you weigh 170 pounds, your 1-MET value is equal to 77 calories. This means that your body uses about 77 calories per hour (1 MET) while quietly at rest. If a 170-pound person was in a 4-MET activity, he/she would be using about 309 calories per hour.

If you know your body's daily energy expenditure while at rest, adding the additional caloric expenditure for your *incremental* activities above your resting expenditure will give you a good estimation of your *total* daily energy expenditure. Most people spend the greatest part of their day in light activities. The *incremental* value of *light* activities is between .5–2 METs. Sitting and standing require slightly more energy than resting (sleeping). The table on page 96 will give you some general guidelines for assigning *incremental* MET values to your physical activities.

If you are using a step counter, you may want to use the MET calculation for those activities that are not recorded by the step counter, like swimming, cycling, resistance training, sitting in a chair, and working at your desk. Let's look at an example.

LIFESTYLE PROFILES

Jack weighs 170 pounds and is in his sixth week of The LEARN Program. Turn to page 101 for an example of Jack's Monitoring Form. We'll be focusing on the middle section, the Daily Activity Record.

Jack is a bookkeeper for a large retail store. Most of his day is spent working at his desk along with small bouts of walking to other offices on the same floor. On this particular day, Jack got up at 6 a.m. and went to bed at 10 p.m. Jack wears the LEARN WalkMaster, and on this particu-

Cindy's Negative Self-Talk

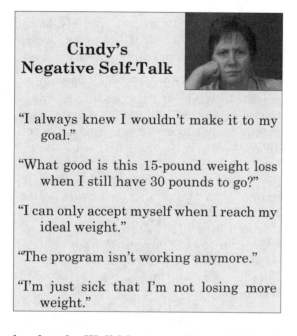

"I always knew I wouldn't make it to my goal."

"What good is this 15-pound weight loss when I still have 30 pounds to go?"

"I can only accept myself when I reach my ideal weight."

"The program isn't working anymore."

"I'm just sick that I'm not losing more weight."

Cindy's More Positive Self-Talk

"A reasonable goal is for me to lose 5–10 percent of my starting weight. I'm actually doing pretty well."

"The 15-pound loss is a big thing for me, and even if I lose no more, I'm a lot better off carrying 15 fewer pounds."

"I don't expect myself to be perfect in other areas of my life. It would be great to be at my ideal weight, but I'll be happier if I focus on being at a 'better' weight rather than at a 'best' weight."

"I still might lose more, but right now I don't want to get discouraged. A good goal for me is to keep off the weight I have lost."

lar day the WalkMaster registered 205 calories and 5,424 steps. Jack also went for a 30 minute bicycle ride with his children when he came home from work and took a 30 minute low-impact water aerobic class at the neighborhood fitness center.

On the first line of his Daily Activity Record, Jack calculated his 1-MET value. Jack's 1-MET value, based on his current weight of 170 pounds is 77. He then estimated how many calories his body uses during a day (24 hours) while at rest. On the third line, Jack estimates his body's energy expenditure from "light" activity of simply being up and moving about for 16 hours (6 a.m. to 10 p.m.). For this he uses an *incremental* value of .5 METs. On the fourth line he records the activity from the step counter, followed by the calorie expenditure from bicycling with his kids and his water aerobic class. From the form you can see that Jack estimates his body used 2,901 calories on this particular day.

The Trap of Negative Self-Talk

All of us have what is referred to as an *internal dialog*. These are the things we say to ourselves and may not share with the outside world. The things you say to yourself can greatly affect your ability to make

*Tape/CD 4
Section 3*

important lifestyle changes. The more upbeat and positive you are when you talk to yourself, the better your chances are to make successful changes. Let's look at an example.

 ### LIFESTYLE PROFILES

A person I know, named Cindy, went through a lot of self-doubt at about this stage of the program. She was discouraged because she wasn't losing more weight and was questioning whether she should keep trying. She was on the verge of giving up. When I asked what type of thoughts she was having, she came up with what you see in the example in the upper left column.

After some discussion, Cindy made a list of more positive ways of looking at things. This helped her get back on track.

Progress In My Program		
Progress I've Made	**Positive Things I've Changed**	**Reasons I Should Maintain the Changes**

She began taking credit for the progress she had made and emphasizing a realistic, attainable set of expectations. Now look at what Cindy was saying to herself in the second example on page 98 in the right column.

Think of your weight like a turnstile that moves in only one direction. Losing weight is like the turnstile moving forward. Wouldn't it be nice if your weight were like a turnstile in that it never moved in the opposite direction? With the right self-management skills, you can have more confidence that your weight will not bounce back up.

Now, of course, expecting a perfect turnstile is unrealistic, because no person who has lost weight maintains a perfectly stable weight. You can expect some weight fluctuation, created in part by fluctuations in your control over eating and activity. One thing that characterizes successful maintainers is that they set an upper limit on how much they allow their weight to increase (usually three to five pounds) before they take corrective action. Hence, the turnstile will move mainly in one direction (weight loss) and will accept a little backward movement before the brakes are applied, but only to a limited degree.

Charting My Progress

Think of the progress you have made since beginning The LEARN Program just a few short weeks ago. Any weight you have lost is a positive change. Also, remember my discussion on the changes in your quality of life. You can measure progress with much more than the scale. Our first order of business is to be sure that these changes are permanent. If you are not continuing to lose 1–2 pounds per week, you may need to work on your self-monitoring skills. Look closely at your Monitoring Forms. Are you completing the forms each day? Are you accurately weighing and measuring your food portion sizes? Are you accurately estimating your body's daily energy expenditure? If the answer to any of these questions is "no" you may want to reread the importance of keeping good records in Lesson One on page 18.

If your weight loss has slowed, try not to be discouraged. Pay attention to all you have achieved rather than what you have left to do. Take a few moments to write down the progress you have made since starting the program and all the positive things you have changed. Also, write down all the positive reasons you can think of to maintain changes you have already made. I have provided the table on page 99 so that you can take a few minutes now to write down your thoughts. So, sharpen your pencil and start writing!

My Weekly Goals

One specific goal you can set is to eat more slowly by putting your fork down between bites and pausing during your meals. This helps most people and is worth making a habit. In addition, think of the personal goals you'd like to set at this point, and try your best to reach these goals. Continue walking and find ways to increase your lifestyle activity. Use the MET method this week to more accurately estimate your daily energy expenditure. You may find this a bit tricky at first, but stick with it, and you'll find it is a very helpful weight management tool.

Make it a goal this week to carefully measure your food portion sizes and estimate the calories as accurately as possibly. Calculate your daily fat intake based on your target calorie level using the form on page 88. Include your fat intake on your Monitoring Form and compare your actual fat intake with your target calculation. Finally, keep an eye out for negative self-talk. Set a goal to counter this negative self-talk with positive thoughts and positive self-talk. Remember to record your weight change for this week on the My Weight Change Record on page 216.

Knowledge Review

Lesson Six

1. T F Eating rapidly helps you enjoy food more because the taste buds get more stimulation.

2. T F Pausing during a meal increases food intake because the body digests food and sends out signals to eat more.

3. T F One and a half ounces of cheese is equivalent to the size of your fist.

4. T F Saturated fat is usually solid at room temperature and is found only in animal foods, such as meats and dairy products made from whole milk or cream.

5. T F The recommended daily intake of dietary fat is 30 percent or less of total calories.

6. T F Because high-fat diets have been linked to heart disease and other health-related risks, it is best to eliminate all fat from your diet.

7. T F Eating 500–1,000 fewer calories each day than your body uses will result in a 3,500–7,000 calorie *deficit* over the course of a week. This caloric deficit should result in about a 1–2 pound weight loss per week.

8. T F One gram of fat contains more than twice the calories of one gram of carbohydrate or protein.

9. T F Climbing stairs requires more energy per minute than taking a casual stroll.

10. T F Accurately estimating food portion sizes is not all that important in a weight management program.

11. T F A MET stands for a metabolism unit and refers to the amount of energy you burn while sleeping.

(Answers in Appendix C, page 221)

Monitoring Form—Lesson Six (*Jack's Example*) **Today's Date:** Feb. 10, 2003

Time	Food and Amount	Calories	Milk & Dairy	Meats & Protein	Vegetables	Fruits	Bread
7:30 am	Apple juice, 6 fl oz	84				✓	
	Special K cereal, 1 oz	115					✓
	Skim milk, 1 cup (8 fl oz)	86	✓				
10:00 am	Banana, 1 med	110				✓	
12:30 pm	Turkey sandwich, 3 oz, wheat, 2 tbs low-fat mayo, lettuce	286		✓	✓		✓✓
	V8 vegetable juice, low sodium, 12 fl oz	90			✓✓		
	Water, 8 fl oz	0					
	Soda crackers, low sodium, 10	130					✓
	Carrots, raw, ½ cup	35			✓		
	Celery, raw, ½ cup	33			✓		
8:00 pm	Salmon, Atlantic, baked, 4 oz	206		✓✓			
	Tossed green salad, 2 tbs fat-free ranch dressing	71			✓✓		
	White rice, ckd, ½ cup	121					✓
	Mashed potatoes, ½ cup, w/ butter buds	100			✓		
	Strawberries, fresh, 1 cup	46				✓✓	
	Skim milk, 1 cup (8 fl oz)	86	✓				
9:30 pm	Apple, raw, 1 med	80				✓	
	Lot fat gingersnap cookies, 10	163					✓
Total Daily Caloric Intake & Food Guide Pyramid Servings		**1,842**	2	3	8	5	6

Daily Activity Record (Caloric Expenditure)

Time	Activity	Calories	Minutes	No. of Steps
	1 MET = 77 calories/hr [170 lb ÷ 2.2 = 77]			
All day	Daily resting energy expend – 77 x 1 MET x 24 hr	1,848		
6am–10pm	Up and moving about – 77 x .5 inc. METs x 16 hr	616		
All day	Steps per step counter	205		5,424
6:00 pm	Bicycling with kids – 77 x 3 inc. METs x .5 hr	116	30 min	
7:00 pm	Water aerobic class – 77 x 3 inc. METs x .5 hr	116	30 min	
Daily Totals		**2,901**	**60 min**	**5,424**

Personal Goals this Week	Most of the Time	Some of the Time	Rarely
1. Meet or exceed walking goal of ___4,600___ steps each day	✓		
2. Put fork down between bites	✓		
3. Pause during meals	✓		
4. Carefully weigh and measure food portions	✓		
5. Eliminate negative self-talk and counter with positive thoughts	✓		
6. Eat less than ___1,800___ calories each day		✓	

Monitoring Form—Lesson Six

*Today's Date:*_____

Time	Food and Amount	Calories	Milk & Dairy	Meats & Protein	Vegetables	Fruits	Bread
Total Daily Caloric Intake & Food Guide Pyramid Servings							

Daily Activity Record (Caloric Expenditure)

Time	Activity	Calories	Minutes	No. of Steps

Personal Goals this Week	Most of the Time	Some of the Time	Rarely
1. Meet or exceed walking goal of _____ steps each day			
2. Put fork down between bites			
3. Pause during my meals			
4. Carefully weigh and measure food portions			
5. Eliminate negative self-talk and counter with positive thoughts			
6. Eat less than _____ calories each day			

Lesson Seven

We are now far enough into The LEARN Program to reflect on what you have learned, the behaviors you have practiced, and the new outlook on dietary, physical activity, and other lifestyle changes you have made. Have some of the techniques become habits? Are you becoming more proficient in using the new skills you have learned? Is this a program you can live with? These are the key questions to consider. In this lesson you will continue to learn new skills and add even more tools to your weight management tool chest.

Thinking Your Way to Success

Tape/CD 3
Section 1

I cannot overstate the importance of your thoughts. Your thoughts determine how you feel about yourself, which in turn affects your behavior, your mood, your interactions with others, and your interpretation of your progress in the program. For example, if you tell yourself, "I've totally blown it. I'm such a failure," how would you feel? What could you do if you think in this way?

People in weight management programs tend to think in certain ways. Examples include expecting too much, being upset with anything less than perfection, and letting small mistakes build to catastrophe. I have seen such thoughts take root in hundreds of people. They get in the way of progress; they can sour a person's outlook; they can be difficult to change. My job is to help you pull these destructive thoughts out by the roots and plant thoughts that are more constructive in their place. This may sound puzzling to do, but stay with me, and I'll explain.

Realistic Goals and Expectations

I discussed goal setting in Lesson One and concluded that having unrealistic expectations can halt your progress. It is time to explore this matter further. We have expectations for practically everything we do.

Tape/CD 2
Section 3

Although we do not always articulate a goal or expectation for every activity, hidden within our minds are ideas of an acceptable outcome. If you mow the lawn, write a letter, buy clothes, or simply talk to a friend, you expect certain standards of performance. If you scalped the lawn,

wrote an unintelligible letter, bought gaudy clothes, or said insensitive things to your friend, you would be upset because you expected more—you did not satisfy your internal standards.

You can see how difficult life would be if your expectations were absurdly out-of-reach. If you expected *Better Homes and Gardens* to lust after your lawn, the National Archives to enshrine your letter, a famous designer to covet your clothes, or your friend to memorialize your words in a book of quotes, you would be crushed by what is otherwise an acceptable performance. Disappointment is often a function of unmet expectations. Unfortunately, people losing weight often set such out-of-reach goals and therefore have unrealistic expectations about eating, exercising, and losing weight. When someone does not satisfy his/her expectations, negative thoughts can trigger negative feelings, which in turn can send the person's progress into a tailspin. These negative responses can be averted if you learn appropriate *coping* skills. Let's look closer at this four-step process.

Learning appropriate coping skills can help you overcome difficult situations and stay on track.

Setting goals and creating expectations come first and are often unconscious. Then comes comparing what you accomplish to the expectation, resulting in either an *acceptable* or *unacceptable* outcome. If the outcome is acceptable, the emotional re-

sponse is usually positive. If the outcome is unacceptable and the individual does not apply appropriate coping skills, the emotional response can be negative. The model below illustrates this four-step process.

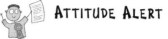

Attitude Alert

Developing appropriate skills to handle difficult situations is a key ingredient of the LEARN approach. This is where the A (Attitudes) comes into play. You learned one important coping skill in Lesson Six where you practiced positive self-talk. Another such skill is learning to *reframe* the outcome of a particular event. In Lesson Ten I will talk about another such coping skill, eliminating the use of *imperative* words such as "always," "never," "must," "should have," and so on. Keep the illustration below in mind as we look at an example.

Lifestyle Profiles

In the early weeks of her program, Susan set a goal to exercise *every* day and to *never* eat fries. During her second week, Susan had to work late at the office. She was tired and very hungry as she drove home. When Susan passed a fast-food restaurant she automatically pulled into the drive-in and ordered a sandwich, fries, and

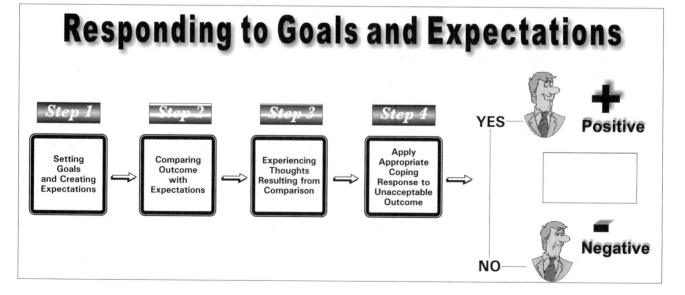

a drink. She was so hungry that she began eating as she drove home, and by the time she pulled into her garage, she had finished. As she walked into the house, Susan began to compare her goals and expectations with her actual behavior and had these thoughts: "I'm so tired, I can't exercise tonight. I've also blown my diet. I am such a failure, I can never lose weight and be happy."

The reality of Susan's example is that skipping an exercise session and eating an order of fries is *insignificant* in the overall scope of her program. What *is* significant are her unrealistic expectations and her negative emotional responses. Two strategies could have prevented Susan's negative responses.

First, Susan could have set more realistic goals. Instead of saying to herself, " I will exercise *every* day" she could have said "I will try my best to exercise most days of the week." Here, she would have avoided imperatives (exercising *every* day) and setting an unrealistic goal. Implicit in her unrealistic goal was that she would exercise every day "no matter what." This is unrealistic.

A second strategy Susan could have used is to reframe the outcome of the situation. Even if she had set an unrealistic goal, Susan could *reframe* her thoughts about not meeting her goal, which would in turn *change* her feelings about skipping a day of exercise, thereby *changing* her nega-

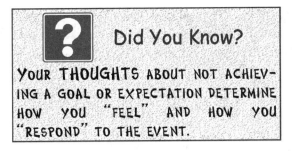

tive response. For example, Susan could have said to herself, "I'm too tired to exercise today, but I did work hard and deserve a rest. I'll schedule another 15 minutes of walking in my day tomorrow." You can see how reframing the outcome allows Susan to view the missed exercise session as something she can handle.

The table below illustrates a few examples of how this process pertains to other unrealistic goals and expectations. These are common examples, so while you are reading, think about whether these or similar situations occur with you.

Negative emotional responses can lead to setbacks. People have enough trouble controlling their eating and exercising without the extra burden of negative thoughts and feelings. You can change the emotional response by altering the two steps that precede it, namely the goals and expectations and the comparison you make to the expectation (coping response).

When you have negative thoughts and feelings, examine them carefully. Trace them to the initial expectations you set. If

Unrealistic Goals and Expectations with No Coping Response			
Goal or Expectation	Comparing/Outcome	Thoughts	Emotional Response
Must exercise every day	Missed a day of exercise	"I'm a failure. I will never lose weight and be happy."	Guilt, stop trying
Will never eat fries	Ate an order of fries	"I'll never be able to stop eating bad foods. Losing this weight is impossible."	Guilt, discouragement, self-doubt
Must never eat more than 1,500 calories a day	Overate at a birthday celebration	"I can never control my appetite. I'm a horrible person."	Self-blame, low self-esteem
Must lose weight every week	Gained a pound	"I'm doomed to be heavy forever. I can't keep from gaining weight."	Self-doubt, resignation

Realistic Goals and Expectations			
Goal or Expectation	**Comparing/Outcome**	**Thoughts**	**Emotional Response**
Will try to exercise on most days of the week	Missed a day of exercise	"It was a busy day at work, and I'm too tired to exercise. But I've still exercised five days this week."	Satisfied, desire to keep exercising
Limit eating fries to a couple times a month	Ate an order of fries	"Those were good fries, but I haven't really missed eating them all that much."	In control, responsible, satisfied
Try to limit caloric intake to 1,500 or fewer calories most days of the week	Overate at a birthday celebration	"That was a fun birthday party. I did overeat, but I have kept my intake to about 1,500 calories most days this week."	In control, high self-esteem, encouraged
Try to lose weight each week	Gained a pound	"I've still lost 10 pounds since starting, and that is good progress."	Encouraged, pleased with progress

you feel guilty because you sneak a Snickers, think about your expectation, which is probably something like, "I should never cheat on this program." Expecting to be perfect can be a real problem.

The table above lists the same outcomes as those in the previous table but with more realistic goals and expectations. Look carefully at how the more realistic goals and expectations affect the thoughts and the resulting emotional responses.

The table below illustrates the same unrealistic goals and expectations and the same outcomes as in the previous tables; the difference here is the use of appropriate coping skills. While you may like to *always* set realistic goals and expectations, we all make slips that can lead to trouble. So, when those unrealistic expectations enter

Unrealistic Goals and Expectations with Coping Responses				
Goal or Expectation	**Comparing/ Outcome**	**Thoughts**	**Coping Response**	**Emotional Response**
Must exercise every day	Missed a day of exercise	"I'm a failure. I will never lose weight and be happy."	*Reframing.* "Missing one day of exercise isn't really all that bad. I walked a lot at work today and I'll take time for a 15-minute walk tomorrow at lunch."	In control, self-confident, pleased with progress
Will never eat fries	Ate an order of fries	"I'll never be able to stop eating bad foods. Losing this weight is impossible."	*Reframing.* "Telling myself I will never eat fries is unrealistic. An occasional order of fries will not make that big a difference over the long run."	Confident, high self-esteem
Must never eat more than 1,500 calories a day	Overate at a birthday celebration	"I can never control my appetite. I'm a horrible person."	*Reframing.* "It would be nice if I could keep my caloric intake below 1,500 each day, but I know this is unrealistic. An occasional slip means it may take just a bit longer to lose the weight I want."	Energized to continue, in control, pleased about coping abilities
Must lose weight every week	Gained a pound	"I'm doomed to be heavy forever. I can't keep from gaining weight."	*Reframing.* "I'd love to lose weight every week, but I know there will be weeks when this may not happen. When I gain weight, I'll focus a bit more on my monitoring forms and my progress."	Pleased with realistic thinking, confident, pleased with progress

the picture, you can head off trouble by using coping strategies you just learned.

Shopping for Food

Let's look back on the ABC approach introduced in Lesson Five. The "A" refers to the antecedents that set the stage for eating. One important antecedent is shopping for food. If you buy healthy foods, you will eat healthy foods. This may sound obvious, but too few people plan their shopping accordingly.

 NUTRITION NOTES

Having problem foods available in the house, office, car, backpack, purse, or pocket can be asking for trouble, even if you vow to "eat only a little." If something threatens your restraint, say fatigue or boredom, you can pay a dear price for the decision you made hours or days earlier to buy the food. On the other hand, if your refrigerator resembles a salad bar because of wise shopping, weakened restraint can inflict only minor damage. You can use several clever methods while shopping to make prudent food choices.

➡ **Shop on a full stomach.** When you are hungry, it is easy to buy impulsively because everything looks appetizing. An innocent trip to the store to buy a few essentials can become a setup for an eating excursion. The supermarket to a hungry person is like water to someone stranded in the Sahara. In addition, stores are designed to tempt you. Your restraint may be high when you first walk in, but little good it does when you are in the produce section! As you move through the store, your restraint weakens just as you pass down the cookie aisle. Desire reaches its peak as you travel down Dessert Drive (the frozen food and ice cream section). To avoid these temptations, shop *after* you have eaten. You will be surprised at how much grief this can prevent.

➡ **Shop from a list**. Prepare a shopping list before you leave the house, and shop

Shopping List

Milk (non-fat)
Chicken breasts (skinned)
Green beans
Green peas
Fresh veggie platter
Orange juice
Apples
Bananas
Potatoes
Bread, whole wheat
Cereal

only from the list. Be sure to prepare your shopping list when you are not hungry. Decide what to buy *before* the foods in the store tempt you.

➡ **Buy foods that require preparation.** In today's age of prepackaged foods, microwave ovens, and fast-food restaurants, you can eat at an instant's notice. Eating requires little thought and can be done impulsively. Buying foods that require preparation can halt this process. Let's use an example of a common food. If you have a hankering for fried chicken, you could visit the Colonel and procure 1,700 calories in an extra crispy three-piece meal. Little time would separate craving from consumption. If you chose the preparation route, you would buy a whole chicken, cut it up, prepare it, and then fry it. You would have time to think about how much you wanted the chicken and may eat less (if you eat it at all). Better still, preparing the chicken yourself would give you the option of baking it, which would result in far fewer calories than deep-frying.

➡ **Buy ready-to-eat fruits and vegetables.** All of us have urges to snack from time to time. Having healthy foods such as fresh fruits and vegetables ready to eat is a great way to control calories and

Shopping from a list can help keep high-risk foods out of the house and make healthy foods readily available.

increase your intake of fruits and vegetables. Most supermarkets now have prepackaged, cut, ready-to-eat fruit and vegetable platters. If you buy items that need to be washed and cut, be sure to do this immediately when you return home from shopping to insure they are available when you're ready for a snack. Remember, your objective is to make it as easy to reach for a nice piece of fruit or vegetables as it is to reach for a cookie or chips.

➡ **Park your shopping cart**. Most people push their shopping cart up and down each aisle in the store. This makes it easy to take something off the shelf and put it into your cart, even when it's not an item on your shopping list. Parking your cart at the end of the aisle and walking back and forth to your cart has two important advantages. First, this strategy gives you more time to think about an item that is not on your shopping list as you carry it down the aisle to your cart. You may be less likely to grab impulse items off the shelf

when you have to carry them back to your cart. Additionally, walking back and forth to your shopping cart is an excellent way to increase your physical activity.

A Shopping Partnership

Partners can often help with your food shopping. There are several ways to do this, as I discuss below. If your partner is also on a program, you can swap shopping duties. If not, the partner can help you shop in exchange for favors from you. This was the case with Tom and Sheila.

 **RELATIONSHIP RESOURCES**

On Saturdays, Tom did yard work while Sheila (the one on a weight loss program) did the food shopping. Sheila had trouble with impulse buying because food beckoned her as the sea nymph sirens beckoned Odysseus. They switched tasks, so Tom did the shopping and Sheila did the yard work. This even added some lifestyle activity to Sheila's routine. Here are a few examples of putting a shopping partnership to work.

➡ **Shop with a partner.** Shopping can become a social event if your partner journeys with you to the supermarket. You can resist the goodies if you know someone has his or her eye on your cart. Your partner can help you prepare your shopping list and carry it in the store.

➡ **Switch tasks with your partner.** This is what Tom and Sheila did in the example earlier. Your partner may be willing to do the shopping in exchange for help with another job.

➡ **Swap shopping duties with your partner.** If your partner is on a program, trade shopping lists. You do your partner's shopping, and your partner does yours. Unless your partner stuffs your bag with treats, you will come away with the foods you need.

Rating Your Diet

In Lesson Two, you completed a short quiz to rate your diet. Now that you are half way through the program, it is a good time to take the same quiz again to see how your diet has changed. On page 235, in Appendix E, is the Rate Your Diet Quiz for this lesson. Take a few moments now to complete the quiz. Record your total score from page 238 in the space provided in Appendix B on page 213. How does your total score now compare with your total score a few weeks ago? Hopefully, your score has improved, and you're on your way to being a nutrition whiz. If your score has not improved, you may want to pay particular attention to food-group servings you are eating from the Food Guide Pyramid. I will discuss each food group in this and upcoming lessons.

The Importance of Food

Tape/CD 3
Section 10

In simple terms, food is energy; it is the fuel our bodies use to live and function. Like most energy sources, quality is as important as quantity, and having the right mixture of nutrients is essential to good health. Some nutrients have energy (calories) and others do not, but both are critical to our bodies. The nutrient needs of our bodies are comparable to the different needs of our automobiles. Gasoline and diesel fuel provide fuel or energy. Oil, water, transmission fluid, and other lubricants are also critical to a car's operation, but they do not provide energy.

Our bodies need over 45 different nutrients every day. These nutrients are essential for our health and must be provided in the food we eat. There are six classes of these nutrients listed in the table on page 111. We can divide them into two categories:

❶ Nutrients with energy (calories)

❷ Nutrients without energy

Nutrients with energy include carbohydrates, proteins, and fats. In Lesson Six, I discussed the role of fat in your diet. I will discuss proteins and carbohydrates in later lessons. The nutrients without energy include minerals, vitamins, and water. Let's take a closer look at these important nutrients.

Nutrients Without Energy

Three classes of nutrients that are essential to our bodies provide no energy (calories). These nutrients include minerals, vitamins, and water. Minerals and vitamins can be compared to the spark plugs in an automobile. Spark plugs are essential to the ignition of the fuel (gasoline). Without them, the fuel cannot be burned, and the car cannot function. If your car has high quality spark plugs in good condition, it will run more efficiently. Similarly, minerals and vitamins are responsible for the metabolism (the burning) of your body's energy (fat, carbohydrate, and protein). If you eat a balanced diet and get the right

Dear Miss know-it-all,

what's the quickest way to lose fifty pounds in a hurry?

GO TO AN ENGLISH GAMBLING CASINO.

MISS KNOW-IT-ALL

6-22

amount of minerals and vitamins, your body will function more efficiently.

Minerals

Our bodies contain over 60 different minerals, 22 of which are essential. The amount needed of the different minerals varies greatly. The 22 essential minerals are classified by the amount needed in the body as either *major minerals* (those needed in larger amounts—more than 100 mg daily) or *trace minerals* (those needed in smaller amounts—less than 100 mg per day). This classification is based upon the amount needed by the body and not on importance. For example, a deficiency in cobalt, which comprises only two parts per trillion of body weight, can have more damaging effects than a deficiency in calcium, which accounts for two percent of body weight.

Minerals serve many functions. They aid in the growth of body tissue, transmit nerve impulses, regulate muscle contraction, maintain water balance in the body, form parts of essential body compounds, maintain the acid-base balance in the cells, and facilitate many biological reactions. Minerals are found together in the foods we eat and interact with each other as well as with other nutrients in the body. Because of this interaction and combination, certain foods are considered better sources.

Vitamins

Vitamins also are essential nutrients needed to sustain life. They are required for the regulation of the body's metabolism and for the transformation of energy (pro-

tein, carbohydrate, and fat) in the body. Some vitamins help to form important enzymes, and others act as catalysts to speed certain chemical reactions. There are two types of vitamins:

❶ Fat soluble

❷ Water soluble

Fat Soluble Vitamins

The four fat soluble vitamins are A, D, E, and K. These vitamins are found in dietary fat and are stored in the body's fat tissue if consumed in excess amounts. Because these vitamins are stored, high doses can be toxic. You should be cautious of people who promote large quantities of these vitamins. Experts suggest no more than the Recommended Daily Allowance (RDA).

Vitamin A is essential for the growth of skin, bones, and teeth. It is also important in vision and immune functions. Vitamin D is essential for bone and tooth development. In addition, it helps the body utilize calcium and phosphorus. Vitamin E is essential for the functioning of red blood cells and immune functioning. Vitamin E also appears to be an antioxidant vitamin. I'll discuss antioxidant vitamins in the next lesson. Vitamin K is used by the liver to produce prothrombin, a factor in blood plasma that combines with calcium to help in blood clotting.

Water Soluble Vitamins

Water soluble vitamins consist of seven primary vitamins: vitamin C and the B complex vitamins that include vitamin B_1

(thiamine), vitamin B_2 (riboflavin), vitamin B_3 (niacin), vitamin B_6 (pyridoxine), folacin, and vitamin B_{12} (cobalamin). Unlike the fat soluble vitamins, these are absorbed in the body's water, and excess amounts are usually excreted.

Vitamin C is used by the body for teeth, bones, cells, and blood vessels; it is essential for the formation of hormones and the healing of wounds. Vitamin C is another antioxidant vitamin.

Vitamin B_1 (*thiamin*) helps produce energy from carbohydrates in all the cells of your body. It also aids in the regulation of nerve impulse transmission. A deficiency of this vitamin can result in beriberi which means "I can't, I can't." Symptoms include depression, weakness, loss of appetite, irritability, nervous tingling, poor arm and leg coordination, and deep muscle pain in the calves.

Vitamin B_2 (*riboflavin*) is intricately involved in the functioning of all cells in the body. It is particularly important in metabolizing fat. Vitamin B_2 is necessary for the skin and helps prevent light sensitivity in the eyes. A deficiency of this vitamin in the diet can result in inflamation of the mouth and tongue. Other symptoms include eye disorders (including cataracts), dry and flaky skin, and other nervous system disorders and confusion.

Vitamin B_3 (*niacin*) plays an important role in the synthesis of fatty acids. It also helps produce energy in all cells of the body and helps enzymes function normally. Deficiencies in vitamin B_3 can lead to pellagra. Symptoms include diarrhea, mental disorientation, and skin problems.

Vitamin B_6 (*pyridoxine*) aids in the metabolism of protein, carbohydrate, and fat. It helps the body make nonessential amino acids (proteins), which are then used to make body cells. Vitamin B_6 also helps in the production of niacin and serotonin (a messenger in the brain). In addition, vitamin B_6 helps produce other body chemicals including insulin, hemoglobin, and antibodies that fight infection. Deficiencies can

The Six Classes of Nutrients

Nutrients with Energy (Calories)

1. **Carbohydrates**—starches, sugar, and fiber

2. **Protein**—includes 22 amino acids

3. **Fats**—saturated, monounsaturated, and polyunsaturated fatty acids

Nutrients without Energy

4. **Minerals**—*22 in total*

7 Major Minerals	*15 Trace Minerals*	
Calcium	Arsenic	Manganese
Chlorine	Boron	Molybdenum
Magnesium	Cobalt	Nickel
Phosphorus	Copper	Selenium
Potassium	Chromium	Silicon
Sodium	Fluorine	Vanadium
Sulfur	Iodine	Zinc
	Iron	

5. **Vitamins**

Fat Soluble	*Water Soluble*
Vitamin A-RDA 5000 IU	Vitamin C-RDA 60 mg
Vitamin D-RDA 100 IU	Vitamin B_1 (thiamine)-RDA 1.5 mg
Vitamin E-RDA 30 IU	Vitamin B_2 (riboflavin)-RDA 1.7 mg
Vitamin K	Vitamin B_3 (niacin)-RDA 19 mg
	Vitamin B_6 (pyridoxine)-RDA 2.0 mg
	Vitamin B_{12} (cobalamin)-RDA 6 μg
	Folacin-RDA 400 μg

6. **Water**

cause convulsions among infants, depression, nausea, greasy, flaky skin, and reduce the efficiency of the immune system.

All nutrients are important for good health and weight management.

Vitamin B_{12} (*cobalamin*) is essential for normal growth and neurological function. This vitamin also helps prevent anemia by working closely with folate to make red blood cells. This vitamin also serves as a vital part of many body chemicals and helps the body use fatty acids and some amino acids. A deficiency may result in anemia, fatigue, nerve damage, a smooth tongue, or very sensitive skin.

Folacin plays a key role in making new body cells by helping to produce DNA and RNA. It works hand-in-hand with vitamin B_{12} to form hemoglobin in red blood cells. This vitamin may also help protect against heart disease. A deficiency affects normal cell division and protein synthesis, impairing growth. Anemia is another symptom caused by malformed blood cells that cannot effectively carry oxygen to the body's cells.

"I'm sorry, but part of the 'Diet Special' is a two-hour wait!"

As a general rule, nutrition experts believe that people in the U.S. receive an adequate supply of minerals and vitamins if they eat a balanced diet. Following the dietary guidelines of the Food Guide Pyramid will help insure a balanced diet with adequate amounts of vitamins and minerals. It is important to watch out for the mega doses promoted by some people, including seemingly credible nutrition stores. If you are eating less than 1,200 calories per day, you may have trouble getting the right nutrients, so check with your doctor. Even people eating more than this level may want to check with their physician because the science on supplement use changes rapidly.

Water

Water makes up about 60 percent of your body and is an essential part of every cell in your body. It plays an important role in temperature regulation, removal of wastes, lubrication and cushioning, and transporting nutrients throughout the body. Yet, many people overlook the importance of water in their diets, not realizing that water is an *essential* nutrient and should be consumed generously.

Weight loss programs commonly recommend that people drink 8 glasses of water per day. Recent research suggests that there may not be much of a scientific basis for this recommendation. So, drinking water when you are thirsty and speaking with your physician for more specific advice makes sense.

Some people report that drinking water helps them curb urges to eat. This can be a helpful strategy, so if you think it may work for you, by all means try it. This would involve recognizing urges to eat and then having water to help the urge go away.

Milk, Yogurt, and Cheese in Your Diet

The second tier of the Food Guide Pyramid represents foods that essentially come from animal sources—milk, yogurt, and cheese; and meat, poultry, fish, dry beans, eggs, and nuts. The focus in this lesson will be on the Milk, Yogurt, and Cheese Group.

Milk, yogurt, and cheese are good sources of protein and carbohydrate, but also they can provide large amounts of unwanted dietary fat (see the food list on page 113). In addition, foods from the Milk Group are good sources of vitamin A, vitamin D, and calcium. Vitamins A and D are essential for the growth and development of skin, bones, and teeth. Calcium is an essential mineral for the growth and development of bones, blood clotting, nerve transmission, and muscle contraction. Deficiencies in calcium can lead to loss of bone and bone fractures. Because the hormone estrogen plays an important role in helping the body absorb calcium, post-menopausal women are at particular risk for deficiencies. Foods from the Milk Group are the best source of dietary calcium and generally supply the greatest amount of calcium in our diet. One cup of milk (8 fl oz), for example, provides 500 International Units (IUs) of vitamin A (10 percent of the 5,000 RDA) and 100 IUs of vitamin D (25 percent of the 400 RDA). The same cup of milk also provides about 313 mg of calcium (24–31 percent of the 1,000–1,300 mg RDIs).

Cheese items have proportionally more calories from protein than carbohydrate. Milk and yogurt, on the other hand, provide more carbohydrate per serving than protein.

How Many Servings?

The Food Guide Pyramid suggests 2–3 servings per day from the Milk Group. For most people, two servings from this group are sufficient; however, for teenagers, young adults, and women who are pregnant, breast feeding, or post-menopausal three servings per day are recommended. Many people may know that servings from this group are important, yet most do not know how many servings are optimal. Use the table on page 80 to help you tailor your servings to your caloric intake.

How Much Is a Serving?

The food chart on the right lists single serving sizes for many common food items from the Milk Group. As a general guide, the following items count as a single serving:

➡ 1½–2 oz processed cheese

➡ 1 cup (8 oz) milk

➡ 1 cup (8 oz) yogurt

➡ 1½ oz natural cheese

➡ 1½ cups ice cream

➡ 2 cups cottage cheese

Watch out for Fat

Most products from the Milk Group come from animal sources. As such, these food items also contain cholesterol and fat. The fat content as well as the number of calories in each serving can vary greatly. For instance, one serving of skim milk (8 fl oz) has 86 total calories, compared to one serving of ice cream (1½ cups) which can have nearly 400 calories. Moreover, the one serving of skim milk has only a trace (less than 1 gram or 4 calories) of fat compared to 198 fat calories in the ice cream.

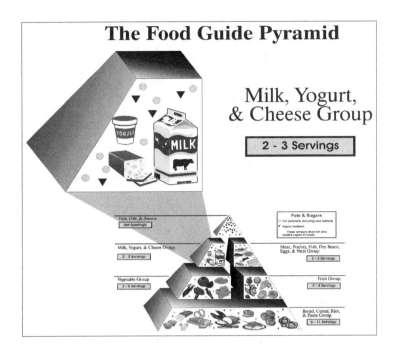

The Food Guide Pyramid

Milk, Yogurt, & Cheese Group

2 - 3 Servings

Milk, Yogurt, and Cheese Group

(One Milk Group Serving Each)

Description	Cal	Pro (g)	Carb (g)	Fat Cal
Cheese, American processed, 2 oz	186	11	4	126
Cheese, cheddar, 1½ oz	171	11	1	127
Cheese, Colby, low-fat, 1½ oz	74	10	1	27
Cheese, cottage, low-fat, 2 cups	324	56	12	41
Cheese, cream, 1½ oz	148	3	1	133
Cheese, mozzarella, whole milk, 1½ oz	135	9	1	94
Cheese, mozzarella, part skim, 1½ oz	119	12	1	66
Cheese, ricotta, whole milk, 1½ oz	74	5	1	50
Cheese, ricotta, part skim, 1½ oz	59	5	2	30
Ice cream, vanilla, 1½ cups	398	7	47	196
Ice cream, vanilla, light, 50% less fat, 1½ cups	275	8	45	77
Ice milk, vanilla, 1½ cups	203	6	31	62
Ice milk, chocolate, 1½ cups	367	9	57	112
Milk, skim, 1 cup	86	8	12	4
Milk, 1% fat, 1 cup	102	8	12	23
Milk, 2% fat, 1 cup	121	8	12	42
Milk, whole, 1 cup	150	8	11	73
Yogurt, vanilla, low-fat, 1 cup	209	12	34	28
Yogurt, plain, 9 oz	156	9	12	75
Yogurt, low-fat, fruit, 1 cup	231	10	43	22
Yogurt, frozen, fruit, vanilla, 1 cup	203	9	37	23

Note: This table should be used only as a guide for the foods listed. Because food values vary by brand name, it is important to read food labels carefully for these foods.

Something for Your Partner to Read

In earlier lessons, I discussed ways to select a partner and to ask for help. One way to help your partner help you is to make specific suggestions. I often encounter partners who ask for guidance on what they can do. Most are genuinely interested in helping and need only a few suggestions.

I wrote this section for both *you and your partner* to read. Have your partner read it, and then discuss the material together. Decide on concrete ways your partner can help and how you can help your partner in return.

Partners can help you with your program in many different ways.

➡ **Partners can model good eating and physical activity habits.** A partner may help you immensely by doing what you are trying to accomplish. Eating slowly is a good example. A partner can exercise with you, help keep food out of sight, and display a positive attitude. This will remind you to do the same and will be a visible sign that your partner is trying to help.

➡ **Partners can praise your efforts.** A pat on the back and a few kind words can go a long way. Your partner should not wait for you to lose weight to be kind to you, and he or she should not focus just on your weight change. When you make positive changes in eating or exercise, your partner can acknowledge them with supportive comments. By waiting only for changes in your weight, your partner misses many opportunities to be supportive.

➡ **Partners can provide practical support.** A partner can watch your children while you go for a walk, exercise with you to an exercise video, or attend your weight management program. A partner also can do your grocery shopping or bring you a healthy take-out meal. Again, these activities will work in some partnerships and not others.

➡ **Partners can help with the weigh-in.** Not everyone on a program will want a partner to know his or her weight, but if the relationship can tolerate this knowledge, having your partner present at a regular weigh-in can help. This gives your partner an idea of how you are doing. You may like this additional motivation. The partner must be forewarned, however, that weight loss will not occur every week. If the weigh-ins are more frequent than once per week, fluid shifts will give false indications about your progress in the program.

➡ **Partners can be rewarded in return.** I explained earlier that you must be kind to your partner in exchange for your partner's support. This is a basic rule of relationships. In fact, many people feel better knowing that they are doing something nice for their partner. I also explained how you should be frank with your partner in asking for support and should be specific in these requests. These same rules apply to the partner. Your partner should tell you in specific terms what you can do to be nice. An example of a specific request might be, "I would like you to go to the movies with me once each week."

Impressive Reasons to Be Active

Tape/CD 2 Section 6

Previously, I mentioned that regularly active people tend to lose weight better and keep it off over the long term. Scientists have used nearly every known psychological and medical test to predict who will lose weight and keep it off. The most consistent finding is that exercise is associated with weight maintenance. In addition, many studies show the benefits of physical activity on our health, psychological well-being, and even the way in which we learn. The table on the right summarizes the many health benefits of regular physical activity.

Weight Maintenance

An impressive example of the research on this topic is a study by Kayman, Bruvold, and Stern published in the *American Journal of Clinical Nutrition*. The researchers studied people in a large health maintenance organization who had participated in a weight loss program. Many months after the program, the researchers contacted the participants to see what distinguished those who had maintained their weight loss from those who had regained.

Of those who maintained their weight loss, 92 percent were getting regular physical activity. Only 34 percent of the regainers were exercising. Other studies have shown similar results.

The National Weight Control Registry provides further evidence as to the power of physical activity in weight management.

Health and Wellness Benefits of Regular Physical Activity

Primary Benefit	Related Benefits

Improves cardiovascular fitness and health	▸ Builds stronger heart muscle
	▸ Lowers resting and exercise heart rate
	▸ Increases oxygen flow to the brain
	▸ Improves circulation
	▸ Increases the blood's oxygen-carrying capacity
	▸ Decreases triglycerides
	▸ Increases high-density lipoprotein (HDL) cholesterol
	▸ May decrease low-density lipoprotein (LDL) cholesterol
	▸ Decreases blood pressure
	▸ Reduces risk of
	  Heart attack
	  High Blood Pressure
	  Stroke

Preserves and increases lean body mass; promotes fat loss	▸ Reduces decline in resting metabolic rate that accompanies calorie restriction ▸ Decreases intra-abdominal body fat (associated with cardiovascular disease (CVD), diabetes, and hypertension) ▸ Improves appearance ▸ Improves self-confidence

Improves strength and muscular endurance	▸ Increases work efficiency
	▸ Reduces the risk of
	  Muscle injury
	  Low back problems
	▸ Improves performance in sports and leisure activities
	▸ Promotes muscle recovery after hard work

Builds and maintains healthy bones, muscles, and joints	▸ Builds greater bone mass in childhood/early adolescence ▸ Maintains peak bone mass in adulthood ▸ Reduces risk of osteoporosis and hip fracture ▸ Relieves symptoms of arthritis
Reduces cancer risk	▸ Reduces risk of breast and colon cancers ▸ May reduce risk of endometrial and prostate cancers
Decreases risk of non-insulin-dependent diabetes	▸ Decreases insulin resistance (i.e., allows glucose (blood sugar) to enter cells) ▸ Decreases blood sugar levels during and after exercise ▸ Improves quality of life for type I diabetics
Improves mood	▸ Relieves symptoms of depression and anxiety ▸ Improves sleep ▸ Decreases stress ▸ Enhances leisure time enjoyment ▸ Improves quality of life ▸ Improves self-esteem ▸ Improves psychological well-being
Increases energy	▸ Decreases fatigue ▸ Improves quality of life ▸ Improves ability to cope with stressors
Improves flexibility	▸ Decreases chance of muscle and joint injury and low back problems ▸ Increases range of motion ▸ Improves balance
Improves cognitive ability	▸ Improves memory ▸ Improves learning ability
Slows effects of aging	▸ Improves physical functioning ▸ Promotes greater mobility and independence ▸ May lower risk of cognitive decline ▸ May reduce the risk of Alzheimer's disease
Other health benefits	▸ Extends life ▸ May improve immune system functioning ▸ Helps some people who have PMS, asthma, and chronic pain

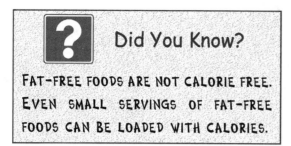

FAT-FREE FOODS ARE NOT CALORIE FREE. EVEN SMALL SERVINGS OF FAT-FREE FOODS CAN BE LOADED WITH CALORIES.

The Registry includes more than 3,000 people who have lost an average of 66 pounds and kept off at least 30 pounds for five years. Participants in the registry complete questionnaires about the strategies they use to maintain their weight loss. Successful weight managers report that they spend about 60 minutes each day in moderate- to vigorous-intensity physical activity. If you would like more information on the Weight Control Registry you can call 1–800–606–NWCR or visit the website at www.nwcr.ws.

The effect of physical activity on weight maintenance can occur in many ways. It affects metabolism and other physical factors, but psychological advantages also occur. When you are active, even in a modest way, you are doing something positive—you are making a statement to yourself that you are committed to lifestyle change. This goes a long way in making you feel good and in boosting your confidence. So, if you are in this for the long run, regular physical activity is one of the best companions you can have.

Learning Ability

Some new studies suggest that regular physical activity may have a positive impact on the brain. In studies with both humans and animals, researchers have found that exercise can increase learning ability, improve mood, and keep brains cells alive longer. Exercise increases blood flow to the brain and the level of a brain-cell growth hormone. This stimulates the growth of new brain neurons while prolonging the survival of existing brain cells. The researchers found that the new brain neurons develop in the part of the brain responsible for new memory.

ACTIVITY ALERT

I cannot emphasize enough the importance of regular physical activity. I hope that you have increased your activity level since beginning this program and that you are now feeling the positive effects of a more active lifestyle. The evidence is now overwhelming that physical activity is both a powerful weight management tool and an important instrument of overall well-being and good health.

Continuing Walking and Lifestyle Activity

Let's review your progress with walking and lifestyle activity. This is a good time to look back at the section on the "Benefits of Physical Activity" from Lesson Two on page 30 and "The Benefits of Exercise" from Lesson Three on page 41. As you may recall, being active brings many physical and emotional benefits. Two of the most important benefits, at this stage of your program, are that exercise may help control appetite and bolster self-confidence.

Remember that exercise is one predictor of who will keep weight off over the long run. On average, people who exercise are more likely to maintain their weight loss long after a program ends. There are exceptions, however. Some people exercise and do not lose weight, and others lose weight without exercising. Where you fit in this scheme may not be evident for many months, but increasing your activity now may pay nice dividends later.

How much are you walking? Are you enjoying your walks? Page 72 in Lesson Five includes ideas for making walking pleasurable, so please review this material if you feel the review would help. You should be walking between 15 and 60 minutes each day or at least 4,800 steps per day. The ultimate goal is for you to make regular increases in the number of steps you take each day. It is best to walk as much as possible without feeling discomfort. If you tire from walking, take several short walks rather than one long one. Having two brisk 30-minute walks or four 15-minute walks can help you as much as a one-hour walk in a single bout.

What types of lifestyle activities have you been doing? Have you found opportunities to use stairs, to park some distance from your destination, or to do some extra walking? These lifestyle activities are nice because they remind you that you are doing something positive.

One reason I use the term *lifestyle* physical activity is the hope of developing permanent habits. Each trip up the stairs may not make you lose a pound, but summed over many days, months, or years, the effect can be powerful. New habits can be difficult to acquire, so it is important to practice and then practice some more. Some of my clients say they now search out stairs wherever they go and feel that they miss an opportunity to be active when they must use an elevator or escalator.

My Weekly Goals

Your monitoring form this week includes goals related to the new behaviors discussed in this lesson. These include three that relate to changes with shopping for food: shop on a full stomach, shop from a list, and park your shopping cart at the end of the aisles. This is also the time to examine your goals and expectations to see if they continue to be realistic.

Your nutrition goals for the week will be to keep your caloric intake at or below your target calorie level, keep your fat intake to 30 percent or less of total daily calories, and to eat 2–3 servings from the Milk Group. Don't forget to record your weight change on the My Weight Change Record on page 216. Good luck this week!

Knowledge Review

Lesson Seven

1. T F   Thoughts and attitudes often occur automatically when we are confronted by certain situations and therefore cannot be changed.

2. F F   Setting goals that are difficult to reach is a good strategy because it motivates you to work harder.

3. T F   It is wise to shop for food when you are hungry to test the new restraint you have learned.

4. T F.   Buying foods that require preparation can increase your awareness of eating and help you eat less.

5. T F   Buying fresh fruits and vegetables that are ready to eat and keeping them readily available is a good way to keep calories under control.

6. T F   All of the nutrients that our bodies need contain calories.

7. T F   One cup (8 fl oz) of milk is equal to one serving from the Milk Group of the Food Guide Pyramid.

8. T F   The recommended number of daily servings from the Milk Group is 2–3.

9 T F   If a partner is working with you to lose weight, it is important to reward him or her for the help he or she provides.

10. T F   Physical activity is important for weight loss but its benefits decline after a person loses weight.

(Answers in Appendix C, page 222)

Monitoring Form—Lesson Seven   *Today's Date:*_____

Time	Food and Amount	Calories	Milk & Dairy	Meats & Protein	Vegetables	Fruits	Bread
Total Daily Caloric Intake & Food Guide Pyramid Servings							

Daily Activity Record (Caloric Expenditure)

Time	Activity	Calories	Minutes	No. of Steps

Personal Goals this Week	Most of the Time	Some of the Time	Rarely
1. Meet or exceed walking goal of _____ steps each day			
2. Shop on a full stomach			
3. Shop from a list			
4. Park shopping cart at the end of the aisles			
5. Eat 2–3 servings from the Milk Group			
6. Eat less than _____ calories each day			

Lesson Eight

Welcome to Lesson Eight. In this lesson, I would like to raise the potentially touchy, but important issue of family relationships. We'll then continue our discussion on physical activity. Thus far, I have spoken mainly of walking as a way of staying physically active. Yet, there are many other activities you might like to try. Having several activities available increases the chance that being active will be fun, and having fun is one key to making physical activity a permanent part of your life. I'll introduce you to an activity formula. We'll continue our discussion on nutrition by turning our attention to today's "toxic" food environment. You will learn more about the Food Guide Pyramid and vitamins, and we will take a close look at reading food labels. We have a lot to cover in this lesson, but it is all very interesting.

For You and Your Family to Read

Some time ago, I traveled to Argentina to speak before a large meeting of a group called FAMALCO in Buenos Aires. Loosely translated, FAMALCO stands for "Families Anonymous of Relatives Fighting Against Obesity." I would like to share what I learned from this experience with you and your family, *so please ask your family to read this.*

The FAMALCO meeting began with moving testimonials from husbands, wives, children, and parents of people struggling with their weight. Some of the family members expressed sorrow about the weight problem, while others related dismay, sympathy, anger, and hostility. One thing common to all was the pain, suffering, and frustration experienced by both the overweight person and the family. FAMALCO allowed the family members to discuss these issues with others in the same situation and provided many opportunities for the families to learn new ways to help the family member and to help themselves.

This meeting reinforced my belief that families can be a great resource for a person losing weight, but that harmony between the individual and the family requires a special effort from both parties. Communication is the first step. The burden falls to the person losing weight to express how he or she feels and how the family can help. This is sometimes diffi-

cult when the person resents the family's response to his or her weight. However, you must communicate by talking to your family and expressing your feelings.

The same responsibility applies to the family. The person with the weight problem may have only a superficial knowledge of how the family feels. When the family members finally express their feelings, the individual is likely to be relieved because the cards are on the table. This permits open discussion, positive communication, and suggestions from both parties about how best to work together. I now recommend that your family and you read the section in Lesson Five, page 75, on "Communicating with Your Partner." You can use the guidelines presented there to begin and sustain the communication with your family.

When I completed my lecture before FAMALCO, the audience responded with a warm, loud ovation. I assured the audience that I had learned at least as much from them as they had learned from me. I was even more certain of this when I listened to the speaker following me, Dr. Alberto Cormillot.

Dr. Cormillot is a prominent physician and public official in Buenos Aires, known all over Argentina for his work on weight loss. He developed a comprehensive approach to weight management that would rival any in the world. In his talk, Dr. Cormillot listed a number of things the family should or should not do. They are as relevant in our country as they are in his.

 **RELATIONSHIP RESOURCES**

Things the Family Should Avoid

➡ *Do not hide food from the person losing weight.* He or she will find it and feel resentful.

➡ *Do not threaten.* Behavior is best changed with a soft touch, not coercion, so be nice.

➡ *Do not avoid social situations because of the person's weight.* This will batter the self-esteem of the family member losing weight and will breed resentment in the family.

➡ *Do not expect perfection or 100 percent recovery.* Weight problems are something a person learns to manage, not cure. There will be periods of misery, weight gain, and overeating. The individual's achievements should be appreciated and the setbacks met with compassion.

➡ *Do not lecture, criticize, or reprimand.* These rarely help. The person needs to feel better, not worse.

➡ *Do not play the role of victim or martyr.* Overweight has many causes, both psychological and physiological. It is not helpful for the family to blame the overweight family member or to feel victimized. Support and encouragement will do more than guilt and shame.

Families can be a great resource for a person losing weight, but that harmony between the individual and the family requires a special effort from both parties.

Things the Family Can Do

➡ *Keep a positive attitude.* This sounds trite but can be very important. It is not easy to be upbeat and encouraging when a program grinds on for months and months. Extra effort from the family can make life much easier for the person losing weight.

➡ *Talk with others in your situation.* Being in a family where a weight problem exists generates strong feelings in the family members. It can help to talk about these with others who deal with the same issues. This process can generate many good ideas.

➡ *Keep the home and family relaxed.* This will permit the person on a program to pay attention to the task at hand, changing eating and exercise habits.

➡ *Learn to ignore and forgive lapses.* The family can react many ways to mistakes, bouts of weight gain, and binges. The person losing weight feels badly when these occur, so it is best for the family to adopt a hands-off policy and to forgive and forget.

➡ *Ask the person losing weight how you can help.* The best way to learn how to help is to ask. Family members are sometimes surprised by what the individual wants.

➡ *Exercise with the person on a program.* This is a wonderful and healthy way to spend time together. Even if you only take daily walks together, this pro- vides time to talk and to help the person with his or her program.

➡ *Develop new interests with the family member losing weight.* There are so many things in life to enjoy, and developing new interests can be good for everybody. Individuals losing weight sometimes feel they are embarking on a new life. New activities can involve the family in this process.

In summary, the family can help the person losing weight in many ways. It begins with communication and proceeds to the things listed above. Both the family and the individual are responsible for making these happen.

An Activity Blueprint

The work of experts in the exercise field has provided a growing body of evidence that regular, moderate-intensity physical activity can result in substantial health benefits. One of the primary benefits is protection against coronary heart disease. Other health benefits may include protection against several other chronic diseases, such as adult-onset diabetes, hypertension, certain cancers, osteoporosis, and depression.

While most of us would readily agree that regular physical activity is beneficial, most Americans are not physically active on a regular basis. According to the National Center for Health Statistics only about 30 percent of adults in the U.S. engage in regular physical activity. About 38 percent of adults are completely inactive, and the remaining 32 percent are not active

As you can see, most American adults do not get enough physical activity.

American Adult Physical Activity

30% are Active
38% are Inactive
32% are NOT Active Enough

enough. With all of the scientific evidence supporting the benefits of exercise, why are we a sedentary nation? Two reasons come to mind.

We live in a high-tech society; this is both a blessing and a curse. Today's technology can do wonderful things. Yet, in the process, we have engineered physical activity out of our daily lives. The more technologically advanced we become, the more inactive we become. Automobiles, garage-door openers, portable telephones, television, remote controls for most electrical devices, the Internet, and many other labor-saving gadgets have changed the way we work, take care of our homes, and spend our leisure time. Technology entices us to be inactive, and our environment presents many barriers to being active. Walking to the corner store is difficult if there are not adequate sidewalks. Riding a bicycle or walking to work is difficult because people living in the suburbs live far from their work. Drive-thru windows at the bank, dry cleaners, and fast-food restaurants keep us in our cars and save time.

People also are inactive because of misconceptions. For years we were told that exercise had to be strenuous and must be done for long periods. This led to the false belief that a person must exercise a tremendous amount to get *any* benefit. We now know this is simply not true. The following guidelines may help to dispel this old myth.

Guidelines for Physical Activity

In July of 1993, the American College of Sports Medicine and the U.S. Centers for Disease Control and Prevention, in cooperation with the President's Council on Physical Fitness and Sports, released new exercise guidelines and recommendations for Americans. These recommend *30 minutes or more* of moderate-intensity physical activity on most days of the week (at least five days). The 1996 Surgeon General's Report on Physical Activity and Health also recommended *at least 30 minutes* of physical activity daily. The important take-home message from these guidelines is that any exercise helps, *more is better,* and the *total* amount of physical activity can be *cumulative.* In other words, you don't have to exercise for 30 minutes all at one time.

This is wonderful news! Six, 5-minute walks throughout the day count as 30 minutes of activity. Remember, your goal here is moderate-intensity activity (walking one mile in about 15–20 minutes). Activities that also can contribute to the 30-minute total include walking up stairs, gardening, cleaning house, raking leaves, and walking part or all of the way to and from work. The recommended 30 minutes of physical activity may also come from planned exercise or recreation, such as jogging, riding a bicycle, playing golf or tennis, or swimming. A brisk two-mile walk is another way to achieve 30 minutes of physical activity.

EXERCISE ESSENTIALS

Thirty minutes of physical activity each day may sound like a lot, but try not to let this discourage you. Remember, *accumulating* only 30 minutes of physical activity provides important health benefits because every bit **counts**. This is why I stress the importance of setting reasonable physical activity goals. Throughout The LEARN Program, you have been gradually increasing your steps or the time you spend being active. You can see why I am a big proponent of using a step counter. It counts every step and gives you credit for the exercise you do.

As you can see, there are many reasons to increase your physical activity. The best advice is to build physical activity into your daily routine—make it part of your lifestyle, just like eating, working, and sleeping. The physical and psychological aspects of a more active lifestyle can be quite rewarding.

Starting a Programmed Activity

Tape/CD 3 Section 9

Physical activity is one key to your success at weight management. It is one of the most powerful means at your disposal to reduce your risk for heart disease and other serious illnesses. Being active can put more life into every step you take, give you more energy, make you feel better about your body, and improve your mood. Best of all, it can help you maintain your weight loss.

Identifying your *barriers* to being physically active can be very helpful. Barriers that often get in the way include embarrassment, being timid about exercise, thinking that you couldn't possibly do as much as necessary, and practical issues such as time. I have given you enough ammunition throughout this program to challenge and defeat each of these obstacles.

Now is a great time to rise above the barriers, and start the activity.

LIFESTYLE PROFILES

Judy has been struggling to meet her physical activity goal of 30 minutes per day, most days of the week. Between working full-time, taking care of her two children, and spending time with her husband, Judy has a difficult time squeezing physical activity into her day. She would like to join a water aerobics class but is afraid that people will snicker behind her back when she puts on a bathing suit. She knows that she can meet her activity goal by taking several short walks during the day, but she doesn't feel like she is reaching her goal. Judy described these exercise barriers to her LEARN program group, who helped brainstorm a list of possible strategies to overcome her barriers (see Judy's example of Physical Activity Barriers and Solutions on page 124). If you are not in a group, you may want to ask your partner, friends, or family members to help you identify solutions. Take a few minutes now to list your barriers in the table on page 125. Think of possible solutions to overcoming each barrier and write them down. Try to incorporate these solutions into your program. When you have finished, let's move on to choosing programmed activities.

Choosing the Best Activity

A terrific definition of the "best" activity is whatever you choose that you enjoy enough to do again. Many activities are available. I discuss several examples below. In making your decision, carefully consider these four things:

➡ **Select something you can do.** Consider your current physical condition when choosing an activity. For example, competitive basketball is strenuous and may not be advisable if you are not in tip-top condition, but friendly, non-competitive activities may be just right for you. Pick something where you can move at your own pace. Walking, cy-

Physical Activity Barriers and Solutions *(Judy's Example)*	
Barrier	**Possible Solution**
Lack of time	1. Get up 15 minutes early and walk before my family wakes up. 2. Politely decline coworkers' invitations to go out to lunch and walk for 20 minutes during my lunch break. 3. Walk around the field during my daughter's soccer game. 4. Ask my husband to pick up the children at their music lessons so I can get to my water aerobics class on my way home from work.
Embarrassed to exercise in public	1. Tell myself that most active people will give me a lot of credit for exercising and not make fun of me. 2. Wear a tee-shirt over my bathing suit. 3. Sign up for a water aerobics class that has other people with weight issues. 4. Buy an exercise video so I can work out in the privacy of my living room.
I don't feel like I'm reaching my exercise goals	1. Wear a step counter so that I get "credit" for the extra physical activity that I do get during the day. 2. Buy a stopwatch so that I can time and keep track of my two-minute walks (they really do add up!). 3. Measure a one-mile route in my neighborhood by driving my car and noting the mileage. 4. Remember to record my 45-minute water aerobics class on my Monitoring Form since the step counter won't record it.

cling, and swimming are good examples.

➡ **Select something you like to do.** Hiking may be something that always caught your fancy, so go ahead and try it. If you are turned off by swimming, don't do it just because you think you should. Remember, choosing activities you enjoy doing is important.

➡ **Select a solo or social activity.** We covered this earlier in our discussion of walking. In your choice of an activity, consider whether you would like to exercise alone (jogging, swimming, cycling) or with other people (tennis, golf, aerobics class, a walking group). If you are a social person, having others around can be an incentive to participate.

➡ **Do not be embarrassed.** This is easier said than done. Many heavy people avoid exercise completely or avoid it when others can see them. They are embarrassed about their bodies, their clothes, and their poor physical condition. If this sounds familiar, try putting this thought aside. Take a deep breath, and ask yourself, "Which is more important, avoiding embarrassment or losing weight?"

A Helpful Tip

Let me pass along a tip drawn from my own experience. I exercise regularly and try to have a number of activities from which to choose. I run, ride a bike, play tennis, and do strength training. Mixing up these activities provides me with choice and variety, both of which help minimize boredom. I can watch TV, listen to music, or both while doing some of these activities, so I sometimes choose to run on the treadmill or ride the stationary bike when I know there is something I might like to see on the television.

Most people can find more than one activity to do. If an outside activity is not possible, then an inside alternative might fit the bill. The key is whether you will still be active months or years from now. Whether this occurs depends in large part on whether you enjoy it, and whether you enjoy it may depend on variety and the pres-

My Physical Activity Barriers and Solutions	
Barrier	**Possible Solution**
	1. 2. 3. 4.
	1. 2. 3. 4.
	1. 2. 3. 4.

ence of other interesting things. If you only enjoy one type of activity, that's fine. Some regular exercisers only do one thing.

Warming Up and Cooling Down

Warming up before exercising and cooling down afterwards is important. This will help stretch your muscles and may avoid strains, pulls, cramps, and discomfort. Warming up also will help your heart and circulatory system make the transition from rest to exercise and then back to rest. You should warm up and cool down at least five minutes for a 30-minute bout of exercise.

In general, a good warm-up for most activities is the same activity performed at lower intensity. For example, walking slowly is a good warm-up for brisk walking, and brisk walking can serve as a warm-up for running. Below are several warm-up exercises. Please note that some exercises may be problematic if you have certain conditions. For instance, trunk twists may be difficult if you have back problems. Choose warm-up exercises that you can comfortably do. Check with your physician or a sports medicine specialist if you have any specific needs or problems.

➡ **Trunk Twists.** Stand with your feet shoulder-width apart. Extend your arms to the side so they are horizontal. Twist your trunk to the right as if you are trying to look over your right shoulder. Then reverse directions, and move your trunk so your left arm extends to your right. Do this exercise slowly or as a held stretch to avoid jerking the muscles.

➡ **Upper back, shoulders, and chest.** Raise your arms above your head, and clasp your hands together loosely. Hold for 10 seconds, then lower your clasped hands in front of you (parallel to the ground) while rounding your back. Hold for 10 seconds. Then clasp your hands behind your back, and pull your shoulders back gently to open up your chest. Another way to stretch your back and shoulders is to sit in a chair and bend forward until your chest touches (or comes close to touching) your knees. Let your arms dangle loosely toward the floor.

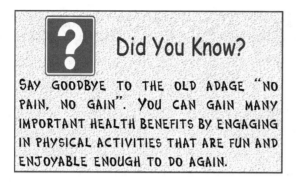

Did You Know?

SAY GOODBYE TO THE OLD ADAGE "NO PAIN, NO GAIN". YOU CAN GAIN MANY IMPORTANT HEALTH BENEFITS BY ENGAGING IN PHYSICAL ACTIVITIES THAT ARE FUN AND ENJOYABLE ENOUGH TO DO AGAIN.

→ **Arm Circles.** In the standing position, hold your arms out to the side of your body in a horizontal position. Roll your arms up, back, and then down to produce backward circles.

→ **Toe Touches.** Stand with your feet a little more than shoulder-width apart. Bend at the waist, and slowly attempt to touch your toes with your fingertips. Keep your knees bent, and do not bounce the upper body. Hold the stretch for a few seconds. Return to the standing position and then repeat. If you have back problems, the following sit-and-reach exercise may present fewer difficulties.

→ **Sit-and-Reach.** Sit on the floor with your legs straight out in front of you. Slowly reach to touch your toes, and hold the reach for a few seconds. As with the toe touches, keeping the legs bent is important to avoid strain on the knees and back.

→ **Quadriceps (thighs).** Stand next to a wall, tree, or chair for balance. Reach back, and slowly pull your right foot up toward your buttocks until you feel a gentle stretch along the front of your thigh. Keep your right knee pointing straight down, and close to your left knee. Hold the foot for 10 or more seconds; release and repeat with the other leg.

→ **Hamstrings.** Stand with one foot on a chair, bench, step, or curb. Keep this knee almost straight, and flex your foot back slightly. Slowly bend forward from the hips, keeping your back straight, until you feel a stretch in the back of your thigh. Slowly straighten up after 10 or more seconds. Repeat with the other leg.

→ **Upper calf muscles stretch.** Stand with one foot about 18 inches in front of the other and 3 to 4 feet from a wall or tree. Lean forward with your back straight and place both hands on the wall or tree. Slowly bring your hips forward while keeping your back leg straight and your heels flat on the floor. Hold the position for 10 or more seconds, then ease your hips back. Repeat with the other leg.

→ **Lower calf muscles and Achilles tendon stretch.** Start with your feet, hands and body in the same position as the upper-calf muscles stretch. Slowly bend your knees, keeping your heels flat on the floor. Hold for 10 or more seconds, then rise slowly. Repeat with the other leg. Alternate this stretch with the upper-calf muscles stretch.

When you begin your programmed activity, be it cycling, swimming, walking, or anything, begin slowly, and gradually increase your pace. To end your exercise session, gradually decrease the pace, and then finish with some combination of the exercises described above. The warming up and cooling down activities are worth the little extra time they take. They can prevent nagging injuries that can keep you away from exercise for a long time.

Cardiovascular Training

Aerobic exercise is the best way to improve your cardiovascular condition—the efficiency of your heart, blood vessels, and general circulatory and respiratory systems. Aerobic activities are rhythmic and use large muscle groups. Brisk walking, hiking, running, swimming, cycling, stair climbing, cross-country skiing, dancing, jumping rope, water aerobics, and skating are examples of aerobic activities. These activities strengthen the heart and lungs and improve the body's ability to use oxygen. Over time, doing aerobic exercise can

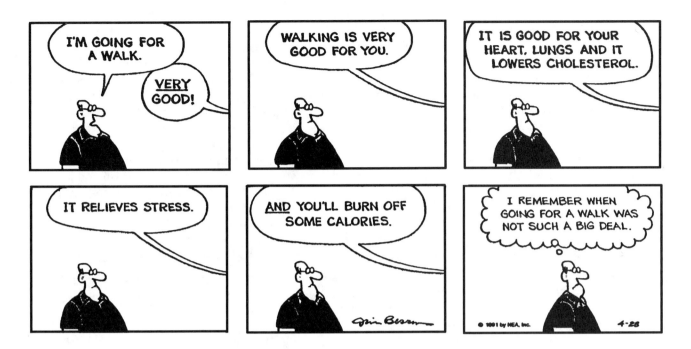

decrease your heart rate and blood pressure and improve your breathing. This type of activity is also associated with greater life expectancy, lowered risk of heart disease, and other health benefits.

How much aerobic exercise do you have to do to improve your cardiovascular condition? Exercise physiologists have done extensive research to answer this question. From this research a formula known to millions of people was born—the F.I.T. principle. This formula describes the *optimal* exercise **F**requency (how often), **I**ntensity (how hard), and **T**ime (how long) to improve cardiovascular conditioning. To achieve *optimal* cardiovascular fitness, the American College of Sports Medicine recommends that you perform an aerobic activity three to five days per week for 20–60 minutes per session at an intensity that is 55–90% of your maximal heart rate (predicted maximal heart rate = 220-age). For example, for someone who is 40 years old, maximum heart rate would be 180 beats per minute (220-40). During a workout, this person would want the heart to beat 99–162 times per minute (this is 55–90 percent of the maximum of 180 beats per minute). If you exercise at the lower end of this heart rate range, your activity session should be closer to 60 minutes. Keep in mind that you will increase your cardiovascular conditioning by performing 30 to 60 minutes of moderate-intensity aerobic activities most days of the week, but to achieve optimal improvements, you may want to increase the intensity and duration of your exercise sessions. I mention cardiovascular fitness here so that you are familiar with commonly used terms and meanings. This may be something you can shoot for a year or more down the road as you lose weight and improve your fitness.

Danger! An Exercise Threshold Attitude

Many people on weight loss programs labor under the insidious influence of a dangerous attitude—the exercise threshold. They feel they must do a magic amount of exercise for it to have any value. One client asked me, "Is it enough that I walked around the block after dinner last night?" Implicit in the word "enough," is that exercising below this threshold has no value. You must banish this concept from your mind!

The threshold concept was born from the cardiovascular training idea discussed above. If you will forgive me for stating it again—*any exercise is better than no exercise*. Walking around the block is not as impressive as running a marathon, but it's better than watching reruns of *Gilligan's Island* and munching on corn chips. If you walk two blocks, it is better than one block, but not as good as three blocks. Do anything to be active. Remember, small amounts of exercise add up, so do not feel you must strain to accomplish some arbitrary level.

Physical Activity Checkup

Now that you are more than half way through the program, let's stop for a moment and assess how you are doing with being more physically active. Before we do, let me first give you a perspective on what others are usually doing at this stage of the program.

Some people, typically those who grew up doing sports, can readily adopt a program of exercise. They may be discouraged by being in poor shape, but they can generally see themselves being more active as their conditioning improves. Others may have been active in the past but feel this is forever gone, given how little exercise they do now. Still, others have never been active and are having a hard time getting mobilized. If you are having difficulty increasing your physical activity, try not to beat yourself up. After all, weight gets in the way of physical activity for both physical and emotional reasons. Becoming active requires a major shift in thinking for many people.

I have spoken a great deal about having reasonable weight goals. Having reasonable physical activity goals also is important. The object is not to have you do some magic amount of exercise, but to increase your level of activity from where you started. If you have been successful thus far, you deserve to be pleased. And remember, being more active is important beyond its effect on your weight—it is good for your health in its own right. So, get as much activity as you can, and have fun at it. You'll benefit in many ways.

Bracing Yourself Against a Toxic Food Environment

Tape/Cd 3
Section 5

Americans face a toxic environment. The temptations to eat are constant, powerful, and compelling, and the barriers to being physically active are numerous. As a nation, we have accepted this without much protest. In the next lesson, I will talk about the toxic activity environment. For now, let's focus on food.

Think of the number of fast-food restaurants you find within a 15-minute drive of your home. In addition to the national chains like McDonald's, Burger King, Wendy's, and KFC, local and regional restaurants abound. Most have drive-thru windows, serve breakfast, may be open 24 hours a day, and some even deliver. Nearly every service station has been remodeled to include a mini-market, and many have teamed up with one or more of the national

fast-food chains. Practically every shopping mall has a food court. Vending machines are everywhere, including schools. Fast-food chains like McDonald's are showing up in airports, airplanes, and even hospital lobbies!

Let's look at one example of how today's environment is so challenging. Many fast-food restaurants offer package meals or combos (McDonald's calls its package a value meal). More calories for less money—some value, eh? They also offer, at a seemingly good price, the opportunity to get extra large drinks and fries, when you "supersize" your meal. This is so much a part of the American landscape that the word "supersize" has become a familiar verb. The value meals and the supersize portions are a powerful and effective means companies use to market their foods.

Food advertising is also a problem. Madison Avenue's brightest minds set to work to convince us that we should eat foods that are high in calories, fat, and sugar. The average American child sees 10,000 food commercials each year, 95 percent of which are for fast foods, sugared cereals, candy, and soft drinks.

It is not stretching the language to say that the environment is toxic. We are exposed to and are encouraged to consume things that can contribute to deadly diseases such as heart disease and cancer. We rail against the tobacco companies for exposing us to temptations to smoke, especially when the inducements are aimed at children, but we remain remarkably quiet when the same thing happens with unhealthy food. I expect that over time the public will begin to develop a more militant attitude toward this.

What does this mean for you? It means that you must find creative ways to resist the environmental pressures to buy unhealthy foods. Part of this lies in developing the right attitude—in some cases an angry one. When you see the drive-thru sign, remember that it is designed to make it easier and more convenient for you to

stop in and spend your money. When you see the junk food stores in the food court, remember that they are in business to sell their food—healthy or not—to as many people as possible. When you fill your car with gas, remember that there is an industry that sells chips, pastries, ice cream, and soft drinks that wants you to succumb. Get mad, and resist! Later in the program I will give you tips for eating away from home. For now I want you to be aware of the thousands of environmental food cues designed to get you to eat more. Again, resist, resist, resist!

The other way to deal with this pressure is be aware of it and avoid exposure as much as possible. When you can, avoid being around these places. If you are at the mall, stay away from the food court or eat before you go shopping. Use a credit card to pay for gas at the pump rather than go inside. Try not to drive by the fast-food places when you are hungry. Most of all, keep alert to these inducements to eat and see that you—not the multi-billion-dollar-a-year food industry—are in charge of your eating and your health.

Counting Grams of Fat

As I discuss earlier in this program, there are many reasons why dietary fat is a central issue in a weight management program. For instance, fat has many calories.

Also, research has related fat intake to risks of heart disease and some cancers. For these reasons, some nutrition experts recommend that individuals keep a record of their fat gram intake—in addition to or in lieu of counting calories.

Your dietary objectives will help you decide whether to count calories or fat grams. If your objective to making dietary changes is to reduce the risk for chronic disease, counting fat grams would be sensible. If weight management is the issue, counting calories is the reasonable choice. A diet high in fat is typically high in calories, and vice-versa, but exceptions exist. For instance, you could drink 25 cans of Coca Cola each day and take in little fat. Yet, you could still gain weight because of the high sugar (calorie) content.

Some individuals who use this program choose to record grams of fat and calories on their Monitoring Forms. Because fat intake is so important, I have provided the grams of fat in the Calorie Guide in Appendix G and calorie values in many tables throughout this manual. Feel free to record fat grams on your Monitoring Forms if you wish, but remember that keeping an accurate record of your calorie intake is essential.

Reduced-Fat Foods

The food companies have been working hard to develop products with less fat. The enormous popularity of reduced-sugar items such as diet soft drinks has led to a frantic search for ways to preserve the taste of foods while lowering the amount of nutrients that may contribute to health problems.

Today, we see more and more food items that have reduced fat, in some cases because they include fat substitutes. For the most part, I believe these are positive developments as they will allow people to enjoy some of the foods they like but with fewer calories and grams of fat. One risk lies in the way people interpret and then make use of terms like "low fat."

Low fat does not mean low calories. In fact, some low-fat cookies now on the market have nearly as many calories as the cookies they hope to replace. True, if one is destined to eat a certain number of cookies, then it would be better to have the reduced-fat versions. Still, we cannot assume this will cut calories. Some people feel that because a food seems healthy that they can eat more. So, if you encounter cookies, crackers, and other foods that are low in fat, be certain to check the calories. For some people, the marketing of these products has had a paradoxical effect—people feel they can eat more and thus *increase* their calorie intake.

Facts about Supplements

Do you take vitamins or other supplements? Chances are the answer is yes. Do you *need* the vitamins you take? Maybe not.

The amount of money made on vitamins and other supplements is unbelievable. The amount of fraud and exploitation is intolerable. An example from my own experience shows this. I once stopped in a health food store hoping to find some fruit. Upon entering, the owner was prescribing an assortment of supplements to a woman who had arthritis and heart disease. She seemed to have little money but was willing to risk it on the hope that the fellow might be right. What he told her was not only false but might possibly have harmed her.

When asked why he thought this would help the woman, his response was "prove that it doesn't." He felt no burden to show that his advice was safe and effective. He then asked if I had cancer, diabetes, poor vision, or impotence (!) and pointed to shelves of supplements that looked like alphabet soup.

This fellow was in his own small business, but similar hoaxes occur in recognized stores, through mail-order companies, and over the internet. Many malls, shopping centers, and downtown shopping

districts have such stores that seem official because of their fancy displays, nice signs, and wholesome appearance. Yet, they may be selling products that exploit and hurt people.

Perhaps some straightforward talk will help clarify this confusing situation. Before I tell you more about vitamins, let me state my beliefs about vitamins and weight loss, a belief shared by every nutrition expert I have consulted:

THERE IS NO EVIDENCE THAT ANY VITAMIN OR COMBINATION OF VITAMINS HELPS PEOPLE LOSE WEIGHT

Thankfully, more research is being done to test the effects of taking vitamins and other supplements. As this science matures, we will learn more and more about what to take. Right now, it's a crap shoot.

The government does a very poor job of regulating supplements. Companies can sell just about whatever they want, can say the most preposterous things in advertisements, and in some cases are allowed to keep selling products even after people start dying. When you see supplement ad-

vertisements making such claims on TV, in newspapers, on fancy internet sites, or even in the national drug store chains, you should have no confidence that it has been tested adequately, that it works, and that it is safe.

With that said, some products are legitimate and have been tested. The safest way to make good decisions is to speak with your doctor and to keep up on objective information. A good source is the *Nutrition Action Healthletter* published by the Center for Science in the Public Interest (www. cspinet.org).

Back to vitamins. To review from Lesson Seven on page 110, vitamins are required for the transformation of energy in the body and for the regulation of metabolism. They do not produce energy themselves, but they are crucial to the body's energy process. Nutrition experts feel, as a general rule, that most people in developed countries, particularly the U.S., receive adequate vitamins if they eat a balanced diet. People may not need vitamin supplements, much less the mega doses prescribed by someone with unproven ideas. Because you are exercising more and eating less, taking a multiple vitamin each day may be a good idea to help remedy any deficiency created by the change in food intake, but again, speak with your doctor.

The Antioxidant Vitamins

You have undoubtedly heard about "antioxidants" and their ability to prevent aging or promote health. Many food manufacturers now fortify their products with antioxidant vitamins such as beta carotene (vitamin A), vitamin C, and vitamin E. Let's take a quick look at the science.

Every cell in your body requires a constant supply of oxygen to utilize the energy (glucose) supplied by the blood. When the body's cells burn oxygen, they form "free radicals" or oxygen by-products. These free radicals can damage body cells and tissues, including DNA. Cigarette smoke, burns, ultraviolet light, and other environmental factors also cause free radicals to form in your body.

Free radicals cause oxidation in your body. Oxidation can easily be seen when you slice an apple and witness the quick browning on the cut. If you dip the apple in orange juice which has vitamin C, it retains its white color and texture. This process is similar in your body. Free radicals cause oxidation or cell damage that may lead to health problems. Antioxidants in your body help to counteract the effects of free radicals. They scavenge or mop up free radicals and convert them to harmless waste products that are eliminated before they can do any damage. Some evidence exists that suggests antioxidants may help undo some of the damage already done to body cells. Research is still mixed on this, however.

The antioxidant vitamins include beta carotene (vitamin A), vitamin C, and vitamin E. Some enzymes that have trace minerals, such as selenium, copper, zinc, and manganese also act as antioxidants. Eating the suggested number of fruit and vegetable servings from the Food Guide Pyramid is the wisest approach to get plenty of antioxidant vitamins and miner-

> **? Did You Know?**
>
> FAT-FREE ON A FOOD LABEL DOES NOT MEAN THE PRODUCT DOES NOT CONTAIN FAT. EACH SERVING CAN STILL HAVE UP TO 0.5 GRAMS OF FAT.

als. Eating at least three servings daily of whole-grain foods containing vitamin E also is important. The debate continues about consuming additional amounts of antioxidants from dietary supplements. Continuing research will unlock the answers to these important questions. In the meanwhile, enjoy a wide variety of plenty of fruits, vegetables, and whole-grain foods with naturally-occurring antioxidants.

Reading Food Labels

By now, it should be apparent that one of the keys to eating right and losing weight is portion control (calorie control). Learning how to use and apply a calorie guide is one way you can control the number of calories you eat each day. Another helpful tool is the food label. The U.S. government has passed legislation requiring almost all food products to include a standardized labeling system. Food labels can be very helpful, and you should know what they mean to you. The following discussion will help you understand how to read and use food labels.

Food label reform was enacted in 1990 to serve three primary purposes. The first is to help Americans choose a more healthful diet. The second is to decrease the confusion about advertising descriptions and other misleading information that had prevailed for years. Finally, the labeling requirements offer an incentive for food companies to improve the nutritional quality of their products.

Nutrition information is voluntary for many raw foods, including the 20 most frequently eaten fresh fruits and vegetables and raw fish. Although currently voluntary, the Nutrition Labeling and Education

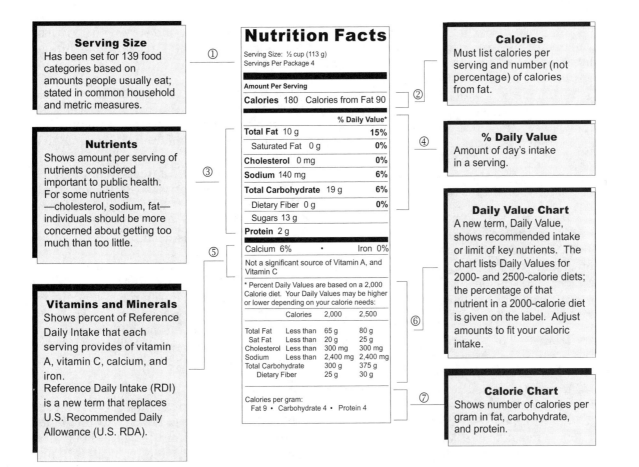

Serving Size
Has been set for 139 food categories based on amounts people usually eat; stated in common household and metric measures.

Nutrients
Shows amount per serving of nutrients considered important to public health. For some nutrients —cholesterol, sodium, fat— individuals should be more concerned about getting too much than too little.

Vitamins and Minerals
Shows percent of Reference Daily Intake that each serving provides of vitamin A, vitamin C, calcium, and iron.
Reference Daily Intake (RDI) is a new term that replaces U.S. Recommended Daily Allowance (U.S. RDA).

Nutrition Facts
Serving Size: ½ cup (113 g)
Servings Per Package 4

Amount Per Serving

Calories 180   Calories from Fat 90

% Daily Value*

Total Fat 10 g	15%
Saturated Fat 0 g	0%
Cholesterol 0 mg	0%
Sodium 140 mg	6%
Total Carbohydrate 19 g	6%
Dietary Fiber 0 g	0%
Sugars 13 g	
Protein 2 g	

Calcium 6%	•	Iron 0%

Not a significant source of Vitamin A, and Vitamin C

* Percent Daily Values are based on a 2,000 Calorie diet. Your Daily Values may be higher or lower depending on your calorie needs:

		Calories	2,000	2,500
Total Fat	Less than		65 g	80 g
Sat Fat	Less than		20 g	25 g
Cholesterol	Less than		300 mg	300 mg
Sodium	Less than		2,400 mg	2,400 mg
Total Carbohydrate			300 g	375 g
Dietary Fiber			25 g	30 g

Calories per gram:
Fat 9 • Carbohydrate 4 • Protein 4

Calories
Must list calories per serving and number (not percentage) of calories from fat.

% Daily Value
Amount of day's intake in a serving.

Daily Value Chart
A new term, Daily Value, shows recommended intake or limit of key nutrients. The chart lists Daily Values for 2000- and 2500-calorie diets; the percentage of that nutrient in a 2000-calorie diet is given on the label. Adjust amounts to fit your caloric intake.

Calorie Chart
Shows number of calories per gram in fat, carbohydrate, and protein.

Act of 1990 (NLEA) states that if voluntary compliance is insufficient, nutrition information for such raw foods may become mandatory.

The Nutrition Facts Panel

The food label includes a nutrition facts panel that has two parts as shown in the diagram above. This title "Nutrition Facts" alerts consumers that the label meets the requirements of the label regulations. The top part (items 1–5 on the sample nutrition label above) of the panel includes product-specific information such as serving size, total calories, calories from fat, and other nutrition information that varies by food product. The second part of the panel (items 6–7 on the sample nutrition label above) is footnote information found only on larger packages. The footnote provides general dietary information about important nutrients. Let's look at the label a little closer.

Item 1—The place to begin when reading the Nutrition Facts panel is the serving size and the number of servings contained in the package. This is a crucial step. If you read incorrectly, you can add many unwanted calories to your diet. The sample nutrition label above, for example, is for ONE serving, and the package contains FOUR servings. Serving sizes are listed for generally familiar units such as cups or pieces, followed by the metric amount. Remember, food label serving sizes are not the same as Food Guide Pyramid serving sizes.

If you mistakenly read the label as the package containing one serving, thinking you will be eating only 180 calories, you would end up eating 720 calories instead.

Item 2—"Calories" and "Calories from Fat" also are important. Both terms are for each serving. Too often, people incorrectly read the "Total Fat" percentage in item 4 as the percentage of total calories per serving coming from fat. This is NOT the case. If you made this error on the sample nutrition label on page 133, you might assume that only 15% of the total calories come from fat. The 15% means *15% of your total daily fat calories* comes from one serving. In reality, for each serving, 90 of the total 180 calories come from fat. In other words, 50% of total calories of this food product come from fat. You can see how this common error can add many unwanted fat calories to your diet.

Item 3—The nutrients listed here are the ones that Americans typically eat in sufficient amounts or too much. Eating too much fat, cholesterol, or sodium may increase your risk for certain diseases like heart disease, high blood pressure, or certain cancers.

Item 4—The percentages on this part of the panel tell you how much of each nutrient *in a single serving* contribute to your *total daily diet* based on the recommended intake of nutrients. As described in the footnote in item 6 of the sample Nutrition Facts panel on page 133, these percentages are based on a daily intake of 2,000 calo-

ries. For example, one serving of this food provides 15% of the *total daily fat* intake, based on a 2,000 calorie per day diet.

The panel includes certain items that are mandatory and other items that are voluntary. Some of the terms included on the panel may be unfamiliar to you. References are made to Daily Values (DV) and comprise two sets of dietary guidelines: Reference Daily Intakes (RDIs) and Daily Reference Values (DRVs). To help make the label less confusing, however, only the term Daily Value is used.

%DVs are based on recommendations for a 2,000 calorie daily diet. The FDA set 2,000 calories as the reference amount for calculating %DVs on food labels. The %DV shows you the percent of the recommended daily amount of a nutrient contained in a single serving of food.

As a general guideline, 5%DV or less is low and 20% or more is high. This means that 5%DV or less is low for all nutrients, those you want to limit (e.g., total fat, saturated fat, sodium, and cholesterol) and those that you want in greater amounts (e.g., fiber, calcium, other vitamins and minerals, etc.).

Item 5—The typical American diet lacks sufficient dietary fiber, vitamin A, vitamin C, calcium, and iron. Thus, you should make sure you get enough of the nutrients listed here. These nutrients can improve health and help reduce the risk of certain diseases.

Reference Daily Intakes

The term Reference Daily Intakes (RDI) replaces the more familiar term U.S. Recommended Daily Allowance (U.S. RDA). The values for the RDIs remain the same as the old U.S. RDAs, at least for now. A major revision is currently underway to replace the RDI with revised recommendations called Dietary Reference Intakes (DRI). Until DRIs can be established for all nutrients, the more familiar RDI values will continue to appear on food labels and will be used by health professionals.

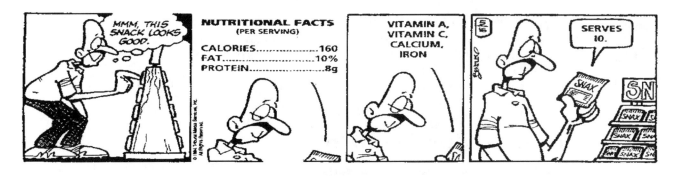

Item 6—Look at the * just after the "%Daily Value" column heading. This refers to the footnote in the lower portion of the nutrition label. The footnote tells you that the %DVs are based on recommendations for a 2,000 calorie diet. This statement is required on all food labels. However, the additional information may not appear on the package if the size of the label is too small. When the complete footnote does appear, it is always the same—it does not change from product to product.

Daily Reference Values

Under the label reform regulations, DRVs are established for nutrients that contain energy (calories). These include fat, carbohydrate (including fiber), and protein. It is important to understand these percentages so that they are not mistaken as percentages of total calories. The DRVs are based on the number of calories consumed per day. As a common reference, 2,000 calories is established as a daily intake. The DRVs for the energy nutrients are calculated in the following manner:

➡ Fat is based on 30 percent of calories.

➡ Saturated fat is based on 10 percent of calories.

➡ Carbohydrate is based on 60 percent of calories.

➡ Protein is based on 10 percent of calories. The DRV for protein applies only to adults and children over four years of age. RDIs for protein have been established for special groups.

➡ Fiber is based on 11.5 grams of fiber per 1000 calories.

The DRVs also include sources for some non-energy nutrients, including cholesterol, sodium, and potassium. In addition, the DRVs for fats, cholesterol, and sodium represent the highest limits that are recommended. These values are as follows:

➡ Total fat: less than 65 g

➡ Saturated fat: less than 20 g

➡ Cholesterol: less than 300 mg

➡ Sodium: less than 2400 mg

Ingredients List

The ingredients list of the food is required on the food label. Food components are listed in order by weight from the most to the least.

Take a few minutes to carefully read through the illustration of the food label on page 133. Knowing how to read a food label can save you time in the grocery store aisles and give you a leg up on good nutrition.

The Importance of Protein

Protein is a popular topic of conversation. We hear about high-protein diets and low-protein diets all the time. I also hear about liquid protein, protein bread, and protein supplements. What is this fuss all about?

Protein is the most abundant material in the body aside from water. It has many functions, and is found in all cells. It plays many roles:

➡ Protein is contained in hemoglobin, which carries oxygen in the blood.

➡ Protein is related to DNA (deoxyribonucleic acid), which provides the genes with the code to transmit heredity.

➡ Protein is used to build muscle and all other body tissue.

➡ Protein is an important part of insulin, which regulates blood sugar.

➡ Protein is used to build the enzymes that digest our food.

What Is Protein?

Proteins are built from approximately 20 amino acids that are put together in long chains. Protein can be synthesized or manufactured by the body, but only if the essential amino acids are present. Of the 20 different amino acids, nine are essential, and the body cannot manufacture them; hence, they must come from the foods we eat. The protein our bodies use best includes these essential amino acids. Our bodies can synthesize the 11 nonessential amino acids, but again, only if the building blocks are present. These building blocks include the nine essential amino acids, nitrogen, and calories.

You may have heard about high-quality and low-quality proteins. High-quality proteins are those the body can use to function properly, because they contain all of the essential amino acids. Low-quality proteins have one or more essential amino acids missing.

Sources of Protein

Meat and dairy products contain high-quality proteins and do not have to be supplemented with other proteins because they contain all nine of the essential amino acids. Plant proteins usually lack one or more of the essential amino acids, but with the right mix of plant sources, one can get adequate amounts of the essential and non-essential amino acids. Vegetarian diets can provide adequate protein if the sources are reasonably varied and the caloric intake is enough to meet the individual's energy needs.

Eating a variety of legumes and grains will provide high-quality protein. Legumes include dried peas and beans, such as black-eyed peas, chick peas (garbanzo beans), kidney beans, lentils, lima beans, navy beans, and soybeans. Soy protein has been shown to be nutritionally equivalent in protein value to proteins of animal origin. Nuts also are in this category, but they contain high amounts of fat. Grains include barley, corn, oats, rice, sesame seeds, sunflower seeds, and wheat.

Protein rarely exists by itself (egg whites or albumin is the exception) and is most often accompanied by mixtures of fat in foods like meat, fish, poultry, and milk products. Protein contains 4 calories per gram; this is the same caloric content by weight as carbohydrates. One ounce (28 grams) of lean meat, fish, or poultry contains approximately 7 grams of protein and 3 grams of fat (a total of 55 calories), whereas protein foods with higher fat content provide as much as 70–120 calories per ounce and 5–10 grams of fat per ounce.

How Much Protein Should You Eat?

Some health experts believe that Americans eat too much protein and that they should cut back. A major benefit would be a reduction in total fat, because the most popular protein foods (meat, fish, and poultry) also provide significant amounts of fat. We must remember, however, that protein in the diet is essential. Recommended amounts of protein range from 10–35 percent of total calories or approximately 50–175 grams of protein per day for adults. To see how your daily protein intake fits the guidelines for a healthy diet, multiply your target calorie level by 20 percent, about the average recommended protein calories per day. For example, if your target caloric intake is 2,000 calories, 2,000 x .20 = 400. Because there are 4 calories in every gram of protein, divide 400 by 4; 400 ÷ 4 = 100. You know that the average recommended daily intake of protein is about 100 grams for your daily calorie intake of 2,000 calories. For most people, the main source of dietary protein will come from the Meat, Poultry, Fish, Dry Beans, Eggs, and Nuts Group of the Food Guide Pyramid.

The Meat, Poultry, Fish, Dry Beans, Eggs, and Nuts Group

The food items in this food group include meat, poultry, fish, dry beans, eggs, and nuts. Meat, poultry, and fish provide good sources of protein, B vitamins, iron, and zinc. Dry beans, eggs, and nuts are similar to meats in providing protein and most vitamins and minerals.

How Much Is a Serving?

Generally, 2–3 oz of cooked lean meat, poultry, or fish count as one serving from the Meat and Protein Group. A 3-oz piece of meat is about the size of a deck of cards or the amount of meat on half a medium chicken breast. For other foods in this group, count 1–2 cups of cooked dry beans, 5 tablespoons of peanut butter, or 3 medium eggs as one serving. As an exam-

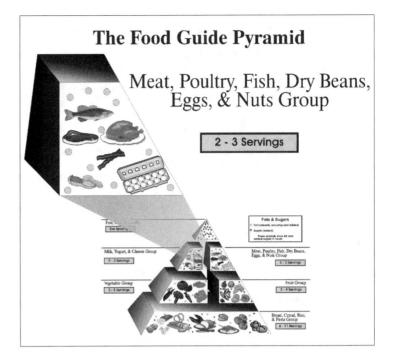

The Food Guide Pyramid

Meat, Poultry, Fish, Dry Beans, Eggs, & Nuts Group

2 - 3 Servings

ple, 6 oz for the day (two servings) may come from:

➡ 1 egg (counts as 1 oz of lean meat) for breakfast;

➡ 2 oz of sliced turkey in a sandwich at lunch; and

➡ 3 oz cooked lean hamburger for dinner.

How Many Servings?

The Food Guide Pyramid suggests two to three servings per day from the Meat and

"Call it McBroccoli if you want to, but I still won't eat it."

Meat, Poultry, Fish, Dry Beans, Eggs, & Nuts Group

(One Meat Group Serving Each)

Description	Cal	Pro (g)	Carb (g)	Fat Cal
Beef:				
Chuck arm roast, braised (2½ oz)	184	21	0	93
Ground (18% fat), broiled (2½ oz)	207	21	0	117
Prime rib, broiled (2½ oz)	286	15	0	223
Round, select, lean, rstd (2½ oz)	110	21	0	22
Sirloin, select, lean, rstd (2½ oz)	120	20	0	34
Lamb:				
Chop, choice, broiled (2½ oz)	224	18	0	147
Loin steak, choice, broiled (2½ oz)	210	18	0	131
Shank half, choice, roasted (2½ oz)	159	19	0	79
Pork:				
Bacon, smoked/cured ckd (2½ oz)	408	22	0	314
Chop, center loin, lean, braised (2½ oz)	143	21	0	53
Ham, whole cured, roasted (2½ oz)	117	16	0	49
Sausage, fresh, ckd (2½ oz)	262	14	1	199
Tenderloin, fresh, broiled (2½ oz)	142	21	0	52
Chicken:				
Breast, w/skin, roasted (2½ oz)	140	21	0	50
Breast, w/o skin, roasted (2½ oz)	117	22	0	23
Dark, w/skin, roasted (2½ oz)	153	19	0	71
Dark, w/o skin, roasted (2.7 oz)	146	21	0	58
Duck:				
Whole, skinless, roasted (2½ oz)	142	17	0	71
Fish/Seafood:				
Catfish filet, baked (2½ oz)	74	13	0	18
Flounder/sole filet, baked (2½ oz)	83	17	0	10
Haddock filet, baked (2½ oz)	79	17	0	6
Lobster, northern, boiled (2½ oz)	69	15	1	4
Orange roughy, baked (2½ oz)	63	13	0	6
Salmon, Atlantic filet, baked (2½ oz)	129	18	0	52
Shrimp, breaded, fried (3.7 oz)	291	12	26	143
Shrimp, broiled (2½ oz)	110	17	1	33
Trout filet, mixed species (2½ oz)	135	19	0	54
Dry Beans:				
Black beans, ckd (1.2 cups)	272	18	49	10
Cowpeas peas, ckd (1.2 cups)	222	14	39	14
Chickpeas beans, ckd (1.2 cups)	323	17	54	46
Great north beans, ckd (1.2 cups)	251	18	45	9
Lima beans, baby, boiled (1.2 cups)	275	18	51	7
Navy beans, ckd (1.2 cups)	310	19	57	11
Pink beans, ckd (1.2 cups)	302	18	57	9
Pinto beans, ckd (1.2 cups)	281	17	53	10
Red kidney beans, ckd (1.2 cups)	263	19	48	2
Soybeans, ckd (2½ cups)	744	72	43	347
Eggs:				
Egg, whole, med, fried (2.8 each)	256	17	2	174
Egg, whole, large, boiled (2.2 each)	198	16	1	122
Nuts:				
Almonds, dry roasted (4.2 oz)	711	26	23	566
Cashews, oil roasted (3.8 oz)	621	17	31	467
Peanut butter, creamy (5 tbs)	474	20	15	367
Peanuts, dry roasted (4.2 oz)	697	28	26	532
Pecan nuts, dry roasted (3.4 oz)	684	9	13	644
Walnuts, dried English (3 oz)	556	13	12	499

Note: This table should be used only as a guide for the foods listed. Because food values vary by brand, it is important to read food labels carefully for these foods.

Protein Group. The total from all servings should be the equivalent of between 5 and 7 oz of cooked lean meat, poultry, or fish per day. The table on the left shows single-serving foods from this food group.

Watch out for Fat

As mentioned earlier, the best sources of protein come from animal products, such as dairy, meat, poultry, fish, and eggs. However, these food sources can be high in saturated fat and cholesterol. These tips will help reduce fat in your diet:

➡ Choose lean meat, fish, poultry without skin, and dried beans and peas. These food choices are low in dietary fat.

➡ Prepare meats in low-fat ways; trim away all the visible fat and boil, roast, grill, or broil these foods instead of frying.

➡ Eat egg yolks sparingly—they are high in cholesterol. Use only one yolk per person in egg dishes and make larger portions by adding extra egg whites.

➡ Remember, nuts and seeds are high in fat, so eat them in moderation.

➡ For beef roasts and steaks of round, loin, sirloin, and chuck arm are lean choices.

➡ For pork roasts and chops of tenderloin, center loin and ham are the leaner choices.

➡ For veal, all cuts are generally lean, except for ground veal.

➡ Lamb roasts and chops of leg, loin, and fore shanks provide the lean cuts.

➡ Fish and shellfish are generally low in fat; however, those canned or marinated in oil are higher.

➡ For chicken and turkey, both light and dark meat are lean choices provided the skin has been removed.

For Vegetarians

Food choices from the Meat and Protein Group will be different if you follow a vegetarian diet. Soy milk is a good source of protein and tofu and tempeh can be substituted for meat, poultry, and fish. If you are a vegetarian, you should consider consulting a registered dietitian to help you plan your meals. A registered dietitian can help you plan your diet to insure that you are eating adequate protein and meeting all of your nutritional needs.

MY WEEKLY GOALS

As you set your personal goals for this lesson, focus on your relationship with other family members. This is also a good time to think about increasing your physical activity. Set reasonable goals that can lead to the recommended levels of physical activity (10,000 steps daily or between 30–60 minutes). Remember that physical activity is associated with long-term weight management, so being active improves your chances of conquering weight and eating problems.

Focus this week on the amount of protein you eat and check to make sure you are eating 2–3 servings from the Meat, Poultry, Fish, Dry Beans, Eggs, and Nuts Group of the Food Guide Pyramid. Practice reading food labels this week and learn all you can about a food product from its label. Share this information with a family member or friend. Teaching someone else is a great way to learn new concepts.

Remember to record your weight change on the My Weight Change Record on page 216. Also, now is a good time to look back at the "My Reasonable Weight Loss" worksheet on page 217 to see how your actual weight change during the first eight weeks compares to what you planned in week two. If you have achieved your reasonable weight loss goals, congratulations! If you have not, now is a good time to re-evaluate your goals and check to make sure they are reasonable.

KNOWLEDGE REVIEW

Lesson Eight

1. T F Involving family members in your weight loss program is not important because behavior changes are all up to you.

2. T F Thirty minutes of incremental moderate-intensity physical activity per day are now recommended for Americans.

3. T F Warming up and stretching before exercise is to strengthen your muscles.

4. T F To improve your cardiovascular fitness you must do the right combination of frequency, intensity, and time.

5. T F Developing a militant attitude about the "toxic food environment" we face can be helpful.

6. T F Most Americans need to take a vitamin supplement because they do not get enough nutrients in the food they eat.

7. T F The Total Fat listed under the heading "% Daily Value" on the Nutrition Facts Panel of the Food Label indicates the percentage of calories from fat for one serving of the food.

8. T F Eating as much protein as you can to manage your weight is fine because protein is good for you.

9. T F The only way to get high-quality protein in your diet is to eat foods from the Meat, Poultry, Fish, Dry Beans, Eggs, & Nuts Group of the Food Guide Pyramid.

(Answers in Appendix C, page 223)

Monitoring Form—Lesson Eight

*Today's Date:*_____

Time	Food and Amount	Calories	Milk & Dairy	Meats & Protein	Vegetables	Fruits	Bread
Total Daily Caloric Intake & Food Guide Pyramid Servings							

Daily Activity Record (Caloric Expenditure)

Time	Activity	Calories	Minutes	No. of Steps

Personal Goals this Week	Most of the Time	Some of the Time	Rarely
1. Meet or exceed walking goal of _____ steps each day			
2. Discuss program with my family			
3. Select a programmed activity to begin			
4. Read food labels of the foods I eat			
5. Eat 2–3 servings from the Meat, Poultry, Fish, Dry Beans, Eggs and Nuts Group			
6. Eat less than _____ calories each day			

Lesson Nine

You have now completed eight lessons of The LEARN Program. I hope the first eight weeks of your program have gone well and that you are well on your way to managing your weight. In this lesson, you will learn more about positive attitudes, techniques for controlling your eating, and nutrition. We have covered a lot of material the past two months. I hope you are pleased with the information you are learning and the progress you are making. We still have much more to cover. The topics we will discuss over the next four weeks are very interesting. So, if you're ready, let's move on.

A Two-Month Review

This lesson marks another milestone in your weight management program. For two months now, you have been using The LEARN Program. I hope you have made meaningful changes in your diet, fitness level, attitudes, and overall health. Congratulations on your progress! You deserve much credit for all your hard work. Let's briefly review your efforts in these important areas.

Your Quality of Life

How is your quality-of-life today, compared with two months ago? Have your attitudes about weight and health in general improved? At this point in the program, many people have begun to change their views, focusing more on healthy lifestyle habits and less on the scale. As they continue to make better food choices and exercise more, they feel better about themselves and their ability to control what they eat. This feeling is a powerful motiva- tional tool.

The key is to make your changes continue to work for you—weaving them into the very fabric of your lifestyle. This way of thinking will help you lose weight, maintain the weight loss you have achieved, and feel better about yourself. On page 142 is a Quality of Life Review that is identical to the reviews you completed before. This review will help you see the important progress you have made and may highlight some areas that need additional work. Take time now to complete this review before continuing with the lesson. Record your scores in the Quality of Life Comparisons worksheet for Lesson Nine provided in Appendix B on page 214. How do your scores compare with your scores from Lesson Five?

Quality of Life Review

Please use the following scale to rate how satisfied you feel now about different aspects of your daily life. Choose any number from this list (1 to 9), and indicate your choice on the questions below.

1 = Extremely Dissatisfied

2 = Very Dissatisfied

3 = Moderately Dissatisfied

4 = Somewhat Dissatisfied

5 = Neutral

6 = Somewhat Satisfied

7 = Moderately Satisfied

8 = Very Satisfied

9 = Extremely Satisfied

1. _____ Mood (feelings of sadness, worry, happiness, etc.)

2. _____ Self-esteem

3. _____ Confidence, self-assurance, and comfort in social situations

4. _____ Energy and feeling healthy

5. _____ Health problems (diabetes, high blood pressure, etc.)

6. _____ General appearance

7. _____ Social life

8. _____ Leisure and recreational activities

9. _____ Physical mobility and physical activity

10. _____ Eating habits

11. _____ Body image

12. _____ Overall Quality of Life[1]

---

[1] Record your Overall Quality of Life score in the space provided in Appendix B, page 213.

Eating and Exercise Habits

We have not reviewed your eating and activity habits in detail for the last few lessons, but I hope you are still focused. Keeping your Monitoring Forms and increasing your physical activity can be two keys to long-term success. Your Monitoring Forms will tell you if you are eating the appropriate number of calories and exercising enough. Continue to use your records to identify patterns in your eating.

Are you measuring and weighing your food portions? This is something you don't have to do everyday, but it is a helpful strategy to do every now and then. People often feel frustrated when they *believe* they are eating 1,500 calories per day and not losing weight, when in reality, they may be eating over 2,000 calories per day. Remember, it is easy to "underestimate" your calorie intake. If you have not been measuring or weighing your food portion sizes, now may be a good time to dust off the food scale and bring out the measuring cups. During a meal at home, fill your plate as you normally would and write down the estimated serving sizes of your meal. Then, before you start to eat, measure each portion size carefully. How close were your *estimated serving* sizes to your actual *portion sizes*?

Some people dislike keeping the Monitoring Forms. They say that it takes too much time, the forms are too bulky to carry through the day, or that monitoring prevents them from enjoying their meals. If this is true for you, then stop using my forms and develop one of your own. You may want to use a 3" x 5" spiral pad or index cards. Similarly, you may want to develop your own records for weekends or times when you usually eat more. There are dozens of ways that you can track the foods you eat. Software programs are also available for your PC if you find them helpful. Find one that works for you if you don't like mine.

I hope that you are enjoying your walking program or whatever other activity you are doing. Remember, the object is to make sure that you enjoy the activities you are doing, set achievable goals, and focus on additional ways of making activity pleasurable. Take a few minutes to review your activity during the past two weeks. Were you as active as you would like to be or could have been? If not, try to determine the barriers that keep you from being active. Review the "Barriers to Physical Activity" section in Lesson Four on page 61 and your solutions to overcoming your particular barriers that you listed on page 125.

Weight Loss

After eight weeks on The LEARN Program, most people have lost about 4 to 6 percent of their starting weight (12–16 pounds). Look back to your "My Weight Change Record" on page 216 and see how you are doing. Also, look back at the "My Reasonable Weight Loss" worksheet you completed on page 217. Is your weight change at the end of week eight close to your goal weight projected on the worksheet? If not, now is a good time to make adjustments in your reasonable weight loss goal for the next four weeks and/or renew your self-monitoring efforts.

If you weighed 200 pounds before the program, I suspect you have lost about 8 to 12 pounds. If you have lost substantially less than this (less than 3 percent of your starting weight) or much more (more than 10 percent of your starting weight), you may want to talk with your doctor. While rapid weight loss is exciting, it can increase the risk of gallstones and other complications.

More likely, your health has continued to improve with weight loss. If you had high blood pressure or blood sugar, these conditions have probably improved even more since the first month of the program.

Honestly assessing your progress at this point in the program is important. If you have done well and feel successful, congratulate yourself, and tell yourself how proud you are of your accomplishments. Too often, people make key lifestyle changes and overlook them or fail to take credit for all their hard work. You deserve the credit and recognition. If you feel there are areas you still need to work on for topics already covered, take time to go back and work on them. Much more information remains in the last four lessons.

"I understand the importance of counting fat and calories, but do you really need a fork with a built-in calculator?"

Cholesterol

Some people mistakenly classify cholesterol as fat. Cholesterol is a waxy, fat-like substance that belongs to a class of molecules called steroids. It is necessary for the body's functioning and is found in many foods, in the bloodstream, and in all body cells. Our bodies also can manufacture cholesterol. Cholesterol is necessary for the formation and maintenance of cell membranes, sex hormones, production of bile salts, and for the conversion of sunlight (when the skin is exposed) into vitamin D.

High blood levels of cholesterol are related to increased risk for heart disease. The blood level of cholesterol is determined, in part, by what you eat.

Lipoproteins carry the cholesterol in the bloodstream. Some of the cholesterol attaches to the walls of the arteries as fatty streaks. When these deposits build, they form a fibrous plaque that restricts the blood flow through the arteries. If the artery narrows enough to stop or seriously restrict the flow of blood, vital tissue can be deprived and die. The result is a heart attack if the coronary arteries are involved or a stroke if the blocked arteries supply blood to the brain.

Knowing your own cholesterol level can be important. The National Cholesterol

Cholesterol Content of Common Foods

Description	Cal	Fat Cal	Fat (g)	Sat Fat (g)	Chol (mg)
Milk Group:					
Cheese, American processed, 2 oz	186	126	14	9	36
Cheese, cheddar, 1.5 oz	171	127	14	9	45
Cheese, Colby, low-fat, 1.5 oz	74	27	3	2	9
Cheese, cottage, low-fat, 2 cups	324	41	5	3	18
Cheese, cream, 1.5 oz	148	133	15	9	47
Cheese, mozzarella, whole milk, 1.5 oz	135	94	10	7	38
Cheese, mozzarella, part skim, 1.5 oz	119	66	7	5	23
Cheese, ricotta, whole milk, 1.5 oz	74	50	6	4	22
Cheese, ricotta, part skim, 1.5 oz	59	30	3	2	13
Ice cream, vanilla, 1.5 cups	398	196	22	14	87
Ice cream, vanilla, light, 50% less fat, 1.5 cups	275	77	9	5	28
Ice milk, vanilla, 1.5 cups	203	62	7	4	28
Ice milk, chocolate, 1.5 cups	367	112	12	8	35
Milk, skim, 1 cup	86	4	0	0	5
Milk, 1% fat, 1 cup	102	23	3	2	10
Milk, 2% fat, 1 cup	121	42	5	3	18
Milk, whole, 1 cup	150	73	8	5	33
Yogurt, vanilla, low-fat, 1 cup	209	28	3	2	12
Yogurt, plain, 9 oz	156	75	8	5	33
Yogurt, low-fat, fruit, 1 cup	231	22	2	2	9
Yogurt, frozen, fruit, vanilla, 1 cup	203	23	3	2	10
Meat and Protein Group:					
Beef:					
Chuck arm roast, braised (2.5 oz)	184	93	10	4	71
Ground (18% fat), broiled (2.5 oz)	207	117	13	5	70
Prime rib, broiled (2.5 oz)	286	223	25	10	61
Round, select, lean, roasted (2.5 oz)	110	22	2	1	49
Sirloin, select, lean, roasted (2.5 oz)	120	34	4	1	57
Lamb:					
Chop, choice, broiled (2.5 oz)	224	147	16	7	71
Loin steak, choice, broiled (2.5 oz)	210	131	15	6	70
Shank half, choice, roasted (2.5 oz)	159	79	9	4	64
Pork:					
Bacon, smoked/cured ckd (2.5 oz)	408	314	35	13	60
Chop, center loin, lean, braised (2.5 oz)	143	53	6	2	60
Ham, whole cured, roasted (2.5 oz)	117	49	5	2	40
Sausage, fresh, ckd (2.5 oz)	262	199	22	8	59
Tenderloin, fresh, broiled (2.5 oz)	142	52	6	2	67
Chicken:					
Breast, w/skin, roasted (2.5 oz)	140	50	6	2	60
Breast, w/o skin, roasted (2.5 oz)	117	23	3	1	60
Dark, w/skin, roasted (2.5 oz)	153	71	8	2	64
Dark, w/o skin, roasted (2.7 oz)	146	58	6	2	72
Duck:					
Whole, skinless, roasted (2.5 oz)	142	71	8	3	63
Fish/Seafood:					
Catfish filet, baked (2.5 oz)	74	18	2	1	51
Flounder/sole filet, baked (2.5 oz)	83	10	1	0	48
Haddock filet, baked (2.5 oz)	79	6	1	0	52
Lobster, northern, boiled (2.5 oz)	69	4	0	0	51
Orange roughy, baked (2.5 oz)	63	6	1	0	18
Salmon, Atlantic filet, baked (2.5 oz)	129	52	6	1	50
Shrimp, breaded, fried (3.7 oz)	291	143	16	3	128
Shrimp, broiled (2.5 oz)	110	33	4	1	131
Trout filet, mixed species (2.5 oz)	135	54	6	1	52
Eggs:					
Egg, whole, med, fried (2.8 each)	256	174	19	5	591
Egg, whole, large, boiled (2.2 each)	198	122	14	4	541

Education Program (NCEP), a nationwide effort of the National Institutes of Health, suggests that the desirable level of total blood cholesterol is below 200 mg/dl. The range from 200–239 mg/dl is considered borderline, and a level above 240 mg/dl is considered high. Where you fall in these categories will indicate how often you should have your cholesterol level checked, the degree to which you should change your diet, and whether special advice from your physician is necessary. Therefore, if you have not done so, you should have your cholesterol checked.

You may have heard talk about different types of cholesterol, particularly HDL (high density lipoprotein) cholesterol and LDL (low density lipoprotein) cholesterol. HDL is thought to protect against heart disease, so higher levels are better. The NCEP classifies HDL lower than 40 mg/dl as low and 60 mg/dl and above as high.

LDL has the opposite effect, so lower levels are better. The NCEP classifies LDL below 100 mg/dl as optimal and 190 mg/dl and above as very high. Scientists are learning more about how diet and exercise can be used to raise HDL and lower LDL. The same methods used to lower total cholesterol appear to have beneficial effects on HDL and LDL.

NUTRITION NOTES

Limiting the amount of fat and cholesterol you eat is important for controlling your cholesterol levels. Cholesterol is found in foods that come from animal products. Foods from plant sources do not contain cholesterol, but they can contain saturated fat. In addition, be aware of the type of fat that you eat. Saturated fat from animal sources (fats from beef, lamb, pork, ham, butter, cream, whole milk, cheese) and saturated fat from vegetable sources (coconut oil, palm oil, cocoa butter) should be limited. Try to limit saturated fats and replace them with polyunsaturated fats, which usually come from vegetable oils. Physical activity is also a powerful way for many people to control their cholesterol levels. This is yet another example of the importance of being physically active.

The table on page 144 may be helpful in guiding you to choose foods low in cholesterol. Remember that reducing saturated fat in the diet can have an even more powerful effect in lowering blood cholesterol than can reducing dietary cholesterol. I discussed dietary fat in Lesson Six.

Serving and Dispensing Food

For some people, simply thinking about food can be a trigger to eat. Here are five questions I like to ask to determine whether a person reacts to the sight, smell, or thought of food.

❶ Do you feel like eating dessert when it looks appetizing, even after eating a large meal?

❷ Do you always have room for something you like?

❸ Do you get excited about a buffet?

❹ If you drive by a bakery or fast-food place and smell the food, do you want to eat, regardless of whether you are hungry?

❺ Do you feel like eating when you see a picture of a delicious dessert in a magazine?

If you answer "yes" to these questions, you may be high in externality. This means you are sensitive to external cues or signals, namely the sight, smell, or suggestion of food. If this describes you, join the crowd. There are millions like you, both heavy and thin. Reducing your exposure to food may be helpful in controlling your eating.

The methods you learned earlier for buying food were designed to reduce exposure to food. We have been moving forward in the sequence of antecedents. We began with the first step (shopping) in Lesson Seven on page 107. We will now move even closer by discussing serving and dispensing

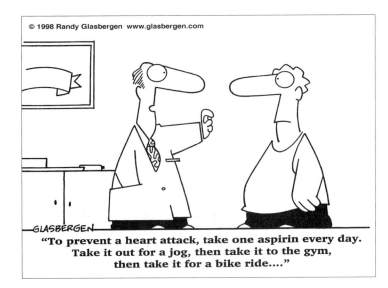

© 1998 Randy Glasbergen www.glasbergen.com

GLASBERGEN

"To prevent a heart attack, take one aspirin every day. Take it out for a jog, then take it to the gym, then take it for a bike ride...."

food. In Lesson Ten we will move a step closer to eating (storing food).

Here, I describe several techniques for serving food. All follow a general principle, which is to interrupt the sequence of events associated with eating. Some techniques will apply to you more than others. You can use the principle to develop techniques of your own.

The following techniques are designed to help you control eating when your exposure to food cues is at its peak. The aim is to minimize your contact with these cues.

➡ ***Remove serving dishes from the table***. After first servings are made, remove the food dishes from the table. Having the food handy is asking for trouble. If the food dishes are in another room or on another table, you can *think* before taking more. This does not prohibit you from having seconds, but it does interrupt the automatic eating that occurs when your plate is a magnet for anything left on the serving dishes.

➡ ***Leave the table after eating***. This may sound antisocial, but leaving the table after you finish eating is helpful for some people. This reduces the time you are exposed to food and to the circumstances of eating. If you finish long before the others, you may be eating too fast, and slowing down will help. If not, perhaps the others can retire to another room with you for the post-meal chat. This technique can work in concert with the previous suggestion to remove serving dishes from the table. If *all* the dishes are gone, it is not necessary to leave the table because exposure to food signals will be low. If food remains, bid the table farewell, and depart for safer surroundings.

➡ *Serve and eat one portion at a time*. Make and serve yourself only one portion of food. If you want two pieces of toast, make one, and eat it before making another. If you want a container of yogurt, put half in a bowl and return for the second half if you still want it. You may find yourself passing up the second portion because you are no longer hungry. Here again is a chance to interrupt automatic eating. This also can help you separate hunger from habit. Just because you have eaten one container of yogurt every morning for 10 years does not mean your body is hungry for that amount every day.

➡ *Follow the five-minute rule*. Wait five minutes before going back for extra helpings. This will help you slow the rate of eating and will give you time to decide how much additional food you really need.

➡ *Avoid being a food dispenser*. Are you the gatekeeper of food in your house? Do the kids get their snacks from you? Do you prepare all the food? If

so, this is a disadvantage because your routine brings you in contact with food many times each day. Drop the job of being a food dispenser. Have the children pack their own lunches, if possible. Your spouse can manage snacks without you and may be willing to help even more by taking on some of the responsibility you have for distributing food.

Carbohydrates and Your Diet

I promised earlier that I would discuss carbohydrates in this lesson. So, let's get to it. Many individuals like to blame carbohydrates for everything. Some people on weight loss programs say that carbohydrates excite the binge center in their brain, and parents blame sugar when their kids misbehave. Much has been said about simple and complex carbohydrates, carbohydrate craving, and low-carbohydrate diets. You, like many others, may be puzzled by all this, so let's clear the air.

What are Carbohydrates?

Stated in technical terms, carbohydrates are a combination of hydrogen, oxygen, and carbon atoms, which join to make single sugars, double sugars, or starches and fibers. The sugars provide energy for the body. Single sugars (like fructose) enter the body's energy supply more quickly than the double sugars or starches found in vegetables and cereals. The body must first break down the double sugars and starches

into single sugars before it can use them as energy.

Many sources of sugars and starches are available in the foods you eat. Sugars consist mainly of sucrose (table sugar), fructose (in fruit and honey), and lactose (in milk). The starches are in foods like cereals, pasta, rice, breads, and vegetables.

Like protein, carbohydrate provides 4 calories per gram. In contrast, fat has more than twice the calories per gram (9 calories per gram). Because the major part of your diet should consist of carbohydrate, it is easy to eat too much. Many carbohydrate-rich foods are of poor nutritional value and contain only calories from sugar. Many soft drinks are like this. Such foods are a poor source of nutrition, hence the term *empty calories*. For example, doughnuts and potato chips contain a lot of empty calories. Foods like these are prime candidates for elimination or reduction for individuals trying to lose or maintain weight.

The National Academy of Sciences Institute of Medicine recommends that adults should have approximately 45–65 percent of their daily calories from carbohydrate. Based on a 1,200 calorie per day diet, this would be 135–195 grams of carbohydrate per day. This would total from 540–780 calories (135–195 grams at 4 calories per gram).

What does all this mean for you? Carbohydrates are essential in the diet and are not necessarily bad. In fact, most people should increase their intake of carbohydrate (starches and fiber). Starches should not have the bad rap they receive. People consider potatoes fattening because they are high in starch, yet potatoes are reasonable to eat because of their nutrition. The amount eaten is usually the problem, along with the goodies that adorn some of these foods. For example, adding sour cream and butter, which are mainly fat, rapidly increases the caloric intake of eating an innocent potato.

It may be unwise to follow a low-carbohydrate diet except under medical supervi-

"When your mother told you to eat something green every day, I don't think she had M & M's in mind."

sion. Some popular diets that restrict carbohydrate to less than 100 grams per day make it very difficult to maintain adequate nutrition. A sensible plan with 45–65 percent of your calories from carbohydrates is consistent with dietary guidelines.

Watch Out for Sugars

Try to be on the lookout for simple sugars in your diet. These tend to come from foods with many calories and little nutrition. Examples are cookies, doughnuts, pastries, soft drinks, candy, and so forth.

These simple sugars stimulate insulin release. Because insulin is related to hunger, you will feel hungry in less time by eating sugars than by eating starches and fiber. An exception to this is fructose, the single sugar found naturally in fruit. Moving away from candy and other sweet foods, and toward vegetables and other complex carbohydrates, is a wise decision.

Carbohydrates and Extra Calorie Burning

For many years, a simple statement ruled in the minds of experts—"A calorie is a calorie." The belief was that the body handles calories in the same way no matter where they came from. For instance, if you ate 3,500 calories of oat bran and tofu, you

Vegetable Group

(One Vegetable Group Serving Each)

Description	Cal	Fat Cal	Pro (g)	Carb (g)
Asparagus, boiled, ½ cup	22	3	2	4
Beets, cooked, ½ cup	37	1	1	8
Broccoli, steamed, ½ cup	22	2	2	4
Brussels sprouts, cooked, ½ cup	32	4	2	7
Cabbage, fresh, raw, ½ cup	8	1	0	2
Carrots, cooked, ½ cup	35	1	1	8
Carrots, chopped, raw, ½ cup	28	1	1	6
Cauliflower, cooked, ½ cup	14	3	1	3
Cauliflower, raw, ½ cup	10	1	1	2
Celery, raw, ½ cup	10	1	0	2
Corn, yellow, cooked, ½ cup	89	9	3	21
Cucumber slices, raw, w/peel, ½ cup	7	1	0	1
Eggplant, cubed, cooked, ½ cup	14	1	0	3
Green snap beans, cooked, ½ cup	22	2	1	5
Lettuce, Romaine, chopped, 1 cup	8	1	1	1
Mixed vegetables, canned, ½ cup	44	3	2	9
Mushroom pieces, cooked, ½ cup	20	3	2	4
Okra, batter fried, 1 cup	175	113	2	14
Okra, boiled, ½ cup	26	1	1	6
Onions, white, raw, chopped, ½ cup	30	1	1	7
Onion rings, breaded & fried, 18 pieces	584	296	8	66
Peas, green, boiled, ½ cup	67	2	4	13
Potato, flesh only, baked, 7/10 cup	79	1	2	18
Potato, fries, frozen, 15 each	236	112	3	30
Potato, hash brown, homemade, ½ cup	163	98	2	17
Potato, mashed w/whl milk & margarine, ½ cup	111	40	2	18
Potato, scalloped w/margarine, ½ cup	105	41	4	13
Pumpkin, mashed, boiled, ½ cup	25	1	1	6
Squash, summer, all varieties, boiled, ½ cup	18	3	1	4
Squash, zucchini, boiled, .4 cup	15	0	1	4
Sweet potato, mashed, boiled, ⅓ cup	103	3	2	24
Vegetable juice, V8, ¾ cup	45	2	8	0

would gain the same weight as you would by eating the same calories from a triple cheeseburger and onion rings. We now know this is not the case.

The body has an easier time (requires less energy) converting fat calories to body fat than it does converting carbohydrate calories to body fat. Between 20–25 percent more energy is required for the body to metabolize carbohydrate than to metabolize fat. As an example, let's say you eat 100 calories of a high-fat food like butter. On another day, you eat 100 calories of a food high in complex carbohydrates, like a whole grain cereal. Your body will use 20–25 percent more calories to metabolize the carbohydrate. Therefore, the calories from fat and carbohydrate are not equal once they enter your body.

This is good news. Foods high in complex carbohydrates are good to eat for health reasons alone. In addition, your body will burn more calories converting them to usable energy. Many people report that it is much easier to lose weight when they cut back on fat and eat more fruits, vegetables, and grains. With this in mind, let's turn our attention to vegetables and the Vegetable Group of the Food Guide Pyramid.

Vegetables in Your Diet

Do you remember your mother saying to you, "Eat your vegetables, they're good for you"? Mom was right—vegetables are good for you. In fact, both fruits and vegetables are *so* important in the diet that the Food Guide Pyramid segregates them into separate groups.

Vegetables are an excellent source of vitamins A, C, and folate. In addition, they provide important minerals, including iron and magnesium, and as I mentioned earlier, they are an excellent source of carbohydrate. Vegetables are also naturally low in dietary fat. This is good news for people losing weight.

Most Americans fall short in their consumption of vegetables, perhaps because adding produce to their diet is inconvenient, time-consuming, or boring. Vegetables may not appeal to everyone's palate, especially in the ways they are usually prepared. Nevertheless, they are an important ingredient in a healthy, low-fat diet.

How Many Servings?

The suggested number of daily servings of vegetables from the Pyramid is three to five. This may sound like a lot, but it is actually less than you may think. For instance, just ½ cup of cooked green beans, one medium carrot, two stalks of celery, or half of a broccoli spear count as one serving.

What Makes a Serving

As a rule, the following will serve as a simple guide to help you include the right amount of vegetable servings in your daily diet:

➡ 1 cup of raw, leafy vegetables (lettuce)

➡ ½ cup of other vegetables, cooked or chopped raw

➡ ¾ cup (6 oz) of vegetable juice

The table on page 148 may help you better understand what counts as a serving. The foods listed in the table count as a single serving.

Serving Tips

Many vegetables are available for you to choose from in our food supply. With a little creativity and planning, vegetables can become a fun and enjoyable part of your everyday diet. Here are some serving tips that you may find helpful:

➡ Fresh vegetables make excellent snacks that you can easily take with you to work, school, or simply enjoy around the house. Celery, carrots, cauliflower, green peppers, cucumbers, and broccoli are good choices.

➡ Steaming vegetables also can be fun and can add variety to your meals. Best of all, it is easy to do and does not leave a big mess. While steaming the vegetables, you can add herbs or other seasonings to enhance flavor, or serve the

The Food Guide Pyramid

Vegetable Group

3 - 5 Servings

steamed vegetables with a splash of lemon.

➡ Think of creative ways to add vegetables to the foods you already eat and enjoy. Adding a slice of tomato, two large leaves of lettuce or spinach, and a pickle on the side turns a sandwich into a meal that includes one serving of vegetables.

➡ When you eat fast food, be creative. Some fast-food establishments now offer vegetable alternatives to French fries. Try a garden salad or baked potato next time. But, be careful with dressings and toppings—make sure they are low fat. Remember to watch out for those *hidden* calories.

More on Physical Activity

We are now in Lesson Nine and have covered much of the introductory information on both lifestyle and programmed physical activity. I have said much about the importance and benefits of regular physical activity.

Are You More Active?

By this time in the program, my hope is that you are fitting lifestyle physical activ-

ity into your daily routine. If this is possible for you, make it your goal, and do your best to make time for exercise each day. Of course, missing a day here and there does not mean you have failed in your program. Daily activity is, however, a nice goal to set.

Look back over your Monitoring Forms and see if your level of exercise has changed. Have you found something you like? Do you use this exercise regularly? Does the exercise help you stick to your eating plan and lose weight?

If you are having trouble with the exercise, read over the exercise sections in the earlier lessons. Let me remind you that people who are still exercising a year or two after they begin a program tend to be the ones who have lost weight and kept it off.

People resist exercise for several good reasons. For some people, exercise is physically difficult to manage. For others, strong negative feelings about sports and exercise present a psychological barrier. Another common problem is a busy lifestyle and the difficulty of budgeting time each day to be physically active. You may want to refer back to the Physical Activity Barriers and Solutions worksheet that you completed on page 125 in Lesson Eight.

These are all understandable reasons not to exercise. I hope you find the reasons in favor of exercise to be more compelling.

"The doctor told my husband to double his physical activity, so now he changes channels with both hands."

Having this mind-set could mean a great deal to you, both now and in the future.

Consider this a pep talk. I really do feel that exercise is important, and I would like to do whatever is possible to encourage you to be active.

Matching Your Activity to Your Goals

In previous lessons, I discussed various reasons to be active. Some people aim to improve their cardiovascular fitness and choose aerobic activities. Some want to increase strength and improve their physique, so they work out with machines or use free weights. Others want to use exercise to speed weight loss, so they do whatever they can to keep moving, usually with walking or jogging. Each type of activity is valuable, but for different purposes.

Cardiovascular fitness improves even in a walking program. This is especially true for overweight, inactive individuals. However, to achieve *optimal* cardiovascular fitness, frequency, intensity, and duration are all important. You may want to review the F.I.T. approach that I discussed on page 127 in Lesson Eight. Keep in mind, however, this type of exercise is not necessary to achieve important health benefits and to manage your weight.

The Myth of Spot Reducing

Many people would need a computer to count the number of sit-ups they have done to tighten the tummy, leg exercises to trim the thighs, and contortions of the neck to wipe out a double chin. The trouble is, these things simply do not work. Yet, millions of people still fall for the slick advertisements or books that promise ways of reducing body fat from specific parts of the body.

Where your body stores fat depends on genetic and hormonal factors. Women tend to store fat below the waist, on their hips, thighs, and buttocks (pear shaped). When they become heavy, they also store it above the waist. Men tend to store fat above the

 Did You Know?

NO EXERCISE WILL GUARANTEE THAT YOU WILL LOSE BODY FAT FROM A PARTICULAR PLACE ON YOUR BODY. DOING 1,000 SIT UPS A DAY DOES NOT MEAN YOU WILL LOSE ABDOMINAL BODY FAT!

waist, in the abdomen (apple shaped). Upper body fat or apple-shaped bodies are associated with a higher risk for cardiovascular disease than pear-shaped bodies. When you lose weight, your body burns fat, but you have little control over where it happens. Recent studies suggest that regular moderate-intensity aerobic exercise not only helps to reduce body weight but may also help prevent fat accumulation in the abdominal area.

Strength training exercises will help you with muscle tone. This can improve appearance somewhat. Doing sit-ups will tighten the muscles in your abdomen and will help you look a little less flabby, but they cannot force your body to take fat from there.

Internal Attitude Traps

Tape/CD 4
Section 3

We all talk to ourselves, albeit silently. I discussed this earlier when I talked about goal setting and emotions and negative self-talk in Lesson Six. How you view your lifestyle changes can help or hinder your progress greatly. How-

ever, you may encounter several common traps.

ATTITUDE ALERT

Your job will be much easier and your success much greater if you are prepared to counter *destructive* thoughts and attitudes with more *constructive* ones. As you have heard me say before, "Your thoughts about an event are as important as the event itself."

Countering the Traps

Visualize the part of yourself that pressures you to eat. You can be more than a match for these pressures but only if you are conscientious and face the problem directly. What follows are some common traps, called *fat thoughts*. I will give you some suggestions for possible counter measures.

Internal Trap Number 1: "The program is the key."

➡ **Fat Thought:** This program is the only reason I have lost weight. When the program is over, I will have real trouble keeping the weight off.

➡ **Counter Thought:** I am losing weight because of my own efforts in learning and practicing new skills. Just because the program ends does not mean my new skills will vanish. The program helped teach me these important skills, but I deserve the credit for all the hard work I have been doing.

Your thoughts and attitudes play a key role in your weight management.

Internal Trap Number 2:
"Is this worth the effort?"

➡ ***Fat Thought:*** I have been on my program for weeks, and I still have lots of weight to lose. I can't wait till this program ends so I can get back to normal.

➡ ***Counter Thought:*** Stop this way of thinking right now! Who said this would be easy? It took a long time to gain the weight, and it will take a long time to lose it. I would like to lose weight quickly and easily, but facts are facts. I don't want to let down now and waste my effort. I can stick with it. I am developing a new and healthy lifestyle that I can maintain for the rest of my life.

Internal Trap Number 3:
"I have done this before."

➡ ***Fat Thought:*** I have heard this nutrition stuff before, and we covered behavior modification in the last program I tried. It didn't help me then, and it will not help me now.

➡ ***Counter Thought:*** I have never been taught these things in such a concentrated way, and my motivation to learn may be different now. I know deep down this is the only way to get permanent results, so putting down the approach just means I have trouble doing the work. Only I can do it, so I must forge ahead.

Try to recognize these and other internal traps. The fat thoughts you have lived with for years will do their best to control your attitudes and eating. Now you can blast them with a counterattack.

 ## MY WEEKLY GOALS

Set goals this week that are personally relevant for you. What will be most helpful in your program? Are there techniques we covered in earlier lessons that are giving you trouble?

Setting specific goals for a regular form of exercise such as walking, jogging, cycling, and swimming is also helpful. The goal you set may be to increase the number of days you engage in this activity, the number of minutes you do the activity, or if you are using a step counter, the number of steps you take. And, as I say in each lesson, keep up the goal setting for the changes you feel are most important.

Focus this week on your eating and activity habits. Practice the techniques I discussed in the serving and dispensing food section of this lesson. Work on countering your internal attitude traps. Try your best to include 3–5 servings daily from the Vegetable Group of the Food Guide Pyramid. Continue to watch your diet for fat, and don't forget to record your weight change on the My Weight Change Record on page 216. Good luck with your goals this week!

KNOWLEDGE REVIEW

Lesson Nine

1. T F Measuring and weighing your food portions are not necessary because most people accurately estimate portion sizes.

2. T F For controlling your blood cholesterol, it is important to limit your intake of saturated fat.

3. T F It is best to take all of what you will eat in one serving so you will not need additional helpings.

4. T F Carbohydrates are not as important as other nutrients, and they should make up only about 30 percent of your daily diet.

5. T F Eating sugars helps you to feel full faster, so you stop eating sooner.

6. T F The Food Guide Pyramid suggests three to five servings each day from the Vegetable Group.

7. T F Because all vegetables have only small amounts of fats, it is not as important to count the amount of fat in these foods as it is to count the dietary fat from meat and dairy products.

8. T F Most Americans eat enough vegetables in their diets.

9. T F No exercise can help you lose fat in specific parts of the body.

10. T F Fat thoughts can hinder a person's efforts to lose weight.

(Answers in Appendix C, page 223)

"Tell me I was born to be fat!"

Monitoring Form—Lesson Nine

*Today's Date:*_____

Time	Food and Amount	Calories	Milk & Dairy	Meats & Protein	Vegetables	Fruits	Bread
Total Daily Caloric Intake & Food Guide Pyramid Servings							

Daily Activity Record (Caloric Expenditure)

Time	Activity	Calories	Minutes	No. of Steps

Personal Goals this Week	Most of the Time	Some of the Time	Rarely
1. Meet or exceed walking goal of _____ steps each day			
2. Leave the table after eating			
3. Avoid being a food dispenser			
4. Counter internal attitude traps			
5. Eat 3–5 servings from the Vegetable Group			
6. Eat less than _____ calories each day			

Lesson Ten

Today's fast-paced environment can trigger stress, which in turn can trigger eating. Stress and eating are often coupled, so I'll spend some time discussing this important issue. On the exercise front, I discuss more good news about physical activity and will then talk about the topic of aerobics. We'll also cover the testy issue of pressures to eat from other people. This can be helpful because offers and demands to eat from others can be hard to resist. We then move to a new category of attitude traps that I briefly mentioned in an earlier lesson—imperatives. In the nutrition arena, you will learn techniques for storing food to help you keep temptation under control, and I'll talk about the key role that fiber and fruit play in a healthy diet. We have a full agenda for this lesson, so if you're ready, let's begin.

Stress and Eating

Tape/CD 4
Section 2

A very interesting and unexplained paradox is that stress makes some people eat more and some people eat less. Although scientists are working to better understand this phenomenon, one thing is clear—people who wish to lose weight often cite stress as a major issue.

When I discuss the complexity of weight loss with clients in my clinic, the issue of stress arises repeatedly. Some people point to a specific stressful event to explain why they gained weight in the first place. Others say that stress makes them want to eat all the time, so they nibble. Many people report that it is difficult to exercise when they are stressed. Still, others feel that stress threatens their ability to maintain weight loss and puts them at risk for relapse.

It is no surprise that stress exerts such an important effect on eating and physical activity. Clear links exist between stress and health. Stress can affect many aspects of health, from the common cold to chronic diseases like heart disease, diabetes, and asthma. It is reasonable to believe that reducing stress would make many people happier and healthier. In addition, less stress would facilitate control over eating, physical activity and weight.

Stress and Eating

Do you feel that stress influences your eating? Here are some questions to ask yourself:

❶ When you feel pressure to accomplish something, do you feel pulled toward food or pushed away from it?

❷ If you were sitting at a desk working on a project that had to be done quickly, would you want to be eating something?

❸ Do you believe food is something you use to feel better when you are stressed?

❹ Does stress make you eat more?

If you answered "yes" to any of these questions, stress and eating might be linked in important ways. The question then is what to do about it.

Two logical solutions come to mind. One is to respond to stress with activities other than eating. For some people, eating helps to soothe difficult feelings. When a person uses food to take the edge off stress, and this behavior is repeated over and over, the association could become automatic. Food may affect the brain in a way that helps with stress. Whatever the reasons, eating is only one way of coping with stress.

Most people can come up with things other than food to make themselves feel better. What does it for you? Is it listening to music, reading a good book, going for a walk, connecting with a friend, meditating, or something else? Having several constructive activities at hand so that you know exactly how to respond when stress triggers the desire to eat can be *very* helpful.

A second solution is to reduce stress. This is an appealing possibility, because stress reduction may affect not only your eating, but other areas of your life as well. Learning stress management techniques may therefore be helpful. It would take another book the size of the LEARN manual to provide a complete stress management program. Even so, I can provide a brief overview about stress and then refer you to materials or programs for more detailed information. At the end of this section, I'll discuss an excellent stress management program you may want to consider—*Mastering Stress 2001—A LifeStyle Approach*. Before I talk about stress management, let's look at the relationship between stress and physical activity.

Stress and Physical Activity

As I mentioned earlier, stress and exercise can be closely linked. Many people tend to forego their physical activities when feeling stressed. When stressful situations arise at work or home, finding the time, energy, or motivation to exercise may seem impossible. Yet, studies have shown that physical activity may be just the ticket to reduce stress. Research has shown that even a single bout of physical activity reduces stress. Many people report short-term improvements in their moods, such as stress and anxiety, and have temporary reductions in muscle tension after a single exercise session. Regular (daily) physical activity is necessary to experience the calming effect on an ongoing basis.

"I'm very sorry, but when I get stressed, I eat."

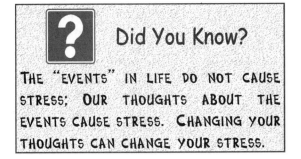

Did You Know?

THE "EVENTS" IN LIFE DO NOT CAUSE STRESS; OUR THOUGHTS ABOUT THE EVENTS CAUSE STRESS. CHANGING YOUR THOUGHTS CAN CHANGE YOUR STRESS.

The good feeling that accompanies exercise is due in part to the release of hormones responsible for improving mood. Many people can relate to the "high" they feel after engaging in physical activity. This improved mood can have a calming effect when stressful events arise. In addition, physical activity fights fatigue and insomnia and can reduce anxiety and depression.

The next time you feel stressed and are tempted to skip an exercise session, remember that physical activity may be just the thing you need to lower your stress and get you going again. Even if you feel rushed, take time for yourself. Just a 10-minute walk can help lower your stress and make you feel better, and most people can find 10 minutes for a quick walk.

Clearly, a short bout of exercise is a terrific alternative to eating when you feel stressed. Not only will you feel better, you will use instead of gain calories in the process.

Stress Is

Stress is a fascinating interplay between the body, mind, environment, and our behavior. We each respond to situations in our environment in a unique way. Events that disturb one person mean nothing to another. Some people respond to stress with a racing heart and anger, while others respond with nausea and fear. Clearly, the way we think and act are key factors in how we handle stress. Therefore, a person can do several different things to manage stress. You can learn stress management skills, much as you are learning weight management skills in this program. I will provide two examples of such skills here.

The first is the use of relaxation training. Good stress management programs teach specific relaxation skills. When stress begins, a person has the ability to halt the process by countering a stress response with relaxation responses. Learning relaxation skills can be very helpful and can help an individual calm down before an undesirable action occurs (like overeating).

The second example deals with what scientists call *appraisal*. When a stressful event occurs in our lives, we appraise the situation and then respond. The appraisal (our thought process) determines how we feel about the event and the subsequent response. One person who receives a negative evaluation from a boss might have a negative appraisal, suffer a blow to self-esteem, become depressed, and overeat. Another person in the same situation may blame the boss, get angry, and strike back in some self-defeating way. Still, another person may make a more constructive appraisal and think of ways to improve work performance. Let's look at a couple of examples.

LIFESTYLE PROFILES

George received a poor performance evaluation from his boss. "I really screwed up this time," he said to himself. "I'll probably get fired for this." George's self-esteem suffered greatly from this negative response to his evaluation. When he got home that evening, he began to eat. At the end of the evening his self-esteem took another blow when he realized how much he had overeaten.

Jerry also received a poor performance evaluation from his boss. "Oops, I goofed this time, but it's not the end of the world," he said to himself. "I'll ask my boss to help me improve my performance." Jerry's more positive and realistic thoughts about his evaluation allowed his self-esteem to rise above the occasion. When he got home that evening, Jerry went for a 30-minute walk.

ATTITUDE ALERT

The way we perceive and interpret events is crucial to the behavior that follows.

Relaxation training and modifying the appraisal process are important components of a good stress management program. So, how do you find one? One possibility is to seek out stress management seminars or training programs. Local hospitals, YMCA's and YWCA's, colleges, and some corporate settings offer stress management programs. Some individuals find they need a formal program in a professional setting, so asking for leads from health professionals you know should be helpful.

Other people do not need a formal program and can use written materials in a very positive way. An excellent guide is a step-by-step manual written by Drs. David Barlow, Ronald Rapee, and Leslie Reisner titled *Mastering Stress 2001—A LifeStyle Approach*. This program is part of the LEARN LifeStyle Program Series® and is published by the American Health Publish-

ing Company (the company that publishes the LEARN manual). You can get more information about this program by calling 1–888–LEARN–41, visiting www.TheLife StyleCompany.com on the internet, or by contacting The LifeStyle Company at the address provided in Appendix H—Supplemental Resources and Ordering Information at the end of this manual on page 257.

Let's Consider Running and Cycling

Society's attitude about exercise has changed over the past two decades, particularly when it comes to running. As recently as the early 1970s, the longest race in most track meets was two miles, and most people had trouble believing that kooks actually raced for six miles in cross-country meets. The picture is quite different today.

Now it seems routine for people to run 3, 5, 10, or even more miles. The number of people who define themselves as runners is amazing. Running magazines, clubs, and even computer software are easily available.

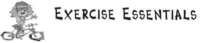

EXERCISE ESSENTIALS

Before we discuss running in more detail, let me emphasize again the virtues of brisk walking. Running is fine, but for people who still have many pounds to lose, brisk walking is easier and affords virtually all the health-related benefits. Running can be helpful to some people, but walking is a fine alternative.

Running

The benefits of running are indisputable. Many positive physical changes occur, as discussed in Lesson Two. However, we often overlook the psychological advantages. I am not talking about a "runner's high," but about a general sense of accomplishment, self-confidence, well-being, and good feelings.

This psychological advantage may come from the running activity itself or may simply result from the mastery of something new. I once lectured on the psychological benefits of exercise at a sports medicine conference in The Netherlands. Dr. John Garrow, an outstanding researcher from England, asked me a telling question. He asked if people would get the same positive effects from something unrelated to exercise, such as learning to play the cello.

Dr. Garrow was questioning whether something inherent to exercise itself would be beneficial or whether the effects were due to the excitement of improving at any activity. This is a difficult question to answer. From a practical standpoint, exercise is a good means for producing this mastery because it carries physical benefits as well. After all, it burns more calories than playing the cello! But in addition, exercise does produce physical changes that act to improve mood. Physical activity has a lot going for it.

Cycling

Cycling has the advantages of running and is more enjoyable for some people. Riding a stationary bicycle indoors or a traditional bike outdoors is good exercise. It spares the knees, ankles, and feet from the pounding they take when running. Cycling is also nice for heavy people because the bike supports the person's weight. It is an excellent method for burning calories. Some people find bicycle seats uncomfortable, and therefore, may hesitate to go riding. Special gel seats are now available to make riding a bicycle more enjoyable and comfortable.

If cycling outdoors is feasible for you, try it. Cycling to work is terrific when possible. If not, consider buying a stationary bicycle for your home. I have one and like to alternate between running, cycling, and playing tennis. Stationary cycling is nice in bad weather, and you can do it while watching the news on television or listening to music.

Running and cycling are not the only aerobic exercises, but they are good ones. These activities (along with walking and

swimming) are top choices among my clients, so please try them. If you are doing something else regularly, stick with it. If you are sporadic in your activity habits or have not tried anything seriously, consider lacing up your shoes to hit the road or jumping on a bike to sail down the street.

Running and cycling are both excellent aerobic physical activities to try.

More about Physical Activity

Tape/CD 3
Section 9

We have focused on lifestyle activity, programmed activity, and more intense types of exercise like running and cycling. Most overweight people can become more physically active by simply walking. By now, you may feel more comfortable with being active and may be ready for more. In Lesson Eight on page 123, I discussed programmed activity, and I covered running and cycling in this lesson.

I expect that about half the people who read this manual will be ready for more intense and varied activities than walking. Others may continue walking and lose more weight before taking on programmed activity. If you are in the second group, reread the section on Starting a Programmed Activity on page 123, and refer back to it when you are ready to increase or vary your activity. In the meantime, continue to increase

your walking by adding steps or time and by increasing the speed at which you walk.

As I mentioned earlier, programmed activities include running, walking, aerobics, racquetball, swimming, cycling, or any regular activity. I also discussed the current guidelines and recommendations for physical activity in earlier lessons. Selecting the right activity (something you enjoy enough to do again) is something of an art. Let's now look at the science behind the current physical activity guidelines and recommendations.

EXERCISE ESSENTIALS

For many people, exercise is a major factor in their long-term prospects for weight management. It is true that some people lose weight without exercise, but for others, exercise makes an enormous difference, especially in keeping the lost weight off. Do you remember the discussion in Lesson Seven on page 115 where I discussed the difference between the maintainers and the regainers? If not, now is a good time to flip back in the manual and review this important information.

Exercise helps people lose weight for both physical and psychological reasons. It burns calories and may boost metabolic rate. Perhaps as important are the ways

exercise makes us feel good. Each time we exercise, we are sending a signal to ourselves that we are making positive changes. Exercise has been shown to reduce stress and may give us more energy for life's other activities (like planning our weekly diet). Some people find exercise especially helpful when they schedule it at times they are most likely to eat.

One bit of very good news about exercise comes from recent research that shows regular moderate-intensity physical activity (walking most days of the week for 30 minutes) reduces the risk of certain diseases and early mortality. In fact, one study examined the impact of physical activity on death rates from cardiovascular disease and other causes in 7,700 men, aged 40–59. Compared to men who were sedentary, men who were moderately physically active had a 50 percent lower risk of death from cardiovascular disease and other causes. Men who were sedentary at the first evaluation and who began at least light activity by the second evaluation 12–14 years later had a 45 percent lower risk of dying than the men who remained sedentary. The take-home message here is that it's *never* too late to start being physically active.

Another study of more than 70,000 postmenopausal women, aged 50–79, found that women who walked briskly at least two and a half hours per week had a 30 percent lower risk of developing heart-related problems, such as heart attack, heart failure, the need for heart bypass surgery, stroke, or death than women who were sedentary. Walking briskly was as effective in reducing cardiovascular risk as vigorous exercise.

Several striking aspects to these studies stand out. First, they are yet another piece to the puzzle showing that people who exercise and are physically active live longer. For our purposes, however, the important news is that even modest levels of physical activity are associated with longevity and greatly reduced disease risk. There is a substantial decline in risk by moving from a sedentary lifestyle to a moderately-active lifestyle. Certainly, gains can be made by increasing physical activity further, but the big drop in risk occurs as people go from being completely sedentary to moderately active.

The moral to this story is that you do not have to knock yourself out to be healthier. Even small amounts of exercise are likely to have a big impact on health and will certainly be helpful for weight loss and maintenance.

How much exercise should you do? If you are counting steps, your ultimate goal should be about *10,000 steps a day or more.* If you are not counting steps, your goal should be 30–60 minutes of regular moderate-intensity physical activity most days of the week.

Remember, any type of activity should be considered exercise. If you take an extra flight of stairs, rake the leaves, walk an extra block, or chase the rabbits out of your vegetable garden, you have exercised and should say so in your own mind. You deserve to feel good about these activities and can feel confident that you are making progress.

Are Aerobics for You?

I remember my school years when coaches and teachers used calisthenics as punishment or as a way to build character. Push-ups, sit-ups, squat thrusts, and leg lifts ranked somewhere below staying after school on my list of favorite activities.

The situation is much different today. Aerobics have now replaced calisthenics,

slimnastics, and the like. This signals not only a change in terminology but also a change in the way we view exercise. In my opinion, the changes are positive.

When aerobic training became popular, using exercise to build strength took a back seat to improving the condition of the heart. This involves getting the heart rate up and keeping it there. Many different movements can accomplish this, hence the use of dance, spinning, kick boxing, and other types of movement in aerobics classes. This makes exercise more interesting and healthier than the calisthenics of old.

Aerobic activities require a large increase in the body's use of oxygen. This is best accomplished by use of large muscle groups, and it involves some form of continuous and rhythmic movement. Walking, running, cycling, swimming, and jumping rope are examples, but so are dancing to fast music and the other movements associated with aerobics classes. As I mentioned before, aerobic activities are the only types of exercise that will improve cardiovascular conditioning. They are not the only exercises that will help you lose weight, but they are certainly among the best.

Aerobics are suitable for almost everybody because they can be done in a variety of ways. If you want to do it alone, there are books, TV shows, videotapes, and DVDs. Most of these workout approaches are aerobic in nature. If you like company, aerobics classes are held at the YMCA, YWCA, exercise centers, and in many companies, churches, and community recreation centers. A variety of classes are available, in-

Aerobic activities can be done in many ways that are fun, enjoyable, and suitable for just about everybody.

cluding non-impact aerobics (NIA), step aerobics, kickboxing, and spinning (stationary cycling in a group). You also may want to take a jazzercise, ballroom dance, or hip-hop class.

The nice thing about aerobics is that you can move at your own pace, even if you are with a group, so don't worry about the shape you're in. Many excellent books on aerobic exercises also are available. I suggest any of the books by Dr. Kenneth Cooper. These books are available in most bookstores. They discuss what to do, how much to do, and how to have fun being physically active.

Many people losing weight use more than one form of exercise. This breaks monotony and gives you a chance to do whatever your mood dictates. You might walk some days, bicycle other days, and do an aerobics class on days when one is scheduled. This allows you to be flexible with your schedule, the weather, and your moods.

Dealing with Pressures to Eat

A major challenge for individuals losing weight is coping with pressure to eat. Friends, relatives, and strangers—some well meaning and some not—can make it difficult to lose weight by encouraging you to eat. I can think of a number of reasons for this. Let's review some of them.

➡ ***They are unaware that offering food to you is a problem.*** Some people are simply unaware of the struggle some individuals have with food. You may need to gently tell these people about what your experience is like and how they can help.

➡ ***They may be uncomfortable eating in front of you.*** People agonize about eating when another person is not. They offer food to be polite, even though they know the offer will not be accepted. You can tell them that you feel comfortable not eating, and that they should eat if they wish.

➡ ***They may be jealous of your success.*** Others with weight problems may be jealous of your success. Thin people may also be jealous that you are accomplishing something and are proud of your achievement. This is their problem, so don't let it become yours by agreeing to eat.

➡ ***They may not want you to succeed.*** This is rare, but it spells trouble for the person on a program. You can spot it in acts of sabotage. The person may develop a sudden craving for your favorite food or may say demoralizing things like, "You have always failed before and will fail again." Several reasons come to mind as to why another person would act this way, but I do not want to launch into a lengthy psychological analysis. You are better off ignoring these comments. Confronting the person rarely helps and can make the situation worse. Again, this is the other person's problem, so don't let it influence you. If this person offers you food or encourages you to eat, refuse in a polite way, but be sure to refuse. Eventually, the person will get the message and will quit trying.

➡ ***They think you are starving.*** These people imagine themselves in your shoes and are certain they would be ravenous. Because so many people associate food with love, encouraging you to eat is one way to show concern. Assure them that you are fine and that they can help by ignoring your diet and by not offering you food.

➡️ **They want to test your determination.** They may want to tease you or to see how serious you are about your program. This seems cruel, but it happens. Show them just how serious you can be.

Be Polite, but Be Firm

When others pressure you to eat, stand up for yourself and refuse. Avoid being aggressive or insulting, even if you suspect evil motives. The polite approach works best. After a few polite refusals, most people will learn that their pressures will not work, and they will quit pestering you.

If Aunt Irma offers you fudge, you might say, "Gee Aunt Irma, I love your fudge, but I'm not very hungry. I would enjoy a cup of tea." If your husband stops to get ice cream with you in the car, say "I hope you enjoy it, but I really don't want the calories."

"It's all your fault. You stopped in front of the bakery store."

If you have trouble being assertive, try to predict the situations where others may pressure you to eat. Plan a response, and practice it so that when the situation arises, you are prepared to be polite but firm.

Imperatives: Another Attitude Trap

Tape/CD 4
Section 3

Let's switch gears now and talk about another type of attitude trap—the imperatives. Imperatives include words that imply perfection or urgency, or allow no room for error. Examples of imperative words include "always," "must," and "never." If you are like most people, you may pepper your vocabulary with imperatives. Using these words can pave the path to trouble. Here are some examples from some of my clients.

➡️ "I will *never* eat more than 1,200 calories."

➡️ "I *must* exercise every day."

➡️ "I *must never* eat cookie dough ice cream again."

➡️ "I *must never* miss an exercise class."

➡️ "I will eat a salad for lunch *every* day."

➡️ "I *must* do at least 30 minutes of exercise, or it won't count."

➡️ "I will *always* meet my daily exercise goals."

➡️ "I *must always* control my cravings for sweets."

➡️ "Chocolate is my downfall, so I will avoid it *always*."

➡️ "I *must* have perfect control of my eating."

➡️ "I will *always* control the moods that make me eat."

These thoughts can float around in your mind waiting to take pot shots at your restraint. If you exceed your calorie level one

CATHY©Cathy Guisewite. Reprinted with permission of Universal Press Syndicate. All rights reserved

Be on the lookout for imperatives—they can get in the way and derail your progress.

day, you can easily recover from the extra calories if your control stays intact. However, the imperatives can get a clean shot at you if your mind cranks out thoughts like, "I should never eat more than I'm told." When this happens, you may be a goner. Disappointment occurs, and you can easily lose sight of many positive accomplishments just because of a few mistakes.

Individuals who feel they should avoid certain foods are especially likely to fall prey to the imperatives. If you forbid yourself peanuts, you will be fine for a week or two. You may then start to crave peanuts, wonder how they would taste, and fantasize about a peanut feast when the program ends. Then you might eat some peanuts, because either someone offers them to you or you break down and buy them. Feeling like a failure may then weaken your restraint even further. Dichotomous thinking (I'll discuss this later in the program) may take over and push you off the ledge, and *you fall* off your program.

Try to find imperatives in your vocabulary. What do you expect of yourself, and how can you banish words like *never* and *al-*

ways from your internal conversations? Replace the imperatives with language that allows some room for error and flexibility. Remember, there is no such thing as a perfect person. This is why I have talked so much about setting *realistic* goals.

The table below illustrates some examples of common imperative statements and some methods to counter them. These may apply to you in one way or another, but if they do not, you can use them as examples to form your own methods of dealing with imperatives. Once again, being prepared can make you ready to deal with most difficult situations.

The imperatives are habits just like other behaviors and attitudes. To develop a new habit, practice is the key. It may seem funny to practice thinking a certain way, but it really works. Once you know what attitudes give you trouble, you can gradually weaken their ability to influence you by replacing them with positive ways of thinking.

Imperative and Counter Statements *(example)*

Imperative Statement	Counter Statement
I will *never* eat candy bars.	I will do my best to eat fewer candy bars, but if I have one, it is a sign to increase my control, not to let down and give up.
I will *never* get depressed because it makes me eat.	Everybody feels down at times. If I get depressed, I will think of reacting with something other than eating—walking may be a good alternative.
I will exercise *every* day.	This is my goal, and I will do my best to reach it. But, when I cannot, I will try harder the next day.

Facts, Fantasies, and Fiber

I remember my parents and grandparents explaining how it was important to eat more "roughage." What they really meant was to eat more fiber. This turned out to be good advice. In the 1970s there was an explosion of interest in fiber. Books and magazines carried fiber diets, and sales of bran cereals increased dramatically. Other high-fiber foods also appeared in the stores. This was a positive development that turned out not to be a fad.

Dietary fiber comes primarily from the tough cell walls of plants. These materials include cellulose, hemicellulose, lignin, and pectin (which is used in home canning to turn fruit juice to jelly). Fiber is not broken down by digestion like other foods and retains its basic structure during transit through the digestive system. The strand-like quality of fiber maintains its rigid structure as it passes through the digestive tract.

Fiber absorbs water during the digestive process. This moisture helps with movement of waste products through the bowel. A brief lesson on digestion should help to clarify this process.

When you chew and swallow food, both the chewing and saliva begin to break down food into smaller nutrients. Stomach acid continues the process as food moves along, then more digestion continues in the small intestine. Toward the end of the line, waste products combine with water in the large intestine and are eliminated as stools. A stool with much water is larger and softer

? Did You Know?

DISAPPOINTMENT IS A FUNCTION OF GOALS AND EXPECTATIONS. THEREFORE, THE MORE REALISTIC AND ACHIEVABLE YOUR GOALS, THE LESS DISAPPOINTMENT YOU WILL EXPERIENCE.

and moves through the colon more easily. A stool with little moisture is small and hard and creates the discomfort of constipation.

Much of the desirable moisture that facilitates movement of the stools comes from water absorbed by fiber. This is why increased fiber is prescribed for people with problems in the gastrointestinal tract such as diverticulitis, irritable bowel syndrome, and constipation. Studies show that fiber also reduces the risk of serious diseases like cancer of the colon.

The study of fiber and health gained momentum with the discovery that Africans living in rural settings rarely get diverticulitis. This occurs when a bubble or mucous membrane pushes out from inside the intestine. The diet of these Africans averages 25 grams of fiber per day, compared to 6 grams per day for the typical American. Cancer of the colon follows a similar pattern—it occurs rarely in rural Africa but is common in industrialized countries. Furthermore, rates for these diseases have increased in the U.S. In the past century, fiber intake has decreased dramatically because of processed foods and less intake of fresh fruits and vegetables.

High-Fiber Vegetables, Fruits, and Cereals

(One Food Guide Pyramid Serving Each)

Description	Cal	Carb (g)	Fiber (g)
Dried Beans:			
Beans, baked (1.2 cup)	282	62	17
Beans, kidney, bld (1.2 cup)	263	48	20
Lentils, bld (1.2 cup)	276	48	19
Vegetables:			
Broccoli, ckd (½ cup)	26	5	3
Broccoli, raw (2 cup)	40	7	4
Brussels sprouts, ckd (½ cup)	32	7	2
Carrots, raw (½ cup)	28	6	2
Cauliflower, raw (½ cup)	13	3	1
Corn, ckd (½ cup)	82	20	2
Lettuce, Romaine (1 cup)	8	1	1
Peas, green bld (½ cup)	62	11	4
Spinach, raw (2 cup)	13	2	2
Tomatoes, raw (.6 cup)	19	4	1
Fruits:			
Apricots, raw (½ cup)	40	9	2
Banana, raw (1 med)	110	29	4
Blackberries, raw (½ cup)	37	9	4
Cherries, fresh (½ cup)	52	12	2
Dates, pitted (½ cup)	245	65	7
Dried fruit, mixed (2.3 oz)	158	42	5
Figs, fresh (2 med)	74	19	3
Guava, raw (2 med)	49	11	4
Kiwi, raw (1 med w/peel)	46	11	3
Orange (1 med)	62	15	3
Peach, raw (1 med)	42	11	2
Pear, raw (1 med)	100	25	4
Prunes, dried (.4 cup)	163	43	5
Raspberries, red, fresh (½ cup)	30	7	4
Bread, Cereal, and Rice:			
Bran cereal, 100% (½ cup)	89	24	10
Bran flakes (1 cup)	100	22	4
Bran cereal, 100% (½ cup)	89	24	10
Oat bran cereal, ckd, (5 oz)	47	13	3
Oatmeal cereal, ckd (½ cup)	73	13	2
Raisin nut bran cereal (½ cup)	105	21	3
Rice, long grain brown (.4 cup)	87	18	1
Shredded Wheat (1 oz)	94	23	4
Whole-wheat cereal, ckd (½ cup)	75	17	2
Whole-wheat bread (1 slice)	69	13	2

Note: Each of the food items listed above counts as one serving from the Food Guide Pyramid. This table should be used as a guide for the foods listed. Because food values vary by size, weight, and brand name, it is important to read the food labels for these foods carefully.

Of course, fiber in the diet is only one of many factors that distinguish the rural Africans from us. One such factor is fat in the diet, which also has been linked to disease. There are dozens of non-dietary factors (stress, etc.) that might be involved. What does this mean for our diet?

Increased fiber in the diet protects against certain diseases. The comparisons between rural and industrialized cultures have now been joined by laboratory and large-scale studies so that government agencies like the National Cancer Institute advocate increased fiber in the diet.

Most Americans should increase their dietary fiber intake. Nutritionists suggest that a healthy goal is to aim for an average intake of 25–35 grams of fiber each day. High-fiber foods may help control your appetite because they add bulk, but they also have health benefits. Fiber comes from vegetables, fruits, and cereals. The table on the left lists some common high-fiber foods. Try to increase the number of these foods in your diet.

Fruit in Your Diet

Fruit and fruit juices are an important ingredient of a well-balanced diet. Fruits are naturally low in sodium and dietary fat, and they are an excellent source of fiber and carbohydrate. They provide generous amounts of vitamins A and C and potassium.

Increasing Fruit in Your Diet

Most Americans fall short in their daily consumption of fruits. This is particularly true of children and adolescents. When this happens, the body suffers from a lack of important vitamins, minerals, and fiber. Here are some tips that may help you add fruit to your diet.

Snacks

Fruit makes a terrific snack—whether in the morning, afternoon, or evening. Canned juices are also convenient and easy to take with you when you are on the go. Instead of a soda or cup of coffee, drink fruit juice. Watch out for the calories in fruit juice, however. One cup of canned orange juice has 105 calories. If you don't have fresh fruit available for a snack, canned fruit will do fine, but watch out for the heavy syrup and added sugars.

Breakfast

Breakfast is an important meal—one that should not be skipped. This is a good opportunity to have a serving of fruit. Six ounces of fruit juice is a good way to start the day. But be careful to make sure you are drinking 100 percent fruit juice. Many of the fruit drinks, aides, and punches on the market contain only a small percentage of actual fruit juice and have a lot of added sugar.

If you have cereal for breakfast, top it off with fresh fruit instead of sugar. Strawberries, blueberries, bananas, and grapes are smart choices and take little time to prepare. You can buy frozen berries when fresh ones are out of season. If you are in a rush, take the fruit with you. Keep fresh oranges, bananas, kiwi, apples, peaches, or pears available to take with you.

Lunch

If you take your lunch to work or school, include some fresh or canned fruit. Fruit is a healthy substitute for dessert. If you eat out, it is still possible to have some fruit. Many restaurants now offer fresh fruit as an appetizer or for dessert, but there are still some that do not offer fruit on the menu. If fruit is not available, ask for fruit juice.

Dinner

Dinner time is a good opportunity to review your fruit intake for the day. If you missed a serving or two during the day, add a glass of fruit juice to your evening menu. Fresh fruit also can be included with your meal (e.g., a fruit salad) or as a dessert.

How Many Servings?

The Food Guide Pyramid suggests two to four servings per day from the Fruit Group. This is less than you may think and should not be difficult to include in your daily diet.

How Much Is a Serving?

Servings from the Fruit Group are relatively easy to remember. The table on page 168 includes food items that count as a single serving. As a general rule, the following count as one serving:

➡ 1 medium apple, orange, banana, peach, or pear

➡ ½ cup of chopped, cooked, or canned fruit

➡ 1 cup of small berries

➡ ¾ cup or 6 oz of fruit juice

Selection Hints

In most parts of the country, certain fruits are seasonal, which makes it necessary to choose from a variety of different fruits. Variety is important because differ-

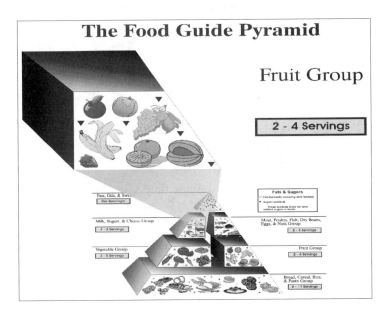

Fruit Group

(One Fruit Group Serving Each)

Description	Cal	Fat Cal	Pro (g)	Carb (g)
Apple, raw, 1 med	80	0	0	22
Apple juice, cnd (6 fl oz)	87	2	0	0
Applesauce, swt, cnd (½ cup)	97	2	0	25
Apricots, raw (½ cup)	40	3	1	2
Apricot nectar (6 fl oz)	105	2	1	27
Banana, raw, 1 med	110	0	1	29
Blackberries, raw (½ cup)	37	3	1	9
Blueberries, raw (½ cup)	41	2	0	10
Cantaloupe, sliced (½ cup)	31	2	1	7
Casaba/Crenshaw melon, sliced (½ cup)	22	1	1	5
Cherries, raw (½ cup)	45	2	1	11
Dates, chopped, pitted (½ cup)	245	4	2	65
Figs, fresh, 2 med	74	3	0	19
Fruit salad, fresh w/citrus (½ cup)	50	3	0	13
Grapefruit, pink, raw (½ cup)	43	1	1	11
Grapefruit juice, fresh (6 fl oz)	72	2	1	17
Grapes, raw (1 cup)	60	6	1	16
Grape juice, cnd (6 fl oz)	94	0	0	24
Guava, raw, 2 med	49	7	1	11
Honeydew melon (½ cup)	31	1	0	1
Kiwi, raw, 2 med	100	9	2	24
Mandarin oranges, sections (½ cup)	43	2	1	11
Mango, fresh (½ cup)	15	1	1	4
Nectarine, raw, 1 med	70	5	1	16
Orange, raw, 1 med	64	1	1	16
Orange juice, fresh (6 fl oz)	84	3	1	19
Papaya, raw, slices (½ cup)	27	1	0	7
Peach, raw, 1 med	40	0	1	11
Peach, cnd/heavy syrup (½ cup)	73	1	0	19
Peach nectar, cnd (6 fl oz)	101	0	1	26
Pear, raw, 1 med	98	6	1	25
Pear halves, cnd/lt syrup (½ cup)	72	0	0	19
Pear nectar, cnd (½ cup)	113	0	0	30
Pineapple, fresh, diced (½ cup)	38	3	0	10
Pineapple juice, cnd (6 fl oz)	105	1	1	26
Raspberries, red, fresh (½ cup)	30	3	1	7
Strawberries, fresh, slices (½ cup)	25	3	1	6
Watermelon, fresh, chpd (½ cup)	25	3	0	6

Note: Each of the food items listed above counts as one serving from the Fruit Group of the Food Guide Pyramid. This table should be used as a guide for the foods listed. Because food values vary by size, weight, and brand name, it is important to read the food labels for these foods carefully.

ent fruits provide different amounts of important nutrients. The following tips may be helpful in your selection:

➡ Choose citrus fruits, melons, and berries regularly—these are rich in Vitamin C.

➡ Choose fresh fruits as often as you can—they do not have added sugars and other preservatives. Try to avoid fruits that are canned or frozen in heavy syrups and sweetened fruit juices—you'll save many unwanted calories this way.

➡ Choose fresh fruit instead of juice whenever possible. As a general rule, the fresh fruit will have fewer calories and more fiber than the juice.

➡ Choose fruit juices that are pure fruit juice and do not contain large amounts of added water and sugars.

Storing Foods: Out of Sight, Out of Mouth

The less you see and think about food, the easier it will be to control your eating. Where and how you store food can influence what and how much you eat.

Let's examine two approaches to the same problem to illustrate this point. Suppose salted nuts are your passion, and you bring home a one-pound bag from Tiny's Nut House. You could make the nuts a constant temptation by keeping them in an open dish, using the classic dodge that, "I need them in case someone drops by."

Another approach would be to keep the nuts out of sight. This would put some distance and effort between you and the nuts. You could lock them in a safe that is stored in your attic behind 24 boxes of old papers and books. In which case would you eat more nuts?

The attic example is far-fetched, but it does show how the accessibility of food can influence your eating. Storing food wisely and keeping it out of sight can be helpful. Here are some ways to follow through.

Hide the High-Calorie Foods

High-calorie impulse foods should be stored out of sight. Put the ice cream under the frozen peas and behind the chicken breasts so you won't see it each time you open the freezer door. Store the cookies on a high shelf behind the seldom-used guest dishes, and put the potato chips on a low shelf behind the colander.

This leads back to Antecedents (discussed in Lesson Five). Bringing problem foods in the house and having them available are steps that precede eating. Of course, it would be preferable to intervene at the earliest step and not buy problem foods at all. If you do buy the foods, keeping them out of sight is the next logical step. Keeping food out of sight serves two purposes. If you don't see it, you may not be stimulated to eat. In addition, putting some effort between you and the food stops automatic eating and gives you time to change your mind. You can help the cause even more by storing problem foods in opaque containers. Keeping the brownies in an opaque plastic bowl will make them less tempting than having them in a clear cookie jar. Store leftovers immediately after eating or, better yet, right after you put servings on your plate. Eating more food will require more time and effort on your part if you later decide to have seconds.

Keep Healthful Snacks Available

Because Sherlock Holmes would now have trouble finding the high-calorie foods in your house, you can use the space vacated by the goodies to store healthful foods. When you buy fresh fruits and vegetables at the store, clean and cut them up immediately when you get home. If you get an urge to eat, reach for the celery, carrot sticks, raisins, apples, cauliflower, bananas, or oranges.

Compulsive Eating and Binge Eating

Tape/CD 2
Section 7

Doctors increasingly recognize that a significant minority of overweight individuals struggle with episodes of compulsive eating or binge eating. Overeaters Anonymous popularized the most widely used term for this problem—compulsive overeating. Researchers call this binge eating.

The official definition of binge eating has two features. The first is eating what

"Anybody seen a box of chocolate-chip cookies?"

others would consider a large amount of food, and the second is feeling out of control. When this happens with sufficient frequency (two times a week or more) and over a sufficient period of time (six months), a person fits the diagnosis called Binge Eating Disorder. I hasten to add that some people have binges many more times than this. Others have fewer or less frequent binges but still have a troubling problem. If you think you may have a problem with Binge Eating, log onto the www.TheLife StyleCompany.com website and complete the Binge Eating Questionnaire. You can find this under the tab "Self-Assessments" on the Home page. Completing this questionnaire can help you decide if you need additional help with binge eating problems.

In the early stages of research on binge eating, some experts felt that individuals who ate compulsively needed treatment specifically for this type of eating disorder. This was in addition to whatever help they needed for weight management. More recently, research has shown that individuals who participate in a weight loss program like LEARN stop binge eating as well as the people who participate directly in a binge-eating program, but in addition lose more weight. Therefore, if you have a problem with binge eating, you may find that this program helps control overeating along with promoting weight loss.

Some people, however, may need additional help. If by this time in the program you are having problems with eating compulsively, you should consider whether additional resources would be helpful. I suggest three approaches.

The first approach is to use a book entitled *Overcoming Binge Eating* written by Dr. Christopher Fairburn, a leading authority from Oxford University in England. The book is an excellent, thoroughly-tested guide, and it brings the best of science to the reader in a useable and friendly format. The book is published by Guilford Press in New York and can be ordered by calling 1–888–LEARN–41. This is the best guide of its type available today.

The second, but more expensive, alternative is to seek counseling. If you choose this option, try to see someone who specializes in treating eating disorders. Several organizations can provide the names of professionals in your area who have experience with eating disorders. Cognitive behavior therapy and interpersonal psychotherapy are two effective approaches for binge eating. As such, you might ask the professional you contact if he or she offers either of these treatment options. A good group to consult is the National Eating Disorders Association at 1–800–931–2237 or on the Internet at www.NationalEatingDisorders.org.

A final approach is to consider help from Overeaters Anonymous (OA). While the OA approach has not been evaluated, it does offer strong support and focuses on compulsive eating. For some people, the support, the around-the-clock help available from a sponsor, and the group meetings can be quite helpful.

MY WEEKLY GOALS

This is an excellent time to reassess your physical activity goals. Consider adding running, cycling, or a new type of aerobic exercise to your exercise program. In the relationship arena, be on the lookout for others trying to pressure you to eat. Remember to be polite, but be firm. Keep alert for imperatives finding their way into your vocabulary, and remember that they leave no room for error. Banish them from your thinking, and replace them with more realistic thoughts.

On the nutrition front, do your best to include 25–35 grams of fiber in your diet every day and to eat 2–4 servings from the Fruit Group of the Food Guide Pyramid. Be alert and hide the high-calorie foods from sight. In addition, think about personal goals you can set from your experience thus far in the program. Which behavior or attitude changes are most important for you? Be sure to continue to record your weight changes on the My Weight Change Record on page 216. Good luck this week!

KNOWLEDGE REVIEW

Lesson Ten

1. T F   If you overeat when you are under stress, the only solution is to avoid the stressful situation.

2. T F   Running and cycling have many benefits. They are good forms of exercise for people trying to lose weight.

3. T F   The best kind of exercise for weight loss is rigorous enough to build muscle, which in turn speeds up metabolism.

4. T F   Aerobic activities are designed to build strength in the shortest possible time.

5. T F   When someone offers you food, it is best to accept it as a sign of their friendship.

6. T F   Imperatives are words like "always" and "never." They leave no room for error.

7. T F   The emphasis on fiber may be dangerous because fiber is indigestible material that can harm the intestinal system.

8. T F   A diet high in fiber may help protect against certain diseases.

9. T F   Fruits, vegetables, and some cereals tend to be high in fiber.

10. T F   A healthy diet should contain between 25–35 grams of fiber each day.

11. T F   Most Americans eat plenty of fruits and should not worry about increasing their daily intake.

12. T F   Keeping high-calorie foods stored out of sight can decrease impulsive eating.

13. T F   Binge eating is characterized by eating large amounts of food with an accompanying sense of loss of control.

(Answers in Appendix C, page 224)

"Mommy says to stop counting by fives."

Monitoring Form—Lesson Ten

*Today's Date:*_____

Time	Food and Amount	Calories	Milk & Dairy	Meats & Protein	Vegetables	Fruits	Bread
Total Daily Caloric Intake & Food Guide Pyramid Servings							

Daily Activity Record (Caloric Expenditure)

Time	Activity	Calories	Minutes	No. of Steps

Personal Goals this Week	Most of the Time	Some of the Time	Rarely
1. Meet or exceed walking goal of _____ steps each day			
2. Use physical activity to reduce stress			
3. Resist pressures to eat from others			
4. Avoid imperative statements when setting goals			
5. Hide the high-calorie foods from sight			
6. Eat 2–4 servings from the Fruit Group and 25–35 grams of fiber each day			
7. Eat less than _____ calories each day			

Lesson Eleven

I hope you had a great week. Two lessons remain in The LEARN Program, yet we still have important areas to cover. In this lesson we will focus on inactivity cues and triggers. As you have learned, many eating cues and triggers abound in today's food environment. In a similar fashion, cues and triggers abound to keep us from being physically active. We'll take a close look at another attitude trap—impossible dream thinking. On the nutrition front, we'll complete our discussion on the Food Guide Pyramid by talking about the bottom tier of the Pyramid, and I will discuss strategies for eating away from home. I'll then talk about food and weight fantasies, a common issue for individuals at this stage of a weight loss program. Finally, we'll peek into the future to see what paths are available to you. We have much to discuss, so let's begin.

Taking Control of Your Physical Activity

In Lesson Nine I discussed the concept of "externality"—being sensitive to external signals related to food. External cues also can influence your exercise behavior. These cues can either work for you—reminding you to be physically active—or against you—encouraging you to be inactive. Here are some strategies to help you keep active:

➡ Make an exercise appointment in your day planner.

➡ Set your computer to beep every hour, reminding you to get up and take a short walk.

➡ Leave yourself a voice-mail reminder to exercise.

➡ Send yourself an e-mail to schedule physical activity time.

➡ Make an activity "date" with your partner.

➡ Keep your walking shoes with you in a bag or in your car.

➡ Put your exercise clothes on the dresser so you see them the first thing in the morning or when you get home in the evening.

➡ Get a dog and take him or her for a walk every day.

→ Set up a regular time to exercise with someone you know.

→ Set up a brief time to be active during the work day.

What are some cues that keep you from being active? For many people, the television can be a powerful cue; for others, their favorite chair in the den beckons them to sit when they walk in after a long day at work. You can counter the inactivity cues, but first, you have to know what they are. Simply turning off the TV or limiting your viewing time may keep you from being inactive. If you do watch TV, try walking around the house, stretching, or doing chores during the commercials. Let the commercials become the cues to be active. Reward yourself by sitting in your favorite chair in the evenings—after you have completed your physical activity goals for the day.

What other cues cause you to be inactive? If your family members are sitting on the couch when you get home, you may be less likely to go take a walk. In this example, both the couch itself and your loved ones sitting on it can cue you to be a couch potato. You may need to avoid the den until after you have exercised. Modern conveniences, including those pesky drive-thru windows, also cue people to be inactive. Resist the urge to save a few minutes, park your car, and walk into the bank, restaurant, or dry cleaners. Friends or family who invite you to last-minute celebrations (typically involving food) may pressure you to skip your exercise session. In this situation, you have several options. You could join them at the restaurant and take a walk after dinner; you could politely decline their invitation and do your physical activity as planned; or you could ask your friends to take a short walk with you before you eat.

Think of the cues that keep you from being active. List them on the My Inactivity Cues and Counters worksheet below. Now, think of ways to counter these inactivity cues and write them down in the second column. This is an important activity, so please take time now to complete this worksheet before you move on.

Pleasurable Partner Activities

Many nice activities are available that you can do with a partner. Use these as re-

My Inactivity Cues and Counters	
Cues	**Counters**
	1.
	2.
	3.
	4.
	1.
	2.
	3.
	4.
	1.
	2.
	3.
	4.

wards from you to your partner, from your partner to you, or as a joint bit of pleasure to acknowledge mutual efforts and support. The list on the right gives many possible activities. Some are appropriate for partners in romantic relationships while others are for any partnership.

Share these ideas with your partner, and use them for special times. If you are working together as a team, it will be nice to have some fun in addition to the hard work you have been doing. Remember that there are many nice partner activities not on the list, so be creative. Add as many ideas to the list as you can.

Impossible Dream Thinking

Along with negative self-talk and internal attitude traps, Impossible Dream Thinking ranks high as an attitude barrier to losing weight. In the next lesson, I'll discuss another attitude trap—Dichotomous Thinking. Impossible Dream Thinking occurs when you fantasize or dream about *impossible* accomplishments. You might have 100 pounds to lose on Thanksgiving and fantasize about wearing a size nine to the office New Year's Eve party.

 ATTITUDE ALERT

Before you turn the page and skip to the next section, let me assure you that most people are not aware of these thoughts. Yet, after some reflection, most see them clearly. Maybe a few more examples will bring this home.

Impossible Dream Thinking occurs when you daydream about how wonderful life will be after weight loss. It is common for those losing weight to imagine an improved marriage, better job, wonderful social life, intimate relationships, and other happy endings to their struggle to lose weight. These things may be possible, but it is unlikely that weight loss alone will make them happen.

Pleasurable Partner Activities

Take a romantic walk	Ride bicycles
Go to a concert	Go window shopping
Plan a day at the park	Go on a picnic
Take a nature walk	Get a puppy or a kitten
Send flowers	Send a card
Pick fresh fruit	Go to a museum
Go bowling	Get a board game
Buy a nice wine	Buy a new book
Play a new sport	Buy a pedometer
See the city	Find a fair or festival
Send a singing telegram	Visit a mutual friend
Plan a mystery weekend	Do your partner's laundry
See a movie	Write a thank you note
Buy cologne or perfume	Plan a surprise party
Get gift certificates	Fix something broken
Get a nice plant	Balance the checkbook
Buy a tape or CD	Watch the sunset
Make Sunday breakfast	Just sit and enjoy each other

Pleasurable Partner Activities I Can Do

_____

_____

_____

_____

_____

_____

This type of thinking also occurs when you imagine succeeding at a program without hard work. When most people begin a program and fantasize about the future, they do not picture the time and effort required for keeping records, changing their eating habits, or exercising regularly.

It does no harm to hope for the best and aspire to improve your life. However, weight loss will usually not make a bad marriage good or shoot you to the top of the corporate ladder. Getting your weight down can actually be a disappointing experience if your *impossible* fantasies are not fulfilled. This is what happened with one of my clients, Audrey.

LIFESTYLE PROFILES

Audrey was one of my first overweight clients. She was 28 years old and was working on an advanced degree in chemistry. Audrey had been heavy since childhood and had been in no serious relationships. She was lonely and yearned to settle down with a stable and loving partner.

Audrey lost weight rapidly and seemed happy about her progress. She spoke often, but in a joking way, about how she would meet the person of her dreams when she got thin. I would easily spot it now, but at the time, I did not realize how serious she was about this fantasy. When she reached her goal, she steadily became more depressed because no spectacular romance evolved. Clearly, there were problems other than weight that prevented the relationships from developing, yet Audrey saw weight loss as her salvation. Fortunately, I worked with Audrey on these problems, and she eventually did find the romance she was seeking.

SIPRESS

This is a dramatic example of Impossible Dream Thinking. This specific case may not parallel your situation, but think honestly about whether you are harboring impossible dreams.

For many people losing weight, life does change in dramatic and positive ways. I hope this happens for you and that what you hope will happen actually occurs. Please remember, however, that weight loss may not automatically change your life.

Here are four ways to deal with Impossible Dream thinking. They can help keep your spirits high.

➡ *Counter the impossible dream.* Pinpoint your Impossible Dreams and counter them with more rational expectations. Methods for developing counter statements were discussed in Lesson Nine on page 151 in the section on Internal Attitude Traps.

➡ *Set realistic short-term goals.* Concern yourself with what you will do today and tomorrow, not what life will be like when you lose weight. This gives you many chances to experience success *now* because you will be making small accomplishments in route to a larger goal. It also will prevent unrealistic fantasies from dominating your thoughts.

➡ *Focus on behavior, not weight.* Remember that your behavior must change before weight can change; so give yourself credit for following the program. You will have something to feel good about every day and will not be so discouraged by weight setbacks.

➡ *Set flexible goals.* If your goals don't work, set new ones. If you vowed to walk three miles each day but cannot, walk one or two miles every other day and work your way up to the three-mile goal. This puts the focus on short-term changes in behavior, so Impossible Dream Thinking will fade to the background.

Cravings vs. Hunger

Tape/CD 3
Section 6

Here is the place where your mind and body may deceive each other, and where the "A" (Attitudes) part of The LEARN Program comes to the fore. When you eat, are you responding to physical hunger or to psychological cravings? Take the Cravings vs. Hunger Quiz on the right to find out which is the mind and which is the body. For each statement, check either true or false.

Cravings vs. Hunger Quiz		
True	False	Statement
		1. Even after a large meal, I still want dessert.
		2. I often have a gnawing feeling in my stomach.
		3. When someone mentions a food I love, I feel like eating.
		4. I feel light-headed after not eating for hours.
		5. When I drive by a fast-food restaurant, I want to eat.
		6. There is a time every day when I feel hungry.

Situations 1, 3, and 5 usually indicate psychological cravings. Situations 2 and 4 signal physical hunger. Situation 6 could be either. Distinguishing cravings from hunger is important. Once you can distinguish the cravings, we will work on special anti-craving techniques.

You can identify cravings by paying careful attention to when you want to eat. Does something stimulate the urge beside actual hunger? Does someone offer you food? Does something make you think about food? Do you have bad feelings that food would help satisfy? You can note these cravings on your Monitoring Form. This will remind you of the situations in which food will be hard to resist.

Conquering the Cravings

The *distraction* approach involves ignoring the cravings. When you know a craving is about to engulf you, do something else. Think about something wonderful, plan a dream vacation, or do anything to take your attention away from the urge to eat. The craving will usually pass.

The distraction method works best for people who have a good imagination or can change activities or thoughts at an instant's notice. You only have to do these things for a few moments, because cravings generally pass within minutes or even seconds. If you are bombarded by cravings throughout the day, confronting the cravings may be most effective.

The *confrontation* approach pits you against the craving. Let's say you want to raid the refrigerator for ice cream. You could pretend the urge is another person trying to convince you to eat the ice cream. Argue with this person and say why you will not give in to the urge. Another approach is to visualize the ice cream container beckoning to you and tempting you with promises of fulfillment. Imagine how silly it is to let the ice cream get the best of you.

A typical confrontation scene might be as follows. You get the urge to stop for a snack while driving home from work. You recognize the craving and decide to get the best of it. You say, "You nasty craving! You

want me to stop for peanut butter cups when I'm not really hungry. I'll show you who's boss. I am in charge of my own life and my weight."

Think of these two approaches now and decide which will work for you. If you are in doubt, experiment with both. Try to arrive at a strategy as soon as possible, be it distraction or confrontation. This will prepare you in advance for the inevitable cravings you will face. Do your best not to give in.

Your Body and Your Self-Esteem

Tape/CD 4
Section 1

How we feel about our bodies can be central to how we feel about ourselves. Our view of our own body is called body image, and unfortunately, body image is negative for most people, especially for women and people who are overweight. This is not surprising considering the enormous pressure in our society to be thin and for women to be valued for how they look rather than for who they are as people. Many, many people internalize these social norms, despair at the difference between the way they look and the way they think they should look, and then hurt themselves emotionally as a result. It really isn't fair, because the social norms present an ideal that is unrealistic and even unhealthy.

 LIFESTYLE PROFILES

Let's look at how this might work for a young woman; I'll call her Ann. As Ann approaches puberty, she is full of energy, is athletic, enjoys being active, has fun, and takes pleasure in what her body can do for her. Yet, she is increasingly aware of the need to be thin. She is not prepared for this pressure to be so intense at the very time puberty causes her body to deposit more fat. Instead of accepting and enjoying the changes in her body, she feels her body is betraying her. Natural processes like eating and exercise become a battleground.

She must restrict what she eats and must now exercise, not for fun, but for the purpose of losing weight. Ann may enter into a fight with her own body that will never end.

As Ann enters her 20s and then passes the 30-, 40-, and 50-year benchmarks, two things are likely to happen. One is that she will be dissatisfied with her body. She will overlook its virtues—that it allows her to be active, to move places, and to feel sensual. Instead, she will focus on the disparity between ideal and actual and will feel it is her fault that she does not look perfect.

The second event is that Ann will let her body image have too much impact on her self-esteem. Our self-esteem is made up of how we evaluate ourselves on many dimensions (as a parent, child, brother or sister, employer or employee, friend, etc.). Our looks influence us all, but for some people, appearance creeps into the heart of self-esteem. It can crowd out other positive influences, so that no matter how good we are at other things, there is always this looming matter of how we look.

Developing a Positive Body Image

Having a positive view of your body, no matter how imperfect, is really important. If you dislike how you look and accept society's unrealistic beauty standards, you will be unhappy with what you accomplish in this program or any other. The risk is that you will make very positive changes in eating, activity, and weight, but feel you are still far from your goal and, therefore, will despair over your lack of success. This is a setup for disappointment, frustration, and giving up.

The Body Image Workbook, written by Dr. Thomas F. Cash for the general public, is an excellent book on this topic. The book is published by New Harbinger Publications and can be purchased by calling 1–800–736–7323. The book contains many good ideas for evaluating how we feel about our bodies, how this affects the way we feel about ourselves in general, and how we can respond.

In his book, Cash discusses fundamental assumptions people make about their appearance and their lives. Some of these are shown in the table on the right, "Faulty Assumptions about Appearance."

These assumptions lead to an overestimation of how appearance governs one's life and to an overemphasis on changing appearance to improve well-being. With these common assumptions, a person can be continually dissatisfied with his or her appearance, and no weight loss is enough.

So, what can you do to be happier about the way you look? The book written by Cash includes exercises and ways to evaluate whether your body image is changing. Here are some ideas that may be helpful.

➡ *Get accustomed to seeing your body.* Most people who do not like their bodies do everything they can to avoid looking at them. Mirrors, especially full-length mirrors, store windows, and other places are avoided. Stop avoiding and find a way to believe that your body can be your friend.

➡ *Challenge the faulty assumptions about your appearance and life.* To equate appearance with happiness is to give the body much more power than it deserves. You can be a smashing success at many things in life (most notably being a good person), irrespective of appearance. Appearance is only one aspect of our lives.

➡ *Confront what is realistic for you as an individual.* Given what you have looked like during your adult life, given how your parents looked, and given how difficult it might be for you to lose to an "ideal" weight, be candid, and consider how you might "realistically" look. Perhaps you can do more, perhaps not.

➡ *Uncouple body image from self-esteem.* The assumption that how you look is who you are can be very damaging.

➡ *Focus on how your body is a gift.* Your body can do many fine things for

Faulty Assumptions about Appearance

1. **Looks are central to who I am.**

2. **People first notice what is wrong with my appearance.**

3. **Appearance reflects the inner person.**

4. **If I looked different, I could be happier.**

5. **By controlling my appearance, I can control my social and emotional life.**

6. **My appearance is responsible for much of what has happened to me.**

7. **The only way I could ever like my looks is to change the way I look.**

Adapted from Cash T. (1997). *The Body Image Workbook.* Oakland, CA: New Harbinger Publications.

you. It allows you to live, to move, to accomplish what you'd like, not to mention how good it feels when you relax, work out, and engage in sensual activities with another person. The body gives you many gifts of living and is, therefore, a gift itself. If you focus on the virtues of your body, it becomes less of an adversary. Being friends with your body is central to your long-term happiness.

None of these will be easy, because how you feel about yourself is the product of years and years of experiences, thoughts, attitudes, and feelings. Just vowing to be happier with the way you look is not enough. You must challenge the faulty assumptions constantly. You must make a concerted effort to reward yourself for looking good, and then practice this new way of thinking for days, weeks, and months. It takes a lot to undo the powerful messages you have been exposed to, so please keep at it. You deserve to feel good about yourself, no matter what you weigh.

Breads, Cereals, Rice, and Pasta in Your Diet

Here we are, at the last tier of the Food Guide Pyramid. Over the last few weeks we have covered a lot of material on nutrition so that you can improve your diet. By now, you should feel very familiar with the Food Guide Pyramid.

Foods from this group of the Pyramid are good sources of complex carbohydrates, such as starch and fiber. These foods are good sources of low-fat energy and provide essential vitamins, minerals, and fiber. Foods from the Bread and Cereal Group should make up the largest part of your daily diet. It is important, however, to watch out for the hidden fats and calories in some of these foods. Bread, cookies, and pastries, for example, typically include

sugar and butter, oil, or margarine. Remember, it is easy to eat many calories from this food group and not get good nutrition. Making wise food choices from this group is important.

Selection Hints

The following guidelines will help you to make good choices from the Bread, Cereal, Rice, and Pasta Group:

➡ Dietary fiber is important for good health, and foods from this food group can be good sources of fiber. Choose several servings a day from whole grains, which are found in whole wheat breads and whole-grain cereals.

➡ Foods that contain low amounts of fat and simple sugars are the best choices for a healthful diet. Choose foods made with small amounts of sugars and fats. These food items include bread, English muffins, rice, and pasta.

➡ Some foods from this group that are made from flour are typically high in fat and sugars. These include cookies, pastries, croissants, doughnuts, and cakes. Keep these foods to a minimum and use fat and sugar substitutes when possible.

➡ Spreads and toppings can add many unwanted calories to the foods in this group while providing little nutrition. The best advice is to leave these items off, or to at least use low-calorie or low-fat toppings, spreads, and sauces.

➡ Most pasta stuffing and sauces use butter or margarine. Use only half of the recipe amount. If milk or cream is called for, use low-fat milk.

➡ If pasta sauces or stuffing call for meat, use lean meat. Trim away any visible fat before cooking, and drain all oil before including in your sauce or stuffing.

How Much Is a Serving?

Servings from this group are simple to remember. As a general rule, the following count as single servings:

Bread, Cereal, Rice, and Pasta Group

(One Bread and Cereal Group Serving Each)

Description	Cal	Fat Cal	Pro (g)	Carb (g)
Bagel, oat bran 1½ (2½")	99	4	4	21
Biscuit, buttermilk, homemade, 1½ (2" ea)	99	41	2	12
Bread, wheat (1 slice)	65	9	2	12
Bread, white, enriched (1 slice)	67	8	2	12
Bread, French (1 small slice)	78	8	3	15
Cereal, clusters (1 oz)	110	16	3	22
Cereal, corn flakes (1 oz)	111	1	2	25
Cereal, cream of wheat, cooked (½ cup)	77	2	2	16
Cereal, honey bran (1 oz)	97	5	2	23
Cereal, rice chex (1 oz)	107	3	2	24
Cookies, chocolate chip (2 ea)	127	53	1	17
Cookies, gingersnap (4 ea)	122	40	2	19
Cookies, Nilla wafers (7 ea)	123	39	1	21
Cookies, oatmeal (2½ ea)	139	53	2	20
Danish, pastry, apple (2½ oz)	210	94	3	27
English muffin (½ ea)	66	5	2	13
Muffins, blueberry (2 oz)	200	36	3	37
Pancake, 4" (1)	86	32	3	11
Pasta/noodles, fresh, cooked (2 oz)	74	5	3	14
Pie, apple, 8" (1/12 piece)	111	46	1	16
Rice, long grain brown, cooked (.4 cup)	87	6	2	18
Rice, long grain white, cooked (½ cup)	103	2	2	22
Waffle, whole grain, 4" (2 ea)	209	79	7	26

➡ 1 slice of bread

➡ 1 oz of ready-to-eat cereal

➡ ½ cup of cooked cereal, rice, or pasta

How Many Servings?

The Food Guide Pyramid suggests 6 to 11 servings each day from the Bread, Cereal, Rice, and Pasta Group. While this may sound like a lot, remember that foods from this group should be the largest part of your daily diet. In addition, the number of servings you select from this food group is dependent upon your daily target calorie goal. The table on page 180 includes common foods from the Bread and Cereal Group that count as a single serving.

A Note
about Breakfast

The discussion above about bread and cereal leads nicely into an important note about breakfast. I mentioned in an earlier lesson that many overweight people skip breakfast. This happens because they may not feel hungry in the morning, they are in a hurry, or they feel that skipping breakfast is a good way to start the day by saving calories. Most people who successfully lose weight resume eating breakfast as they lose weight. This prevents the situation where you find yourself famished later in the day.

Eating breakfast is consistent with the prevailing wisdom among health experts. Research findings support this view. Researchers at the University of Minnesota gave individuals one of five cereals varying in fiber content, plus milk and orange juice,

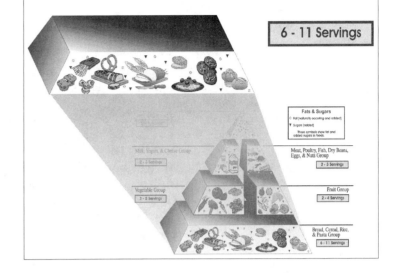

The Food Guide Pyramid
Bread, Cereal, Rice, and Pasta Group

6 - 11 Servings

for breakfast at 7:30 a.m. At 11:00 a.m., the study participants ate a buffet lunch. The amount eaten at lunch was carefully measured and recorded. The individuals who had the high-fiber cereals ate fewer calories at lunch than did the people eating the low-fiber cereals. Especially important is that the people eating the high-fiber cereals ate fewer total calories (combining breakfast and lunch) than those individuals who ate the low-fiber cereals.

Starting the day with breakfast, especially a breakfast high in fiber, may help control calorie intake the rest of the day. In the research study I just described, individuals who ate the high-fiber cereals ate less at lunch even when they felt just as hungry as those participants having the other cereals. So, beginning the day with breakfast

may help you eat less. Read the food labels on cereal boxes carefully so you can choose those high in fiber and low in sugar and calories. In addition to helping you eat less, the fiber may have other positive health benefits such as I discussed in Lesson Ten.

Indeed, breakfast could be the foundation to developing overall healthy eating habits. This is especially true for children, because many habits learned as children carry over into adulthood. You can use many creative ways to make breakfast fun, fast, and easy; it just takes a little planning and dedication. If you are a breakfast-skipper, the breakfast tips that follow may help you incorporate breakfast as an important part of your day. If you are still not convinced, try it for a couple of weeks. The benefits may surprise you.

➡ *No time?* Try getting up a few minutes earlier—10 minutes will do fine; once you are up and going, you will not miss the time. This is plenty of time to have a glass of juice, a bowl of cereal, and some fruit.

➡ *Still no time?* Plan breakfast around foods that are ready to eat or take little time to prepare. Examples include canned or fresh fruit, juices, milk, instant-breakfast mixes, ready-to-eat cold cereals, yogurt, cheese, bagels, or toast.

➡ *Take it to go.* If you still find yourself short on time, pack yourself a breakfast-to-go the night before and eat it the following morning when you have a few extra minutes. Try celery stuffed with cheese, fresh or dried fruit, packaged juice or milk, breakfast bars, a bagel, or English muffin.

➡ *Be creative.* Top cereals with fresh fruit; add jelly or jam to toast, biscuits, or rolls; and add chopped nuts to hot cereals.

➡ *Not hungry?* Drink some juice, and take something with you for a snack later in the morning. Bread, crackers or a piece of fruit will do fine. You may

wish to add some cheese or yogurt. Then drink some milk or water.

➡ *Plan your breakfast the night before.* Make as much advanced preparation as possible. This way you are not confronted with the decision of what to prepare, and much of your meal can be ready and waiting for you when you wake up.

➡ *Start a breakfast partnership.* Enjoy the company of your spouse, a child, or a friend. Take turns making healthy breakfast choices. You also can take turns preparing breakfast with a breakfast partner.

I cannot overstate the importance of a good breakfast. If you are a breakfast-skipper, think of ways to overcome this behavior.

Eating Away from Home

Trips to restaurants can be a minefield of temptation. The best intentions can crumble when you are enjoying yourself with people who feast on delicious foods. Two aspects of this concern me. The first is how much you eat; however, there are methods for keeping eating under control. The second is to control your response to the event.

ATTITUDE ALERT

One trip to a restaurant never torpedoed any weight management program with its calories alone. An extraordinary, massive meal of 5,000 calories could bring only 1½ pounds of weight. The *response* to those calories, however, could lead to trouble. Your attitudes, thoughts, and beliefs about these events are as important as what you eat.

Eating at Restaurants

It is hard to be virtuous at restaurants. This is a real problem for people in business or those whose lifestyle includes eating away from home.

What should you do when dessert comes with the meal? What about a waitress who pours 14 gallons of dressing on your salad? How do you deal with a hot loaf of bread or the basket of chips the waiter delivers before the meal even begins? What do you do about huge portions? How can you refuse when the dessert cart rolls up like a Brink's truck ready to unload its treasures? Let's look at some strategies that may help.

➡ ***Order from the appetizer or salad section of the menu.*** If you find something healthy among the appetizers, or find a salad you like, try ordering this for your meal. There may well be enough food to fill you up and make you feel like you are having a nice meal out.

➡ ***Order à la carte meals.*** You may be inclined to order full meals because the cost is less than for the sum of its parts. This group plan is a booby trap because you order more than you need simply because the price seems attractive. The "value" meals at fast-food restaurants are classic examples of this problem. However, the logic is faulty.

The regular price for a roast beef sandwich might be $5, but for $6 you could get fries and Cole slaw that would normally cost $1 each. The package deal makes sense only if you wanted the other two items anyway. If not, you are saving money you never would have spent. Most of these extras are high-calorie foods like fries. Order just what you want and no more.

➡ ***Share meals or get a doggie bag before the meal.*** Sharing a meal with someone can be a great idea because often there is enough food for two. This is worthwhile even if the restaurant charges you for the extra plate. And, getting a doggie bag before the meal and putting in a portion of the food when it's served insures that it's out of sight and won't tempt you.

➡ ***Watch the salad dressing.*** Because salad dressing is high in fat (oil), eating more than you need really boosts the calories. Ask for salad dressing "on-the-side" so you are not at the mercy of a heavy-handed server. Better yet, leave the salad dressing off completely.

If you need dressing, consider bringing your own bottle of low-fat dressing. Many people do this, and unless you're at the White House for an awards banquet, you shouldn't be embarrassed. I usually order dressing on the side and then dip my fork in the dressing before putting a bite of salad on my folk. It's amazing how little dressing this uses and how much of the good taste you can still have.

➡ ***Watch for hidden calories.*** Many foods contain calories that are added in subtle ways. These hidden calories are important to consider. Think about rich sauces added to meats and vegetables in restaurants, oils added in Italian restaurants, and things breaded and fried in any restaurant. If you cannot guess what is in a dish, ask the waiter or waitress.

➡ ***Watch the Alcohol.*** As I will discuss later in the lesson, alcohol is loaded with calories; it is easy to consume more

9-25 © Jim Jenger, dist. by United Media 1998

"I'm learning to slow my eating."

than you want in the spirit of being social. This is a real temptation when you sit in the bar area waiting for a table in the restaurant.

When you order alcohol, avoid the hard liquor and sweetened drinks. A jigger of whiskey has 110 calories and a Tom Collins has 180 calories. White wine is a better choice, and better yet is a white wine spritzer. You could also order club soda or tomato juice.

Alcohol generally has *empty* calories. Its sugar brings calories with little or no nutrition. You can estimate the calories in alcohol by remembering that the following drinks have about 100 calories each:

➤ 12 oz of light beer

➤ 8 oz of regular beer

➤ 3½ oz of wine

➤ 1 shot of liquor

You may want to refer to the table on page 186 as a reminder of calories in alcohol.

➡ ***Beware of the breadbasket.*** Keep an eye out for that wondrous basket. It comes when you are hungry and excited about being at the restaurant. You can refuse the breadbasket, but if one arrives against your will, let it rest across the table. If you are still tempted, imagine there is a mousetrap under the napkin that covers the bread!

Some people may actually benefit from the breadbasket. They are the ones who use a piece of bread (without butter) to take the edge off their hunger, so that they will eat less of higher-calorie foods later in the meal. You might try this approach, but don't use it as an excuse to eat lots of bread and then eat what you would anyway.

Bread does not have empty calories. It is an important part of your diet—breads and cereals comprise the largest of the five food groups of the Food Guide Pyramid. The purpose of watching the breadbasket is not to cut down on bread, but to avoid eating lots of bread and butter just because it's there.

➡ ***Be wise with dessert.*** Do you deserve dessert when you eat out? After all, you don't get special desserts often, so why not enjoy yourself? Ignore this rationalization, and get dessert under two conditions: you are still hungry, or you have planned it in your day's calories. Think about fresh fruit or sorbet. Both taste good and have far fewer calories than traditional choices.

➡ ***Engage your partner.*** Restaurants are a place where your partner can help. This can begin before you arrive for the meal. Some individuals decide with their partners what to order in advance, before their restraint is weakened by the smells and atmosphere of a nice restaurant. Some even have their partner order for them. At the restaurant, the partner can keep the breadbasket in a safe place and can help by not pushing drinks or desserts.

➡ ***Watch your emotional response.*** If you eat more than you plan, be careful not to consider it a catastrophe. One client used to say, "A 200-calorie doughnut doesn't have to turn into a 3,000-calorie day." We have been working to avoid the attitude traps, such as considering some foods illegal and setting unrealistic goals of never overeating. If you feel guilty, reread the earlier material, and be prepared to rebound from a bout of overeating by eating less, not more. Do *not* use this as a rationalization to overdo it, but keep these events in perspective and use them as a sign that you can do better the next meal or the next day.

These are techniques that people use to control their eating in restaurants. You may think of others yourself. For example, you might drink extra water to help fill up before the meal comes. I have provided a

| My Challenges and Techniques for Eating Out ||
My Challenge	My Technique

worksheet above for you to list your challenges and techniques that will be helpful for you when dining out. Take a few minutes now to complete the worksheet. Feel free to make a copy and carry it with you. When you find yourself eating out, take out your chart and review it before going into the restaurant. Also, if you discover additional difficulties, write down techniques that may be helpful in the future. Have fun, but keep control!

Warning:
Alcohol and Calories

As you will see from the table provided on page 186, alcohol is packed with calories. Each gram of alcohol contains 7 calories—almost twice that of carbohydrate and protein. A can of light beer will have 100 calories; the count for regular beer is 150 calories, about the same as a can of Coke or Pepsi. Mixed drinks and cordials are higher yet. Think of a daiquiri with more than 200 calories and a pina colada over 250.

Some people can have a successful time with weight loss simply by eliminating or greatly reducing their alcohol intake. Many just decide the pleasure they derive from the drinks does not justify all the calories.

Remember that you get plenty of calories and no nutrition with alcohol. If you use up part of your day's allotment of calories with alcoholic drinks, there will not be much room in the remaining calories to pack in the nutrients you need for healthy living. If the drinks are important to you, use the skills you are learning to help keep the amount under control. Pour small amounts, taste every bit (calories should be tasted, not wasted), and be certain to drink only things that are special to you. Don't drink out of habit, and don't continue taking in calories just because you have done so in the past.

One other factor to be alert for is the "disinhibiting" effect of alcohol. Alcohol releases inhibitions in some people, and they do things they might not do when not drinking. You are working to inhibit your calorie intake, and drinking may make you vulnerable to the "what the heck" phenomenon in which you relax your guard and eat more than you might like.

Calorie Values of Alcohol

Beverage	Serving Size (oz)	Calories
Beer or ale	12	140–160
Beer, light	12	100
Bloody Mary	5	116
Bourbon and soda	4	105
Brandy or cognac	1	65–80
Champagne	4	90
Coffee-flavored creme liqueur	1.5	154
Cold Duck	4	120
Cordials and liqueurs, 34 to 72 proof	1	102–125
Creme de Menthe	1.5	186
Daiquiri (with lime)	4	222
Distilled spirits:		
Gin, vodka, rum, whiskey; 80 to 100 proof	1.5	95–124
Gin and tonic	7.5	171
Manhattan	2	128
Martini	2.5	156
Pina colada (canned)	4.5	346
Screwdriver	7	174
Sherry	3	125
Tequila sunrise	5.5	89
Tom Collins	7.5	121
Vermouth, dry	1	32
Vermouth, sweet	1	45
Wine, dry white	4	79
Wine, red	4	85
Wine, dessert (sweet)	4	181
Wine, light	4	52
Wine, nonalcoholic	6	60
Wine cooler	12	220

Note: The calorie values here are approximations only and may vary depending on a drink's proof, specific sweetness, age, and amount of ice used.

Food and Weight Fantasies

Tape/CD 3 Section 10

Many individuals have fantasies of foods. It is common, for example, to fantasize about having a celebration or "letting go" meal when the program ends. Some people even think about specific foods or the ability to eat large quantities again. Weight fantasies are also common. These usually are visions of a sleek body and huge weight losses.

Food or weight fantasies are a sign of unrealistic expectations. Weight loss is not easy, and pounds do not fly off as we'd like. Food fantasies reveal an expectation that the rigors of going through a program will end some magic day and old eating habits will return.

You must keep up what you learn. You can eat your favorite foods now, and you will be able to eat them later. You will not, however, be able to return to uncontrolled eating. Identify what you want to eat and eat a small quantity in a controlled manner. Most of all, enjoy it. By not overeating, you will not feel guilty; by eating a small portion, you will not deprive yourself and feel resentful.

A Look into the Future

As you conclude your reading of Lesson Eleven, you may be thinking or even worrying about The LEARN Program ending. Some people wonder how they will manage after the program ends. But remember, the primary focus of the program is to help you develop a new way of thinking and a new way of living—now and in the future. In this sense, the program does *not* end; your new life is just beginning.

In three short months, you have learned many new skills to help you change attitudes and behaviors that have developed over your lifetime. Your continuing mission is to become more proficient in the use of these skills and to develop new skills as you continue to learn. In a sense, the end of this program is like a high school or college "commencement." Although a commencement ceremony signifies the ending of formal training and the recognition of the mastery of key concepts and skills, it also represents a *time of beginning*.

As you prepare to complete the last lesson of this program, think about what you are beginning. Some people continue to lose weight after this initial 12 weeks while others focus on maintaining their new behaviors and stabilizing their current weight. The path you choose is up to you.

Losing weight is difficult enough, but keeping it off ranks up there with finding a compassionate auditor from the Internal Revenue Service; it can be a real challenge. For this reason I have developed a follow-up program for stabilization and maintenance. I'll talk more about this program in the next lesson, but I want to mention it to you now in case you want to have a copy of it in hand when you finish this manual. You can order a copy of *The LEARN Weight Stabilization and Maintenance Guide* by calling toll-free 1–888–LEARN–41 or on the internet at www.TheLifeStyle Company.com.

 ## MY WEEKLY GOALS

This is a good time for you to identify those things in your life that keep you from being active. Use the skills and techniques you have learned in this program to overcome these inactivity cues. Continue to increase your daily activity level. Do your best this week to identify any fantasies or impossible dreams you may have about what life will be like once you lose weight. Root these from your mind right now!

In the nutrition arena, continue to keep your fat intake to 30 percent or less of total calories. In addition, keep track of your fiber intake; you should be eating between 25–35 grams of dietary fiber every day. Use the information in this lesson to help you distinguish between cravings and hunger and use your new skills to conquer the cravings. Be sure to eat between 6–11 servings each day from the Bread, Cereal, Rice, and Pasta Group of the Food Guide Pyramid. Make it a point to eat breakfast everyday. Remember, eating breakfast each day can actually help in your weight loss efforts. Alcohol has many calories, and these calories do not provide your body with nutrients. So, if you drink alcohol, do so in moderation and record the calories on your Monitoring Form. Continue to complete your Monitoring Form each day, and remember to record your weight change for the week on the My Weight Change Record on page 216.

 ## KNOWLEDGE REVIEW

Lesson Eleven

1. T F Turning off the TV or limiting your viewing time can help you to be more physically active.

2. T F Impossible Dream Thinking is having fantasies and images about weight loss, life as a thin person, etc.

3. T F Overweight people do not experience hunger, only psychological cravings for food.

4. T F To conquer food cravings, distraction will be helpful for some people and confrontation will be helpful for others.

5. T F Many people internalize society's unrealistic standards for beauty, weight, and shape and are likely to have a negative body image.

6. T F It is possible to weigh more than the "ideal," and even be fairly heavy, and still have good self-esteem and a positive body image.

7. T F Foods from the Bread, Cereal, Rice, and Pasta Group are good choices of complex carbohydrates, but they may contain hidden fat.

(Answers in Appendix C, page 224)

Monitoring Form—Lesson Eleven   *Today's Date:*_____

Time	Food and Amount	Calories	Milk & Dairy	Meats & Protein	Vegetables	Fruits	Bread
Total Daily Caloric Intake & Food Guide Pyramid Servings							

Daily Activity Record (Caloric Expenditure)

Time	Activity	Calories	Minutes	No. of Steps

Personal Goals this Week	Most of the Time	Some of the Time	Rarely
1. Meet or exceed walking goal of _____ steps each day			
2. Overcome inactivity cues and triggers			
3. Eat breakfast every day			
4. Control eating while eating away from home			
5. If you drink alcohol, do so in moderation and record calories from alcohol			
6. Eat 6–11 servings from the Bread, Cereal, Rice, and Pasta Group			
7. Eat less than _____ calories each day			

Lesson Twelve

Here we are, the final lesson of The LEARN Program. I hope that you have enjoyed your journey so far and have acquired the knowledge and skills to use for lasting changes. In this lesson, I will discuss a few final steps. But, perhaps even more important, we'll look ahead to your future. Let's finish this stage of your journey with a flurry of excitement!

Taking Stock of Your Progress

Tape/CD 3
Section 7

If you have been reading one lesson each week, you should now be completing the third month of the program. This is an important landmark. Three months is a long time, so you deserve much credit for working hard this long. Many people give up before this point; perhaps you have done so in the past yourself. But, persistence pays off.

What also pays off is being a student of your life circumstances. If you understand the circumstances that prompt you to eat well and be active, and the triggers that cue you to *eat more* and be *inactive*, you are poised to act. Acting means having a plan so that you place yourself in the circumstances where you can cope with problems in a constructive way. Let's take stock of where you are with each part of The LEARN Program.

Your Lifestyle Achievements

A key concept I introduced in Lesson Five dealt with the ABC's (Antecedents, Behaviors, and Consequences) of behavior. This is a scheme for thinking about the events that occur before, during, and after eating or physical activity. This is a great time to reapply that scheme to your eating and activity patterns.

You may have confronted situations in which you were and were not successful at sticking with your program. Can you think about what precedes the situations in which you have trouble (the antecedents)? For many people, negative feelings such as anger, loneliness, depression, or jealousy make a person want to eat or be inactive. The time of day may matter and so may whether other people are eating or exercising in your presence. Have you developed a plan to change the situations that promote eating or inactivity? Think also about changing the behavior itself (your eating or inactivity) or the conse-

quences (such as your reaction to making a mistake). Then you can implement the ABC plan to its fullest.

What lifestyle change techniques are most important to you? Perhaps eating slowly, sticking with an eating schedule, making an appointment to exercise, keeping a Monitoring Form, or other techniques work best for you? If they work, use them. But go beyond this to understand why they work. This will enable you to adopt additional strategies and techniques for remaining in charge.

Your Exercise Achievements

A great deal has been said about physical activity throughout the program. Let's review a few of the key points.

➡ Being physically active is one of the strongest predictors of long-term success at weight management.

➡ Physical activity has benefits far beyond weight management; it is associated with reduced risk of a number of serious diseases, including heart disease. People who are active live longer and are healthier than those who are not.

➡ We now know that rigorous activity is not necessary to derive important health benefits from physical activity.

➡ Several bouts of activity during the day are as good as one long bout.

➡ The best type of activity is something you enjoy and, hence, will continue doing over and over again.

➡ Anything you do to be active, no matter how small, should "count" in your mind as activity. This makes you feel like an "exerciser" and helps you realize that you are making progress.

I talked about how and why physical activity is linked to weight loss (Lesson Two, page 31 and Lesson Three, page 41) and weight maintenance (Lesson Seven, page 115). Have you found activities that you enjoy? Are you meeting your exercise goals? If not, reread the sections on perfecting your walking program (Lesson Five, page 72), making physical activity count (Lesson Six, page 92), starting a programmed activity (Lesson Eight, page 123, and aerobic exercise (Lesson Ten, page 161). What can you do to overcome the barriers that interfere with being regularly active? You may need to use cues to remind yourself to be more active (Lesson Eleven, page 173). If you have not been exercising with a partner, you may want to give it a try. What lifestyle physical activities have you added to your daily routine? Declare in the space on page 191 what you plan to do to increase and maintain your physical activity.

Your Attitude Achievements

It comes as no accident that the A (Attitudes) is at the center of LEARN. How we think is central to who we are as people.

My Commitment to Be Physically Active
1. I will
2. I will
3. I will
4. I will
5. I will

How we think affects how we feel, and our thoughts and feelings are key drivers of our behavior. Eating and exercising are behaviors, so thinking right goes a long way toward acting right.

If you accept the proposition that attitudes are key, then you are in a good position to spot troublesome thoughts and to develop more helpful ways to think positively. By thinking positively, I do not mean you should love everyone, expect world peace, and write smiley faces when you sign your name. I mean interpreting your progress in a realistic way; having positive, but realistic expectations; recovering from slips; and thinking about your weight, your eating, your physical activity, and your body in a constructive way.

Think back on your experience of the last few months. You should be able to remember thoughts that have hindered or helped your progress. They may relate to

how you thought about your rate of weight loss, how you felt when you had setbacks, or how much confidence you had in coping with difficult situations. In the space on page 192, list some of your positive and negative thoughts. When you have identified the helpful, positive thoughts, practice them. The negative thoughts have probably occurred many hundreds of times over many years, so you may have to work hard to counter them. The more you repeat the new thoughts to yourself, the more real they will become, even if the process seems artificial at first.

Your Relationship Achievements

Support from others can be a real asset. Not everyone wants or needs this support, but if used the right way, it can make a real difference for some people. In Lesson Four on page 57, I discussed how to decide whether you would benefit from social support (remember the distinction between social and solo changers?). Have you been asking for support if you feel that it would help?

You may want to go back and read the information on Relationships in Lesson Four to ask again whether you are the type of person who would benefit from support, and if so, what you can do to get and keep support from others. Also, social support is not an all-or-none matter. You may not need support under ordinary circumstances but may want to call for it in a pinch. Let's say you start to slip off the program, or you feel your control is threatened

Changing My Thoughts to Help My Progress

Thoughts That Have Hindered My Progress	More Positive Thoughts That Will Help

because of some upsetting events in your life. Support can often be used as crisis intervention.

There are formal ways to get support, if you feel they might help. Overeaters Anonymous provides a great deal of support, to the point where you can have a sponsor you can call day or night. Other programs can provide support from group members or from a leader or counselor, and of course, support can come from a professional like a psychologist or dietitian.

Your Nutrition Achievements

As with the other LEARN components, awareness in the nutrition area is important. You can go a long way toward correct nutrition if you use common sense, eat a variety of foods, and follow some plan like the Food Guide Pyramid. The two key issues to remember are a balanced diet and calorie control. And remember, the key to calorie control is to accurately measure serving sizes and record them on your Monitoring Form.

Calorie control is necessary for weight loss and maintenance. By now you should know the calories in most foods and should be pretty good at estimating portion sizes. If the calories you take in are less than what your body burns, you will lose weight. If you eat more than you need, you will gain. Eat the exact amount the body needs, and your weight will be stable. This principle may sound simple, and it is!

Eating a balanced diet is necessary for good health. You could have a low calorie intake and lose weight, but still eat a terrible diet. The weight loss is gratifying, but you will pay a price in energy level and the general condition of your body. You can eat a balanced diet and keep the calories low.

This satisfies your need for both weight management and good health.

There is no magic in nutrition. I can offer an iron-clad guarantee you will continue to see diet books, magazine articles, and the like that promise some new discovery. Some will tell you to eat lots of certain nutrients (like protein or carbohydrate) and little of others. Others will say that the time at which you eat foods makes a difference, or that certain foods have special fat-burning qualities. Many of these are old diet plans packaged by a new huckster with new hype.

What is common to most of these is that they promise what people want to hear—a new solution and something that sounds like magic. They may spin a rationale that sounds good, talking about insulin, hormones, brain chemicals, and things like food addiction and carbohydrate craving. When you get lucky, you will find a plan that won't hurt you. Some might hurt you. Think of how many such plans you have read or heard about in your lifetime. How many could you name? Where are they now? How much would you be willing to bet that any of those that are popular now will still be around in a year or two? If they worked, they'd be around forever, and everyone in the world would want a copy. Few have been tested, and if they ever get tested, my guess is that none will be superior to most other programs.

Are you eating a balanced diet? If not, refer back to the sections on the Food Guide Pyramid. You may also want to repeat the Rate Your Diet quiz in Appendix E from time to time. Are you meeting your calorie goal? You can expect better and worse days, so remember that what counts is how these balance out and how you do over a longer period, such as a week or a month.

Remember a Reasonable Weight

Tape/CD 1
Section 6

In the very beginning of this program, I discussed the concept of achieving a "reasonable weight." Most people begin programs with expectations of what they will weigh that are based on arbitrary and unrealistic beauty ideals or even on landmarks in their lives (when they got married, finished school, etc.). What should be viewed as terrific progress gets dismissed.

 ### LIFESTYLE PROFILES

Let me tell you a story about Susan. She began a program at 185 pounds saying she wanted to be 125. Susan weighed 125 when she got married, but she began gaining weight after she had children and had been no less than 150 most of her adult life. In the 52 weeks on the program, Susan lost 25 pounds and weighed 160. Instead of celebrating the 25 pounds she lost, she focused on the remaining weight she still wanted to lose. How reasonable is it for her to think that 125 is the only acceptable weight?

You may have lost as much weight as you set out to lose, but if not, which is the case with many people, it is important to view what you have done in a positive context. There is no reason to expect perfection. We do not expect to be the perfect employee, the perfect parent, the perfect child, or expect to win the world's fashion award. Why, then, are we only satisfied with *perfect* weight loss? The answer is that society teaches us that weight is under total control of the individual; hence, we have ideals that are highly unrealistic. It would be like saying there is only one acceptable hair style and that people with other styles were imperfect and weren't trying hard enough to change the way they looked.

You may be one of the many people who would like to weigh much less but will not or can not. The choice, then, is whether to wage a wholesale assault on your self-esteem by feeling there is something wrong with you or to accept what is reasonable and feel good about the progress you have made. You know which path I favor.

A great deal of research has been done on goal setting, and I have talked a lot about goal setting in this program. This is such an important concept that it warrants mentioning again. It won't surprise you to hear that people get frustrated, disappointed, and even depressed when they do not reach their goals. Goals, therefore, have to be challenging, but not impossible to reach. By setting realistic goals and rewarding yourself for reaching them, your self-esteem will increase, and you will be in a much better position to sustain changes you make.

Bringing It All Together: The Behavior Chain

Tape/CD 4
Section 4

You have learned a lot about the five key components of The LEARN Program: Lifestyle, Exercise, Attitudes, Relationships, and Nutrition. We need to now organize the information in this program into a logical picture. I have covered ways to identify problem situations, along with techniques (more than 200 by now) to help you control your eating, increase your physical activity, change your attitudes, and improve your relationships. You are still left with an important challenge—knowing which technique to use in which situation.

What each person needs is a mental card file or computer database to summon the right technique to counter the triggers and cues that lead to overeating, inactivity, or harmful thoughts and attitudes. For example, if being home alone on the weekend when the weather is bad is a high-risk situation for overeating and being inactive, you could look in your file under "Being Home Alone on the Weekend in Bad Weather" for a list of techniques. The card in your file

would list different aspects of this situation that would help you determine its degree of risk. These aspects may include how stressful your week was, what time of day it is, how hungry you are, how well your program has been going, and so forth. Then, when a rainy weekend arises and other triggers for overeating and inactivity occur (perhaps your mother-in-law calls or your favorite movie is playing on HBO), your card would list several possible strategies to avoid overeating, not exercising, or negative thinking.

The Behavior Chain is the path to this process. It is a method for breaking eating, exercising, and thinking episodes into discrete parts. When you examine each part, ideas emerge for stopping an episode in its tracks. The ideas that follow can truly increase your understanding of your behavior.

A Chain and its Links

We can view eating and exercise as a chain that contains many links. The links string together like an ordinary chain. We can use a familiar phrase: "*A chain is only as strong as its weakest link.*" The good news is that you can break this chain, so attacking at the *weakest link* is ideal.

If we return to the example of being home alone on the weekend when the weather is bad, overeating and skipping an exercise session resides at the end of a long chain. Preceding it were links like the weather being bad, turning on the television, sitting in your favorite chair in the den, having snack foods readily available in the house, and so forth. Both the overeating chain and the inactivity chain could be broken at any of these points.

A Sample Behavior Chain

Let's illustrate the chain concept with the example of Bill. In his chain, Bill had a stressful day at work, skipped his exercise session, overate when he got home, and wound up skipping his exercise the rest of the week. Bill's eating and inactivity occurred in a chain that included many links

before the first slip. We could help Bill control his eating, meet his physical activity goal, and change his attitudes by reviewing this chain. Remember that this is an example to illustrate the principal of a chain. Think about how this concept applies to your situation.

 ## LIFESTYLE PROFILES

Bill's chain began early in the day when he overslept and missed his morning walk. Due to a work deadline, skipping lunch, and working late, Bill felt stressed, tired, and hungry at the end of the day. He skipped his evening exercise session, overate, and skipped his planned healthy dinner. Feeling guilty and like a failure, Bill decided to forego his exercising and meal planning for the rest of the week. We can find 12 links in Bill's chain. These are listed in the table on page 196 along with link-breaking techniques for each link. The page numbers for LEARN link-breaking techniques are shown in parentheses. Bill's Behavior Chain also is illustrated in the figure on page 197.

These are the 12 links in Bill's Behavior Chain example. It started when 1) Bill overslept and was assigned an unexpected rush project at work. He had planned on going for a 15-minute walk before getting ready for work, but because he'd overslept, he didn't take his walk before going to work. He then 2) skipped breakfast, lunch, and his breaks during the day to meet the deadline. Bill 3) worked late to finish the project, and 4) left work feeling tired, stressed, and hungry.

Bill 5) drove straight home where he immediately 6) changed into lounging clothes and 7) went to the kitchen for a snack. He pulled out a whole bag of chips. Bill then 8) went to the den and sat in his favorite chair where he ate chips while watching TV. Because he was tired, stressed, and hungry, Bill 9) ate rapidly until he was full, then 10) felt guilty and like a failure. This 11) weakened his restraint even further until he 12) ate even more while he watched TV the rest of the evening, skipping physical activity altogether.

Is Bill an innocent victim of an inevitable chain of life's events keeping him from exercising, compelling him to overeat, and inducing him to abandon his plan? Can he do something to interrupt the chain's events at critical points? As you probably guessed, Bill has many options for interrupting the chain. Before we discuss these, think of your own lifestyle and the things in your life that trigger you to overeat or skip planned exercise sessions. How do they exist as chains, and what are the links in the chains?

Identifying Your Behavior Chains

Take some time now to form a picture of a behavior chain that applies to you. Use the blank chain provided on page 198 to fill in the details. You can use Bill's chain as an example, but make the situation specific to you. Pick a high-risk situation that really gives you trouble. Examples may include controlling your eating or fitting in exercise when you are traveling, feeling sad, very busy, and so on.

Breaking a Behavior Chain (*Bill's Example*)

(Numbers in parentheses refer to pages where the technique is discussed)

The Link	Link-Breaking Techniques
1. Overslept and skipped exercise, assigned a rush project at work	➲ Get up 30 minutes early to walk (63) ➲ Make an exercise appointment (173) ➲ Ask a coworker for practical support (57) ➲ Take brief walks throughout the day (174)
2. Skipped breakfast, lunch, and breaks	➲ Eat on a schedule (77) ➲ Keep ready-to-eat breakfast foods available (181) ➲ Make appointment to take a walking break (173) ➲ Keep healthy snacks available (169)
3. Worked late	➲ Keep physically active to lower stress (157) ➲ Avoid negative self-talk (98) ➲ Walk after work (63) ➲ Eat a healthy dinner after work (27)
4. Left work tired, stressed, and hungry	➲ Exercise throughout the day to lower stress (157) ➲ Set brief time to be active during the work day (174) ➲ Eat on a schedule (77) ➲ Keep healthy snacks available (169)
5. Drove straight home without exercising	➲ Set daily step goals (43) ➲ Stop at the mall or hardware store for a walk (45) ➲ Keep walking shoes in the car or at work (173) ➲ Ban perfectionist attitudes (164)
6. Changed to lounging clothes, skipping exercising	➲ Put exercise clothes on dresser (173) ➲ Engage in a pleasurable partner activity (174) ➲ Exercise with a partner (184) ➲ Use the ABC approach to alter antecedents (70)
7. Went to kitchen, got bag of chips	➲ Distinguish between cravings and hunger (177) ➲ Hide the high-calorie foods (168) ➲ Keep healthy snacks available (169) ➲ Confront or ignore the cravings (177)
8. Ate chips while watching TV	➲ Eat in one place (78) ➲ Do nothing else while eating (77) ➲ Pause during eating (84) ➲ Take walks during commercials (63)
9. Ate rapidly until full; skipped exercise	➲ Put food down between bites (173) ➲ Pause during eating (84) ➲ Serve only a few chips at one time (146) ➲ Stop automatic eating (28, 145) ➲ Follow the five-minute rule (146) ➲ Ask a partner to exercise with you (63)
10. Felt guilty, like a failure	➲ Review your progress (67, 189) ➲ Set realistic goals (13, 105, 176) ➲ Banish imperatives (163) ➲ Ban perfectionist attitudes (164) ➲ Avoid negative self-talk (98)
11. Restraint weakened further	➲ Review your progress (67, 189) ➲ Stop dichotomous thinking (200) ➲ Read the LEARN manual for ideas (3) ➲ Enlist support from others to get back on track (57)
12. More eating and no exercise	➲ Examine Behavior Chain, use link-breaking techniques to break the links (199) ➲ Beware of attitude traps (98, 127, 151, 200) ➲ Ban perfectionist attitudes (164) ➲ Make an appointment to walk with your partner tomorrow (173)

Bill's Sample Behavior Chain

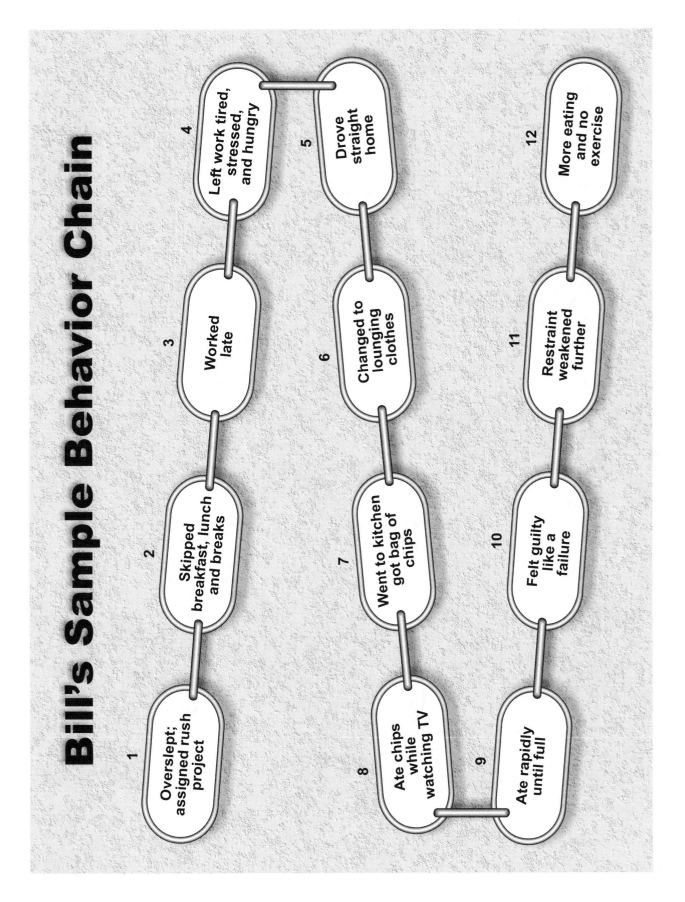

1. Overslept; assigned rush project
2. Skipped breakfast, lunch and breaks
3. Worked late
4. Left work tired, stressed, and hungry
5. Drove straight home
6. Changed to lounging clothes
7. Went to kitchen got bag of chips
8. Ate chips while watching TV
9. Ate rapidly until full
10. Felt guilty like a failure
11. Restraint weakened further
12. More eating and no exercise

My Behavior Chain

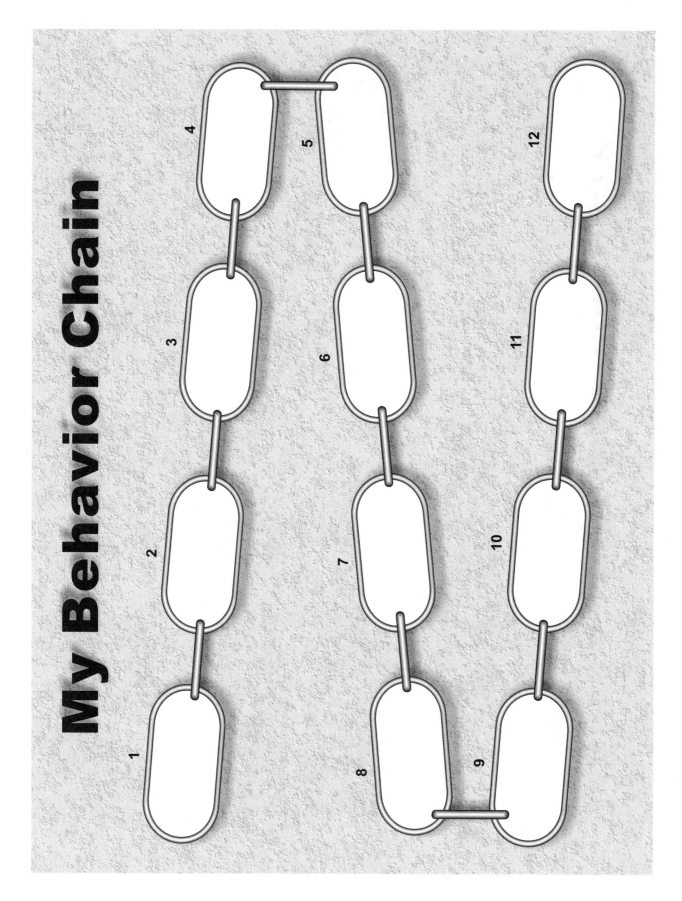

Your chain can contain fewer links or more links than the blank chain permits, but try to include each important detail. You will see how the links are inextricably tied together to form a sequence of events that is hard to stop once it gets started. If you come armed with techniques for dismantling the chain, you will increase your control.

Analyzing Your Behavior Chain

This chain concept can be a key part of your program. If you can analyze your eating and inactivity according to the chain notion, you can devise many ways to meet your goals and stay on track. Contrast this with the common approach that relies solely on *willpower* once the chain advances and the chips and couch beckon.

Now we can go to work on your chain. Look at each of the links in your chain and write down at least two ways that you could break the chain at each link. With Bill's chain, we listed 51 link-breaking ideas (see page 196). Use the information you have learned in the program to think of your own techniques. You might refresh your memory on techniques by referring to your Monitoring Forms from previous weeks or to the Master List of LEARN Techniques in Appendix A.

When listing ideas that may help you break links in your behavior chain, remember several points. The first is to concentrate on the weakest links. For instance, if skipping exercise is the final link in your chain, it might be easier to plan to exercise early in the day than to count on fitting in exercise after your day gets "crazy." This leads to the second point, which is to interrupt the chain as early as possible. This does not diminish the importance of interrupting the steps late in the chain, but starting early in the chain gives you more links to work with.

I know what often happens when an author asks us to fill something out. We think it's not worth the effort, and we read ahead. You may feel that you need not go through this exercise, and you might be correct. Re-member, however, that the act of writing these things down will make you think and analyze your high-risk situations like never before.

Fast Food

Fast-food restaurants are part of the American landscape. In 1970, there were 30,000 fast food outlets, rising to 140,000 by 1980. In 1997, there were 23,132 McDonald's alone, with three new McDonald's opening every day. Within a 15-minute drive of where I live in Connecticut, I bet I could find 25 fast-food restaurants, and an ocean occupies half of the available space! In addition to McDonald's, I would find other restaurants, such as Burger King, KFC, Wendy's, Popeye's, and heaven knows what else. And with 24-hour service, breakfast, and drive-thru windows, convenience has reached new levels. If you can believe it, 7 percent of the American population eat at McDonald's every day.

The world of fast food has undergone many interesting, and in a few cases, positive changes. Chicken has found its way onto the menu, but in some cases, in better form than others (broiled chicken vs. chicken nuggets). Healthier oils are being used to cook fries in some places, yet people are consuming fries (and, therefore, fat and calories) in record amounts. Some developments, such as drive-thru windows and

package deals ("value meals"), very likely increase the number of customers and amount eaten per customer.

Fast foods vary widely in their nutritional value. Appendix F includes menu items from some of the common fast-food restaurants. Foods from these restaurants can be high in saturated fat, sodium, cholesterol, and calories, and low in calcium, vitamins A and D, and fiber. The news is not all bad, however. One can walk into some fast-food chains and escape with a reasonable meal, but you need to plan ahead so that you are not tempted by colorful signs and the aroma.

Some places have a salad bar or prepared salads so you can load up with vegetables (ask for low-fat dressing). Grilled chicken sandwiches are better than fried ones, and you can save yourself calories and fat by not having cheese and sauces. You also can control portion sizes. If you have a hankering for fries, get the small size. A hamburger or cheeseburger will have fewer calories than a bacon double cheeseburger, a quarter pounder, or the deluxe burger that requires a forklift. And, if you are used to regular soft drinks, switch to diet drinks, have skim milk or juice, or drink water. Most soft drinks have no nutrition and loads of calories, especially the large sizes.

Dichotomous (Light Bulb) Thinking

This is the classic attitude problem that plagues many people on weight loss programs. It involves viewing the world and losing weight as either right or wrong, perfect or terrible, good or bad, friend or foe, legal or illegal. I see this in nearly every client I work with.

Dichotomous thinking occurs when you slip and feel you have blown the program. A slight transgression can send you into a tailspin. For example, you may have six straight days in which you meet your calorie goal and then splurge the seventh day by eating cake and boosting your calorie to-

tal to 2,000. The common response would be "I really blew it now. I am off my program."

Notice the phrase "off my program." This is the dichotomous view that you are either perfect or terrible, that you are either *on* or *off* a program. This is where the term *Light Bulb Thinking* was born, because a light bulb is either on or off.

The danger is not the slip but the despair that you feel about making inevitable mistakes. Having 2,000 calories is insignificant in your total calorie intake for a week, month, or year. However, your *reaction* to those calories can be devastating. If you feel guilty and depressed, the likely response to soothe the feelings is eating.

Another example is the tendency for people to classify foods as good or bad, dietetic or fattening, and legal or illegal. The specific foods that are good or bad vary from person to person. For you, ice cream might be the illegal food, but for another person it might be corn chips, beer, donuts, potato chips, or fast food. I do not like the notion of any forbidden food. All foods, in moderation, can fit into a healthy eating plan.

Being aware of your dichotomous thoughts is essential. Have you made internal rules about foods that you can and *cannot* eat, a calorie level you *must* maintain, things you must do to stay "on the program," or what constitutes proper dietary behavior? Notice how you feel when you violate the rules. Negative feelings usually indicate dichotomous thinking.

You can contend with dichotomous thinking by talking back to yourself. For example, instead of saying, "I really blew it now. I'm off my program," try telling yourself something like, "One bad day doesn't mean I'm a failure. I'll get back on track tomorrow." Try to replace your dichotomous thoughts with more realistic thoughts.

Please realize that attitudes are habits just like any other. Simply reading this material and knowing that attitudes might be hindering your progress are not enough.

It will help to practice the new thinking and then to practice again. Try not to be a passive recipient of my advice. Be active and search for these thoughts, and be poised to counter them when they occur.

In the spaces below, write down your most common dichotomous thoughts and write a counter statement for each. You can then be prepared in advance when dichotomous thinking occurs.

Is your thinking like a light bulb—either on or off?

Preventing Lapse, Relapse, and Collapse

Tape/CD 4
Section 6

Far too often, a minor slip propels a person to misery. The guilt from a slip makes a person susceptible to more slips and can ultimately lead to loss of all control. This is a gloomy picture, but good news is around the corner! There are ways to turn the tables.

Everyone makes mistakes. Some people bounce back and use the slip as a signal to increase control. It is common, however, for the slip to cause a negative emotional reaction (guilt and despair) that builds until all control is lost.

Maintenance of weight loss may be the greatest challenge facing overweight persons. Losing weight is difficult enough, but keeping it off can be really tough. Most overweight people have lost and regained weight many times, so something must be done to interrupt these cycles. The trick is to prevent slips from occurring and to respond constructively when they do occur.

Two paths to success are possible. The first is to avoid or prevent slips and mistakes, and the second is to respond to slips with coping techniques that put you in control. I discuss these paths in great detail in *The LEARN Weight Stabilization and Maintenance Guide.*

Countering Dichotomous (Light Bulb) Thinking	
My Dichotomous Thoughts	**My Counter Statements**
1.	
2.	
3.	
4.	
5.	
6.	
7.	
8.	

Much of our discussion on this topic is drawn from the excellent work of Dr. G. Alan Marlatt from the University of Washington. He has studied the situations associated with relapse in overweight persons, alcoholics, smokers, drug addicts, and compulsive gamblers. He also proposes methods for preventing relapse.

Distinguishing Lapse, Relapse, and Collapse

I have used several terms to describe deviating from your program: mistake, lapse, slip, error, etc. Relapse implies something different, and collapse is yet another matter. We fuss with these words because the terms we use can be important.

In recovering alcoholics, one slip or lapse is considered by many to be a relapse (i.e., "one drink, a drunk"). Some think the same is true for people who stop smoking. Having a single cigarette begins an inevitable path to relapse. However, there is abundant evidence that this is not true.

Many recovering alcoholics have had at least one drink since their reformation, and it is a rare ex-smoker who has not had a cigarette. Yet, they recover from their lapses and prevent a relapse. The same is unquestionably true with overweight individuals.

A *lapse* is a slight error or slip, the first instance of backsliding. It is a discrete event like eating a forbidden food, exceeding a calorie level, or skipping an exercise session. *Relapse* occurs when lapses string together and the person returns to his or her former state. When relapse is complete and there is little hope of reversing the negative trend, *collapse* has occurred.

The most important message is that

**A Lapse Does Not
Always Lead to Relapse**

The person who can view a lapse for what it is, an unfortunate but temporary problem, is prepared to respond positively to life's inevitable setbacks. Talking back to yourself after a slip can help prevent a lapse from turning into a relapse.

Interpreting Your Progress

*Tape/CD 3
Section 2*

At this stage in the program, individuals have had different experiences and weight losses. Some people have done well and attained their goal, and others still have weight to lose. There are those who struggled at times and succeeded at others, and are now on their way to a positive outcome. Others struggled throughout and lost no weight at all. Let's reflect on your progress and use it to forge a picture of the future.

Making the transition from the structure of the program to *free living* can be tricky for some people. If you are fearful of this transition or have had difficulty in the past when ending a program, some work in the "A" (Attitudes) part of the LEARN model might help.

Some people who complete programs have an unfortunate way of not taking credit when credit is due. When they do well on a program they attribute their success to the program, but if they flounder, they blame themselves. I hear people say, "Weight Watchers really helped me lose weight" and later say, "The Weight Watchers program was good, I just couldn't stick with it." This attitude can eventually wear away a person's confidence.

I prefer a different attitude. If you do well on a program, the credit is yours. The program only provides ideas and techniques, but you have the responsibility for implementing them. It is similar to using tools to build a house. Having the right tools can help, but someone has to make the effort to put it all together. Giving the program credit for weight loss is like giving the hammer credit for building the house. When we hear a virtuoso perform a masterpiece on the piano, do we give the piano credit? Whatever you have achieved is yours to boast about. You deserve to feel good and to remember that your efforts were at work. What does this mean?

If you have been responsible for making progress, the progress can continue. If you believe that the *program* has been responsible, it would be natural for you to fall apart when the program ends. This is not the case, obviously, but beware of the tendency to give the program credit when the credit is yours.

If you have achieved less than you expected, what can you conclude? Again, the natural tendency is to despair and blame yourself. I do not feel this is fair. Over the course of a lifetime, overweight individuals go through periods of being very motivated and having the strength to try a program, then periods where nothing seems to work and starting a program is a series of false starts.

There are peaks of success and valleys of disappointment, with lots of terrain in-between. Individuals begin programs at many points in these stages. The ones who do best, of course, are those at the peaks. Those in the valleys have trouble. Others fall somewhere in the middle.

For a person who has not done well, I recommend two approaches. The first is to consider waiting until a peak comes along and then try again. The right timing can be important. The second is to consider trying a different program. This program is not right for everyone, so if something else meets your needs, by all means, try it.

Losing weight is like being a batter on a baseball team. You need not hit a home run on every pitch. Even if you strike out, you will have other chances at bat; even if you go hitless in one game, there will be other games. You just want to avoid a prolonged slump! So, keep a positive attitude and keep trying.

Making Your Habits Permanent

There are several keys to developing permanent habits. *Practice* is one such key. The lessons in this program may not provide enough time for all your habits to change. Eating and physical activity habits develop over years and years, so you must be patient for the changes to become permanent. By the time a person is 40, at least 40,000 meals have been consumed. This is lots of practice, so new habits may take time.

Another key is awareness. Try to continue to be a student of your eating and exercise habits. Be aware of what stimulates your eating and inactivity and of techniques for turning the tide. Continuing to complete the Monitoring Forms is a great way to continue your awareness and to help you find eating and inactivity cues.

Using the Master List of LEARN Techniques

Appendix A, beginning on page 209, contains a summary list of all the techniques I introduced throughout the program. Use this list to review your progress and to determine which techniques are important for you. Some techniques will be more applicable to you than others. If you do no food shopping, the techniques in this area may not be relevant; however, you may wish to share these techniques with the person who does the shopping. Focus on those most pertinent for you. They may be the techniques you struggled with most, which is one sign that the habits they targeted are difficult to change.

Go through the list in Appendix A, and circle the techniques that have been the most important in changing your lifestyle. Each technique is referenced by page number in the manual. These are not necessarily the behaviors that are easiest for you. They should be the ones that are the keys to your future success. Circle any behavior you feel fits this bill. Think back carefully over your experience with earlier parts of the program and consider programs you have been on in the past. Circle the behaviors that help you control your eating and increase your exercise.

Quality of Life Review

Now we come to the point in the program when it's time once again to review your quality of life. Use the form on page 205 to check your quality of life. This is the same form you have completed on previous occasions. Compare your scores now with your scores earlier in the program. Use the Quality of Life Review Comparisons—Lesson Twelve on page 215 to help with your review.

What areas of your life are you most satisfied with now? I would be surprised if you do not have more energy, a more positive mood, greater mobility, and fewer health complications. Think about how remarkable this is. In just three months, you have achieved some impressive benefits.

Compare your current responses to those before the program. This comparison will remind you just how much you have changed. Sometimes people lose sight of their accomplishments. I won't let you forget yours!

For those areas in which you are not more satisfied, what can you do to improve things? I suggest that you identify one area and start there. For instance, if you are not satisfied with your leisure and recreational activities, identify a concrete goal that you would like to achieve. It should be something specific such as reading for 30 minutes a day, going for a bike ride with friends on the weekend, or decorating the downstairs bathroom. Make a specific plan concerning what you will do, when, and with whom. That's the best way to get new behaviors going. Use the worksheet below titled Quality of Life Improvement Worksheet to help you identify specific areas and develop a specific plan of action.

Where to Go from Here

Tape/CD 4
Section 10

As you are reading this final lesson, you may be thinking "I still want to lose 20 more pounds. What do I do now?" You may be happy with the weight you have lost but are concerned about keeping it off. A number of options are available for you to consider for losing more weight, for maintaining the weight that you have lost, or for getting back on track if you falter. These are just

Quality of Life Improvement Worksheet		
Area to Improve	**How to Improve**	**When to Improve**

suggestions— you might have better ideas of your own.

The key is to have a plan, to know what path you will follow, and to know when the plan should be put into action. Here are some paths to consider.

Use The LEARN Program Again

You may start at the beginning and follow this program through as if you were doing it for the first time. Many people do this. This is not a sign that you failed the first time around. Instead, it shows that you know what works for you and that you have made a conscious choice to go back and do it again.

An alternative to starting at the beginning is to use sections in the manual that are most pertinent to you at this time. For example, if you are having difficulty staying physically active, you should reread the sections on physical activity and follow the suggestions made throughout this material.

You may want to pay special attention to the goals you set at the end of each lesson (in the "My Weekly Goals" sections). The idea of these sections was to encourage you to experiment with different lifestyle-change techniques and find goals that were particularly useful and important for you. Chances are, these goals may still be important for you. Focusing on them is a good way to keep your motivation high and your weight management efforts moving along as you wish.

Use The LEARN Stabilization Guide

Some people can successfully manage their weight on their own after The LEARN Program ends. These individuals have already mastered the skills they need to maintain their new eating and exercise behaviors, and they have reshaped their attitudes and relationships to help them keep off the lost weight. However, for most people, it takes longer than 12 weeks for these new behaviors and attitudes to really take root. Remember, you have spent the past 12 weeks trying to change habits that have

Quality of Life Review

Please use the following scale to rate how satisfied you feel now about different aspects of your daily life. Choose any number from this list (1 to 9), and indicate your choice on the questions below.

1 = Extremely Dissatisfied

2 = Very Dissatisfied

3 = Moderately Dissatisfied

4 = Somewhat Dissatisfied

5 = Neutral

6 = Somewhat Satisfied

7 = Moderately Satisfied

8 = Very Satisfied

9 = Extremely Satisfied

1. _____ Mood (feelings of sadness, worry, happiness, etc.)

2. _____ Self-esteem

3. _____ Confidence, self-assurance, and comfort in social situations

4. _____ Energy and feeling healthy

5. _____ Health problems (diabetes, high blood pressure, etc.)

6. _____ General appearance

7. _____ Social life

8. _____ Leisure and recreational activities

9. _____ Physical mobility and physical activity

10. _____ Eating habits

11. _____ Body image

12. _____ Overall Quality of Life[1]

[1] Record your Overall Quality of Life score in the space provided in Appendix B, page 213.

been evolving over your entire lifetime. It should be no surprise that uprooting a lifetime of embedded behaviors, planting new ones, and nurturing them along to last you a lifetime may take more than 12 short weeks.

The LEARN Weight Stabilization and Maintenance Guide is designed to follow The LEARN Program and to help your new habits become even more rooted and permanent. This program expands upon the skills you have already learned while teaching you new techniques to maintain those healthy behaviors you have adopted. The focus of The LEARN Stabilization Guide is to help you stabilize or lose more weight if you desire, while maintaining those behaviors that helped you lose weight in the first place.

When you began The LEARN Program, your motivation was probably very high, but it may have waned over time; this is normal. The LEARN Stabilization Guide can help you recapture your initial motivation and inspiration. You will learn how to set an acceptable weight range for stabilization and what corrective actions you can take when your weight moves too far out of range. In addition, you will learn when it is best to work on stabilizing your weight and when the time may be right for further weight loss. Having the right mind-set at the right time can enhance self-esteem, encourage continued success, and prevent relapse.

The LEARN Stabilization Guide is designed to help you develop new skills and to practice old ones to prevent and cope with lapses and prevent relapse. Successful long-term weight maintenance depends on being able to get back on track after the inevitable detours and roadblocks that arise along the weight management path.

Like The LEARN Program, The LEARN Stabilization Guide is a step-by-step, lesson-by-lesson weight stabilization and maintenance program that you can use over and over again. It is designed to be used with the assistance of a health professional either in a one-on-one setting or group setting, or as a self-help program. Flexibility is the key ingredient of The LEARN Stabilization Guide.

Enlist Social Support

If you find your motivation flagging, enlisting a friend or a support partner might be just the thing you need. Two people working together can produce a synergy where each motivates the other and in turn enhances self-motivation. Besides, working with another person on some common goal can really be fun. There is abundant material in this manual about how to identify support people, enlist their help, and communicate in positive ways to keep the support flowing.

 MY WEEKLY GOALS

Much of this lesson focused on reviewing your progress in the program and the Behavior Chain. Be sure to complete at least one blank Behavior Chain in this lesson and devise plans to break as many links in the chain as possible. Be aware of the fast foods you eat and their caloric content. Try to avoid dichotomous thinking by developing counter thoughts. Distinguish lapses from a relapse. Continue to eat the appropriate number of servings from each of the five groups of the Food Guide Pyramid.

Finally, continue to set physical activity goals. If you are using a step counter, the ideal goal is to walk at least 10,000 steps each day. Record your weight change on the My Weight Change Record on page 216. If you are ready to move on to *The LEARN Weight Stabilization and Maintenance Guide* and you have not done so, you may want to call 1–888–LEARN–41 to get your copy.

My Salute to You!

If you have been following the LEARN lessons as they were designed, it should now be about three months (or 12 weeks) since you started the program. Let's place this in context. Some people start programs and give up the same day. Others last a few days, perhaps a few weeks, or on rare occasions, a few months. Why?

Many programs are fads, and people find quickly that they are impossible to follow or simply don't work. And let's face it—sticking to any program for a long time is difficult. A person in for the long haul encounters many challenges, may feel deprived, may think "it's not fair when other people can eat all they want," and may get frustrated by slow progress. Hence, many people get off the train before it has reached its final destination.

I salute you for staying with the program! It is a REALLY good sign that you have been able to think of your weight management plan as something that requires persistence and flexibility over the long term. I am delighted that you have made the effort and hope that the rewards have been and will continue to be substantial. If I could be there with you right now, I'd be giving you a standing ovation!

Ending Where We Began

Tape 4
Section 9

We can end where we began—emphasizing the most important principles of all. You may recall that one of the first things I mentioned was a concept called self-efficacy. This concept tells us that the people most likely to make successful, long-term changes are those with the skills and confidence to do so. You have learned many skills—skills to help you confront difficult situations, handle setbacks, make changes you can live with, and enjoy the whole process. You hold your weight management future in your hands. Use the skills you have learned, and you will do just fine.

You should feel confident in your abilities. Give yourself a pep talk when you need it. If you were your own coach, think about what you would need to hear to be most effective and then inspire yourself in that way.

Saying Farewell

Tape/CD 4
Section 10

Let me offer my sincere hope that you enjoyed this program and that you are on your way to accomplishing your weight loss goals. I know it can be a struggle, but with the right attitude

and skills, you can be successful. Keep up the spirit! If you are continuing with The LEARN Stabilization Guide, I look forward to taking this next step along with you.

 KNOWLEDGE REVIEW

Lesson Twelve

1. T F Being a student of your own life circumstances is important for making and maintaining positive lifestyle changes.

2. T F Exercise is not a good predictor of who will keep weight off over the long run, but the health benefits are reason enough to be active.

3. T F A Behavior Chain, like any chain, is only as strong as its weakest links.

4. T F Once the behavior chain begins, it is not possible to stop because the links are so strong.

5. T F It is best to interrupt a behavior chain at one of the last links.

6. T F Light bulb or dichotomous thinking refers to your own bright ideas about losing weight.

7. T F When a person lapses, relapse is close behind because nothing can interrupt the negative cycle of lapses and out-of-control eating.

8. T F Certain techniques are essential for all individuals controlling their weight.

(Answers in Appendix C, page 225)

Monitoring Form—Lesson Twelve

*Today's Date:*_____

Time	Food and Amount	Calories	Milk & Dairy	Meats & Protein	Vegetables	Fruits	Bread
Total Daily Caloric Intake & Food Guide Pyramid Servings							

Daily Activity Record (Caloric Expenditure)

Time	Activity	Calories	Minutes	No. of Steps

Personal Goals this Week	Most of the Time	Some of the Time	Rarely
1. Meet or exceed walking goal of _____ steps each day			
2. Sketch my behavior chains			
3. Be aware of fast-foods I eat and their calorie content			
4. Counter Dichotomous Thinking			
5. Distinguish between lapse, relapse, and collapse			
6. Eat appropriate daily servings from each of the five food groups of the Food Guide Pyramid			
7. Eat less than _____ calories each day			

Appendix A

Master List of LEARN Techniques

ATTITUDE TECHNIQUES

RELATIONSHIP TECHNIQUES

Nutrition Techniques

Appendix B

My Personal Charts and Forms

This appendix is a new addition to The LEARN Program. Here, you can summarize the many worksheets, quizzes, and forms that you complete throughout the program. My hope is that by having this information in a single, easy-to-use, convenient location, you can more readily see your progress. Refer to this section often. I hope that it will provide encouragement, inspiration, and motivation to you as you go through the program.

Quality of Life Review Scores

_____ Overall Quality of Life score from the Introduction and Orientation, page 9.

_____ Overall Quality of Life score from Lesson Five, page 68.

_____ Overall Quality of Life score from Lesson Nine, page 142.

_____ Overall Quality of Life score from Lesson Twelve, page 205.

Rate Your Diet Quiz Scores

_____ Total score from your Rate Your Diet Quiz—Lesson Two from Appendix E, page 234.

_____ Total score from your Rate Your Diet Quiz—Lesson Seven from Appendix E, page 238.

Quality of Life Review Comparisons—Lesson Five

(a) Category	(b) Scores from Orientation (page 9)	(c) Scores from Lesson Five (page 68)	(d) Change in Scores (column c less column b)
1. Mood (feelings of sadness, worry, happiness, etc.)			
2. Self-esteem			
3. Confidence, self-assurance, and comfort in social situations			
4. Energy and feeling healthy			
5. Health problems (diabetes, high blood pressure, etc.)			
6. General appearance			
7. Social life			
8. Leisure and recreational activities			
9. Physical mobility and physical activity			
10. Eating habits			
11. Body image			
12. Overall quality of life			

Quality of Life Review Comparisons—Lesson Nine

(a) Category	(b) Scores from Lesson Five (page 68)	(c) Scores from Lesson Nine (page 142)	(d) Change in Scores (column c less column b)
1. Mood (feelings of sadness, worry, happiness, etc.)			
2. Self-esteem			
3. Confidence, self-assurance, and comfort in social situations			
4. Energy and feeling healthy			
5. Health problems (diabetes, high blood pressure, etc.)			
6. General appearance			
7. Social life			
8. Leisure and recreational activities			
9. Physical mobility and physical activity			
10. Eating habits			
11. Body image			
12. Overall quality of life			

Quality of Life Review Comparisons—Lesson Twelve			
(a) **Category**	**(b)** **Scores from** **Lesson Nine** **(page 142)**	**(c)** **Scores from** **Lesson Twelve** **(page 205)**	**(d)** **Change in** **Scores (column** **c less column b)**
1. Mood (feelings of sadness, worry, happiness, etc.)			
2. Self-esteem			
3. Confidence, self-assurance, and comfort in social situations			
4. Energy and feeling healthy			
5. Health problems (diabetes, high blood pressure, etc.)			
6. General appearance			
7. Social life			
8. Leisure and recreational activities			
9. Physical mobility and physical activity			
10. Eating habits			
11. Body image			
12. Overall quality of life			

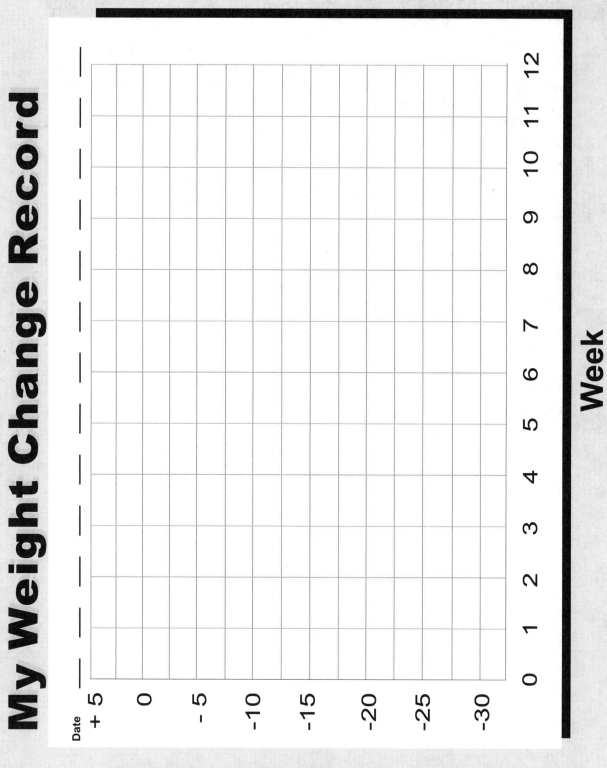

My Weight Change Record

Date

Weight Change (in pounds)

Week

My Reasonable Weight Loss

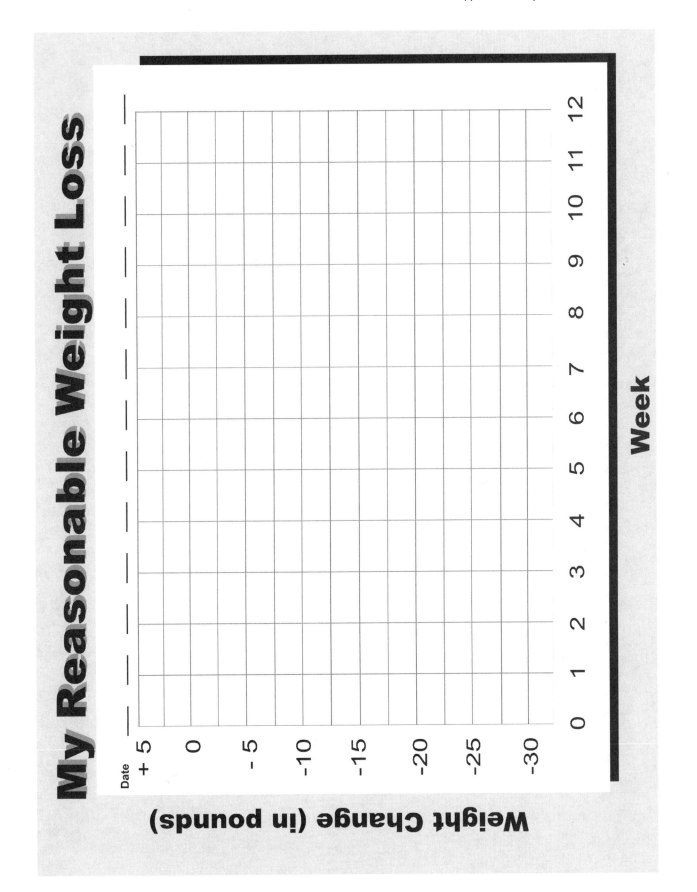

Date

Weight Change (in pounds)

+ 5 / 0 / - 5 / -10 / -15 / -20 / -25 / -30

0 1 2 3 4 5 6 7 8 9 10 11 12

Week

Appendix C

Answers for Knowledge Review Questions

Lesson One

1. *True* The LEARN Program focuses on making gradual, sustainable, and *permanent* changes in your eating, exercise, thinking, and feeling. Diets, on the other hand, are quick, temporary fixes that require effort over the short term.

2. *False* This program aims for a slow, steady weight loss of 1–2 pounds per week. Losing weight slowly allows you to make lasting changes. In addition, losing 5 pounds of body fat in a week is impossible for most people.

3. *False* Setting goals that you cannot achieve can easily lead to discouragement, low self-esteem, and poor self-confidence. This is a setup for failure. Establishing more realistic goals that you can reasonably attain can enhance motivation, self-esteem, self- confidence, and help keep you on track.

4. *True* People who have lost weight and maintained their loss often report that record keeping was one key to their success.

5. *False* Keeping track of the calories you eat is *very* important for weight loss. To lose weight, you *must* eat fewer calories than your body uses; so, it is crucial to know how many calories you consume.

6. *False* One study showed that individuals who increased their lifestyle physical activity lost as much weight as people who took a step aerobics class three times a week. This study underscores the importance of lifestyle physical activity.

7. *True* One study found that people losing weight who observed common foods and estimated quantity and calories averaged errors of 60 percent. Therefore, using a calorie guide, measuring tools, and a food scale is important.

8. *False* A step counter is an excellent tool to help you keep up with your daily physical activity. Moreover, it can help motivate you by showing you just how much physical activity you are doing each day.

9. *False* The Weight Change Record is designed for you to track your *progress* by recording your weekly weight *change*, not your actual weight per se. By recording your weight change instead of your weight, you can post your record in a public place, such as your refrigerator.

Lesson Two

1. *False* Psychological problems are not at the root of all cases of overweight. There is no evidence that uncovering these causes helps with weight loss.

2. *False* People who have been overweight in childhood may have excessive fat cells, but other overweight persons may not. They have fat cells that are too large.

3. *False* Wide variations in metabolic rate exist among different people. Some are cursed with a slow metabolism and may be prone to easy gains in body weight.

4. *False* Being on a weight management program does not mean you have to forgo great tasting meals. By learning all about calories, you can enjoy every bit of your food.

5. *True* Many overweight people eat without paying attention to all they consume. They miss the taste in much of what they eat.

6. *True* Make the meals that you do eat count. Your meals should be satisfying, good tasting, and nutritious. Otherwise, you'll feel deprived when there is no need to, and your body won't get enough good nutrients.

7. *True* The Monitoring Form helps you discover times, foods, feelings, and activities associated with eating. Understanding your eating patterns is a key in changing lifelong habits.

8. *False* Any physical activity can be helpful, including short walks of 2–5 minutes in duration. Small bouts of physical activity accumulated over the course of a day can add up.

9. *False* You decide how frequently to weigh yourself. Some people benefit from daily weighing, but others do not. It is your call.

Lesson Three

1. *True* Your Monitoring Form will allow you to identify times, places, feelings, activities, and other events which are frequently associated with overeating. Identifying these situations will allow you to intervene appropriately.

2. *False* Exercise has many benefits aside from the calories you burn. It is one of the most important aspects of weight management.

3. *False* We now know that moderate-intensity physical activity can be very beneficial for health and weight management. This means that you can set aside the notion that only high-intensity exercise is necessary for improved health and weight management. A three-mile walk burns about the same number of calories as a three-mile run.

4. *True* Physical activity maximizes the loss of fat and can prevent the loss of muscle. Physical activity combined with diet is preferable to diet alone for weight loss.

5. *True* How far you go is more important than how fast you go. This is one reason that walking is an ideal form of physical activity. Of course, running will get the job done faster!

6. *True* Using a step counter can help you to realize the progress you are making in being more active. Often, you may be more active than you realize. Using a step counter that tells you that you have been active can be a powerful motivational tool at the end of a long day.

7. *False* Expensive exercise clothes contain no special materials and have no advantage over clothes most people have anyway. Their only advantage is cosmetic.

8. *False* A calorie is a measure of the energy your body gets from a food. Fat supplies some of these calories in some foods, but so do carbohydrate and protein.

9. *False* Different numbers of servings are recommended for each of the five food groups. It is this combination of a different number of servings from each of the five food groups that provides a balanced diet.

Lesson Four

1. *False* Many people do profit from exercising with a partner, but many enjoy doing their exercise alone. It is a matter of individual preference.

2. *True* Many overweight people are embarrassed to exercise, but this is something you need to banish from your mind. Most people give heavy people much credit for increasing their physical activity.

3. *True* Modest weight losses of 5–10 percent of body weight can improve blood pressure, diabetes, high cholesterol, sleep disturbances, and a variety of other medical problems.

4. *False* Dropping your calories below 1,000 calories per day is not advisable because you may be losing weight at the expense of good nutrition. Diets of less than 1,000 calories per day should be supervised by a physician.

5. *False* Increasing your physical activity by 30 minutes all at once may lead to injuries if you have not been exercising regularly. In addition, you may not be able to maintain this new activity level. This can lead to discouragement, despair, and a blow to self-esteem. Increasing your physical activity gradually and working your way up is important to prevent injuries and discouragement.

6. *False* A step counter is very simple to use and is an easy way to keep track of your daily physical activity. Moreover, it is a nice way to see if you're getting more activity. Because it counts every step as activity, this feedback can be motivational.

7. *True* It takes about 3,500 calories to equal one pound of body weight. So, if you decrease your intake by 500 calories a day, this is equal to 3,500 calories per week—that's about one pound of weight loss per week.

8. *False* Shaping refers to making gradual progress in a step-by-step fashion so that goals are attainable.

Lesson Five

1. *False* Weight loss is one measure of success. Equally, if not more important, are improved health, fitness, and overall quality of life.

2. *False* Behavioral weight loss programs produce slow, gradual weight losses of 1–2 pounds per week. During the first month, women typically lose 4–6 pounds and men lose about 6–8 pounds.

3. *False* The ABC approach stands for Antecedents, Behavior, and Consequences. This approach shows the importance of what occurs before, during, and after eating or being inactive.

4. *False* Gradual increases in your physical activity are important so that you do not become injured, frustrated, and discouraged. You should add 5–10 minutes of walking each day *per* week until you reach your ultimate goal of 30–60 minutes of physical activity each day.

5. *False* Many people do benefit from having a weight management partner, but not everyone falls into this category. This decision is best left up to you.

6. *True* Do not expect your partner to read your mind. Tell your partner exactly what he or she can do to help. Remember, be specific, ask for positive changes, and be nice to your partner in return.

7. *True* As few as 10 calories make a difference when added up over a year.

8. *False* Eating on a schedule helps define the times you eat so that you minimize the times of the day associated with eating.

9. *True* It is wise to break the habit of cleaning the plate so you, and not the server, determine how much you eat. By cleaning the plate, you have no control and eat whatever is in front of you.

Lesson Six

1. *False* Taste buds catch nothing but a blur if the food shoots past like a rocket. Slowing down can help you enjoy food more.

2. **False** Pausing gives the body a chance to signal that enough has been eaten so you can be satisfied with less food.

3. **False** No such luck! One and a half ounces of cheese is equivalent to the size of a pair of dice.

4. **False** It is true that saturated fats are generally solid at room temperature, but is not true that saturated fats are found *only* in animal products. Coconut and palm oils also contain saturated fats.

5. **True** Fat, as a *percentage* of total calories eaten, should be 30 percent or less of your daily diet.

6. **False** Fat plays an important role in the body and should not be *eliminated* from your diet. Dietary fat is important for good health; however, most people eat too much fat.

7. **True** It takes about 3,500 calories to equal one pound of body weight. Therefore, creating a 500–1,000 calorie *deficit* per day would allow you to lose about 1–2 pounds per week.

8. **True** One gram of fat contains 9 calories while 1 gram of carbohydrate or protein contains only 4 calories.

9. **True** Climbing stairs uses about twice the number of calories as a casual walk. This is an excellent way to burn calories.

10. **False** Many people underestimate the calories they eat. Part of this error may result from not accurately measuring portion sizes. The more accurately you record the calories you eat, the better you will be at providing your body with just the right amount of fuel.

11. **False** A MET is an abbreviation for metabolic equivalent and refers to the energy you expend while resting quietly. METs are important to help you estimate the total number of calories your body uses in a day.

Lesson Seven

1. **False** Changing thoughts we have had for years can be difficult, but with repeated practice, old thoughts can give way to new, constructive, and more helpful thoughts.

2. **False** Having unrealistic goals that are difficult to reach creates unrealistic expectations. When these expectations are not achieved, negative thoughts can trigger negative feelings, which in turn can send your motivation into a tailspin.

3. **False** Shopping on an empty stomach is asking for trouble. You will do less impulse buying if you shop after eating.

4. **True** Taking the time to prepare foods will give you a chance to make a determined decision to eat. Many times the food will not be worth the effort, so you can ask yourself how important eating really is.

5. **True** Having healthy foods such as fresh fruits and vegetables readily available to eat is a great way to control calories and increase your intake of fruits and vegetables.

6. **False** Vitamins, minerals, and water are essential nutrients for our bodies, yet they contain no calories.

7. **True** One serving from the Milk Group is equal to one cup or 8 ounces of milk. Remember, drinking skim or low-fat (1%) milk will help keep the calories down.

8. **True** The Food Guide Pyramid recommends 2–3 servings each day from the Milk Group.

9. **True** Behavior, even helping behavior, fades away if it is not rewarded (people like to be appreciated). So, if a partner helps you, show your appreciation in creative ways—his or her desire to help you will continue.

10. *False* Physical activity is important for both weight loss and weight loss maintenance. In fact, studies have shown that regular physical activity is associated with weight maintenance.

Lesson Eight

1. *False* Families can be a great resource for a person losing weight, but the harmony between the individual and the family requires a special effort.

2. *True* Thirty minutes of incremental physical activity on most days (at least five) are now recommended for people to reach a moderate level of physical fitness.

3. *False* The two purposes of stretching and other warm up exercises are to loosen the muscles to avoid strain and to permit the heart and circulatory system to make a gradual transition from rest to hard work. You should warm up and cool down for at least five minutes each time you exercise.

4. *False* You will increase your cardiovascular fitness by performing 30–60 minutes of moderate-intensity aerobic activities most days of the week. Achieving *optimal* cardiovascular fitness requires more attention to frequency, intensity, and time.

5. *True* Just like many people get angry at tobacco companies trying to peddle their products, it can be helpful to think of the food environment as a risky place. It is fine to get mad at inducements to overeat. Resist!!!

6. *False* Most people in the U.S. receive adequate vitamins if they eat a balanced diet. Because you are exercising more and eating less, taking a multiple vitamin each day may be a good idea to help remedy any deficiency created by the reduction in food intake. Check with your doctor to find out if a vitamin supplement is right for you.

7. *False* The amount of Total Fat listed under the heading "% Daily Value" of the food label represents the amount of a day's intake in a serving of the food, based on a 2,000 calorie-per-day diet.

8. *False* Protein is important for good health, but too much protein can lead to certain health problems. Most experts agree that between 10–35 percent of your total daily calories should come from protein.

9. *False* Eating a variety of legumes and grains will also provide high-quality protein.

Lesson Nine

1. *False* It is easy to "underestimate" your calorie intake. Measuring and weighing your food portions are helpful strategies to do every now and then to increase the accuracy of your food records.

2. *True* Saturated fat can raise your cholesterol level, so it is important to control the intake of foods high in cholesterol *and* foods high in saturated fat.

3. *False* It is best to take one portion at a time because it gives you time to decide whether you need more, and it interrupts automatic eating.

4. *False* Carbohydrates should make up the largest portion of your daily diet (between 55 and 60 percent of total calories). It is important, however, to watch for *hidden* calories in these foods and limit the *added* calories, such as toppings, butter, and dressings.

5. *False* Sugars stimulate insulin release, so you will feel hungry in less time by eating sugars than by eating starches and fiber. Limit your intake of sugars, which tend to come from foods with many calories and little nutrition.

6. **True** The Food Guide Pyramid suggests between three and five servings each day from this group.

7. **False** It is important to be familiar with the fat content of all foods. Vegetables are generally low in fat; however, nuts and avocados are examples of vegetables that are very high in fat.

8. **False** Most Americans fall short in their consumption of vegetables. The Food Guide Pyramid recommends 3–5 servings from the Vegetable Group each day.

9. **True** Spot reducing is a myth. Your body adds and removes fat according to genetic and hormonal factors. You can reduce fat in general, but you cannot dictate where it will come off.

10. **True** Each of us holds internal conversations, and many overweight individuals have fat *thoughts*. These thoughts and attitudes can greatly hinder weight loss efforts if they are not countered.

Lesson Ten

1. **False** If stress and eating are linked for you, you can respond to stress with activities other than eating, such as going for a walk. In addition, you can learn alternative stress management techniques to help you reduce stress.

2. **True** Running and cycling have both psychological and physical benefits. They are ideal for many people who are losing and maintaining weight.

3. **False** There are many kinds of exercise that can help with your weight loss. The best kind is the kind you enjoy enough to do again—now and in the future. Doing something rigorous is fine, if you keep it up. But, low-level activities will be better if you can stick with them over the long term.

4. **False** Aerobic activities do little for strength. They increase the body's use of oxygen and improve the condition of your heart. They are valuable for both health and weight loss.

5. **False** It is nice to be friendly, but it is more important that *you* control what you eat. Be polite, but be firm in not yielding to pressure to eat.

6. **True** These words are a setup for failure because they represent standards that no person can meet.

7. **False** Precisely because fiber is indigestible, it facilitates movement of food and waste products through the digestive system.

8. **True** Increased fiber in the diet protects against certain diseases.

9. **True** These foods are naturally high in fiber and are good additions to your diet if you wish to increase fiber intake.

10. **True** Most nutritionists suggest that a healthy goal is to aim for an average intake of 25–35 grams of fiber each day.

11. **False** Most Americans do not eat the recommended number of servings of fruit on a daily basis. Hence, most people should increase their intake of fruit.

12. **True** Remember, the refrigerator battle cry, "Out of Sight, Out of Mouth!"

13. **True** A significant number of overweight persons suffer from binge eating. The LEARN Program may help with this problem, as may other resources described in Lesson Ten.

Lesson Eleven

1. **True** The television can be a powerful cue that keeps people from being active. Turning off the TV may help you become and stay more physically active.

2. **True** These images and fantasies can distract a person from the day-to-day behaviors needed to lose weight, can lead to serious disappointment when

the individual loses weight, and can cause significant life issues.

3. **False** Overweight people experience physical hunger. However, they often confuse psychological cravings for this hunger and eat when there is no physical need.

4. **True** One size does not fit all. Different approaches to food cravings will help different people.

5. **True** With the "ideal" being extremely thin, shaped, and sculpted, it is virtually impossible for most people to look like they think they should—no matter how much dieting and exercising they do. People deserve to feel good and positive about their bodies, and the first step is to have a realistic standard.

6. **True** It's not easy, because society places so much importance on being thin. However, many people uncouple weight from their self-esteem and manage to appreciate their personal qualities and to accept their body for the pleasure it can bring them.

7. **True** Foods from this group are very high in complex carbohydrates, and most people should increase their intake from this food group. Breads, cakes, cookies and so forth, however, have *hidden* calories, and it is important to watch out for these.

Lesson Twelve

1. **True** If you understand the circumstances that prompt you to eat well and be active, and the circumstances that make you eat more and be inactive, you are poised to make positive lifestyle choices.

2. **False** Exercise is one predictor of who will keep weight off in the long run.

3. **True** A Behavior Chain can be broken at any link. Concentrate on the weakest links, where the chain is easiest to break.

4. **False** People losing weight may sometimes feel that the chain is out of control. However, a chain *can* be broken by using the right techniques at the proper time in a given situation.

5. **False** Interrupting a chain at one of the final links can be difficult because the momentum created by the earlier links can be powerful. Consider breaking the links earlier, before the process gets rolling.

6. **False** This refers to thinking that you are on or off a program, perfect or terrible with your behavior, and legal or illegal in your eating. Try to replace these thoughts with more rational perspectives.

7. **False** Some people *think* that a lapse leads to relapse because they feel guilty at any mistake. By using special coping techniques, you can see that a lapse can be a signal to do better, not worse.

8. **False** Different people respond to different techniques. Selecting a small number of techniques that work for *you* and focusing on them are the best strategies.

Appendix D

Guidelines for Being a Good Group Member

Many programs deal with participants in groups. This is done for an important reason. Members of the group can provide tremendous help to one another. The help may come in the form of encouraging words, a pat on the back, ideas to solve a specific problem, or just the knowledge that others in similar circumstances care about you.

Importance of the Group

From a problem-solving perspective, a group provides a shared experience that can help you develop an effective program. Still, beyond providing information, group members can provide support and encouragement. Most people losing weight experience times when their motivation is high. At other times, however, they find it difficult to move in the right direction. When you take a detour from your program, the group can help the motivation return. When you are highly motivated yourself, you can encourage someone else in the group who may have trouble.

Good Chemistry and Teamwork

When a group has the right chemistry, it functions like a well-oiled machine. The meetings are enjoyable, informative, and motivational. Each group member receives as much as he or she gives, and all are better off for the effort.

The analogy of a sports team is especially appropriate. Let's take a basketball team, for example. We all know of teams with great individual players, but the team goes nowhere if the players do not work together. One player may have an opportunity to take a shot, but passing to a teammate who has a better shot will help

the team. Teams with far less individual talent win championships by working together and helping one another. This intangible team spirit motivates everyone to work harder. Each player gives and receives, and all members of the team benefit in the process.

Being a good group member is the responsibility of everyone entering the group. Yet, more than duty, it is the best way to lose weight and keep the weight off. Entering a group with a spirit of cooperation and the willingness to help others will insure

A good group is like a sports team. The team goes nowhere if the players do not work together and help one another.

that the help comes back to you. In the end, you emerge a winner.

To be a good group member means following specific guidelines. There are things to do, things to say, and ways to act. The guidelines that follow can make this happen.

Guidelines and Responsibilities

Attend Meetings and Be Punctual

People in a group are responsible for attending meetings, not only for themselves but also for others. When a group member misses a meeting, others in the group may worry about the person, may wonder if the absence is a sign of trouble, or may be disappointed that the person wasn't there to provide support. Group members do become attached to each other and depend on one another for information and support.

You will undoubtedly face times when you question whether you should attend a meeting. You may have overdone it on the nacho chips,  it may be rainy and miserable outside, or you may have had a difficult time with work or with the kids. These are the times when your continued success may be most in jeopardy. So, it is important to attend the meeting. The group functions best when all attend, so remember that by joining a group you are agreeing to do your level best to attend all of the meetings. If you cannot attend, be sure to call your group leader and let him or her know that you will not be at the meeting.

Being on time is another key factor. When you arrive late for a group, you draw attention to yourself, disrupt the proceedings, miss what has happened to that point, and force the group leader to either ignore what you have missed or cover it again. Showing up late, especially if it occurs chronically, is a sign of disrespect for other members of the group.

Sometimes, of course, being late is inevitable. You may have just arrived in town on the flight from Tokyo where you were thinking of acquiring SONY or Toyota. If you live in Arizona, the Abominable Cactus may have attacked you. Alternatively, you may have some more common reason like a traffic jam, a late baby sitter, or deadlines at the office. These things happen, but when you can avoid being late and you still arrive late, it is a possible sign of trouble—a sign that you may need the group support the most!

Being late can be a sign of many things. Some people are always late because they fall into the Type A behavior pattern. They are always rushing and want to get in every bit of activity before departing for the group. Such a person would cringe at sitting around for a few minutes with nothing to do. My advice is to go ahead and cringe, but be on time. If you worry about wasting time by arriving early, you can always spend that time reading the next lesson in your LEARN manual.

Sometimes group members are late because they have done poorly and want to avoid facing the group or speaking with the group leader. Others may be angry with the group leader or dissatisfied with the program or their progress. These things are usually not done on a conscious level. Yet, if you look closely at your reasons for being late, these things may be the driving factors. If you find yourself being late, or *wanting* to be late, think about the reasons.

Really Listen

Sure, we all listen in a group, but do we *really* listen? Are you tuned in to what is happening? Do you hear the emotions behind the words of other group members?

It is quite apparent when someone in the group is not listening. Yawning, rolling the eyes, looking out the window, or daydreaming are all giveaways. Becoming distracted is sometimes easy, especially if what is being discussed is not relevant to you, or if something else important is occupying your thoughts. It takes a real effort to listen carefully.

Being a good listener involves watching the people who are speaking. Do they look like they are expressing some strong emotions? Is the topic a sensitive one? Have you experienced a similar situation or feeling? Have you found some approach helpful with the problem? It is fine to ask questions if you don't understand what the person is trying to say, and it is certainly fine to respond with supportive statements or suggestions. You will appreciate it when others in the group do this for you, so start by really listening.

Be Non-judgmental

This may sound like psychological jargon, but here is what it means to be non-judgmental. Sometimes you may feel that what another group member says or does is wrong, silly, or even stupid. There is a tendency to come down on these people or to point out the folly in their ways. The risk lies in being too negative, which can antagonize the person on the other end and make the remaining group members mad at you for being critical.

This does not mean that you are in a group where *everything is wonderful* and that you cannot express negative emotions. It is important to remember, however, that there are different ways of saying things. What others say can be used as an opportunity for growth or an occasion to create bad

feelings. The basic concept is for group members to accept one another. In such a climate, people in the group feel free to say things they may otherwise hide, for fear of being criticized.

The chart provided below gives some examples of judgmental and non-judgmental statements. As you can see, the non-judgmental statements are supportive and understanding. They open the door for further discussion. These statements show others that you care about them and are willing to help.

Be an Active Participant

In any group, some people are more active than others. This is fine, and can reflect differences in personalities. Not everyone has to be talkative to benefit from the group. However, opening up to be an active participant can help both you and the other members of the group.

Being silent in a group sometimes reflects being shy or reserved. In other cases, it shows that a person is angry, resentful, or bored. Whatever the reason, try to speak up when you have something worth saying. If you would like to share some of your own experiences, ask if anyone has a solution to a particular problem you face, or provide ideas of your own about an issue, speak up. Many times, what you have to say will be listened to with all the attention given to a group leader, and you might have ideas that the leader or others in the group do not have.

Non-judgmental statements are supportive, understanding, and open the door for further discussion.

Being Non-Judgmental		
One person says	**Judgmental Response**	**Non-Judgmental Response**
"I just couldn't exercise this week."	"You must be getting lazy."	"It's hard to keep motivated to exercise."
"I don't think this group is helping."	"You are just making excuses."	"Can we do something to help?"
"Others here don't understand me."	"You talk too much."	"I would like to. What can I do?"

If you are the silent type, don't feel pressured to be exceptionally talkative. Not everyone will participate equally or will speak the same amount. When you do have something to offer, please share it with the others.

Share the Air Space

Think of the air in the room as the territory around an airport. If too many planes enter the air space, the situation becomes dangerously confusing. If one jet occupies more than its share of the air space, say by circling in an erratic pattern, it would be tough going for the others.

In a group, only so much air space is available. Only so many voices can be heard and so many things said in the course of a group session. For members of the group who are particularly verbal, there can be a tendency to monopolize the conversation and to crowd others from the air space.

Think of group space as air space in a hot-air balloon festival. The air space is limited. Only so many voices can be heard during the course of a group session.

Again, not everyone speaks the same amount, so if some people are naturally more vocal in the group, there is no need to pull in the reins. But, if such a person interrupts or always speaks first, there may be a problem with sharing the air space. If the person takes a long time to make a point or has to say something during every discussion, it may be time to open the air space to others. Look at the way you speak

in the group, and see if any of these apply to you. If so, try to pull back, and think before speaking. By all means, speak up when you have something to say, and say what you feel, but try not to speak just because there is an opportunity.

Be Supportive

One of the fundamental reasons groups exist is for group members to support each other. This can be motivating and encouraging. In fact, sometimes a  kind word or a supportive gesture will mean more coming from a fellow group member than the exact same word or gesture coming from the group leader.

Group members should try to be nice, helpful, and understanding. When something is troubling another group member, do what you can to show that you understand. You can offer moral support by showing that you understand that the person faces a difficult situation. Share similar experiences you may have had, and most of all, give some constructive suggestions if you can think of ways to help.

In Summary

When you enter a group, you enter a situation in which you can reap impressive rewards. You have the opportunity to not only learn the facts and techniques of the program, but also to support and be supported, learn and instruct, help and be helped. This does not happen automatically, so you must be serious about your responsibilities as group members. In so doing, other group members will benefit from you and you will benefit from them. All will be better off, and the long-term result can be permanent weight loss.

Rate Your Diet Quiz—Lesson Two

The following questions will give you a rough sketch of your typical eating habits. The (+) or (–) number for each answer instantly pats you on the back for good eating habits or alerts you to problems you didn't even know you had. The quiz focuses on fat, saturated fat, cholesterol, sodium, sugar, fiber, and fruits and vegetables. It doesn't attempt to cover everything in your diet. Also, it doesn't try to measure precisely how much of the key nutrients you eat.

Next to each answer is a number with a + or – sign in front of it. Circle the number that corresponds to the answer you choose and write that score (e.g., +1) in the space provided in front of each question. That's your score for the question. If two or more answers apply, circle each one. Then average them to get your score for the question.

How to average. In answering question 19, for example, if your sandwich eating is equally divided among tuna salad (–2), roast beef (+1), and turkey breast (+3), add the three scores (which gives you +2) and then divide by three. That gives you a score of + ⅔ for the question. Round it to +1.

Pay attention to serving sizes, which are given when needed. For example, a serving of vegetables is ½ cup. If you usually eat one cup of vegetables at a time, count it as two servings. If you're ready, let's begin.

Fruits, Vegetables, Grains, and Beans

____ 1. How many servings of fruit or 100% fruit juice do you eat/drink per day? (*OMIT fruit snacks like fruit roll-ups and fruit-on-the-bottom yogurt. One serving = one piece or ½ cup of fruit or 6 oz of fruit juice.*)

    –3   None
    –2   Less than 1 serving
    0   1 serving
    +1   2 serving
    +2   3 serving
    +3   4 or more servings

____ 2. How many servings of non-fried vegetables do you eat per day? (*One serving = ½ cup. Include potatoes.*)

    –3   None
    –2   Less than 1 serving
    0   1 serving
    +1   2 serving
    +2   3 serving
    +3   4 or more servings

____ 3. How many servings of vitamin-rich vegetables do you eat per week? (*One serving = ½ cup. Only count broccoli, Brussels sprouts, carrots, collards, kale, red pepper, spinach, sweet potatoes, or winter squash.*)

    –3   None
    +1   1 to 3 servings
    +2   4 to 6 servings
    +3   7 or more servings

____ 4. How many servings of leafy green vegetables do you eat per week? (*One serving = ½ cup cooked or 1 cup raw. Only count collards, kale, mustard greens, romaine lettuce, spinach, or Swiss chard.*)

    –3   None
    –2   Less than 1 serving
    +1   1 to 2 servings
    +2   3 to 4 servings
    +3   5 or more servings

____ 5. How many times per week does your lunch or dinner contain grains, vegetables, or beans, but little or no meat, poultry, fish, eggs, or cheese?

    –1   None
    +1   1 to 2 times
    +2   3 to 4 times
    +3   5 or more times

____ 6. How many times per week do you eat beans, split peas, or lentils? (*Omit green beans.*)

    –3   None
    –1   Less than 1 time
    0   1 times
    +1   2 times
    +2   3 times
    +3   4 or more times

____ 7. How many servings of grains do you eat per day? (*One serving = 1 slice of bread, 1 oz of crackers, 1 large pancake, 1 cup pasta or cold cereal, or ½ cup granola, cooked cereal, rice, or bulgur. Omit heavily sweetened cold cereals.*)

    –3   None
    0   1 to 2 servings
    +1   3 to 4 servings
    +2   5 to 7 servings
    +3   8 or more servings

____ 8. What type of bread, rolls, etc., do you eat?

    +3   100% whole wheat as the only flour
    +2   Whole-wheat flour as 1st or 2nd flour
    +1   Rye, pumpernickel, or oatmeal
    0   White, French, or Italian

Rate Your Diet—Lesson Two (*continued*)

_____ 9. What kind of breakfast do you eat?

+3   Whole-grain (like oatmeal or Wheaties)

0   Low-fiber (like Cream of Wheat or Corn Flakes)

−1   Sugary low-fiber (like Frosted Flakes or low-fat granola)

−2   Regular granola

Meat, Poultry, and Seafood

_____ 10. How many times per week do you eat high-fat red meats (*e.g., hamburgers, pork chops, ribs, hot dogs, pot roast, sausage, bologna, steaks other than round steak, etc.*)?

+3   None
+2   Less than 1 time
−1   1 time
−2   2 times
−3   3 times
−4   4 times

_____ 11. How many times per week do you eat lean red meats (*e.g., hot dogs or luncheon meats with no more than 2 grams of fat per serving, round steak, or pork tenderloin*)?

+3   None
+1   Less than 1 time
0   1 time
−1   2 to 3 times
−2   4 to 5 times
−3   6 or more times

_____ 12. After cooking, how large is the serving of red meat you eat? (*To convert from raw to cooked, reduce by 25 percent. For example, 4 oz of raw meat shrinks to 3 oz after cooking. There are 16 oz in a pound*).

−3   6 oz or more
−2   4 to 5 oz
0   3 oz or less
+3   Don't eat red meat

_____ 13. If you eat red meat, do you trim the visible fat when you cook or eat it?

+1   Yes
−3   No

_____ 14. What kind of ground meat or poultry do you eat?

−4   Regular ground beef
−3   Ground beef that's 11 to 25% fat
−2   Ground chicken or 10% fat ground beef
−1   Ground turkey
+3   Ground turkey breast
+3   Don't eat ground meat or poultry

_____ 15. What chicken parts do you eat?

+3   Breast
+1   Drumstick
−1   Thigh
−2   Wing
+3   Don't eat poultry

_____ 16. If you eat poultry, do you remove the skin before eating?

+2   Yes
−3   No

_____ 17. If you eat seafood, how many times per week? (*Omit deep-fried foods, tuna packed in oil, and mayonnaise-laden tuna salad. Low-fat mayo is okay.*)

0   Less than 1 time
+1   1 time
+2   2 times
+3   3 or more times

Mixed Foods

_____ 18. What is your most typical breakfast? (*Subtract an extra 3 points if you also eat sausage.*)

−4   Biscuit sandwich or croissant sandwich

−3   Croissant, Danish, or doughnut

−3   Eggs

−1   Pancakes, French toast, or waffles

+3   Cereal, toast, or bagel (no cream cheese)

+3   Low-fat yogurt or low-fat cottage cheese

0   Don't eat breakfast

_____ 19. What sandwich fillings do you eat?

−3   Regular luncheon meat, cheese, or egg salad

−2   Tuna or chicken salad or ham

0   Peanut butter

+1   Roast beef

+1   Low-fat luncheon meat

+3   Tuna or chicken salad made with fat-free mayo

+3   Turkey breast or hummus

_____ 20. What do you order on your pizza? (*Subtract 1 point if you order extra cheese, cheese-filled crust, or more than one meat topping*).

+3   No cheese with at least one vegetable topping

−1   Cheese with at least one vegetable topping

−2   Cheese

−3   Cheese with one meat topping

+3   Don't eat pizza

____ 21. What do you put on your pasta? (*Add one point if you also add sautéed vegetables.*)

  +3 Tomato sauce or red clam sauce
  −1 Meat sauce or meat balls
  −3 Pesto or another oily sauce
  −4 Alfredo or another creamy sauce

____ 22. How many times per week do you eat deep-fried foods (*fish, chicken, French fries, potato chips, etc.*)?

  +3 None
   0 1 time
  −1 2 times
  −2 3 times
  −3 4 or more times

____ 23. At a salad bar, what do you choose?

  +3 Nothing, lemon, or vinegar
  +2 Fat-free dressing
  +1 Low- or reduced-calorie dressing
  −1 Oil and vinegar
  −2 Regular dressing
  −2 Cole slaw, pasta salad, or potato salad
  −3 Cheese or eggs

____ 24. How many times per week do you eat canned or dried soups or frozen dinners? (*Omit lower-sodium, low-fat ones.*)

  +3 None
   0 1 time
  −1 2 times
  −2 3 to 4 times
  −3 5 or more times

____ 25. How many servings of low-fat calcium-rich foods do you eat per day? (*One serving = ⅔ cup low-fat or non-fat milk or yogurt, 1 oz low-fat cheese, 1½ oz sardines, 3½ oz canned salmon with bones, 1 oz tofu made with calcium sulfate, 1 cup collards or kale, or 200 mg of a calcium supplement.*)

  −3 None
  −1 Less than 1 serving
  +1 1 serving
  +2 2 servings
  +3 3 or more servings

____ 26. How many times per week do you eat cheese? (*Include pizza, cheeseburgers, lasagna, tacos or nachos with cheese, etc. Omit foods made with low-fat cheese.*)

  +3 None
  +1 1 time
  −1 2 times
  −2 3 times
  −3 4 or more times

____ 27. How many egg yolks do you eat per week? (*Add 1 yolk for every slice of quiche you eat.*)

  +3 None
  +1 1 yolk
   0 2 yolks
  −1 3 yolks
  −2 4 yolks
  −3 5 or more yolks

Fats & Oils

____ 28. What do you put on your bread, toast, bagel, or English muffin?

  −4 Stick butter or cream cheese
  −3 Stick margarine or whipped butter
  −2 Regular tub margarine
  −1 Light tub margarine or whipped light butter
   0 Jam, fat-free margarine, or fat-free cream cheese
  +3 Nothing

____ 29. What do you spread on your sandwiches?

  −2 Mayonnaise
  −1 Light mayonnaise
  +1 Catsup, mustard, or fat-free mayonnaise
  +2 Nothing

____ 30. With what do you make tuna salad, pasta salad, chicken salad, etc.?

  −2 Mayonnaise
  −1 Light mayonnaise
   0 Fat-free mayonnaise
  +2 Nothing

____ 31. What do you use to sauté vegetables or other food? (Vegetable oil includes safflower, corn, sunflower, and soybean.)

  −3 Butter or lard
  −2 Margarine
  −1 Vegetable oil or light margarine
  +1 Olive or canola oil
  +2 Broth
  +3 Cooking spray

Beverages

____ 32. What do you drink on a typical day?

  +3 Water or club soda
   0 Caffeine-free coffee or tea
  −1 Diet soda
  −1 Coffee or tea (up to 4 a day)
  −2 Regular soda (up to 2 a day)
  −3 Regular soda (3 or more a day)
  −3 Coffee or tea (5 or more a day)

Rate Your Diet—Lesson Two (*continued*)

____ 33. What kind of "fruit" beverage do you drink?

+3   Orange, grapefruit, prune, or pineapple juice

+1   Apple, grape, or pear juice

0   Cranberry juice blend or cocktail

−3   Fruit "drink," "ade," or "punch"

____ 34. What kind of milk do you drink?

−3   Whole

−1   2% fat

+2   1% low-fat

+3   skim

____ 35. What do you eat as a snack?

+3   Fruits or vegetables

+2   Low-fat yogurt

+1   Low-fat crackers

−2   Cookies or fried chips

−2   Nuts or granola bar

−3   Candy bar or pastry

____ 36. Which of the following "salty" snacks do you eat?

−3   Potato chips, corn chips, or popcorn

−2   Tortilla chips

−1   Salted pretzels or light microwave popcorn

+2   Unsalted pretzels

+3   Baked tortilla or potato chips or homemade air-popped popcorn

+3   Don't eat salty snacks

____ 37. What kind of cookies do you eat?

+2   Fat-free cookies

+1   Graham crackers or reduced-fat cookies

−1   Oatmeal cookies

−2   Sandwich cookies (like Oreos)

−3   Chocolate coated, chocolate chip, or peanut butter cookies

+3   Don't eat cookies

____ 38. What kind of cake or pastry do you eat?

−4   Cheesecake

−3   Pie or doughnuts

−2   Cake with frosting

−1   Cake without frosting

0   Muffins

+1   Angle food, fat-free cake, or fat-free pastry

+3   Don't eat cakes or pastries

____ 39. What kind of frozen dessert do you eat? (*Subtract 1 point for each of the following toppings: hot fudge, nuts, or chocolate candy bars or pieces.*)

−4   Gourmet ice cream

−3   Regular ice cream

−1   Frozen yogurt or light ice cream

−1   Sorbet, sherbet, or ices

+1   Nonfat frozen yogurt or fat-free ice cream

+3   Don't eat frozen desserts

____   **Total Score** (add scores from 1–39)[1]

[1] Record this score in the space provided in Appendix B, on page 213.

If your score is:

1 to 29:   Don't be discouraged. Eating healthy is tough, but you can learn to eat healthier.

30 to 59:   Congratulations. You are doing just fine. Pin your Quiz to the nearest wall.

60 or above: Excellent. You're a nutrition superstar. Give yourself a big pat on the back.

Source: Adapted with permission from *Nutrition Action Healthletter*, May 1996, V23/N4. (*Nutrition Action Healthletter*, 1875 Connecticut Ave., N.W., Suite 300, Washington DC 20009-5728. $24 for 10 issues.)

Rate Your Diet Quiz—Lesson Seven

The following questions will give you a rough sketch of your typical eating habits. The (+) or (–) number for each answer instantly pats you on the back for good eating habits or alerts you to problems you didn't even know you had. The quiz focuses on fat, saturated fat, cholesterol, sodium, sugar, fiber, and fruits and vegetables. It doesn't attempt to cover everything in your diet. Also, it doesn't try to measure precisely how much of the key nutrients you eat.

Next to each answer is a number with a + or – sign in front of it. Circle the number that corresponds to the answer you choose and write that score (e.g., +1) in the space provided in front of each question. That's your score for the question. If two or more answers apply, circle each one. Then average them to get your score for the question.

How to average. In answering question 19, for example, if your sandwich eating is equally divided among tuna salad (–2), roast beef (+1), and turkey breast (+3), add the three scores (which gives you +2) and then divide by three. That gives you a score of + ⅔ for the question. Round it to +1.

Pay attention to serving sizes, which are given when needed. For example, a serving of vegetables is ½ cup. If you usually eat one cup of vegetables at a time, count it as two servings. If you're ready, let's begin.

Fruits, Vegetables, Grains, and Beans

____ 1. How many servings of fruit or 100% fruit juice do you eat/drink per day? (*OMIT fruit snacks like fruit roll-ups and fruit-on-the-bottom yogurt. One serving = one piece or ½ cup of fruit or 6 oz of fruit juice.*)

   –3 None
   –2 Less than 1 serving
   0 1 serving
   +1 2 serving
   +2 3 serving
   +3 4 or more servings

____ 2. How many servings of non-fried vegetables do you eat per day? (*One serving = ½ cup. Include potatoes.*)

   –3 None
   –2 Less than 1 serving
   0 1 serving
   +1 2 serving
   +2 3 serving
   +3 4 or more servings

____ 3. How many servings of vitamin-rich vegetables do you eat per week? (*One serving = ½ cup. Only count broccoli, Brussels sprouts, carrots, collards, kale, red pepper, spinach, sweet potatoes, or winter squash.*)

   –3 None
   +1 1 to 3 servings
   +2 4 to 6 servings
   +3 7 or more servings

____ 4. How many servings of leafy green vegetables do you eat per week? (*One serving = ½ cup cooked or 1 cup raw. Only count collards, kale, mustard greens, romaine lettuce, spinach, or Swiss chard.*)

   –3 None
   –2 Less than 1 serving
   +1 1 to 2 servings
   +2 3 to 4 servings
   +3 5 or more servings

____ 5. How many times per week does your lunch or dinner contain grains, vegetables, or beans, but little or no meat, poultry, fish, eggs, or cheese?

   –1 None
   +1 1 to 2 times
   +2 3 to 4 times
   +3 5 or more times

____ 6. How many times per week do you eat beans, split peas, or lentils? (*Omit green beans.*)

   –3 None
   –1 Less than 1 time
   0 1 times
   +1 2 times
   +2 3 times
   +3 4 or more times

____ 7. How many servings of grains do you eat per day? (*One serving = 1 slice of bread, 1 oz of crackers, 1 large pancake, 1 cup pasta or cold cereal, or ½ cup granola, cooked cereal, rice, or bulgur. Omit heavily sweetened cold cereals.*)

   –3 None
   0 1 to 2 servings
   +1 3 to 4 servings
   +2 5 to 7 servings
   +3 8 or more servings

____ 8. What type of bread, rolls, etc., do you eat?

   +3 100% whole wheat as the only flour
   +2 Whole-wheat flour as 1st or 2nd flour
   +1 Rye, pumpernickel, or oatmeal
   0 White, French, or Italian

Rate Your Diet—Lesson Seven (*continued*)

___ 9. What kind of breakfast do you eat?

+3   Whole-grain (like oatmeal or Wheaties)

0   Low-fiber (like Cream of Wheat or Corn Flakes)

−1   Sugary low-fiber (like Frosted Flakes or low-fat granola)

−2   Regular granola

Meat, Poultry, and Seafood

___ 10. How many times per week do you eat high-fat red meats (*e.g., hamburgers, pork chops, ribs, hot dogs, pot roast, sausage, bologna, steaks other than round steak, etc.*)?

+3   None

+2   Less than 1 time

−1   1 time

−2   2 times

−3   3 times

−4   4 times

___ 11. How many times per week do you eat lean red meats (*e.g., hot dogs or luncheon meats with no more than 2 grams of fat per serving, round steak, or pork tenderloin*)?

+3   None

+1   Less than 1 time

0   1 time

−1   2 to 3 times

−2   4 to 5 times

−3   6 or more times

___ 12. After cooking, how large is the serving of red meat you eat? (*To convert from raw to cooked, reduce by 25 percent. For example, 4 oz of raw meat shrinks to 3 oz after cooking. There are 16 oz in a pound*).

−3   6 oz or more

−2   4 to 5 oz

0   3 oz or less

+3   Don't eat red meat

___ 13. If you eat red meat, do you trim the visible fat when you cook or eat it?

+1   Yes

−3   No

___ 14. What kind of ground meat or poultry do you eat?

−4   Regular ground beef

−3   Ground beef that's 11 to 25% fat

−2   Ground chicken or 10% fat ground beef

−1   Ground turkey

+3   Ground turkey breast

+3   Don't eat ground meat or poultry

___ 15. What chicken parts do you eat?

+3   Breast

+1   Drumstick

−1   Thigh

−2   Wing

+3   Don't eat poultry

___ 16. If you eat poultry, do you remove the skin before eating?

+2   Yes

−3   No

___ 17. If you eat seafood, how many times per week? (*Omit deep-fried foods, tuna packed in oil, and mayonnaise-laden tuna salad. Low-fat mayo is okay.*)

0   Less than 1 time

+1   1 time

+2   2 times

+3   3 or more times

Mixed Foods

___ 18. What is your most typical breakfast? (*Subtract an extra 3 points if you also eat sausage.*)

−4   Biscuit sandwich or croissant sandwich

−3   Croissant, Danish, or doughnut

−3   Eggs

−1   Pancakes, French toast, or waffles

+3   Cereal, toast, or bagel (no cream cheese)

+3   Low-fat yogurt or low-fat cottage cheese

0   Don't eat breakfast

___ 19. What sandwich fillings do you eat?

−3   Regular luncheon meat, cheese, or egg salad

−2   Tuna or chicken salad or ham

0   Peanut butter

+1   Roast beef

+1   Low-fat luncheon meat

+3   Tuna or chicken salad made with fat-free mayo

+3   Turkey breast or hummus

___ 20. What do you order on your pizza? (*Subtract 1 point if you order extra cheese, cheese-filled crust, or more than one meat topping*).

+3   No cheese with at least one vegetable topping

−1   Cheese with at least one vegetable topping

−2   Cheese

−3   Cheese with one meat topping

+3   Don't eat pizza

21. What do you put on your pasta? (*Add one point if you also add sautéed vegetables.*)

   +3   Tomato sauce or red clam sauce
   −1   Meat sauce or meat balls
   −3   Pesto or another oily sauce
   −4   Alfredo or another creamy sauce

22. How many times per week do you eat deep-fried foods (*fish, chicken, French fries, potato chips, etc.*)?

   +3   None
    0   1 time
   −1   2 times
   −2   3 times
   −3   4 or more times

23. At a salad bar, what do you choose?

   +3   Nothing, lemon, or vinegar
   +2   Fat-free dressing
   +1   Low- or reduced-calorie dressing
   −1   Oil and vinegar
   −2   Regular dressing
   −2   Cole slaw, pasta salad, or potato salad
   −3   Cheese or eggs

24. How many times per week do you eat canned or dried soups or frozen dinners? (*Omit lower-sodium, low-fat ones.*)

   +3   None
    0   1 time
   −1   2 times
   −2   3 to 4 times
   −3   5 or more times

25. How many servings of low-fat calcium-rich foods do you eat per day? (*One serving = ⅔ cup low-fat or nonfat milk or yogurt, 1 oz low-fat cheese, 1½ oz sardines, 3½ oz canned salmon with bones, 1 oz tofu made with calcium sulfate, 1 cup collards or kale, or 200 mg of a calcium supplement.*)

   −3   None
   −1   Less than 1 serving
   +1   1 serving
   +2   2 servings
   +3   3 or more servings

26. How many times per week do you eat cheese? (*Include pizza, cheeseburgers, lasagna, tacos or nachos with cheese, etc. Omit foods made with low-fat cheese.*)

   +3   None
   +1   1 time
   −1   2 times
   −2   3 times
   −3   4 or more times

27. How many egg yolks do you eat per week? (*Add 1 yolk for every slice of quiche you eat.*)

   +3   None
   +1   1 yolk
    0   2 yolks
   −1   3 yolks
   −2   4 yolks
   −3   5 or more yolks

Fats & Oils

28. What do you put on your bread, toast, bagel, or English muffin?

   −4   Stick butter or cream cheese
   −3   Stick margarine or whipped butter
   −2   Regular tub margarine
   −1   Light tub margarine or whipped light butter
    0   Jam, fat-free margarine, or fat-free cream cheese
   +3   Nothing

29. What do you spread on your sandwiches?

   −2   Mayonnaise
   −1   Light mayonnaise
   +1   Catsup, mustard, or fat-free mayonnaise
   +2   Nothing

30. With what do you make tuna salad, pasta salad, chicken salad, etc.?

   −2   Mayonnaise
   −1   Light mayonnaise
    0   Fat-free mayonnaise
   +2   Nothing

31. What do you use to sauté vegetables or other food? (Vegetable oil includes safflower, corn, sunflower, and soybean.)

   −3   Butter or lard
   −2   Margarine
   −1   Vegetable oil or light margarine
   +1   Olive or canola oil
   +2   Broth
   +3   Cooking spray

Beverages

32. What do you drink on a typical day?

   +3   Water or club soda
    0   Caffeine-free coffee or tea
   −1   Diet soda
   −1   Coffee or tea (up to 4 a day)
   −2   Regular soda (up to 2 a day)
   −3   Regular soda (3 or more a day)
   −3   Coffee or tea (5 or more a day)

Rate Your Diet—Lesson Seven (*continued*)

____ 33. What kind of "fruit" beverage do you drink?

+3   Orange, grapefruit, prune, or pineapple juice

+1   Apple, grape, or pear juice

0   Cranberry juice blend or cocktail

−3   Fruit "drink," "ade," or "punch"

____ 34. What kind of milk do you drink?

−3   Whole

−1   2% fat

+2   1% low-fat

+3   skim

____ 35. What do you eat as a snack?

+3   Fruits or vegetables

+2   Low-fat yogurt

+1   Low-fat crackers

−2   Cookies or fried chips

−2   Nuts or granola bar

−3   Candy bar or pastry

____ 36. Which of the following "salty" snacks do you eat?

−3   Potato chips, corn chips, or popcorn

−2   Tortilla chips

−1   Salted pretzels or light microwave popcorn

+2   Unsalted pretzels

+3   Baked tortilla or potato chips or homemade air-popped popcorn

+3   Don't eat salty snacks

____ 37. What kind of cookies do you eat?

+2   Fat-free cookies

+1   Graham crackers or reduced-fat cookies

−1   Oatmeal cookies

−2   Sandwich cookies (like Oreos)

−3   Chocolate coated, chocolate chip, or peanut butter cookies

+3   Don't eat cookies

____ 38. What kind of cake or pastry do you eat?

−4   Cheesecake

−3   Pie or doughnuts

−2   Cake with frosting

−1   Cake without frosting

0   Muffins

+1   Angle food, fat-free cake, or fat-free pastry

+3   Don't eat cakes or pastries

____ 39. What kind of frozen dessert do you eat? (*Subtract 1 point for each of the following toppings: hot fudge, nuts, or chocolate candy bars or pieces.*)

−4   Gourmet ice cream

−3   Regular ice cream

−1   Frozen yogurt or light ice cream

−1   Sorbet, sherbet, or ices

+1   Nonfat frozen yogurt or fat-free ice cream

+3   Don't eat frozen desserts

____   **Total Score** (add scores from 1–39)[1]

[1] Record this score in the space provided in Appendix B, on page 213.

If your score is:

1 to 29:   Don't be discouraged. Eating healthy is tough, but you can learn to eat healthier.

30 to 59:   Congratulations. You are doing just fine. Pin your Quiz to the nearest wall.

60 or above: Excellent. You're a nutrition superstar. Give yourself a big pat on the back.

Source: Adapted with permission from *Nutrition Action Healthletter*, May 1996, V23/N4. (*Nutrition Action Healthletter*, 1875 Connecticut Ave., N.W., Suite 300, Washington DC 20009-5728. $24 for 10 issues.)

Fast Food Guide

Description	Calories	Pro (g)	Carb (g)	Fat (g)
Arby's				
Roast Beef Sandwiches				
Arby's Melt w/Cheddar	340	16	36	15
Arby-Q®	360	16	40	14
Beef 'N Cheddar	480	23	43	24
Big Montana®	630	47	41	32
Giant Roast Beef	480	32	41	23
Junior Roast Beef	310	16	34	13
Regular Roast Beef	350	21	34	16
Super Roast Beef	470	22	47	23
Other Sandwiches				
Chicken Bacon 'N Swiss	610	31	49	33
Chicken Breast Fillet	540	24	47	30
Chicken Cordon Bleu	630	34	47	35
Grilled Chicken Deluxe	450	29	37	22
Roast Chicken Club	520	29	38	28
Hot Ham 'N Swiss	340	23	35	13
Sub Sandwiches				
French Dip	440	28	42	18
Hot Ham 'N Swiss	530	29	45	27
Italian	780	29	49	53
Philly Beef 'N Swiss	700	36	46	42
Roast Beef	760	35	47	48
Turkey	630	26	51	37
Market Fresh Sandwiches				
Roast Beef & Swiss	810	37	73	42
Roast Ham & Swiss	730	36	74	34
Roast Chicken Caesar	820	43	75	38
Roast Turkey & Swiss	760	43	75	33
Roast Turkey Ranch & Bacon	880	48	74	44
Market Fresh Ultimate BLT	820	24	72	49
Market Fresh Salads (without dressing)				
Turkey Club Salad	350	33	9	21
Caesar Salad	90	7	8	4
Grilled Chicken Caesar	230	33	8	8
Chicken Finger Salad	570	30	39	34
Caesar Side Salad	45	4	4	2
Light Menu				
Light Grilled Chicken	280	29	30	5
Light Roast Chicken Deluxe	260	23	33	5
Light Roast Turkey Deluxe	260	23	33	5
Salads (without dressing)				
Roast Chicken Salad	160	20	15	2.5
Grilled Chicken Salad	210	30	14	4.5
Garden Salad	70	4	14	1
Side Salad	25	2	5	0
Side Items				
Cheddar Curly Fries	460	6	54	24
Curly Fries (small)	310	4	39	15
Curly Fries (med)	400	5	50	20
Curly Fries (large)	620	8	78	30
Homestyle Fries (child-size)	220	3	32	10
Homestyle Fries (small)	300	3	42	13
Homestyle Fries (med)	370	4	53	16
Homestyle Fries (larger)	560	6	79	24
Potato Cakes (2)	250	2	26	16
Jalapeno Bites™	330	7	30	21
Mozzarella Sticks (4)	470	18	34	29
Onion Petals	410	4	43	24
Chicken Finger Snack (with Curly Fries)	580	19	55	32
Chicken Finger 4-Pack	640	31	42	38
Baked Potato w/Butter & Sour Cream	500	8	65	24
Broccoli 'N Cheddar Baked Potato	540	12	71	24
Deluxe Baked Potato	650	20	67	34

Description	Calories	Pro (g)	Carb (g)	Fat (g)
Desserts				
Apple Turnover (iced)	420	4	65	16
Cherry Turnover (iced)	410	4	63	16
Drinks				
Vanilla Shake	470	10	83	15
Chocolate Shake	480	10	84	16
Strawberry Shake	500	11	87	13
Jamocha Shake	470	10	82	15
Breakfast Items				
Biscuit w/butter	280	5	27	17
Biscuit with Ham	330	12	28	20
Biscuit with Sausage	440	10	27	33
Biscuit with Bacon	320	7	27	21
Croissant with Ham	310	13	29	19
Croissant with Sausage	420	11	28	32
Croissant with Bacon	300	8	28	20
Sourdough with Ham	220	12	30	7
Sourdough with Sausage	330	10	29	19
Sourdough with Bacon	380	14	66	7
Add Egg	110	5	2	9
Add Slice Swiss Cheese	45	3	0	3
French Toastix (no syrup)	370	7	48	17
Condiments				
Arby's Sauce® Packet	15	0	4	0
BBQ Dipping Sauce	40	0	10	0
Au Jus Sauce	5	<1	<1	<1
BBQ Vinaigrette Dressing	140	0	9	11
Bleu Cheese Dressing	300	2	3	31
Bronco Berry Sauce™	90	0	23	0
Buttermilk Ranch Dressing	360	1	2	39
Buttermilk Ranch Dressing Reduced Calorie	60	1	13	0
Caesar Dressing	310	1	1	34
Croutons, Cheese & Garlic	100	3	10	6
Croutons, Seasoned	30	1	5	1
German Mustard Packet	5	0	0	0
Honey French Dressing	290	0	18	24
Honey Mustard Sauce	130	0	5	12
Horsey Sauce® Packet	60	0	3	5
Italian Dressing, Reduced Calorie	25	0	3	1
Italian Parmesan Dressing	240	1	4	24
Ketchup Packet	10	0	2	0
French Toast Syrup	130	0	32	0
Mayonnaise Packet	90	0	0	10
Mayonnaise Packet Light, Cholesterol-Free	20	0	1	2
Marinara Sauce	35	1	4	1
Tangy Southwest Sauce™	250	0	3	26
Thousand Island Dressing	290	1	9	28
Blimpies				
Cold Subs (6" Regular)				
BLIMPIE® Best®	476	30	52	16
Club	440	28	51	12
Ham & Cheese	436	28	52	13
Roast Beef	468	37	49	14
Seafood	355	14	58	8
Tuna	493	24	51	23
Turkey	424	25	49	11
Hot Subs (6" Regular)				
BLT	588	28	49	32
Grilled Chicken	373	29	50	9
Buffalo Chicken	400	32	50	13
Meatball	572	28	55	27
Pastrami	507	36	53	17
Steak & Onion Melt	440	29	49	16

Description	Calories	Pro (g)	Carb (g)	Fat (g)
MexiMax™	425	23	65	9
ChikMax™	511	29	71	13
VegiMax™	395	24	60	7
Grilled Subs (6" Regular)				
Beef, Turkey & Cheddar	600	28	49	31
Cuban	462	30	50	12
Pastrami Special	462	32	52	14
Reuben	630	31	55	33
Ultimate Club	724	33	51	42
Wraps				
Chicken Caesar	646	25	56	35
Beef & Cheddar	714	34	57	37
Southwestern	674	26	54	35
Steak & Onion	716	30	64	37
Ultimate BLT	831	34	60	50
Zesty Italian	638	26	74	33
Salads				
Antipasto	244	23	10	13
Chef	212	20	9	9
Grilled Chicken (w/Caesar dressing)	347	18	9	27
Seafood	122	6	16	4
Tuna	261	16	8	20
Zesto Pesto™ Turkey	370	20	31	19
Chili Olé™	480	21	42	27
Roast Beef 'n Bleu™	390	31	29	16
Cole Slaw	180	1	13	13
Macaroni Salad	360	4	25	25
Mustard Potato Salad	160	2	21	5
Potato Salad	270	2	19	19
Toppings/Sauces/Dressings				
Provolone Cheese (1 slice)	80	6	0	6
Swiss Cheese (1 slice)	80	7	0	6
Cheddar Cheese (1 slice)	52	3	0	5
Oil & Vinegar Topping	36	0	1	4
Guacamole (1½ oz)	194	2	7	18
Caesar (1½ oz)	208	1	2	22
Cracked Peppercorn (1½ oz)	237	1	2	25
Pesto Dressing (1 oz)	132	0	1	13
GourMayo Wasabi Horseradish (1 T)	50	0	1	5
GourMayo Sun Dried Tomato (1 T)	50	0	1	5
GourMayo Chipotle Chili (1 T)	50	0	1	5
French's Honey Mustard (1 T)	5	0	1	0
Frank's RedHot Buffalo Sauce (1 oz.)	13	<1	2	<1
Soups (8 oz)				
Chicken Soup with White & Wild Rice	230	10	21	12
Tomato Basil with Raviolini	110	4	22	1
Grande Chili with Beans & Beef	250	18	30	7
Vegetable Beef	80	4	13	2
Cream of Potato	190	5	24	9
Homestyle Chicken Noodle	120	7	18	3
Cream of Broccoli & Cheese	190	6	15	12
Garden Vegetable	80	5	14	1
Cookies (1)				
Chocolate Chunk	200	2	26	10
Macadamia White Chunk	210	2	26	10
Oatmeal Raisin	190	3	27	8
Peanut Butter	220	4	23	12
Sugar	330	3	24	17

Burger King

Description	Calories	Pro (g)	Carb (g)	Fat (g)
Burgers				
Original Whopper®	760	35	52	46
w/o mayo	600	34	52	28
Original Whopper® w/ cheese	850	39	53	53
w/o mayo	690	39	53	36
Original Double Whopper®	1,060	59	52	69
w/o mayo	900	59	52	51

Description	Calories	Pro (g)	Carb (g)	Fat (g)
Original Double Whopper® w/ cheese	1,150	64	53	76
w/o mayo	990	64	53	59
Original Whopper Jr.®	390	17	32	22
w/o mayo	310	17	31	13
w/ cheese	440	19	32	26
w/cheese, w/o mayo	360	19	32	17
BK Homestyle™ Griller	480	26	35	27
BK Smokehouse Cheddar™ Griller	720	39	32	48
King Supreme™ Sandwich	550	30	32	34
BK ¼ lb Burger™	490	26	50	21
Hamburger	310	17	31	13
Cheeseburger	360	19	31	17
Double Hamburger	450	28	31	24
Double Cheeseburger	540	32	32	31
Bacon Double Cheeseburger	580	35	32	34
Sandwiches/Side Orders				
BK Big Fish® Sandwich	710	24	66	39
Chicken Whopper®	580	39	48	26
w/o mayo	420	38	47	9
Chicken Whopper Jr.®	350	26	30	14
w/o mayo	270	25	30	6
Specialty Chicken Sandwich	560	25	52	28
w/o mayo	460	25	52	17
Chicken Tenders®, 4 pieces	170	11	10	9
5 pieces	210	14	13	12
6 pieces	250	16	15	14
8 pieces	340	22	20	19
BK Veggie™ Burger	330	14	45	10
w/o reduced fat mayo	290	14	44	7
Fries (small)	230	3	29	11
(medium)	360	4	46	18
(large)	500	6	63	25
(king)	600	7	76	30
Onion Rings (small)	180	2	22	9
(medium)	320	4	40	16
(large)	480	7	60	23
(king)	550	8	70	27
Salads/Dressings				
Chicken Caesar (w/o dressing and croutons)	160	25	5	6
Garden Salad (w/o dressing)	25	1	5	0
Kraft® Catalina Dressing	180	0	10	16
Signature® Creamy Caesar Dressing	140	1	4	13
Kraft® Ranch Dressing	220	0	2	23
Kraft® Thousand Island Dressing	110	1	7	9
Light Done Right® Light Italian Dressing	50	0	4	5
Croutons (¾ oz.)	90	2	14	3
Parmesan Cheese (½ oz.)	45	4	0	4
Dipping Sauces				
Barbecue	35	0	9	0
Honey Flavored	90	0	23	0
Honey Mustard	90	0	9	6
Sweet and Sour	40	0	10	0
Ranch	140	1	1	15
Zesty Onion Ring	150	0	3	15
Desserts				
Dutch Apple Pie	340	2	52	14
Hershey®'s Sundae Pie	310	3	33	18
Hot Fudge Brownie Royale	440	6	62	19
Fresh Baked Cookies	440	4	57	21
Breakfast				
Croissanwich® w/sausage, egg & cheese	520	19	24	39
Croissanwich® w/sausage & cheese	420	14	23	31
Croissanwich® w/egg & cheese	320	12	24	19
Eggwich™ w/Canadian bacon, egg & cheese	420	18	36	23
Eggwich™ w/Canadian bacon & egg	380	15	35	19
Eggwich™ w/egg & cheese	410	15	36	23

Description	Calories	Pro (g)	Carb (g)	Fat (g)
French Toast Sticks–5 sticks	390	6	46	20
Cini-minis (w/o vanilla icing) 4 rolls	440	6	51	23
Hash Brown Rounds (small)	230	2	23	15
(large)	390	3	38	25
Drinks				
Vanilla Shake (small)	560	11	56	32
(medium)	720	15	73	41
Chocolate Shake (small)	620	12	72	32
(medium)	790	15	89	42
Strawberry Shake (small)	620	11	71	32
(medium)	780	15	88	41

Dairy Queen

Burgers/Sandwiches/Side Orders

Description	Calories	Pro (g)	Carb (g)	Fat (g)
DQ Homestyle® Hamburger	290	17	29	12
DQ Homestyle® Cheeseburger	340	20	29	17
DQ Homestyle® Dbl Cheeseburger	540	35	30	31
DQ Homestyle® Bacon Dbl Cheeseburger	610	41	31	36
DQ Ultimate® Burger	670	40	29	43
Hot Dog	240	9	19	14
Chili 'n' Cheese Dog	330	14	22	21
Chicken Breast Fillet Sandwich	500	19	48	26
Grilled Chicken Sandwich	310	24	30	10
Chicken Strip Basket	1,000	35	102	50
Crispy Chicken Salad w/ Honey Mustard Dressing	700	27	36	51
Crispy Chicken Salad w/ Fat Free Italian Dressing	460	26	27	28
Grilled Chicken Salad w/ Honey Mustard Dressing	470	26	22	32
Grilled Chicken Salad w/ Fat Free Italian Dressing	230	26	13	9
Fries (small)	350	4	42	18
(medium)	440	5	53	23
Onion Rings	320	5	39	16

Frozen Treats

Description	Calories	Pro (g)	Carb (g)	Fat (g)
DQ® Vanilla Soft Serve, ½ cup	140	3	22	5
DQ® Chocolate Soft Serve, ½ cup	150	4	22	5
Vanilla Cone (small)	230	6	38	7
(medium)	330	8	53	9
(large)	410	10	65	12
Chocolate Cone (small)	240	6	37	8
(medium)	340	8	53	11
Dipped Cone (small)	340	6	42	17
(medium)	490	8	59	24
Chocolate Malt (small)	650	15	111	16
(medium)	880	19	153	22
Chocolate Shake (small)	560	13	94	15
(medium)	770	17	130	20
Frozen Hot Chocolate	860	14	127	35
Misty® Slush (small)	220	0	56	0
(medium)	290	0	74	0
Chocolate Sundae (small)	280	5	49	7
(medium)	400	8	71	10
Banana Split	510	8	96	12
Peanut Buster® Parfait	730	16	99	31
Pecan Mudslide™ Treat	650	11	85	30
Strawberry Shortcake	430	7	70	14
Brownie Earthquake™	740	10	112	27
DQ® Sandwich	200	4	31	6
Chocolate Dilly® Bar	210	3	21	13
Buster Bar®	450	10	41	28
Starkiss®	80	0	21	0
DQ® Fudge Bar–no sugar added	50	4	13	0
DQ® Vanilla Orange Bar–no sugar added	60	2	17	0
Lemon DQ Freez'r®, ½ cup	80	0	20	0
Chocolate Sandwich Cookie Blizzard® (small)	520	10	79	18
(medium)	640	12	97	23
Chocolate Chip Cookie Dough Blizzard® (small)	660	12	99	24
(medium)	950	17	143	36

Description	Calories	Pro (g)	Carb (g)	Fat (g)
Heath® DQ Treatzza Pizza®, 1/8th	180	3	28	7
M&M's® DQ Treatzza Pizza®, 1/8th	190	3	29	7
DQ® Frozen 8" Round Cake, 1/8th	370	7	56	13
DQ® Layered 8" Round Cake, 1/8th	330	6	49	12

Hardee's

Breakfast

Biscuits

Description	Calories	Pro (g)	Carb (g)	Fat (g)
Made From Scratch®	390	6	44	21
Jelly	440	6	57	21
Apple Cinnamon 'N' Raisin™	250	2	42	8
Sausage	550	12	44	36
Sausage & Egg	620	19	45	41
Bacon, Egg, & Cheese	520	17	45	30
Country Ham	440	14	44	22
Ham	410	13	45	20
Biscuit 'N' Gravy™	530	10	56	30
Omelet	550	20	45	32
Chicken	590	24	62	27
Steak	580	15	56	32
Frisco™ Breakfast Sandwich (Ham)	450	22	42	22
Regular Hash Rounds™ (16)	230	3	24	14
Orange Juice (10 fl oz)	140	2	34	<1

Burgers/Sandwiches

Description	Calories	Pro (g)	Carb (g)	Fat (g)
Famous Star™	570	24	41	35
Six Dollar Burger®	949	38	58	62
Super Star®	790	40	47	53
All Star	660	29	41	43
Frisco® Burger	720	37	37	49
Monster Burger®	1,060	49	37	79
Hamburger	270	13	29	11
Chicken Fillet Sandwich	480	24	44	23
Grilled Chicken Sandwich	350	23	28	16
Bacon Swiss Crispy Chicken	670	24	45	44
Regular Roast Beef	310	17	26	16
Big Roast Beef™ Sandwich	410	24	26	24
Monster Roast Beef	610	35	26	39
Hot Ham 'N Cheese™ Sandwich	300	16	34	12
Fisherman's Fillet™ Sandwich	530	25	45	28
Hot Dog (with condiments)	450	15	25	32

Chicken/Sides

Description	Calories	Pro (g)	Carb (g)	Fat (g)
Chicken Breast	370	29	29	15
Wing	200	10	23	8
Thigh	330	19	30	15
Leg	170	13	15	7
Cole Slaw (small)	240	2	13	20
Gravy	20	<1	3	<1
Mashed potatoes (small)	70	2	14	<1
Fries, regular	340	4	45	16
large	440	5	59	21
monster	510	6	67	24
Crispy Curls, medium	340	5	41	18
large	520	7	62	28
monster	590	8	70	31

Desserts

Description	Calories	Pro (g)	Carb (g)	Fat (g)
Peach Cobbler	310	2	60	7
Shake (vanilla)	350	12	65	5
Shake (chocolate)	370	13	67	5
Twist Cone	180	4	34	2
Apple Turnover	270	4	38	12

Description	Calories	Pro (g)	Carb (g)	Fat (g)
Jack in the Box				
Breakfast				
Bacon	20	2	0	2
Breakfast Jack®	310	14	34	14
Extreme Sausage Sandwich	720	26	35	53
French Toast Sticks (4-Piece)	430	8	57	18
Hash Brown	150	1	13	10
Sausage Biscuit	380	11	25	27
Sausage Croissant	680	18	41	50
Sausage, Egg & Cheese Biscuit	760	25	33	60
Sourdough Breakfast Sandwich	450	18	36	26
Supreme Croissant	570	19	41	37
Ultimate Breakfast Sandwich	730	30	66	40
Burgers				
Chili Cheeseburger	430	24	32	23
Double Cheeseburger	410	20	32	22
Hamburger	250	12	30	9
Hamburger with Cheese	300	14	31	13
Junior Bacon Cheeseburger	540	22	33	36
Philly Cheesesteak	530	30	53	20
Bacon Bacon Cheeseburger	910	38	58	59
Bacon Ultimate Cheeseburger	1,120	52	59	75
Big Cheeseburger	700	26	59	40
Big Texas Cheeseburger	610	26	55	32
Jack's Western Cheeseburger	660	24	59	37
Jumbo Jack®	600	22	58	31
Jumbo Jack® with Cheese	690	26	60	38
Sourdough Jack®	700	30	36	49
Ultimate Cheeseburger	990	41	59	66
Chicken/Fish				
Chicken Breast Pieces (5)	360	27	24	17
Chicken Fajita Pita	330	24	35	11
Chicken Sandwich	410	15	39	21
Chicken Supreme	710	30	62	39
Chicken Teriyaki Bowl	550	26	103	3
Fish & Chips	610	18	66	31
Grilled Chicken Fillet	430	23	34	22
Jack's Spicy Chicken®	650	26	67	31
Sourdough Grilled Chicken Club	520	33	33	28
Tacos/Sides				
Bacon Cheddar Potato Wedges	770	21	52	53
Cheese Sticks (3)	240	11	21	12
Cheese Sticks (5)	400	18	35	21
Chili Cheese Curly Fries	630	13	54	40
Egg Rolls (1)	130	5	15	6
Egg Rolls (3)	400	14	44	19
Fries, regular	330	3	44	16
jumbo	410	4	55	20
super scoop	580	6	77	28
Monster Taco	280	10	22	17
Onion Rings	500	6	51	30
Seasoned Curly Fries	400	6	45	23
Side Salad	50	3	5	3
Stuffed Jalapeños (3)	230	7	22	13
Stuffed Jalapeños (7)	530	15	51	30
Taco	180	7	16	10
Taquitos (3 pce)	320	14	28	17
Taquitos (5 pce)	480	19	47	24
Sauces/Dressings				
Barbecue Dipping Sauce	45	1	11	0
Blue Cheese Dressing	260	1	5	26
Buttermilk House Dipping Sauce	130	0	3	13
Buttermilk House Dressing	310	1	3	33
Frank's Red Hot Buffalo® Dipping Sauce	10	0	2	0
Low Calorie Italian Dressing	15	0	4	0
Marinara Sauce	15	0	3	0
Soy Sauce	5	0	1	0
Sweet & Sour Dipping Sauce	45	0	11	0
Taco Sauce	0	0	0	0
Tartar Sauce	210	0	2	22
Thousand Island Dressing	160	1	12	12

Description	Calories	Pro (g)	Carb (g)	Fat (g)
Shakes/Desserts				
Apple Turnover	320	3	41	16
Cappuccino Shake (16 oz.)	640	10	85	28
Cheesecake	310	7	34	16
Chocolate Shake (16 oz.)	660	11	89	29
Double Fudge Cake	310	3	49	11
Oreo Cookie Shake (16 oz.)	670	11	81	33
Strawberry Shake (16 oz.)	640	10	84	28
Vanilla Shake (16 oz.)	570	12	65	29
KFC				
Chicken				
Original Recipe® Chicken, wing	145	11	5	9
breast	370	40	11	19
drumstick	140	14	4	8
thigh	360	22	12	25
Extra Crispy™ Chicken, wing	190	10	10	12
breast	470	34	19	28
drumstick	160	12	5	10
thigh	370	21	12	26
Hot & Spicy Chicken, wing	180	11	9	11
breast	450	33	20	27
drumstick	140	13	4	9
thigh	390	22	14	28
Colonels Crispy Strips® (3)	340	28	20	16
Spicy Crispy Strips (3)	335	25	23	15
Honey BBQ Strips (3)	377	27	33	15
Blazin Strips (3)	315	26	21	16
Popcorn Chicken, small	362	17	21	23
large	620	30	36	40
Chunky Chicken Pot Pie	770	29	69	42
Hot Wings™ Pieces (6)	471	27	18	33
Honey BBQ Pieces (6)	607	33	33	38
Sandwiches				
Original Recipe® Sandwich w/sauce	450	29	33	22
Original Recipe® Sandwich w/o sauce	360	29	21	13
Triple Crunch® Sandwich w/sauce	490	28	39	29
Triple Crunch® Sandwich w/o sauce	390	25	29	15
Triple Crunch® Zinger Sandwich w/sauce	550	28	39	32
Triple Crunch® Zinger Sandwich w/o sauce	390	25	36	15
Tender Roast® Sandwich w/sauce	350	32	26	15
Tender Roast® Sandwich w/o sauce	270	31	23	5
Honey BBQ Flavored Sandwich	310	28	37	6
Twister®	600	22	52	34
Blazin Twister	719	30	56	43
Crispy Caesar Twister	744	27	66	41
Honey BBQ Crunch Melt	556	33	48	26
Vegetables/Sides				
Mashed Potatoes w/Gravy	120	1	17	6
Potato Wedges	376	6	53	15
Macaroni & Cheese	180	7	21	8
Corn on the Cob	150	5	35	2
BBQ Baked Beans	190	6	33	3
Cole Slaw	232	2	26	14
Potato Salad	230	4	23	14
Green Beans	45	1	7	2
Mean Greens®	70	4	11	3
Biscuit (1)	180	4	20	10
Desserts				
Double Chocolate Chip Cake	320	4	41	16
Little Bucket Parfait				
Fudge Brownie	280	3	44	10
Lemon Crème	410	7	62	14
Chocolate Cream	290	3	37	15
Strawberry Shortcake	200	1	33	7

Description	Calories	Pro (g)	Carb (g)	Fat (g)
Colonel's Pies (slice), Pecan	490	5	66	23
Apple	310	2	44	14
Strawberry Crème	280	4	32	15

Long John Silver's

Fish/Seafood/Chicken

Description	Calories	Pro (g)	Carb (g)	Fat (g)
Battered Chicken (1 piece)	130	6	9	8
Battered Fish (1 piece)	230	11	16	13
Battered Shrimp (1 piece)	45	2	3	3
Breaded Clams	240	8	22	13
Fish Sandwich	440	17	48	20
Ultimate Fish Sandwich	480	20	51	22

Sides

Description	Calories	Pro (g)	Carb (g)	Fat (g)
Cheesesticks (3 sticks)	140	4	12	8
Clam Chowder (1 bowl)	220	9	23	10
Cole Slaw	200	1	15	15
Corn Cobbette	90	3	14	3
Crumblies	170	1	14	12
Hushpuppies (1 pup)	60	1	9	3
Fries, regular	230	3	34	10
large	390	4	56	17
Rice	180	3	34	4

Desserts

Description	Calories	Pro (g)	Carb (g)	Fat (g)
Chocolate Cream Pie	310	5	24	22
Pecan Pie	370	4	55	15
Pineapple Cream Pie	290	4	39	13

McDonald's

Sandwiches/Chicken/Fries

Description	Calories	Pro (g)	Carb (g)	Fat (g)
Big Mac®	590	24	47	34
Big N' Tasty®	530	24	37	32
Big N' Tasty® with Cheese	580	26	37	37
Cheeseburger	330	15	35	14
Chicken McGrill®	400	25	37	17
Crispy Chicken	500	22	46	26
Double Cheeseburger	480	25	37	27
Double Quarter Pounder® w/cheese	760	46	38	48
Filet-O-Fish®	470	15	45	26
Grilled Chicken Flatbread	520	28	54	22
Hamburger	280	12	35	10
Hot 'n Spicy McChicken®	450	15	39	26
McChicken®	430	14	41	23
Quarter Pounder® w/cheese	530	28	38	30
Quarter Pounder®	420	23	36	21
Chicken McNuggets® (10 piece)	510	25	30	33
Chicken McNuggets® (20 piece)	1,030	49	61	65
Chicken McNuggets® (4 piece)	210	10	12	13
Chicken McNuggets® (6 piece)	310	15	18	20
Fries, small	210	3	26	10
McValue®	320	5	40	16
medium	450	6	57	22
large	540	8	68	26
Super Size®	610	9	77	29

Sauces (1 pkg)

Description	Calories	Pro (g)	Carb (g)	Fat (g)
Barbeque Sauce	45	0	10	0
Honey	45	0	12	0
Honey Mustard Sauce	50	0	3	5
Hot Mustard Sauce	60	<1	7	4
Light Mayonnaise	45	0	<1	5
Sweet 'N Sour Sauce	50	0	11	0

Salads/Dressings

Description	Calories	Pro (g)	Carb (g)	Fat (g)
Bacon Ranch Salad (w/o chicken)	140	9	7	10
Butter Garlic Croutons	50	1	8	2
Caesar Salad (w/o chicken)	90	7	7	4
California Cobb Salad (w/o chicken)	160	11	7	11
Crispy Chicken Bacon Ranch Salad	370	26	20	21
Crispy Chicken Caesar Salad	310	23	20	16
Crispy Chicken California Cobb Salad	380	27	20	23
Grilled Chicken Bacon Ranch Salad	270	28	11	13
Grilled Chicken Caesar Salad	210	26	11	7
Grilled Chicken California Cobb Salad	280	30	11	14
Side Salad	15	1	3	0
Newman's Own® Cobb Dressing	120	1	9	9
Newman's Own® Creamy Caesar Dressing	190	2	4	18
Newman's Own® Light Balsamic Vinaigrette	90	0	4	8
Newman's Own® Ranch Dressing	290	1	4	30

Breakfast

Description	Calories	Pro (g)	Carb (g)	Fat (g)
Bacon, Egg & Cheese Biscuit	480	21	31	31
Bagel (plain)	260	9	54	1
Big Breakfast	710	24	45	48
Biscuit	240	4	30	11
Egg McMuffin®	300	18	29	12
English Muffin	150	5	27	2
Ham, Egg & Cheese Bagel	550	26	58	23
Hash Browns	130	1	14	8
Hotcakes (2 pats margarine & syrup)	600	9	104	17
Sausage	170	6	0	16
Sausage Biscuit	410	10	30	28
Sausage Biscuit with Egg	490	16	31	33
Sausage Breakfast Burrito	290	13	24	16
Sausage McMuffin®	370	14	28	23
Sausage McMuffin® with Egg	450	20	29	28
Scrambled Eggs (2)	160	13	1	11
Spanish Omelette Bagel	710	27	59	40
Steak, Egg & Cheese Bagel	700	38	57	35
Apple Danish	340	5	47	15
Cheese Danish	400	7	45	21
Cinnamon Roll	340	5	52	15

Desserts/Shakes

Description	Calories	Pro (g)	Carb (g)	Fat (g)
Baked Apple Pie	260	3	34	13
Butterfinger® McFlurry™ (12 oz)	620	16	90	22
Butterfinger® McFlurry™ (16 oz)	900	23	131	31
Chocolate Chip Cookie	170	2	23	9
Chocolate Triple Thick™ Shake (12 oz)	430	11	70	12
Shake (16 oz)	580	15	94	17
Shake (21 oz)	750	19	123	22
Shake (32 oz)	1,150	30	187	33
Fruit 'n Yogurt Parfait	380	10	76	5
Fruit 'n Yogurt Parfait (w/o granola)	280	8	53	4
Hot Caramel Sundae	360	7	61	10
Hot Fudge Sundae	340	8	52	12
M&M® McFlurry™ (12 oz)	630	16	90	23
M&M® McFlurry™ (16 oz)	910	23	131	33
McDonaldland® Chocolate Chip Cookies (2 oz)	280	3	37	14
McDonaldland® Cookies (2 oz.)	230	3	38	8
Nestle Crunch® McFlurry™ (12 oz)	630	16	89	24
Nestle Crunch® McFlurry™ (16 oz)	920	23	129	35
Nuts (for Sundaes)	40	2	2	4
Oreo® McFlurry™ (12 oz)	570	15	82	20
Oreo® McFlurry™ (16 oz)	820	22	119	29
Snack Size Fruit 'n Yogurt Parfait	160	4	30	2
Snack Size Fruit 'n Yogurt Parfait (w/o Granola)	130	4	25	2
Strawberry Sundae	290	7	50	7
Strawberry Triple Thick™ Shake (12 oz)	420	11	67	12
Shake (16 oz)	560	14	89	16
Shake (21 oz)	730	19	116	21
Shake (32 oz)	1,120	28	178	32
Vanilla Reduced Fat Ice Cream Cone	150	4	23	5
Vanilla Triple Thick™ Shake (12 oz)	430	11	67	12
Shake (16 oz)	570	14	89	16

Description	Calories	Pro (g)	Carb (g)	Fat (g)
Shake (21 oz)	750	18	116	21
Shake (32 oz)	1,140	28	178	32

Pizza Hut

Pizza (1 slice)

Description	Calories	Pro (g)	Carb (g)	Fat (g)
Cheese				
Hand Tossed	240	12	28	10
Thin 'N Crispy	200	10	22	9
Stuffed Crust	360	18	39	16
Stuffed Crust Gold	440	21	44	20
The Big New Yorker	410	20	46	18
Pan	290	12	28	14
Personal Pan (1 pizza)	630	28	71	28
Beef Topping				
Hand Tossed	330	16	29	17
Thin 'N Crispy	270	13	22	15
Stuffed Crust	390	19	40	18
Stuffed Crust Gold	490	24	44	24
The Big New Yorker	500	25	47	26
Pan	330	14	29	18
Personal Pan (1 pizza)	710	31	71	35
Pepperoni				
Hand Tossed	280	13	28	13
Thin 'N Crispy	190	9	21	9
Stuffed Crust	360	17	39	16
Stuffed Crust Gold	430	20	43	20
The Big New Yorker	390	18	46	17
The Chicago Dish	390	18	34	20
Pan	280	11	28	14
Personal Pan (1 pizza)	620	26	70	28
Sausage				
Hand Tossed	340	16	28	18
Thin 'N Crispy	290	12	22	17
Stuffed Crust	400	19	40	20
Stuffed Crust Gold	520	24	44	27
The Big New Yorker	530	24	47	29
Pan	340	13	29	20
Personal Pan (1 pizza)	740	31	71	39
Meat Lover's®				
Hand Tossed	320	14	28	17
Thin 'N Crispy	310	14	22	19
Stuffed Crust	470	22	40	25
Stuffed Crust Gold	550	27	44	29
The Chicago Dish	470	21	35	27
Pan	360	14	29	21
Veggie Lover's				
Hand Tossed	220	9	29	8
Thin 'N Crispy	190	8	24	7
Stuffed Crust	340	16	42	14
Stuffed Crust Gold	420	19	46	18
The Big New Yorker	480	19	57	22
The Chicago Dish	370	17	36	18
Pan	270	10	30	12
Supreme				
Hand Tossed	270	13	29	12
Thin 'N Crispy	250	12	23	13
Stuffed Crust	410	20	41	20
Stuffed Crust Gold	490	24	45	24
The Big New Yorker	470	23	48	23
The Chicago Dish	420	20	36	23
Pan	320	13	29	17

Pasta/Sandwiches

Description	Calories	Pro (g)	Carb (g)	Fat (g)
Spaghetti w/Marinara Sauce	490	18	91	6
w/Meat Sauce	600	23	98	13
w/Meatballs	850	37	120	24
Cavatini® Pasta	480	21	66	14
Cavatini Supreme® Pasta	560	24	73	19
Ham and Cheese Sandwich	550	33	57	21
Supreme Sandwich	640	34	62	28

Sides

Description	Calories	Pro (g)	Carb (g)	Fat (g)
Mild Buffalo Wings (5 pieces)	200	23	<1	12
Hot Buffalo Wings (4 pieces)	210	22	4	12
Garlic Bread (1 slice)	150	3	16	8
Breadstick (1 serving)	130	3	20	4

Description	Calories	Pro (g)	Carb (g)	Fat (g)
Breadstick Dipping Sauce	30	<1	5	<1

Sauces/Dressings

Description	Calories	Pro (g)	Carb (g)	Fat (g)
Blue Cheese Dressing	150	1	1	15
Buffalo Wing Blue Cheese Dip'n Dressing	220	2	2	24
Buffalo Wing Ranch Dip'n Dressing	220	1	2	24
Buttermilk Dressing	130	0	1	13
Creamy Caesar Dressing	150	0	1	15
Creamy Cucumber Dressing (Reduced Calorie)	70	0	3	7
French Dressing	160	0	10	13
Garlic Parmesan Mayonnaise Dressing	190	1	1	21
Italian Dressing	140	0	2	14

Desserts

Description	Calories	Pro (g)	Carb (g)	Fat (g)
Cinnamon Sticks (2 pieces)	170	4	27	5
Apple Dessert Pizza (1 slice)	250	3	48	5
Cherry Dessert Pizza (1 slice)	250	3	47	5
White Icing Dipping Cup (2 oz.)	190	0	46	0

Subway

Sandwiches (6")

Description	Calories	Pro (g)	Carb (g)	Fat (g)
BMT®	480	23	46	24
Cold Cut Trio	440	21	47	21
Meatball	530	24	53	26
Seafood & Crab®	410	16	52	16
Steak & Cheese	390	24	48	14
SUBWAY Melt	410	25	47	15
Tuna	450	20	46	22
Sweet Onion Chicken Teriyaki	380	26	59	5
Red Wine Vinaigrette Club	350	24	53	6
Honey Mustard Ham	310	18	52	5
Dijon Horseradish Melt	470	26	47	21
Southwest Turkey Bacon	410	22	48	16
Ham	290	18	46	5
Roast Beef	290	19	45	5
Roasted Chicken Breast	320	23	47	5
SUBWAY Club®	320	24	46	6
Turkey Breast	280	18	46	5
Turkey Breast & Ham	290	20	46	5
Veggie Delite®	230	9	44	3

Deli Sandwiches

Description	Calories	Pro (g)	Carb (g)	Fat (g)
Ham	210	11	35	4
Roast Beef	220	13	35	5
Tuna	330	13	36	16
Turkey Breast	220	13	36	4

Condiments/Extras

Description	Calories	Pro (g)	Carb (g)	Fat (g)
Vinegar (1 tsp)	0	0	0	0
Mustard (2 tsp)	5	0	1	0
Light Mayonnaise (1 T)	45	0	1	5
Mayonnaise (1 T)	110	0	0	12
Bacon (2 strips)	45	3	0	4
Olive Oil Blend (1 tsp)	45	0	0	5
American Cheese (2 triangles)	40	2	0	4
Provolone Cheese (2 half circles)	50	4	0	4
Swiss Cheese (2 triangles)	50	4	0	4
Pepperjack Cheese (2 triangles)	40	2	0	4
Cheddar Cheese (2 triangles)	60	4	0	5
Fat Free Honey Mustard Sauce	30	0	7	0
Southwest Sauce	90	0	2	9
Fat Free Red Wine Vinaigrette	30	0	6	0
Fat Free Sweet Onion Sauce	40	0	9	0
Dijon Horseradish Sauce	90	0	1	10

Breakfast Sandwich

Description	Calories	Pro (g)	Carb (g)	Fat (g)
Cheese & Egg	320	14	34	15
Bacon & Egg	320	15	34	15
Ham & Egg	310	16	34	13
Western Egg	300	14	36	12
Steak & Egg	330	19	35	14

Salads

Description	Calories	Pro (g)	Carb (g)	Fat (g)
BMT®	280	16	11	19
Cold Cut Trio	230	14	11	15

Description	Calories	Pro (g)	Carb (g)	Fat (g)
Meatball	320	17	17	20
Seafood & Crab®	200	9	17	11
Steak & Cheese	180	17	12	8
SUBWAY Melt	200	18	11	10
Tuna	240	13	10	16
Ham	110	11	11	3
Roast Beef	120	12	10	3
SUBWAY Club®	150	17	12	4
Turkey Breast & Ham	120	13	11	3
Veggie Delite®	50	2	9	1
Roasted Chicken Breast	140	16	12	3

Salad Dressings
Description	Calories	Pro (g)	Carb (g)	Fat (g)
Fat Free French	70	0	17	0
Fat Free Italian	20	0	4	0
Fat Free Ranch	60	0	14	0

Soup (1 Cup)
Description	Calories	Pro (g)	Carb (g)	Fat (g)
Roasted Chicken Noodle	90	7	7	4
Vegetable Beef	90	5	14	2
Golden Broccoli Cheese	180	6	12	12
Cream of Potato with Bacon	210	5	20	12
Cheese with Ham and Bacon	230	8	13	16
Minestrone	70	3	11	1
New England Style Clam Chowder	140	5	19	5
Chicken and Dumpling	130	7	16	5
Potato Cheese Chowder	210	7	22	10
Tomato Bisque	90	1	15	3
Brown and Wild Rice with Chicken	190	6	17	11
Black Bean	180	9	27	5
Chili Con Carne	310	17	28	14
Cream of Broccoli	130	5	15	6

Fruizle Express (small)
Description	Calories	Pro (g)	Carb (g)	Fat (g)
Berry Lishus	110	1	28	0
Sunrise Refresher	120	1	29	0
Pineapple Delight	130	1	33	0
Peach Pizazz	100	0	26	0
Berry Lishus (with Banana)	140	1	35	0
Pineapple Delight (with Banana)	160	1	40	0

Cookies
Description	Calories	Pro (g)	Carb (g)	Fat (g)
Chocolate Chip	220	2	30	10
Oatmeal Raisin	200	3	30	8
Peanut Butter	220	4	26	12
M & M	220	2	30	10
White Macadamia Nut	220	2	28	11
Sugar	230	2	28	12
Chocolate Chunk	220	2	30	10
Double Chocolate	210	2	30	10

Taco Bell

Tacos
Description	Calories	Pro (g)	Carb (g)	Fat (g)
Taco	170	9	13	10
Taco Supreme®	220	9	15	14
Soft Taco, Beef	220	10	21	10
Soft Taco, Chicken	190	13	20	7
Soft Taco Supreme®, Beef	260	11	23	14
Soft Taco Supreme®, Chicken	240	14	21	11
Grilled Steak Soft Taco	290	13	20	17
DOUBLE DECKER®, Taco	340	14	39	14
DOUBLE DECKER®, Taco Supreme®	380	15	41	18

Gorditas
Description	Calories	Pro (g)	Carb (g)	Fat (g)
Gordita Supreme®, Beef	320	13	29	17
Gordita Supreme®, Chicken	300	16	28	13
Gordita Supreme®, Steak	300	15	28	14
Gordita Baja®, Beef	360	13	30	21
Gordita Baja®, Chicken	340	16	28	18
Gordita Baja®, Steak	340	15	28	18
Gordita Nacho Cheese, Beef	310	12	30	16
Gordita Nacho Cheese, Chicken	290	15	29	13
Gordita Nacho Cheese, Steak	290	14	28	13

Chalupas
Description	Calories	Pro (g)	Carb (g)	Fat (g)
Chalupa Supreme, Beef	370	13	26	25
Chalupa Supreme, Chicken	350	16	24	21
Chalupa Supreme, Steak	350	14	24	22
Chalupa Baja, Beef	410	13	26	29
Chalupa Baja, Chicken	390	16	25	26
Chalupa Baja, Steak	390	14	24	26
Chalupa Nacho Cheese, Beef	360	12	27	24
Chalupa Nacho Cheese, Chicken	340	15	25	20
Chalupa Nacho Cheese, Steak	340	13	25	21

Burritos
Description	Calories	Pro (g)	Carb (g)	Fat (g)
Bean Burrito	370	13	56	11
7-Layer Burrito	520	16	66	22
Chili Cheese Burrito	390	16	41	18
Burrito Supreme®, Beef	440	17	52	18
Burrito Supreme®, Chicken	420	20	50	15
Burrito Supreme®, Steak	410	19	50	15
Fiesta Burrito, Beef	400	14	47	17
Fiesta Burrito, Chicken	370	17	46	14
Fiesta Burrito, Steak	370	15	46	14
Grilled Stuft Burrito, Beef	730	28	78	35
Grilled Stuft Burrito, Chicken	690	34	76	28
Grilled Stuft Burrito, Steak	680	31	75	29

Specialties
Description	Calories	Pro (g)	Carb (g)	Fat (g)
Tostada	250	10	29	10
Mexican Pizza	550	20	43	35
Enchirito®, Beef	370	18	34	18
Enchirito®, Chicken	350	21	33	15
Enchirito®, Steak	350	20	33	15
MexiMelt®	290	15	23	16
Taco Salad with Salsa	830	29	66	51
Taco Salad with Salsa w/o Shell	410	24	33	21
Express Taco Salad with Chips	610	26	61	30
Cheese Quesadilla	490	19	38	29
Chicken Quesadilla	550	27	39	31
Steak Quesadilla	550	26	39	31
Extreme Cheese Quesadilla	470	20	40	26
Zesty Chicken BORDER BOWL™	720	22	58	45
Zesty Chicken BORDER BOWL™ w/o Dressing	460	20	55	19
Southwest Steak Bowl	660	28	66	33

Nachos/Sides
Description	Calories	Pro (g)	Carb (g)	Fat (g)
Nachos	350	5	30	23
Nachos Supreme	470	13	40	28
Nachos BellGrande®	810	20	76	48
Pintos 'n Cheese	180	9	20	7
Mexican Rice	190	5	21	10
Cinnamon Twists	150	1	27	5

Breakfast
Description	Calories	Pro (g)	Carb (g)	Fat (g)
Breakfast Gordita	400	12	28	25
Breakfast Burrito	530	17	48	26
Breakfast Steak Burrito	530	22	40	27
Breakfast Quesadilla	420	15	38	21
Breakfast Steak Quesadilla w/Green Sauce	470	22	39	23

Sauces/Condiments
Description	Calories	Pro (g)	Carb (g)	Fat (g)
Border Sauce	0	0	0	0
Picante Sauce	0	0	<1	0
Red Sauce	10	0	2	0
Green Sauce	10	0	2	0
Nacho Cheese Sauce	110	2	4	10
Pepper Jack Cheese Sauce	80	<1	1	8
Fiesta Salsa	5	0	1	0
Sour Cream	40	<1	1	4
Guacamole	35	0	1	3
Cheddar Cheese	25	2	0	2
Three Cheese Blend	25	2	0	2

Wendy's

Sandwiches
Description	Calories	Pro (g)	Carb (g)	Fat (g)
Classic Single® w/everything	410	24	37	19
Big Bacon Classic®	570	34	46	29
Jr. Hamburger	270	14	34	9
Jr. Cheeseburger	310	17	34	12
Jr. Bacon Cheeseburger	380	20	34	18
Jr. Cheeseburger Deluxe	350	17	37	16
Hamburger, Kids' Meal	270	14	33	9

Description	Calories	Pro (g)	Carb (g)	Fat (g)
Cheeseburger, Kids' Meal	310	17	34	12
Grilled Chicken Sandwich	300	24	36	7
Chicken Breast Fillet Sandwich	430	27	46	16
Chicken Club Sandwich	470	30	47	19
Spicy Chicken Sandwich	430	27	47	15
Fries				
Kids' Meal	250	3	36	11
Medium	390	4	56	17
Biggie®	440	5	63	19
Great Biggie®	530	6	75	23
Hot Stuffed Baked Potatoes				
Plain	310	7	72	0
Bacon & Cheese	580	18	79	22
Broccoli & Cheese	480	9	81	14
Sour Cream & Chives	370	7	73	6
Whipped Margarine (1 pkt)	60	0	0	7
Chili				
Small	200	17	21	6
Large	300	25	31	9
Cheddar Cheese, shredded (2T)	70	4	1	6
Crispy Chicken Nuggets™				
5 Piece	220	11	13	14
4 Piece Kids' Meal	180	9	10	11
Barbecue Sauce	40	1	10	0
Honey Mustard Sauce	130	0	6	12
Sweet & Sour Sauce	45	0	12	0
Garden Sensations™ Salads/Dressings				
Caesar Side Salad	70	7	2	4
Homestyle Garlic Croutons	70	0	1	3
Caesar Dressing	150	1	1	16
Side Salad	35	2	7	0
Chicken BLT Salad	310	33	10	16
Honey Mustard Dressing	310	1	12	29
Mandarin Chicken Salad	150	20	17	2
Roasted Almonds	130	4	4	12
Crispy Rice Noodles	60	1	10	2
Oriental Sesame Dressing	280	2	21	21
Spring Mix Salad	180	11	12	11
Honey Roasted Pecans	130	2	5	13
House Vinaigrette Dressing	220	0	9	20
Taco Supremo Salad	360	27	29	17
Taco Chips	220	3	25	11
Sour Cream	60	1	1	6
Salsa	30	1	6	0
Blue Cheese	290	2	3	30
Creamy Ranch	250	1	5	25
Fat Free French Style	90	0	21	0
Low Fat Honey Mustard	120	0	23	4
Reduced Fat Creamy Ranch	110	1	7	9
Frosty™				
Junior (6 oz.)	170	4	28	4
Small (12 oz.)	330	8	56	8
Medium (16 oz.)	440	11	73	11

The Calorie Guide

This calorie guide is designed to help you better understand the caloric nutrient values of many common foods and beverages. In addition, it lists serving sizes from the five food groups of the Food Guide Pyramid. The guide is not all-inclusive; other, more complete calorie guides are available in most bookstores. The foods listed here should help you as you go through The LEARN Program. Helpful measures and conversions are listed on page 256 for your convenience. Remember to use the information from food labels if you have them because they will be the most accurate.

The Calorie Guide is divided into six columns as follows:

Description—This column describes the food or beverage item and the serving size for the caloric nutrients listed.

Cal—This column lists the total calories of the food or beverage item listed.

Pro—This column lists the protein content of the food or beverage item listed in grams. To convert this number to calories, simply multiply the number of grams by 4.

Carb—This column lists the carbohydrate content of the food or beverage item listed in grams. To convert this number to calories, simply multiply the number of grams by 4.

Fat—This column lists the TOTAL amount of fat for the food or beverage item listed in grams. To convert this number to calories, simply multiply the number of grams by 9.

FGP—This column indicates the number of servings of the food or beverage item listed from the five food groups of the Food Guide Pyramid. Servings of .9 and .1 are rounded to the nearest whole number. The five food groups are abbreviated as follows:

b = Bread, Cereal, Rice, and Pasta Group

v = Vegetable Group

f = Fruit Group

p = Meat, Poultry, Fish, Dry Beans, Eggs, & Nuts Group

m = Milk Group

As an example, one medium apple is one serving from the fruit group, so the FGP column will indicate 1f. For combination foods, the two food groups with the highest number of servings are listed. For example, nachos with beef, beans, and cheese contain 1 serving from the bread group (1b), .4 servings from the vegetable group (.4v), .3 servings from the protein group (.3p), and .3 servings from the milk group (.3m); however, the listing will read 1b, .4v because these two groups have the highest number of servings. The Food Guide Pyramid servings were determined using the Food Processor software.

Abbreviations

Below are some common abbreviations used throughout the Calorie Guide.

choc = chocolate
ckd = cooked
cnd = canned
hmd = homemade
med = medium
swt = sweetened
unckd = uncooked
unswt = unsweetened

Description	Cal	Pro (g)	Carb (g)	Fat (g)	FGP
A					
Alcohol (*see beverages*)					
Almonds					
dry roasted (4 oz)	677	24	22	60	1p
oil roasted (4 oz)	704	25	14	66	1p
Apples					
raw, w/skin (1 med)	81	0	21	0	1f
raw, w/o skin (1 med)	73	0	19	0	1.2f
baked, unsweetened (1 med)	102	0	26	1	1.2f
Apple juice, cnd (6 oz)	80	0	20	0	1f
Apple sauce					
cnd, unswt (½ cup)	52	0	14	0	1f
cnd, swt (½ cup)	97	0	25	0	1f
Apricots					
raw (2 med)	34	1	8	0	1f
cnd in water (⅓ cup)	15	0	4	0	1f
cnd in heavy syrup (3 halves)	100	1	26	0	1f
dried, unckd (⅖ cup)	172	2	40	0	1f
Apricot nectar, cnd (6 oz)	95	1	25	0	1f
Artichoke, ckd (¾ med)	45	3	10	0	1v
Artichoke hearts, boiled (½ cup)	42	3	9	0	1v
Asparagus					
boiled (½ cup)	22	2	4	0	1v
cnd (½ cup)	23	3	3	1	1v
frozen, boiled (6 spears)	25	3	4	0	1v
Avocado (⅓ med)	83	2	5	8	1v
B					
Bacon					
ckd (10 med pieces)	365	19	0	31	1p
Canadian, grilled (3 slices)	129	17	1	6	1p
turkey (5 pieces)	175	11	1	14	1p
Bagels					
oat bran, 2½" (1½)	99	4	21	1	1b
plain, 3" (½)	78	3	15	0	1b
Baking powder (1 t)	2	0	1	0	
Baklava (⅘ of piece)	269	4	23	18	1b
Bamboo shoots, raw (½ cup)	20	2	4	0	1v
Banana (1 med)	110	1	29	0	1f
Barbecue sauce (1 T)	12	0	2	0	
Bass					
freshwater, baked (2½ oz)	103	17	0	3	1p
sea, baked (2½ oz)	88	17	0	2	1p
Beans					
green, fresh, ckd (½ cup)	22	1	5	0	1v
green, cnd (½ cup)	20	1	4	0	1v
green, frozen, ckd (½ cup)	19	1	4	0	1v
kidney, ckd (1.2 cups)	270	18	48	1	1p
kidney, cnd (⅓ cup)	62	4	11	0	1p
lima, ckd (1.2 cups)	259	18	47	1	1p
lima, cnd (1.2 cups)	228	14	43	0	1p
navy, boiled (½ cup)	50	5	10	1	1p
navy, cnd (1.2 cups)	355	24	64	1	1p
northern, boiled (1.2 cups)	251	18	45	1	1p
northern, cnd (1.2 cups)	358	23	66	1	1p
pinto, cnd (1.2 cups)	248	14	44	2	1p
refried, cnd (1.2 cups)	285	17	47	4	1p
white, ckd (1.2 cups)	299	21	54	1	1p
white, cnd (1.2 cups)	368	23	69	1	1p
yellow snap, ckd (½ cup)	22	1	5	0	1v
yellow snap, cnd (½ cup)	14	1	3	0	1v
Bean sprouts, raw (½ cup)	43	5	3	2	1v
Beef					
bologna (2½ oz)	221	9	1	20	1p
brisket, lean, (2.7 oz)	185	23	0	10	1p
chipped, dried (6 oz)	226	13	12	14	1p
chuck pot roast, lean (2½ oz)	153	23	0	6	1p
chuck blade roast, lean (2½ oz)	178	22	0	9	1p
corned beef brisket (2½ oz)	178	13	0	13	1p
flank steak, lean (2½ oz)	147	19	0	7	1p
ground, 9% fat (2½ oz)	120	15	0	6	1p

Description	Cal	Pro (g)	Carb (g)	Fat (g)	FGP
ground, 10% fat (2½ oz)	154	19	0	8	1p
ground, 16% fat (2½ oz)	181	18	0	12	1p
ground, 21% fat (2½ oz)	205	17	0	15	1p
porterhouse steak, lean (2½ oz)	137	19	0	6	1p
ribeye steak, lean (2½ oz)	159	20	0	8	1p
round steak, lean (2½ oz)	128	22	0	3	1p
sirloin steak, lean (2½ oz)	143	22	0	6	1p
tenderloin, lean (2½ oz)	167	19	0	9	1p
T-bone steak, lean (2½ oz)	134	18	0	6	1p
Beef stew, cnd (8 oz)	213	11	15	12	1v,½p
Beef stir fry w/rice and vegetables (6 oz)	182	11	30	2	1b,½v
Beef stroganoff (⅘ cup)	326	20	12	22	1p
Beer (*see beverages*)					
Beets					
boiled (½ cup slices)	37	1	8	0	1v
cnd (½ cup slices)	26	1	6	0	1v
Beverages (nonalcoholic)					
cider, apple (6 oz)	90	0	23	0	1f
choc milk, 1% fat (1 cup)	158	8	26	3	1m
choc milk, 2% fat (1 cup)	180	8	26	5	1m
choc milk, whole (1 cup)	208	8	26	8	1m
coffee, black (1 cup)	5	0	1	0	
eggnog (10 oz)	383	11	38	21	1m
lemonade, frozen conc (8 oz)	99	0	26	0	
lemonade, from powder (8 oz)	103	0	27	0	
milk, skim (8 oz)	90	9	13	0	1m
milk, 1% fat (8 oz)	110	9	13	3	1m
milk, 2% fat (8 oz)	122	8	12	5	1m
milk, whole (8 oz)	150	8	11	8	1m
milk shake, thick vanilla (8 oz)	254	9	40	7	1m
milk shake, choc (10 oz)	405	9	68	11	1m
soft drinks (12 oz)					
cola	139	0	35	0	
cola, diet	3	0	0	0	
cream soda	174	0	45	0	
fruit punch	160	0	40	0	
ginger ale	116	0	30	0	
grape soda	146	0	38	0	
orange soda	163	0	42	0	
orange soda, diet	0	0	0	0	
root beer	139	0	36	0	
tea, black (1 cup)	0	0	0	0	
Beverages (alcoholic)					
beer and lager (12 oz)					
beer, regular	139	1	13	0	
beer, light	95	1	4	0	
lager	102	1	6	0	
distilled spirits					
brandy, 100 proof (1 oz)	84	0	0	0	
gin, 100 proof (1½ oz)	125	0	0	0	
rum, 100 proof (1½ oz)	125	0	0	0	
vodka, 100 proof (1½ oz)	125	0	0	0	
tequila, 100 proof (1½ oz)	125	0	0	0	
whiskey, 90 proof (1½ oz)	112	0	0	0	
liqueurs and cordials (1 oz)					
anisette	100	0	13	0	
brandy, cherry	72	0	9	0	
creme de menthe	105	0	12	0	
drambuie	100	0	13	0	
triple sec	100	0	13	0	
mixed drinks					
daquiri (3½ oz)	185	0	7	0	
manhattan (3½ oz)	124	0	3	0	
margarita (7 oz)	437	0	28	0	
martini (3½ oz)	113	0	2	1	
pina colada (7 oz)	345	1	45	4	
screwdriver (7 oz)	169	1	17	0	
tequila sunrise (5½ oz)	171	1	13	0	
tom collins (7 oz)	81	0	6	0	
whiskey sour (3½ oz)	148	0	13	0	
wines & wine beverages (3½ oz)					
dessert, dry	125	0	4	0	

Description	Cal	Pro (g)	Carb (g)	Fat (g)	FGP
dessert, sweet	152	0	12	0	
red	71	0	2	0	
rose	70	0	1	0	
white	67	0	1	0	
wine cooler	49	0	6	0	
Biscuits					
buttermilk, commercial (1)	127	2	17	6	1b
buttermilk, hmd, 2½" (½)	106	2	13	5	1b
Blackberries					
raw (½ cup)	37	1	9	0	1f
cnd, heavy syrup (½ cup)	118	2	30	0	1f
frozen, unswt (½ cup)	48	1	12	0	1f
Blackeyed peas (cowpeas)					
ckd (1.2 cups)	239	16	43	1	1p
cnd (1.2 cups)	222	14	39	2	1p
Blueberries					
raw (½ cup)	41	0	10	0	1f
cnd, heavy syrup (½ cup)	113	1	28	0	1f
frozen, unswt (½ cup)	40	0	9	0	1f
Bluefish, baked/broiled (2½ oz)	113	18	0	4	1p
Blintz, fruit filled	124	4	17	4	1b
Bologna (see beef and sausage)					
Bouillon					
beef broth (8 oz)	7	1	1	0	
chicken broth (8 oz)	21	1	1	1	
Brains, simmered beef (2.8 oz)	127	9	0	10	1p
Bran flakes (1 oz)	98	5	22	1	1b
Braunschweiger (see sausage)					
Breads					
bread sticks (3 sticks)	124	4	21	3	1b
cinnamon raisin (1 piece)	80	3	14	2	1b
corn (½ of 2½ x 2½ x 1½" piece)	76	2	11	2	1b
cracked wheat (1 piece)	65	2	12	1	1b
French (4/5 of piece)	70	2	13	1	1b
garlic bread (1 piece)	160	5	14	10	1b
hoagie or submarine roll (¼ roll)	97	3	17	2	1b
Italian (1 piece)	81	3	15	1	1b
matzoh crackers (1)	112	3	24	0	1b
mixed grain (1 piece)	65	3	12	1	1b
oatmeal (1 piece)	73	2	13	1	1b
oatmeal, reduced cal (1.2 pieces)	58	2	12	1	1b
pita pocket (4"), white (1 pocket)	77	3	16	0	1b
pumpernickel (1 piece)	80	3	15	1	1b
raisin (1 piece)	71	2	14	1	1b
rye (1 piece)	83	3	15	1	1b
rye, reduced calorie (1.2 pieces)	56	3	11	1	1b
white (1 piece)	67	2	12	1	1b
white, reduced calorie (1.2 pieces)	57	2	12	1	1b
whole wheat (1 piece)	69	3	13	1	01
Breadcrumbs (⅓ cup)	128	4	23	2	1b
Bread pudding (½ serving)	238	7	33	8	1b
Bread stuffing (⅓ cup)	107	2	13	5	1b
Broccoli					
raw (7/10 cup chopped)	14	1	3	0	1v
ckd (½ cup)	22	2	4	0	1v
Brunswick stew (8 oz)	158	14	19	3	1v,½p
Brussels sprouts, cnd (½ cup)	32	2	7	0	1v
Buns, cinnamon (1 bun)	220	4	31	10	1p
Burritos					
bean and cheese (8 oz)	347	12	49	12	1p,.6p
beef and cheese (4 oz)	259	12	32	9	1b,.2p
chicken (4 oz)	207	11	30	5	1b,.3p
Butter (1 T)					
stick	100	0	0	11	
whipped	68	0	0	8	
whipped, light	35	0	0	4	

C

Description	Cal	Pro (g)	Carb (g)	Fat (g)	FGP
Cabbage, green					
raw (4/5 cup chopped)	18	1	4	0	1v
ckd (½ cup shredded)	17	1	3	0	1v
Cakes					
angel food (2 oz)	146	3	33	0	1b
boston cream pie (4 oz)	286	3	49	10	1b
carrot cake (4 oz)	481	4	53	28	1b
cheesecake (1/6 of cake)	257	4	20	18	1b
choc, w/choc icing (1/8 of cake)	235	3	35	11	.8b
coffee cake (1/9 of cake)	263	4	29	15	1b
cupcake, choc (1)	131	2	29	2	.8b
devils food (1½ pieces)	225	3	41	5	1b
fruit cake (1/8 of cake)	156	3	26	5	1b
German choc, from mix (1/12 of cake)	300	2	37	16	1b
gingerbread, hmd (1/9 of cake)	263	3	36	12	1b
pineapple upside-down (1/9 of cake)	367	4	58	14	1b
pound cake (2½ pieces)	275	4	35	14	1b
spice cake	368	5	62	12	1b
sponge cake (1/8 of cake)	165	3	35	2	1b
white cake, coconut icing (1/12 of cake)	399	5	71	12	1b
yellow cake, vanilla icing (1/8 of cake)	239	2	38	9	.8b
Cake Icing					
choc (½ cup)	560	0	84	24	
white (½ cup)	346	2	30	25	
Calamari, fried (2½ oz)	124	13	6	5	1p
Candy					
almond joy (1.7 oz bar)	231	2	29	13	
baby ruth (1.2 oz bar)	164	3	22	7	
butterfinger (1.6 oz bar)	218	6	30	8	
butterscotch (1 oz)	111	0	26	1	
candy corn (1 oz)	105	0	26	0	
caramels (1 oz)	108	1	22	2	
chocolate					
almonds, coated (1 oz)	149	4	13	11	
bar (1½ oz)	225	3	26	13	
chips, semisweet (1 oz)	136	1	18	9	
cherries, coated (2 pieces)	105	1	17	4	
fudge, hmd (1 oz)	117	1	22	3	
kisses (9 pieces)	218	3	25	13	
milk choc chips (1 oz)	145	2	17	9	
mints, choc covered (1 oz)	135	1	20	6	
peppermint patties, small (3)	196	1	41	4	
semi-sweet (1 oz)	151	1	18	8	
sweet (1 oz)	143	1	17	10	
gumdrops (1 oz)	109	0	28	0	
hard candy (1 oz)	112	0	28	0	
jelly beans (1 oz)	104	0	26	0	
marshmallows (1 large)	22	0	5	0	
mints (1 oz)	111	0	28	0	
peanut brittle (1 oz)	136	2	20	5	
peanut butter chips (1 oz)	141	5	13	8	
peanut butter candy, Reeses (1 oz)	146	3	16	9	
Cannelloni w/Cheese & Spinach (5 oz)	228	10	25	10	1b,1m
Cantaloupe, raw (½ cup)	27	1	7	0	1f
Carrots					
raw (1 med)	26	1	6	0	1v
ckd (½ cup slices)	35	1	8	0	1v
cnd (½ cup slices)	20	0	4	0	1v
Carrot juice, cnd (6 oz)	68	2	16	0	1v
Casaba melon, raw (½ cup)	22	1	5	0	1f
Cashew Nuts					
salted (4 oz)	704	20	27	59	1p
oil roasted (4 oz)	659	19	34	54	1p
Catfish					
channel, raw (2½ oz)	67	12	0	2	1p
breaded & fried (2½ oz)	162	13	6	9	1p
Catsup (see ketchup)					
Cauliflower					
raw (½ cup)	13	1	3	0	1v
ckd (½ cup)	14	1	3	0	1v
Caviar, black & red (5 T)	202	20	3	14	1p

Description	Cal	Pro (g)	Carb (g)	Fat (g)	FGP
Celery					
raw, 1 stalk (7" long)	10	1	3	0	1v
ckd (½ cup diced)	14	1	3	0	1v
Cereal (1 oz)					
all-bran	74	4	21	1	1b
all-bran buds	71	2	23	1	1b
almond delight	110	2	23	2	1b
alpha bits	111	2	25	1	1b
bran, 100%	81	4	22	1	1b
bran chex	90	3	23	1	1b
bran flakes	98	5	22	1	1b
cap'n crunch	114	1	24	2	1b
cheerios	105	3	21	2	1b
cinnamon toast crunch	120	1	22	3	1b
cocoa krispies	108	1	25	1	1b
cocoa puffs	111	1	25	1	1b
corn chex	106	2	24	0	1b
corn flakes	111	2	25	0	1b
cream of rice, ckd (4 oz)	59	1	13	0	1b
cream of wheat, ckd (4 oz)	73	2	15	0	1b
farina, ckd (4 oz)	57	2	12	0	1b
fiber one	56	2	23	1	1b
froot loops	111	1	25	1	1b
frosted mini wheats	96	3	23	0	1b
fruit & fiber	109	2	22	2	1b
golden grahams	105	1	24	1	1b
granola, hmd	132	4	15	7	1b
granola, lowfat	110	2	23	2	1b
grape nuts	102	3	23	1	1b
honey comb	112	1	25	1	1b
honey nut cheerios	106	3	23	1	1b
kashi go lean	89	6	20	1	1b
kashi go lean crunch	107	5	19	2	1b
kix	107	2	24	1	1b
life	106	3	22	1	1b
lucky charms	108	2	24	1	1b
malt o meal, ckd (4 oz)	58	2	12	0	1b
maypo, ckd (4 oz)	81	3	15	1	1b
oatmeal, instant, plain, ckd (4 oz)	67	3	12	1	1b
product 19	103	2	24	0	1b
puffed rice	117	2	25	0	1b
puffed wheat	94	3	23	0	1b
rice chex	107	2	24	0	1b
rice krispies	110	2	25	0	1b
shredded wheat	96	3	24	0	1b
special K	107	6	20	0	1b
sugar frosted flakes	111	2	26	0	1b
super sugar crisp	106	2	26	0	1b
total raisin bran	88	2	21	1	1b
total wheat	92	2	21	1	1b
trix	111	1	25	1	1b
wheat chex	98	3	23	1	1b
wheaties	101	3	23	1	1b
Cheese (1½ oz)					
American, processed (2 oz)	186	11	4	14	1m
blue, crumbled (1.4 oz)	142	9	0	11	1m
brick	150	11	2	12	1m
Camembert	128	8	0	10	1m
cheddar	171	11	1	14	1m
Colby	168	10	1	14	1m
cottage, creamed (2 cups)	433	52	11	19	1m
cream cheese	148	3	1	15	1m
cream cheese, light	93	4	3	7	1m
edam	152	11	1	12	1m
fontina	147	9	1	12	1m
Gouda	151	11	1	12	1m
Gruyere	176	13	0	14	1m
Limburger	139	9	0	12	1m
Monterey jack	159	10	0	13	1m
mozzarella, part-skim	119	12	1	7	1m
mozzarella, whole milk	135	9	1	10	1m
Muenster	156	10	0	13	1m
neufchatel	111	4	1	10	1m

Description	Cal	Pro (g)	Carb (g)	Fat (g)	FGP
Parmesan, grated (1 T)	23	2	0	2	m
Parmesan, hard	167	15	1	11	1m
pimento, processed (2 oz)	213	13	1	18	1m
provolone	149	11	1	11	1m
ricotta	59	5	2	3	1m
Romano	165	14	2	11	1m
Roquefort	157	9	1	13	1m
Swiss	160	12	1	12	1m
Velveeta (2 oz)	172	9	6	12	1m
Cherries					
raw (½ cup)	52	1	12	1	1f
sour, cnd in light syrup (½ cup)	95	1	24	0	1f
sour, cnd in water (½ cup)	44	1	11	0	1f
sweet, cnd in light syrup (½ cup)	84	1	22	0	1f
sweet, cnd in water (½ cup)	57	1	15	0	1f
Chewing gum (1 stick)	10	0	3	0	
Chicken Parts					
breast, fried w/skin (½)	182	17	6	9	1p
breast, fried w/o skin (1)	161	29	0	4	1.2p
breast, roasted w/skin (¾)	145	22	0	6	1p
breast, roasted w/o skin (1)	143	27	0	3	1.2p
drumstick, fried w/skin (1½)	289	24	9	17	1p
drumstick, fried w/o skin (1½)	123	18	0	5	1p
drumstick, roasted w/skin (1½)	168	21	0	9	1p
drumstick, roasted w/o skin (1)	181	26	0	8	1.2p
thigh, fried w/skin (1)	162	17	2	9	1p
thigh, fried w/o skin (1½)	170	22	1	8	1p
wing, fried	318	19	11	21	1b,1p
wing, roasted	197	18	0	13	1p
Chicken a lá king, Stouffer's (8 oz)	257	15	33	8	1b,1v
Chicken cacciatore (3 oz)	160	15	4	9	1p
Chicken pot pie, Swanson (1 pie)	410	10	43	22	2.3b,1v
Chickpeas (garbanzo beans)					
ckd (1.2 cups)	323	17	54	5	1p
cnd (1.2 cups)	343	14	65	3	1p
Chili con carne					
cnd, w/beans (12 oz)	391	31	38	12	1p
w/o beans (6 oz)	235	17	14	13	1p
Chili powder (1 t)	8	0	1	0	
Chocolate syrup (2 T)	102	1	24	0	
Chop Suey					
beef, w/o noodles (½ cup)	136	11	6	8	1.3v,.4p
beef, w/ noodles (¾ cup)	316	17	23	18	1½v,1b
chicken, w/o noodles (1 cup)	193	20	10	8	1v,.8p
Cider (*see beverages*)					
Clams (2½ oz)					
raw	52	9	2	1	1p
steamed/boiled	105	18	4	1	1p
fried	143	10	7	8	1p,.2b
Clam Sauce					
red (5 oz)	68	5	9	1	1v,.3p
white (4 oz)	128	6	5	9	.4p
Coconut, shredded & swt (2½ oz)	355	2	34	25	1p
Codfish (2½ oz)					
raw	58	13	0	0	1p
baked/broiled	74	16	0	1	1p
fried	124	12	5	6	1p
Coffee (*see beverages*)					
Cola (*see beverages*)					
Coleslaw					
hmd (1 cup)	83	2	15	3	1v
fast food (½ cup)	98	1	9	7	1v
Collards, ckd (½ cup chopped)	25	2	5	0	1v
Cookies					
animal crackers (25 pieces)	139	2	23	4	1b
applesauce (1½ large)	99	1	17	3	1b
fudge walnut brownie (½)	185	3	26	9	1b
butter (6)	140	2	21	6	1b
choc chip (2)	127	1	17	6	1b
choc covered graham cracker (2½ pieces)	169	2	23	8	1b
choc dipped marshmallow (2 cookies)	109	1	18	4	1b

Description	Cal	Pro (g)	Carb (g)	Fat (g)	FGP
choc sandwich (2)	130	1	18	7	1b
fig newtons (2)	120	2	20	3	1b
fig newtons, fat free (1)	68	1	16	0	.8b
gingersnap (4)	122	2	19	5	1b
lady finger (2)	80	2	13	2	1b
macaroon (2)	194	2	35	6	1b
molasses (2)	129	2	22	4	1b
nilla wafers (8)	140	1	24	5	1b
nutter butter peanut butter (2)	130	3	19	6	1b
oatmeal (2)	111	1	16	5	.8b
oatmeal raisin (2)	131	2	21	5	1.2b
oreo (2½)	133	2	19	6	1b
peanut butter (2)	143	3	18	7	1b
shortbread (2)	80	1	10	4	1b
snackwell's devils food (2)	98	2	24	0	1b
snackwell's fudge (2)	106	2	24	0	1b
sugar (2)	143	2	20	6	1b
vanilla wafers (8)	147	2	22	6	1b
Cooking oil (*see oils*)					
Corn grits, yellow					
dry (¾ oz)	79	2	17	0	1b
ckd (4 oz)	68	2	15	0	1b
Corn, yellow					
ckd (½ cup)	89	3	21	1	1v
cnd, cream style (½ cup)	92	2	23	1	1v
cnd, vacuum pack (½ cup)	83	3	20	1	1v
Cornbread (*see breads*)					
Corn muffins (*see muffins*)					
Corn oil (*see oils*)					
Cornstarch (1 T)	30	0	7	0	
Cornsyrup (*see syrup*)					
Cottage cheese (*see cheese*)					
Crab, Blue (2½ oz)					
raw	62	13	0	1	1p
ckd	84	17	0	1	1p
cnd	70	15	0	1	1p
Crackers (1 oz)					
cheese (1.2 oz)	171	3	20	9	1b
graham	120	2	22	3	1b
oyster	123	3	20	3	1b
Ritz	139	2	18	6	1b
saltines	123	3	20	3	1b
soda	123	3	20	3	1b
triscuits	137	3	19	5	1b
wheat thins	133	2	20	6	1b
Cranberries, raw (²/₅ cup)	22	0	6	0	1f
Cranberry juice (6 oz)	97	0	24	0	1f
Cranberry sauce, jellied (½ cup)	200	0	52	0	1f
Crayfish (2½ oz)					
raw	55	11	0	1	1p
steamed/boiled	58	12	0	1	1p
Cream & Cream Substitutes					
creamer, non-dairy liquid (½ oz)	71	0	7	4	
creamer, non-dairy powder (1 t)	9	0	2	0	
half and half (1 T)	20	1	1	2	
heavy whipping (1 T)	51	0	0	6	
light (1 T)	29	0	1	3	
light whipping (1 T)	44	0	0	5	
sour, light (1 oz)	32	1	4	2	
sour, nonfat (1 oz)	27	1	4	0	
sour, regular (1 oz)	57	1	2	6	
Cream puff w/filling (¾)	220	5	20	13	1b
Cucumber (½ cup slices)	7	0	1	0	1v
Curry (6 oz)					
beef	314	20	9	23	1p, .3v
chicken	212	20	7	12	1p
Custard flan (1 serving)	398	12	49	18	1.2m

D

Description	Cal	Pro (g)	Carb (g)	Fat (g)	FGP
Danish pastry, apple (2 oz)	210	3	27	11	1b
Dates (½ cup chopped)	245	2	65	0	1f
Dips (1 oz)					
bacon	55	2	2	5	

Description	Cal	Pro (g)	Carb (g)	Fat (g)	FGP
blue cheese	170	1	3	18	
blue cheese, low calorie	89	1	6	6	
clam	55	1	3	4	
hummus	47	2	4	3	
onion	41	1	2	4	
ranch	55	1	3	4	
Doughnuts (1 each)					
cake	310	4	28	20	1.2b
choc glazed cake	250	3	29	14	1.3b
glazed yeast	160	3	23	7	.8b
jelly filled	240	4	32	10	1.2b
powdered sugar	210	3	24	11	1b
raised/yeast	170	4	23	7	1b
Duck, roasted (2½ oz)					
w/skin	239	13	0	20	1p
w/o skin	142	17	0	8	1p

E

Description	Cal	Pro (g)	Carb (g)	Fat (g)	FGP
Eggs					
boiled, hard/soft (2½ large)	194	16	1	13	1p
fried (2½ large)	229	16	2	17	1p
omelette, spinach (2½)	276	19	6	19	1v,1p
poached (2½ large)	186	16	2	12	1p
scrambled (2½ large)	249	16	2	19	1p
white, fresh/frozen (4 large)	67	14	1	0	1p
yolk, fresh/frozen (1 large)	59	3	0	5	p
Eggnog (*see beverages*)					
Eggplant					
raw (½ cup cubed)	11	0	2	0	1v
ckd (½ cup cubed)	14	0	3	0	1v
Eggplant Parmesan					
casserole (¼ cup)	80	4	4	6	1v,.3p
Egg roll					
meatless (1½)	151	4	15	9	1b,.7v
meat (1)	113	5	9	6	1b,1p
Enchilada, beef (5 oz)	250	8	28	12	1b,.3m

F

Description	Cal	Pro (g)	Carb (g)	Fat (g)	FGP
Fajitas					
beef (6 oz)	305	17	27	14	1b, 1v
chicken (6 oz)	277	15	34	9	1b, 1v
Falafel patty (2½ oz)	236	9	23	13	1p
Farina (*see cereals*)					
Fettuccini Alfredo,					
Stouffer's (4 oz)	188	7	22	8	1b, .2m
Figs					
raw (1½ med)	60	1	14	0	1f
dried (3 figs)	145	2	37	1	.8f
Fish (*see individual kinds*)					
Fish fillets, frozen,					
batter dipped (3 pieces)	510	21	48	30	.8p,2.2b
Fish sticks, frozen					
heated (2½ oz)	193	11	17	9	1p
batter-dipped (3 oz)	209	6	21	12	1p, .8b
Flounder/sole (2½ oz)					
raw	64	13	0	1	1p
baked/broiled	83	17	0	1	1p
fried	158	14	6	8	1p
Flour (.75 oz)					
white	77	2	16	0	1b
wheat	72	3	15	0	1b
Frankfurters (*see sausage*)					
French toast (2 pieces)	166	7	27	4	1b
Fried rice (3 oz)	139	3	18	6	1b
Frog legs, steamed (2½ oz)	75	17	0	0	1p
Frostings (*see cake icing*)					
Fruit (*see individual listings*)					
Fruit cocktail (½ cup)					
cnd, heavy syrup	91	0	23	0	1f
cnd, light syrup	69	0	18	0	1f
cnd, juice pack (¾ cup)	82	1	21	0	1f

Description	Cal	Pro (g)	Carb (g)	Fat (g)	FGP
cnd, water	38	0	10	0	1f

G

Description	Cal	Pro (g)	Carb (g)	Fat (g)	FGP
Garbanzo beans (see chickpeas)					
Garlic, raw (3 cloves)	13	1	3	0	v
Guacamole (1½ oz)	50	1	3	4	1f
Gelatin (½ cup)					
plain	81	2	19	0	
fruit flavors	80	2	19	0	
low calorie	9	1	1	0	
Gin (see beverages)					
Ginger ale (see beverages)					
Gingerbread (see cakes)					
Ginger root, raw (½ cup)	33	1	7	0	1v
Gnocchi (5 oz)					
cheese	259	14	12	17	1b, 1m
potato	202	4	25	10	1b, .8v
Granola Bars					
soft, uncoated (1.3 oz)	157	3	24	6	1b
chewy, honey nut, low fat (1.3 oz)	119	3	27	2	1b
fat free (1 oz)	95	1	24	0	1b
Grape juice, unswt (6 oz)	104	1	25	0	1f
Grapefruit (½ cup)					
raw, pink & red	43	1	11	0	1f
raw, white	43	1	10	0	1f
cnd, juice pack	46	1	11	0	1f
Grapefruit juice, unswt (6 oz)	65	1	15	0	1f
Grapes, raw (1 cup)	60	1	16	1	1f
Gravy (½ cup)					
beef	62	4	6	3	
chicken	94	2	6	7	
mushroom	60	1	7	3	
Grits (see corn grits)					
Gum (see chewing gum)					

H

Description	Cal	Pro (g)	Carb (g)	Fat (g)	FGP
Haddock (2½ oz)					
raw	62	13	0	1	1p
broiled	79	17	0	1	1p
smoked	82	18	0	1	1p
breaded and fried	155	14	6	8	1p
Halibut (2½ oz)					
raw	78	15	0	2	1p
broiled	169	13	0	13	1p
battered	248	10	17	16	1p, .8b
Ham (see pork)					
Hamburger (see beef, ground)					
Herbs	0	0	0	0	
Herring, Atlantic (2½ oz)					
raw	112	13	0	6	1p
baked, broiled	144	16	0	8	1p
pickled	186	10	7	13	1p
Hollandaise sauce (½ cup)	342	4	1	36	.2p
Hominy, cnd (½ cup)					
white	59	1	12	1	1v
yellow	58	1	11	1	1v
Honey (1 T)	64	0	17	0	
Honeydew melon, raw (½ cup)	30	0	8	0	1f
Horseradish sauce (1 T)	30	0	1	3	
Hushpuppy mix, dry (¾ oz)	72	2	15	0	1b

I

Description	Cal	Pro (g)	Carb (g)	Fat (g)	FGP
Ice Cream (1½ cups)					
choc	428	8	56	22	1m
strawberry	380	6	55	17	1m
vanilla	398	7	47	22	1m
vanilla, French, soft serve	555	11	57	34	1m
sherbet, orange	306	2	67	4	.8m
Ice cream bar, vanilla w/ choc (3)	497	6	37	36	.8m
Ice cream cone, plain (3)	50	1	9	1	.8b

Description	Cal	Pro (g)	Carb (g)	Fat (g)	FGP
Ice cream sandwich (5)	718	13	109	28	1m
Ice milk, vanilla (1½ cups)	203	6	31	7	1m
Icings (see cake icing)					

J

Description	Cal	Pro (g)	Carb (g)	Fat (g)	FGP
Jams/preserves (1 T)	56	0	14	0	
Jellies (1 T)	54	0	13	0	
Jello (½ cup)					
fruit	80	2	19	0	
fruit, sugar free	10	1	0	0	
Juice (see types)					

K

Description	Cal	Pro (g)	Carb (g)	Fat (g)	FGP
Kale, boiled (½ cup chopped)	18	1	4	0	1v
Ketchup (1 T)	16	0	4	0	
kiwifruit, raw (1 med)	46	1	11	0	1f
Knockwurst (see sausage)					
Kumquats, raw (5 med)	60	1	16	0	1f

L

Description	Cal	Pro (g)	Carb (g)	Fat (g)	FGP
Lamb (2½ oz)					
leg, roasted, lean	172	19	0	10	1p
loin, roasted, lean	143	19	0	7	1p
loin chop, broiled, lean	153	21	0	7	1p
Lard (1 T)	115	0	0	13	
Lasagna					
meatless (4 oz)	159	8	21	5	1b, ½v
w/meat (8 oz)	363	21	37	14	1b, ½p
Leeks (½ cup chopped)					
raw	27	1	6	0	1v
boiled	16	0	4	0	1v
Lemon, raw (2 med)	30	0	10	0	1f
Lemonade (see beverages)					
Lemon juice					
fresh (1 T)	4	0	1	0	f
fresh (7/10 cup)	43	1	15	0	1f
Lentils, boiled (1.2 cups)	276	21	48	1	1p
Lettuce, fresh, raw (1 cup)					
bibb	7	1	1	0	1v
iceberg	7	1	1	0	1v
leaf	10	1	3	0	1v
looseleaf	10	1	2	0	1v
romaine	8	1	1	0	1v
Lima beans (see beans)					
Lime, raw (2 med)	40	0	14	0	1f
Liver, ckd (2½ oz)					
beef	114	17	2	4	1p
chicken	111	17	1	4	1p
Liverwurst (see sausage)					
Lobster, steamed (2½ oz)	69	15	1	0	1p
Lobster newburg (5 oz)	355	17	7	29	1p
Lox (see salmon)					
Luncheon meats (see sausage)					

M

Description	Cal	Pro (g)	Carb (g)	Fat (g)	FGP
Macadamia nuts, dried (4 oz)	814	9	16	86	1p
Macaroni, ckd					
shells, small (3/5 cup)	97	3	20	1	1b
spirals (½ cup)	94	3	19	0	1b
Macaroni & cheese (½ cup)	205	6	25	9	1b, .2m
Mackerel, broiled (2½ oz)	186	17	0	13	1p
Mandarin oranges, cnd (½ cup)					
juice pack	46	1	12	0	1f
light syrup	77	1	20	0	1f
Mango, raw (1.2 cups)	129	1	34	1	1f
Manicotti, cheese (6 oz)	240	13	23	11	1m, 1b
Margarine (1 T)	101	0	0	11	
Marshmallow (see candy)					
Mayonnaise (see salad dressing)					
Meatloaf (see sausage)					

Description	Cal	Pro (g)	Carb (g)	Fat (g)	FGP
Meats (*see beef, lamb, pork*)					
Melba toast (3 slices)	59	2	12	1	1b
Milk, cow (8 oz)					
whole (3.3% fat)	139	8	11	8	1m
skim	79	8	11	0	1m
1% fat	95	8	11	2	1m
low-fat (2% fat)	113	8	11	4	1m
dry, whole, w/water	146	8	11	8	1m
Milkshake (*see beverages*)					
Molasses (1 T)	55	0	14	0	
Moussaka (2½ oz)	68	5	4	4	1v, .2p
Muffins					
blueberry (¾ large)	157	3	27	4	1b
bran, raisin (2 oz)	120	4	26	2	1b
corn (2 oz)	173	3	29	5	1b
English (½)	67	2	13	1	1b
oat bran (2 oz)	153	4	27	4	1b
wheat bran (2 oz)	117	2	21	4	1b
Mushrooms					
raw (²/₅ cup)	10	1	2	0	1v
boiled (½ cup pieces)	21	2	4	0	1v
cnd (3 oz)	20	2	4	0	1v
Mussels, blue (2½ oz)					
raw	61	8	3	2	1p
steamed	122	17	5	3	1p
Mustard, Dijon (1 T)	19	1	2	1	
Mutton (*see lamb*)					

N

Description	Cal	Pro (g)	Carb (g)	Fat (g)	FGP
Nachos					
beef, beans, and cheese (5 oz)	316	11	31	17	1b, .4v
cheese (2½ oz)	217	6	23	12	1b, .2m
Nectarine, raw (1 med)	70	1	16	1	1f
Noodles					
egg, ckd (½ cup)	106	4	20	1	1b
chow mein, dry (½ cup)	119	2	13	7	1b
Nuts (*see individual kinds*)					
Nuts, mixed (4 oz)					
dry roasted	674	20	29	58	1p
oil roasted	700	19	24	64	1p

O

Description	Cal	Pro (g)	Carb (g)	Fat (g)	FGP
Oat Bran					
ckd (½ cup)	44	4	13	1	1b
dry (¼ cup)	58	4	16	2	1b
Oatmeal (*see cereal*)					
Ocean Perch (2½ oz)					
raw	67	13	0	1	1p
broiled	86	17	0	2	1p
breaded & fried	160	14	6	8	1p
Oils, all vegetable (1 T)	120	0	0	14	
Okra, boiled (½ cup slices)	26	2	6	0	1v
Olives, pitted (2½ oz)	199	1	7	19	1v
Omelette (*see eggs*)					
Onion					
raw (⁷/₁₀ cup)	31	1	7	0	1v
boiled (½ cup)	46	1	11	0	1v
cnd (½ cup)	21	1	5	0	1v
Onion rings, frozen (5 rings)	122	2	11	8	1v
Orange, raw (1 med)	70	1	21	0	1.2f
Orange juice, fresh (6 oz)	77	1	18	0	1f
Oysters (2½ oz)					
raw	48	5	3	2	1p
steamed	116	13	7	3	1p
cnd	49	5	3	2	1p
breaded & fried (3 oz)	168	8	10	11	1p, ½b

P

Description	Cal	Pro (g)	Carb (g)	Fat (g)	FGP
Pad thai, w/chicken & shrimp (8 oz)	422	22	30	26	1v, .7p

Description	Cal	Pro (g)	Carb (g)	Fat (g)	FGP
Pancakes (4")					
from mix (¾ of a pancake)	55	2	11	1	1b
frozen (1 pancake)	82	2	16	1	1b
Papaya, raw (½ a small)	30	1	8	0	1f
Parsley (1 cup chopped)	22	2	4	1	1v
Parsnips, boiled (½ cup)	63	1	15	0	1v
Pastries					
Cream puff w/custard filling (½)	168	4	15	10	.8b
Danish, cheese (¾)	199	4	20	12	1b
Danish, raspberry (1½ small)	195	3	25	10	1b
Peach					
raw (1 med)	42	1	11	0	1.2f
cnd, heavy syrup, halves (1)	73	0	20	0	.8f
cnd, light syrup (½ cup)	68	1	18	0	1f
cnd, juice pack (½ cup)	55	1	14	0	1f
cnd, water pack (½ cup)	29	1	8	0	1f
Peach nectar, cnd (6 oz)	92	1	24	0	1f
Peanuts					
boiled (¾ cup)	429	18	29	30	1p
dry roasted (¾ cup)	641	26	24	54	1p
oil roasted (¾ cup)	628	28	20	53	1p
Peanut Butter					
creamy/smooth (5 T)	474	20	15	41	1p
creamy, reduced fat (5 T)	475	20	38	30	1p
chunky/crunchy (5 T)	471	19	17	40	1p
crunchy, reduced fat (5 T)	475	20	38	30	1p
Pear					
raw (1 med)	98	1	25	1	1f
cnd, heavy syrup (½ cup)	90	0	22	0	1f
cnd, juice pack (½ cup)	80	0	21	0	1f
cnd, light syrup (½ cup)	80	1	20	0	1f
Peas, green					
raw (½ cup)	59	4	11	0	1v
boiled (½ cup)	67	4	13	0	1v
cnd (⅓ cup)	51	3	9	0	1v
frozen (½ cup)	55	4	10	0	1v
Pecans, dried (⅓ cup chopped)	247	3	5	26	1p
Peppers, sweet					
raw, chopped (⅓ cup)	12	0	3	0	1v
boiled (½ cup)	19	1	5	0	1v
cnd (½ cup)	13	1	3	0	1v
Perch (*see ocean perch*)					
Pickles					
bread and butter (3 oz)	91	0	21	0	1v
dill (1½ med)	12	1	2	0	1v
sweet (3 oz)	122	0	30	0	1v
sweet relish (1 T)	20	0	5	0	v
Pies (⅛ of 9" pie)					
apple	411	4	58	19	1b, 1f
banana cream	387	6	47	20	1b
blueberry (¹/₁₆ pie)	180	2	25	9	1b, .2f
cherry (¹/₁₆ pie)	243	3	35	11	1b, .3f
choc cream	344	3	38	22	1b
coconut cream (¼ of 7" pie)	286	2	36	16	1b
coconut custard	203	5	24	10	1b
lemon meringue	227	1	40	7	1b
mincemeat	477	4	79	18	1b
peach (¹/₁₆ pie)	177	2	27	8	1b, .3f
pecan	503	6	64	27	1b
pumpkin	316	7	41	14	1b, .3v
strawberry cream	294	2	38	16	1b, .6f
sweet potato	295	6	36	14	1b, .3v
Pie crust (⅛ of 9" shell)	82	1	8	5	.8b
Pike, northern, broiled (2½ oz)	80	18	0	1	1p
Pizza (*see Pizza Hut*)					
Pineapple					
raw (½ cup)	38	0	10	0	1f
cnd, heavy syrup (½ cup)	99	0	26	0	1f
cnd, juice pack (¼ cup)	37	0	10	0	.8f
Pineapple juice, unswt (6 oz)	95	1	23	0	1f
Pistachios, shelled (¾ cup)	535	20	27	43	1p
Plum					
raw (1 med)	40	1	10	1	.8f

Description	Cal	Pro (g)	Carb (g)	Fat (g)	FGP
cnd, extra heavy syrup (½ cup)	132	1	34	0	1f
cnd, water pack (4 oz)	46	0	13	0	1f
Pomegranate, raw (½ med)	52	1	13	0	1f
Popcorn					
air-popped (3½ cups)	107	3	22	1	1b
oil-popped (3 cups)	165	3	19	9	1b
microwave, low fat (5 cups)	119	4	21	3	1b
Popover (1 med)	189	7	18	10	1b
Pork (2½ oz)					
bacon (*see bacon*)					
ham, cnd	96	15	0	4	1p
ham, cured, roasted	111	18	0	4	1p
ham, fresh, roasted	193	19	0	13	1p
ham, 11% fat, sliced	129	12	2	8	1p
ham, spread, deviled	203	10	0	18	1p
loin, broiled	142	21	0	6	1p
loin, chops	143	21	0	6	1p
spareribs, braised	281	21	0	22	1p
Pork and beans, cnd (1 cup)	281	13	53	4	.8p
Potatoes					
au gratin, w/margarine (½ cup)	162	6	14	9	1v
raw (½ med)	50	2	13	0	1v
baked, w/o skin (½ med)	73	2	17	0	1v
baked, w/ skin (½ med)	80	2	18	0	1v
cnd, new (½ cup)	45	1	10	0	1v
French fried, frozen (15 pieces)	150	2	23	6	1v
mashed, flakes (½ cup)	119	2	16	6	1v
mashed, fresh (½ cup)	111	2	18	4	1v
scalloped, fresh (½ cup)	105	4	13	5	1v
sweet, baked (¾ med)	119	2	28	0	1v
sweet, candied (3 oz)	117	1	24	3	1v
sweet, cnd (½ cup)	106	1	25	0	1v
Potato chips (1 oz)	152	2	15	10	1v
Potato salad (½ cup)	179	3	14	10	1v
Pretzels					
hard (1 oz)	108	3	23	1	1b
soft (1)	190	5	38	2	1b
sticks (1 oz)	106	3	22	0	1b
Prunes					
cnd, heavy syrup (7 prunes)	123	2	46	0	1f
dried (8 prunes)	161	2	42	0	1f
dried, stewed (²/₅ cup)	106	1	28	0	1f
Prune juice (6 oz)	121	1	30	0	1f
Puddings (1½ cups)					
banana	463	12	87	8	1m
butterscotch snack cups (4)	520	8	84	20	1m
choc	463	14	83	9	1m
rice	390	12	63	9	1m
tapioca	444	12	83	7	1m
vanilla	424	12	78	7	1m
Pumpkin					
boiled (½ cup mashed)	25	1	6	0	1v
cnd (½ cup)	136	2	30	1	1v
Pumpkin seeds (2 oz)	253	11	31	11	1p

Q					
Quail, breast (1)	69	13	0	2	.8p
Quesadilla (3 oz)	289	10	29	15	1p, .6m
Quince (2 med)	105	1	28	0	1f

R					
Rabbit, roasted (2½ oz)	140	21	0	6	1p
Radishes, raw (5 med)	11	1	2	0	1v
Raisins					
seedless (½ cup)	248	3	65	0	1f
seeded (½ cup)	244	2	65	0	1f
Raspberries					
raw (½ cup)	30	1	7	0	1f
frozen, swt (½ cup)	129	1	33	0	1f
Ravioli					
cheese, w/ tomato sauce (6 oz)	232	10	26	10	1b, 1m
meat, w/ tomato sauce (5 oz)	223	12	21	10	1b, .4p

Description	Cal	Pro (g)	Carb (g)	Fat (g)	FGP
Red beans and rice, low-fat (6 oz)	195	6	34	4	1b
Relish (*see pickles*)					
Rice, ckd (½ cup)					
brown, long-grain	87	2	18	1	1b
white, long-grain	103	2	22	0	1b
wild	83	3	18	0	1b
Rice mixes, commercial					
beef (5 oz)	125	8	20	2	1b, .3p
chicken (5 oz)	227	17	25	6	1b, .6p
fried (6 oz)	191	4	30	6	1b, .8v
Risotto, chicken, dry (¼ cup)	115	4	22	1	1b
Rockfish, broiled (2½ oz)	86	17	0	1	1p
Rolls and buns					
brown & serve (⅓)	108	5	20	1	1b
dinner (1½)	75	4	10	2	1b
French (1)	130	4	25	2	1b
hoagie or submarine (¼)	97	3	17	2	1b
hamburger bun (¾)	92	3	16	2	1b
hotdog bun (¾)	92	3	16	2	1b
kaiser (½)	84	3	15	1	1b
sweet (1)	223	4	31	10	1b
Root beer (*see beverages*)					
Roughy, orange, broiled (2½ oz)	63	13	0	1	1p
Rum (*see beverages*)					

S					
Safflower oil (*see oils*)					
Salad dressings (1 T)					
blue cheese	77	1	1	8	
blue cheese, low cal	15	1	0	1	
Caesar	52	1	0	5	
French	67	0	3	6	
French, low cal	22	0	4	1	
mayonnaise	100	0	0	11	
mayonnaise, light	50	0	1	5	
mayonnaise, fat free	11	0	2	0	
ranch	90	0	1	10	
ranch, fat free	24	0	5	0	
thousand island	59	0	2	6	
thousand island, low cal	24	0	3	2	
vinegar and oil	70	0	0	8	
Salad oil (*see oils*)					
Salads					
coleslaw (*see coleslaw*)					
chicken (2½ oz)	177	7	6	14	1p
fruit, mixed, cnd in heavy syrup (½ cup)	111	1	29	0	1f
fruit, mixed, cnd in light syrup (½ cup)	80	0	21	0	1f
fruit, mixed, cnd in water (½ cup)	37	0	10	0	1f
gelatin (*see gelatin*)					
macaroni (⅓ cup)	118	2	15	6	.8b
tuna (4 oz)	212	18	11	11	1p, .3v
Salmon (2½ oz)					
atlantic, raw	101	14	0	5	1p
atlantic, broiled	129	18	0	6	1p
chinook, smoked (lox)	83	13	0	3	1p
Salt	0	0	0	0	
Sardines, cnd in oil (6 sardines)	150	18	0	8	1p
Sauces and Toppings (1 T)					
barbecue	12	0	2	0	
butterscotch	52	0	14	0	
chili	20	0	5	0	
cheese (5 oz)	247	10	10	19	1m
choc	51	0	12	0	
cream, half and half	20	1	1	2	m
soy	10	2	0	0	
tartar	45	0	2	5	
tomato (½ cup)	37	2	9	0	1v
worcestershire	11	0	3	0	
Sauerkraut, cnd (¾ cup)	20	1	5	0	1v
Sausage, cold cuts (2½ oz)					
beef, link	221	10	2	19	1p

Description	Cal	Pro (g)	Carb (g)	Fat (g)	FGP
bologna, pork	175	11	1	14	1p
Braunschweiger	254	10	2	23	1p
frankfurter, beef (1½ links)	221	8	3	20	1p
knockwurst	218	8	2	20	1p
liverwurst	231	10	2	20	1p
meatloaf, beef and pork	141	12	4	8	1p
minced ham (1 oz)	75	5	1	6	.8p
mortadella	220	12	2	18	1p
Polish sausage	222	9	2	19	1p
pork sausage, ckd	198	17	1	14	1p
pork sausage, Italian, ckd	229	14	1	18	1p
salami, beef	259	13	0	23	1p
salami, pork	301	15	1	26	1p
turkey sausage	164	11	1	13	1p
Scallops, broiled (2½ oz)	95	14	2	3	1p
Sesame seeds, dried (¾ cup)	662	30	11	62	1p
Shad, baked (2½ oz)	179	15	0	13	1p
Sherbet (see ice cream)					
Shishkabob, lamb, braised (2½ oz)	158	24	0	6	1p
Shortbread (see cookies)					
Shortcake biscuit (2 oz)	196	4	28	8	1b
Shortening (1 T)	115	0	0	13	
Shrimp					
raw (2½ oz)	75	14	1	1	1p
breaded & fried (3 oz)	236	10	21	13	1b, .8p
steamed (2½ oz)	70	15	0	1	1p
cnd (2½ oz)	58	13	0	0	1p
cocktail (5 oz)	134	17	13	2	1p
Sorbet (½ cup)					
citrus fruit	92	1	23	0	
non citrus fruit	82	1	20	0	
Soup, cnd					
asparagus (½ cup)	43	1	5	2	1v
bean, black (1 cup)	116	6	20	2	.8p
beef broth (½ cup)	20	3	0	1	
beef noodle (2 cups)	166	10	18	6	1b, .3p
celery, cream (½ cup)	45	1	4	3	1v
chicken broth (¼ cup)	20	3	1	1	
chicken, cream (1½ cups)	176	5	14	11	1b
chicken gumbo (½ cup)	28	1	4	1	1.2v
chicken noodle (1 cup)	75	4	9	3	1b
chicken w/ rice (4 cups)	241	14	29	8	1b, ½p
chicken vegetable (½ cup)	37	2	4	1	1v
clam chowder, Manhattan (½ cup)	39	1	6	1	1v
clam chowder, N E (4 cups)	381	19	50	12	1p
egg drop (2 cups)	146	15	2	8	1p
gazpacho (½ cup)	23	4	2	0	1v
green pea (½ cup)	83	4	13	2	1p
hot & sour (½ cup)	81	8	3	4	1v
minestrone (½ cup)	41	2	6	1	.8v
mushroom, cream (½ cup)	65	1	5	5	1v
onion (½ cup)	29	2	4	1	1v
split pea w/ham (1 cup)	190	10	28	4	1p
tomato (½ cup)	43	1	8	1	1v
tortilla soup w/chicken (1 cup)	220	10	19	11	1p, .6b
turkey noodle (2 cups)	137	8	17	4	1b, .4p
vegetable (½ cup)	39	1	7	1	1v
vegetable beef (½ cup)	39	3	5	1	1v, ½b
wonton (1 cup)	182	14	14	7	1.3v, 1b
Soy nuts (4 oz)	480	48	36	16	1p
Soybean tofu, raw (1.2 cups)	182	20	5	11	1p
Soybean oil (see oils)					
Soybeans					
green, boiled (1.2 cups)	305	27	24	14	1p
mature, boiled (2.2 cups)	655	63	38	34	1p
Soy sauce (see sauces)					
Spaghetti					
ckd (½ cup)	99	3	20	1	1b
w/meatballs (1 cup)	370	19	28	18	1b,1v,1p
Spaghetti meat sauce, cnd (½ cup)	89	4	10	4	1v, .3p
Spanish rice (½ cup)	108	3	21	2	1b

Description	Cal	Pro (g)	Carb (g)	Fat (g)	FGP
Spinach					
raw (1½ cups chopped)	10	1	2	0	.8v
boiled (½ cup)	21	3	3	0	1v
cnd (½ cup)	25	3	4	1	1v
Spring roll, fresh (1)	113	5	9	6	1b, 1p
Squash (½ cup)					
acorn, baked	57	1	15	0	.8v
acorn, boiled, mashed	42	1	11	0	1v
crookneck, boiled	18	1	4	0	1v
hubbard, boiled, mashed	35	2	8	0	1v
scallop, boiled, mashed	19	1	4	0	1v
zucchini, raw	9	1	2	0	1v
zucchini, boiled	14	1	4	0	1v
Stew (see beef stew)					
Strawberries					
raw (½ cup)	25	1	6	0	1f
cnd in heavy syrup (⅓ cup)	70	0	18	0	1f
Stuffing, cornbread (½ cup)	160	3	19	8	1b
Sturgeon, broiled (2½ oz)	96	15	0	4	1p
Succotash (½ cup)					
boiled	110	5	23	1	1v
cnd	102	4	23	1	1v
Sugar					
brown (1 cup)	827	0	214	0	
white (1 cup)	774	0	200	0	
white (1 t)	16	0	4	0	
white (1 packet)	23	0	6	0	
powdered (1 cup unsifted)	467	0	119	0	
powdered (1 t unsifted)	10	0	3	0	
Sunflower seeds, hulled (4 oz)					
dry roasted	660	22	27	57	1p
oil roasted	697	24	17	65	1p
sweet potatoes (see potatoes)					
Sweet & sour pork (2½ oz)	72	5	8	3	1p
Swordfish (2½ oz)					
raw	86	14	0	3	1p
baked/broiled	110	18	0	4	1p
Syrups (1 T)					
choc	51	0	12	0	
corn, light or dark	58	0	16	0	
maple	52	0	13	0	
molasses	55	0	14	0	
sorghum	41	1	9	0	
T					
Tabouli salad (½ cup)	294	9	61	2	1b
Taco salad, w/o shell (¾ cup)	140	7	12	7	1v
Tamale, meat (1½)	201	10	17	11	1b, 1p
Tangerine, raw (1 med)	50	1	15	1	1f
Tapioca (see puddings)					
Tartar sauce (see sauces)					
Tea (see beverages)					
Tomatoes					
green, raw (1 med)	22	1	5	0	1v
red, raw (1 med)	19	1	4	0	1v
red, boiled (½ cup)	32	1	7	1	1v
red, cnd (½ cup)	23	1	5	0	1v
red, paste, cnd (½ cup)	107	5	25	1	1v
red, stewed, cnd (½ cup)	35	1	8	0	1v
puree (½ cup)	50	2	12	0	1v
Tomato juice (6 oz)	29	1	7	0	1v
Tomato juice cocktail (6 oz)	39	2	8	0	
Tomato ketchup (see ketchup)					
Toppings (see candy & sauces)					
Tortillas, 6" diameter					
corn (1)	58	2	12	1	.8b
Flour (1½)	156	4	27	3	.8b
Trout (2½ oz)					
mixed species, raw	74	12	0	3	1p
rainbow, raw	84	15	0	3	1p
rainbow, baked	106	16	0	4	1p
Tuna (2½ oz)					
cnd in oil, light	140	21	0	6	1p

Description	Cal	Pro (g)	Carb (g)	Fat (g)	FGP
cnd in oil, white	132	19	0	6	1p
cnd in water, light	82	18	0	1	1p
cnd in water, white	91	17	0	2	1p
Tuna noodle casserole (¾ cup)	301	20	24	13	1b, 1p
Tuna salad (*see salads*)					
Turkey, roasted (2½ oz)					
dark, w/skin	157	20	0	8	1p
dark, without skin	133	20	0	5	1p
white, w/skin	140	20	0	6	1p
white, without skin	111	21	0	2	1p
Turnip, boiled (¾ cup)	25	1	6	0	1v
Turnip greens					
raw (1 cup)	15	1	3	0	1v
boiled (½ cup)	14	1	3	0	1v
cnd (½ cup)	16	2	3	0	1v

V

Description	Cal	Pro (g)	Carb (g)	Fat (g)	FGP
Veal (2½ oz)					
ground, broiled	122	17	0	5	1p
loin chop, lean, braised	160	24	0	7	1p
rib, lean, braised	155	24	0	6	1p
Veal marsala (6 oz)	473	21	11	35	1p
Veal parmigiana (6 oz)	335	25	15	20	.8p, .7v
Vegetable juice (6 oz)	42	1	8	0	1v
Vegetables (*see types*)					
Vegetables, mixed (½ cup)	54	3	12	0	1v
Vegetable stew (6 oz)	168	14	15	5	1v, .6p
Venison, roasted (2½ oz)	112	21	0	2	1p
Vinegar, white (1 cup)	64	0	16	0	
Vodka (*see beverages*)					

W

Description	Cal	Pro (g)	Carb (g)	Fat (g)	FGP
Waffles, 7" diameter (1)	218	6	25	11	1b
Walnuts, dried (2 oz)	350	14	6	34	1p
Water chestnuts, raw (1 cup)	70	1	17	0	.8v
Watermelon (½ cup)	25	1	6	0	1f
Wheat (*see cereal, flour*)					
Wheat germ, crude (¼ cup)	104	7	15	3	1b
Whiskey (*see beverages*)					
Whitefish (2½ oz)					
raw	95	14	0	4	1p
baked, broiled	122	17	0	5	1p
smoked	77	17	0	1	1p
Wine (*see beverages*)					

Y

Description	Cal	Pro (g)	Carb (g)	Fat (g)	FGP
Yeast, baker's, dry (½ oz)	15	2	1	0	
Yogurt (1 cup)					
fzn, choc, low-fat (1.3 cups)	285	13	54	5	1m
frozen, vanilla or fruit	203	9	37	3	1m
plain, low-fat	154	13	17	4	1m
plain, whole milk	149	9	11	8	1m
strawberry, low-fat	240	10	45	3	1m
vanilla, low-fat	208	12	34	3	1m

Helpful Measures

Below are some measurements and conversions that may be helpful to you in understanding portion and serving sizes.

3t = 1T	= ½ fl oz	
16T = 1 cup	= 8 fl oz	= ½ pint
2 cups = 1 pint	= ½ quart	= ¹/₈ gallon
1 quart = 2 pints	= ¼ gallon	= .946 liter
1 gallon = 4 quarts	= 3.785 liter	
1 liter = 1.057 quarts		
1 oz = 28.35 g		
1 lb = 16 oz	= 453.59 g	

Supplemental Resources and Ordering Information

T his manual and the other materials distributed by The LifeStyle Company are not available in bookstores. You may write, call, or visit us on the Internet to obtain current pricing and shipping information. Discounts are available for bulk orders. Below is a sampling of other materials and services available from The LifeStyle Company.

The LifeStyle Company

The LifeStyle Company, a division of American Health Publishing Company, was established to respond to the increasing demand for scientifically sound, state-of-the-art publications, training courses, and services. The LifeStyle Company is dedicated to the development of health and wellness materials, including audio tapes, CDs, professional training guides, and leadership training programs.

For your ordering convenience, a toll-free telephone number is available and may be called 24 hours a day. In addition, you can order via the Internet at www.TheLifeStyleCompany.com. For your convenience, we accept all major credit cards, checks, or money orders.

All orders are shipped within 24 hours of receipt, and next day and second day delivery service is available. As you use our publications, we sincerely welcome any comments you may have to improve these materials, and we encourage you to tell us how we are doing.

For ordering or general information, please write or call us at:

The LifeStyle Company
P.O. Box 610430, Dept. 70
Dallas, Texas 75261–0430

Telephone (In the U.S.)   1-888–LEARN–41
Telephone (Outside the U.S.)   817–545–4500

Fax   817–545–2211
E-mail address:
      LEARN@TheLifeStyleCompany.com
Internet address:
      www.TheLifeStyleCompany.com

The LEARN Institute for LifeStyle Management

The LEARN Institute was established to provide state-of-the-art training and education programs to health professionals working with clients seeking to improve their health and well-being through lifestyle change. The LEARN Institute is the first to offer specific training and certification in the fields of weight and stress management. The LifeStyle Counselor Certification Program™ provides a comprehensive cross-disciplinary training program to health professionals working in the fields of weight and stress management.

Two certification training programs are currently offered and include:

Certification in Weight Management
Certification in Stress Management

For more detailed information on The LifeStyle Counselor Certification Program or a free brochure call or write to:

The LEARN Institute for LifeStyle Management
P.O. Box 610430, Dept. 50
Dallas, Texas 75261–04308
Telephone (In the U.S.)   1-888–LEARN–50

Telephone (Outside the U.S.)   817–545–4500
Fax   817–545–2211
E-mail address:
                TheInstitute@TheLifeStyleCompany.com
Internet address:
                www.TheLifeStyleCompany.com

The American Association of LifeStyle Counselors

The American Association of LifeStyle Counselors is a nonprofit corporation dedicated to providing its members and the public with the most current, safe, and sound lifestyle-management programs and services. Individuals who complete the LifeStyle Counselor Certification Program become eligible for membership in the American Association of LifeStyle Counselors (AALC). Only members of the AALC can use the Certified LifeStyle Counselor® title. If you would like to locate a Certified LifeStyle Counselor in your area you may write, call, or visit the AALC's Internet site as follows:

The American Association of
LifeStyle Counselors
P.O. Box 610410, Dept. 55
Dallas, Texas 76261–0410
Telephone   817–545–3220
Fax   817–545–2211
E-mail address   AALC@AALC.org
Internet address   www.AALC.org

Other Materials

Publications and products currently available from The LifeStyle Company are as follows:

Weight Management

The LEARN Program Cassettes/CDs, by Kelly D. Brownell, Ph.D.

The LEARN Program for Weight Management—10ᵗʰ Edition, by Kelly D. Brownell, Ph.D.

The LEARN Weight Stabilization and Maintenance Guide (available spring 2004).

The LEARN Program for Weight Control—Special Medication Edition, by Kelly D. Brownell, Ph.D. and Thomas A. Wadden, Ph.D.

The LEARN Program Monitoring Forms

The LifeStyle Counselor's Guide for Weight Control, by Brenda L. Wolfe, Ph.D., et al.

Eating Disorders

Overcoming Binge Eating, by Christopher Fairburn, M.D.

Stress Management

Mastering Stress 2001—A LifeStyle Approach, by David H. Barlow, Ph.D., Leslie Reisner, Ph.D., Ronald M. Rapee, Ph.D.

Mind Over Mood, by Dennis Greenberger, Ph.D. and Christine A. Padesky, Ph.D.

Other Materials

The Body Image Workbook, by Thomas F. Cash, Ph.D.

Motivational Interviewing, by William R. Miller and Stephen Rollnick.

The LEARN WalkMaster

The LEARN Program Index

About the Author

Kelly D. Brownell, Ph.D., is an internationally known expert on weight management. He received training at Purdue University, Rutgers University, and Brown University. After serving on the faculty of the University of Pennsylvania School of Medicine for 13 years, he joined the faculty at Yale University, where he is Professor and Chairman of Psychology, Professor of Epidemiology and Public Health, and Director of the Yale Center for Eating and Weight Disorders. He served six years as Master of Silliman College at Yale. Dr. Brownell has written 13 books and more than 200 research papers and book chapters, and holds appointments on 10 editorial boards.

Tape/CD 1
Section 3

Dr. Brownell has received awards from the American Psychological Association and the New York Academy of Sciences, and has been awarded research grants from the National Institutes of Health, the MacArthur Foundation, and the National Institute of Mental Health. He has been the President of the Society of Behavioral Medicine, the Division of Health Psychology of the American Psychological Association, and the Association for the Advancement of Behavior Therapy. He has been an advisor to the U.S. Navy, American Airlines, Johnson & Johnson and other organizations.

He has appeared on the *Today Show, Good Morning America, Nightline, Nova* and *20/20,* and his work has been featured in the *New York Times, Washington Post, Glamour, Redbook, Family Circle, Vogue,* and other publications.